CONTEMPORARY
AMERICAN LITERATURE

BIBLIOGRAPHIES AND STUDY OUTLINES

BY

JOHN MATTHEWS MANLY

AND

EDITH RICKERT

INTRODUCTION

AND REVISION BY

FRED B. MILLETT

GREENWOOD PRESS, PUBLISHERS
WESTPORT, CONNECTICUT

Library of Congress Cataloging in Publication Data

Manly, John Matthews, 1865-1940.
    Contemporary American literature.

    Reprint of the 1929 ed. published by Harcourt, Brace,
New York.
    Includes indexes.
    1. American literature--20th century--Bio-bibliogra-
phy. 2. American literature--Outlines, syllabi, etc.
I. Rickert, Edith, 1871-1938, joint author. II. Title.
[PS221.M3 1975]   016.810'9'005   73-17631
ISBN 0-8371-7254-3

This edition originally published in 1929 by Harcourt,
Brace and Company, New York

Reprinted in 1975 by Greenwood Press,
a division of Williamhouse-Regency Inc.

Library of Congress Catalog Card Number 73-17631

ISBN 0-8371-7254-3

Printed in the United States of America

CONTENTS

iii

FOREWORD

This book is not so much a revision of the *Contemporary American Literature* published in 1922 as it is a new book. Every feature of the original book has undergone the most searching scrutiny and revision, many new authors have been included, and hundreds of books and critical entries have been added. The new book aims to give a systematic account of contemporary American literature since 1900, a classified bibliography of all the significant writers of the period, with biographical information, suggestions for reading, and carefully chosen studies and reviews for each author of major importance. Limitations of space have forced the exclusion of a number of living authors who have produced no particularly significant work since 1914.

The critical introduction that precedes the bibliographies has been contributed to this edition by Mr. Fred B. Millett. Those whose critical opinions have already taken form will find much therein with which to disagree. To those who wish a background for haphazard and undirected reading, we trust that this tentative survey will prove of some service. For those who enter upon a similar undertaking with greater knowledge and more certain taste, this initial effort may serve at least as a guide to the avoidance of errors.

The *Bibliographies* aim, with certain specific exceptions, at completeness. The following items have *usually* been omitted: (1) books privately printed; (2) separate editions of works included in larger volumes; (3) works not of a distinctly literary character; (4) English reprints; (5) editions other than the first; (6) books primarily for children.

The *Suggestions for Reading* given in the case of the more important authors are intended for students who need or

Foreword—*Continued*

desire guidance. It is our hope that these hints and questions may lead to discussions and differences of opinion, for dissent is the guidepost to truth.

The *Studies and Reviews* are the meager result of long search in periodical and critical literature. Every entry in the original volume has been reconsidered, and those which seemed unworthy have been eliminated. Every entry has been checked and rechecked to secure the maximum degree of accuracy in the presentation of an infinite number of details. A conscientious attempt has been made to bring the *Studies and Reviews* up to the latest possible date before publication, but to include only those which would prove genuinely helpful to the critical or curious student or reader.

Supplementary to the alphabetical list of authors with material for study are the classified indexes. These are intended for use in planning courses of study. The classification according to form includes poets, dramatists, novelists, short story writers, essayists, critics, writers on country life, travel, and nature, humorists, and writers of biography and autobiography. In this connection should be noted the supplementary list of poets whose work can be studied in one or more of the anthologies indicated.

The classification according to birthplace furnishes material for the study of local groups of writers.

The classification according to subject matter (including the use of local color and background), although it is necessarily incomplete, will, it is hoped, suggest courses of reading on these bases.

Following the alphabetical list of authors are bibliographies of different types: lists of indexes and critical periodicals; general works of reference discussing the period; collections of poems, plays, short stories, and essays; and bibliographies of short plays and short stories.

Our thanks are due to numerous students and helpers for assisting us in collecting the material, for checking and rechecking the countless details involved, and for offering many suggestions to increase the usefulness of the book. We trust that this volume will prove of value not only as a reference book and a textbook, but as a guide to the countless readers who desire to relate their current reading to the development of literature in our generation.

No one can appreciate the problems involved in making a survey of contemporary American literature except the student who has attempted the impossible and thankless task. First of all, he is confronted repeatedly with the acute problem of selection. Of the hundreds of books which pour monthly from the presses, of the dozens of writers who have won a little reputation, a brief fame, which shall be chosen for discussion, which ignored? Is it the part of wisdom to consider a popular author who seems essentially trivial, and ignore an unpopular author who may have a trace of distinction? A wide literary popularity has a meaning, at least in a democratic society. The question is whether that meaning belongs to the history of literature or to social history. Should one devote a page to Harold Bell Wright and a footnote to H. D.?

And when the repeated problems of selection have been solved, at least to one's own satisfaction, how shall one impose order and form upon these masses of material? Grant that an author is to be discussed, where does he belong? He may refuse steadfastly to fit into any of the conventional literary categories. The tone, the style, the technique of his work may be so experimental that no hitherto respected category will longer suffice. Further, the young author may fit neatly into a system until his next book reveals an unsuspected facet of his nature. Is Sherwood Anderson to be considered as a short story writer or as a novelist? Is Heywood Broun an essayist or a "columnist"? Is E. E. Cummings a poet?

But after all, the crucial problem in all critical activity is evaluation, and certainly the evaluation of contemporaries is extra-hazardous. Happy the man whose lot it is to discuss

Foreword—*Continued*

established reputations. His own taste or the lack of it may be corrected or confirmed by the judgments of his predecessors. He will escape calumny so long as he is content to modify or echo the judgments of the respectable. But in the evaluation of contemporaries, each man's judgment is as good as another's. The critic of contemporaries sails an uncharted sea, and the monsters ready to devour him are his fellow readers and his fellow critics. He risks a thousand shipwrecks.

CONTEMPORARY AMERICAN LITERATURE

INTRODUCTION TO
CONTEMPORARY AMERICAN LITERATURE

THE NOVEL

The Old Masters: Howells and James

At the turn of the century William Dean Howells was in his sixty-third year, and Henry James, his friend and master-disciple, was in his fifty-seventh. After 1900 Howells issued twenty or more volumes, but none of them except perhaps *The Kentons* (1902) and *The Leatherwood God* (1916) approached the distinguished work he had done in the eighties and nineties, or modified the conceptions critics had already formed of his ideas, his practice, and his service to American literature. The publication in 1900 of his autobiographical pieces, *Literary Friends and Acquaintances* and *A Personal Retrospect of American Authorship* indicated that Howells had arrived at the time when a man looks back over his achievement rather than forward to it.

Howells's agreeable but somewhat uneventful life is of interest only in so far as it influenced his theory and practice of literature. Born at Martins Ferry, Ohio, in 1837, he spent his childhood under pioneer conditions that gave him little formal education. He educated himself sturdily, however, in varied journalistic activities, and gradually acquired a knowledge of six languages, and a zest for reading which had not a little to do with the formation of his literary taste and the direction of his creative work. As a reward for writing a campaign biography of Lincoln, he was appointed United States consul at Venice, where he lived from 1861 to 1865. After a year on the staff of the *Nation*, he became assistant editor of the *Atlantic Monthly*, 1866, and its editor from 1872 to 1881, that is to say, the arbiter of the most severe American taste of the period. Later he became an editorial writer for *Harper's Magazine* (1886–91), and finally the writer of "The Editor's Easy Chair" for the same magazine. He died in 1920, after long and distinguished serv-

3

ice as novelist, essayist, critic, and encourager of talents as
diverse as those of Mark Twain and Henry James.

Howells's literary theories were a blend of audacity and
timorousness. His wide acquaintance with European literature brought him in touch with realism of varying degrees
of intensity. The main tenets of the realistic doctrine he
adopted, he attempted to propagate and to practise. He insisted that literature must be faithful to life, that it must
not permit itself to indulge in flights of extravagant fancy.
He strove painstakingly in his own work to eschew the un-
usual and the improbable, and to cling to the familiar and
the possible. On the other hand, Howells's deep admiration
for the dominant culture of New England, and that prolonged contact with it which made him more Bostonian than
the Bostonians, provoked in him a fastidious reaction from
the extremities of naturalism. It is not to his discredit that
he wrote that if "a novel flatters the passions, and exalts
them above the principles, it is poisonous." It is, however, of
considerable importance to Howells's influence and reputation that in his novels he steadily restricted his characters
to gentlemanly and ladylike emotions, and rather bodiless
emotions at that. His realism insisted on being respectable.

The material for his fiction Howells found in his own
boyhood in Ohio, in his long literary life in Boston and New
York, and in his frequent journeys to Europe. This material
he treated with seriousness and artistry, in a style not brilliant but graceful and agreeable, in a form that was conscious
if rather conventional. The best of his work offers problems
of character and conduct soundly envisaged, and made real
by his painstaking representation of the *milieu*, the accurate
rendition of the surfaces of his story.

There is no question as to the influence of Howells upon
the men of his own generation. In the earlier part of our
period, Howells's example both in criticism and in creative
work assisted considerably in making realism the dominant
literary mode. If the publication of Dreiser's *Sister Carrie*

in 1900 indicates the emergence of a more daring realism, its suppression suggests that the restrained and decent realism of Howells was still a standard of taste. There is reason, however, to believe that before the end of his career his influence was waning. As an artist, Howells will continue to occupy a respectable position. His good taste and his native inhibitions make him unfashionable at the moment, but both historically and aesthetically he has probably more significance than any other American novelist of the last quarter of the nineteenth century in America except Henry James.

RECOMMENDED READING

The Lady of the Aroostook. 1879.
A Modern Instance. 1882.
The Rise of Silas Lapham. 1884.
Indian Summer. 1885.
A Hazard of New Fortunes. 1889.
The Quality of Mercy. 1892.
The Kentons. 1902.
The Leatherwood God. 1916.

RECOMMENDED CRITICISM

Boynton, P. H.: *A History of American Literature.* 1919.
Clemens, S. L.: *What is Man? and Other Essays.* 1917.
Cooke, Delmar G.: *William Dean Howells.* 1922.
Firkins, Oscar W.: *William Dean Howells.* 1924.
Harvey, A.: *William Dean Howells.* 1917.
Howells, Mildred: *Life and Letters of William Dean Howells.* 1928.
Macy, John A.: *The Spirit of American Literature.* 1913.
Underwood, J. C.: *Literature and Insurgency.* 1914.
Van Doren, Carl: *The American Novel.* 1921.
Vedder, Henry C.: *American Authors of Today.* 1895.

Henry James

The outer life of Henry James is even less interesting and eventful than that of his friend and critic, Howells. He was born in New York City in 1843, and with his older brother,

Henry James—*Continued*

William James, he was educated unsystematically both at home and abroad. Prevented by uncertain health from participating in the Civil War, he studied casually at the Harvard Law School, but under the influence of the New England literary tradition still strong in Cambridge he turned toward literature. A passion for the rich experience and the complex culture of Europe drew him again and again to the Continent, and ultimately led to his settling down in England in 1876, first at London, and then in greater seclusion at Lamb House, Rye. His very deep love for England induced him, early in the Great War, to become a British subject. In 1916, the year of his death, he received the Order of Merit, the highest honor conferred on literary men in England.

In the deepest sense, James's attitude toward art was a by-product of his attitude toward life. Both temperament and early experience attracted him to the attitude of spectator rather than that of participant. His quest for the comely and charming life is reflected in his preoccupation with the upper reaches of society at home and abroad, and his untiringly curious study of the life and types he loved is manifest on every page of his novels and tales. He felt that the novel should be the result of the most scrupulous and honest observation of human beings, and that if the observation were accurate, the meaning and value of life would become apparent even though no moral were deliberately indicated.

A typical novel by James represents a group of persons in an intimate and complicated series of relations. The characters are studied with infinite pains in order to bring to light the ultimate truth of their relationships. James's artistic conscience frequently led him to represent this psychological drama in terms of an incidental observer whose most intense emotion seems, as in James himself, to be curiosity. The pattern of his novels illustrates one or another of his major themes, alone or in combination. His earlier work, like *The American* (1877) and *The Portrait of a Lady*

Henry James—*Continued*

(1881), is a series of studies of the impact of European characters upon Americans. Later, in *The Tragic Muse* (1892) and in numerous tales such as "The Death of the Lion" and "The Figure in the Carpet," he turned to a consideration of the artist and his plight in a civilized but Philistine society. Finally, as he came to realize with some sinking at heart the weaknesses of his glamorous Europeans, he studied the basic conflict between integrity and depravity, in *What Maisie Knew* (1897), *The Wings of the Dove* (1902), and *The Golden Bowl* (1904).

All this significant subject matter, these rich and inexhaustible psychological data, he rendered in a style which is at once the joy and the despair of his readers. The style changed from a lithe simplicity to a complexity that exhausts the reader's attention if it does not frighten him away. The secret of this amazing development is to be sought, perhaps, in his increasing fastidiousness and in his passion for utterly honest statement. The first motive led him from the banal to the fresh, from the simply direct to the indirectly complex. The second developed in him the habit of qualification, the multiplication of adverbial phrases and clauses until the essential assertion is often almost hidden from sight. The style became, in the critical prefaces to the New York edition of his carefully chosen works, a mode of concealment rather than one of revelation of thought. It became an astounding instrument for infinitesimal psychological notation, but it lost the eminently desirable qualities of simplicity and clarity.

The work of James is more significant in itself than in relation to the history of the contemporary novel. Condemned by temperament and experience to an increasing remoteness from crude vitality, he created a number of novels perfect in their kind, but inevitably limited in their appeal. The unequaled seriousness of his attitude toward his work distinguishes him from all his American contemporaries and successors. He persuaded a few people, as no one

Henry James—*Continued*
had succeeded in doing, that the novel as an art-form should
be considered with prayerful respect. He contributed, in
both Europe and America, to the intensification of the
psychological element in the novel, an intensification that
may be said to have begun with George Eliot and not yet
to have reached its end.

RECOMMENDED READING

The American. 1877.
The Portrait of a Lady. 1881.
Terminations. 1895. (Tales.)
What Maisie Knew. 1897.
The Two Magics. 1898. (Tales.)
The Wings of the Dove. 1902.
The Ambassadors. 1903.
The Golden Bowl. 1904.
The Altar of the Dead. 1909. (Tales.)
The Letters of Henry James. 1920. (Selected and edited by Percy
Lubbock.)

RECOMMENDED CRITICISM

Beach, J. W.: *The Method of Henry James.* 1918.
Brooks, Van Wyck: *The Pilgrimage of Henry James.* 1925.
Cambridge History of American Literature.
Cary, Elizabeth L.: *The Novels of Henry James.* 1905.
Edgar, Pelham: *Henry James.* 1927.
Elton, Oliver: *Modern Studies.* 1907.
Follett, H. T. and W.: *Some Modern Novelists.* 1918.
Hackett, Francis: *Horizons.* 1918.
Hueffer, Ford Madox: *Henry James: a Critical Study.* 1913.
Lubbock, Percy: *The Craft of Fiction.* 1921.
Macy, J. A.: *The Spirit of American Literature.* 1913.
Perry, Bliss: *The American Spirit in Literature.* 1918.
Sherman, Stuart P.: *On Contemporary Literature.* 1917.
Underwood, J. C.: *Literature and Insurgency.* 1914.
Van Doren, Carl: *The American Novel.* 1921.
West, Rebecca: *Henry James.* 1916.

Cf. also *Cambridge History of American Literature,* III (IV), 674.
Quarterly Review, 212 ('10): 393; 226 ('16): 60; 234 ('20): 188.

THE NEW MASTERS: WHARTON, DREISER, CABELL, CATHER, ANDERSON

Edith Wharton

Of the novelists who have come into prominence since 1900, the position of Mrs. Edith Wharton (q. v.) is perhaps the most assured. Both her theory and her practice link her with the old masters, for consciously and passionately she has declared herself a disciple of Henry James, whom she regards as the first really artistic English novelist. Her long friendship with James, his constant critical interest, and his approbation of her literary methods, confirmed her in her natural inclination to an attitude toward life and art steadily parallel with his. If her work has proved to be at once more popular and less distinguished, the reason is to be sought in the inevitable divergence of their personalities and their talents.

With James, Mrs. Wharton shares the conviction that the novel should have a carefully constructed pattern, presenting a moral problem involving subtle and unsubtle personalities against a highly civilized setting. With James, she shares a distaste for the shambling methods of the great English novelists from Fielding to Thackeray, and an almost romantic enthusiasm for old lands and for a rich tradition of manners and character. They are alike, too, in their aloofness, in their preoccupation with moral problems of such a rarity as to lay them open to the charge of unreality and casuistry. They are alike, finally, in their distaste for the banal, the commonplace in life and art, for the vulgar, the shabby, the crude. Both have the loftiest conception of the function of the artist and of art in a civilized society, and regard their creative activity with immense conscientiousness.

9

Edith Wharton—*Continued*

Mrs. Wharton's work in the novel is probably more significant than her work in the tale or short story.[1] Her novels fall into several fairly distinct classes. Her earliest novel, *The Valley of Decision* (1902) is an elaborate and industrious attempt at the historical novel in an eighteenth century setting. The effect is praiseworthy but frigid. Her short novels of rural New England life, *Ethan Frome* (1911) and *Summer* (1917), demonstrate her ability to understand and present the lives of people out of her own class, and the former is one of her most impressive works. Her fiction inspired by the Great War, notably *The Marne* (1918), *A Son at the Front* (1923), and *The Mother's Recompense* (1925), is made comparatively negligible by her conventional attitude toward the experiences represented. The major part of her work concerns the upper levels of American society, more frequently than in the case of James, and at home rather than abroad. In this vein are *The House of Mirth* (1905), the foundation of her popularity; *The Custom of the Country* (1913), a venomous portrait of a social climber, Undine Spragg; and *The Age of Innocence* (1920), a subtle reconstruction of the tone and manner of the New York society of Mrs. Wharton's childhood.

Aside from the qualities she shares with her master, Henry James, Mrs. Wharton brings to her work an at first uncontrolled epigrammatic brilliance, a deep vein of irony, and a faculty for the brilliant pictorial rendition of the settings of civilized life in America and Europe.

Theodore Dreiser

In the novel of our time, a hardly more striking contrast could be drawn than between the work of Mrs. Wharton and that of Theodore Dreiser (q. v.). They differ radically in personality, philosophy, and artistry. Yet it is probable that, with the exception of Mrs. Wharton, no other novelist has done such significant if not distinguished work.

[1] See below, p. 39.

Theodore Dreiser—*Continued*

The long struggle of Dreiser for recognition, a struggle notably aided by the persistent enthusiasm of H. L. Mencken, and crowned by the great success of *An American Tragedy* (1925), is to be explained primarily by the gulf between Dreiser's philosophy and that of the American reading public. Both by temperament and by experience Dreiser belongs to the naturalistic movement, led by the somewhat outmoded Zola, and only very belatedly manifesting its influence in America on Dreiser and some of the post-war novelists. The ideal of the naturalists was to record what they saw without moral or ethical bias, to set down all the facts that they could collect, with as little artistic selection as possible. In point of practice, however, most of the naturalists, Dreiser among them, have tended to see human life in terms of animal life. If they did not identify the two, they made their readers steadily aware of the animal elements in human behavior.

Dreiser's reading of the American scene is then inevitably different from the moral earnestness of Winston Churchill and the cheery sentimentality of Booth Tarkington. Dreiser, like Zola himself, feels the intricate confusion of modern industrial society, and has seen numbers of individuals fail through weakness, and others succeed in their coarse determination to exact what they desire from the social organism. In the intense economic struggle, he sees how strong-willed financiers or "geniuses" trample their way to eminence. He is also aware of the misery and poverty in which many people are condemned to live under the present industrial régime. This struggle between powerful and impotent individuals fills Dreiser, not with exultation and admiration, but with a sense of pathos and despair. Moreover, he does not enjoy the large consolation of beauty. To the beauty of nature he is curiously blind, and the luxury and elegance which he sometimes depicts are frequently ugly and tasteless. The world through which Dreiser's characters move is shabby and grim and precarious.

Theodore Dreiser—*Continued*

This somewhat grim view of life is only imperfectly trans-
mitted by Dreiser's art. Its most obvious weakness is the
wretchedness of his style. There is much justice in the
charge that the style is awkward and sometimes unbearably
commonplace and conventional in word and phrase. His
control of grammar is imperfect, and his feeling for the fresh
and delightful word or phrase is almost negligible. A more
essential weakness is his inability to distinguish between the
significant and the insignificant detail. He collects facts
for the facts' sake, and though the effect is undeniably
massive, the weight of inconsequential details impedes the
movement of the narrative and obscures the essential events.
Probably the most damning charge against Dreiser is that
his view of life is limited. He is almost unaware of beauty
in nature or in character, and though he sees life steadily,
he certainly does not see it whole.

On the other hand, the virtues of Dreiser go a considerable
distance in counterbalancing his weaknesses. He has a
dogged devotion to the collection of material, an immense
honesty to the contemplation of human motives, and a pene-
tration into the subterfuges and sufferings of weak characters,
which make him the most skilful among Americans in evoking
a pity and a terror that he has demonstrated may belong
even to naturalistic tragedy. *An American Tragedy* is not
only a remarkable representation of some obscure phases
of the American scene, but an oppressively powerful study
of a youth who at first seems despicably weak, but who
through the intensity of his suffering becomes a heart-
breaking symbol of the dilemma of humanity. It is not
merely American, but universal.

James Branch Cabell

Possessed of a philosophic outlook and a theory of art
diametrically opposed to those of Dreiser, James Branch
Cabell (q. v.) rivals him in the mass and the distinction of
his achievement as well as in his conflicts with the moralists

James Branch Cabell—*Continued*

and the violence of his partizan followers. Cabell has expressed his views of life and art most directly in his series of essays *Beyond Life* (1919) and in the somewhat more cynical *Straws and Prayerbooks* (1924), but his basic ideas are implicit in everything that he has written since his earliest period of pure and popular romanticism. Cabell is a romanticist with a difference. He extols the glamorous and colorful past, the adventurous existence, the flowing gesture, and above all, the idolatry of woman. The qualifications of his devotion arise from his consciousness that none of these objects of worship is quite worth the emotion that it arouses. Though the illusion of art and love and religion is what makes life endurable, it is bound in subtle natures to end in disillusionment, and in simple natures like Jurgen's in a welcome return to unimaginative domesticity. So all Cabell's heroes in whatever age go a-questing, and though they meet with diverse and absorbing adventures, they return with pleasant memories and a more or less bitter awakening to the light of common day or to the approach of death. Numerous objections may be made to this reading of life: it is certainly un-American, and it is likewise mildly profane. The chief aesthetic objection to it is its monotony in the hands of Cabell. Situations and characters recur even under the most outlandish disguise, and the repetition of motifs becomes wearisome. Yet the music built up on these restricted themes is like none composed in these days by an American prose master.

Cabell's style is what we should expect from a romantic ironist, elaborate, rhythmical, and sophisticated. He has read in strange rare books, and from them he brings esoteric learning and the vocabulary of ancient romance. He delights in odd flowers and jewels and metals; he is fascinated by exotic names that stir the imagination. He scatters them over his page so thickly that one pines for a less connotative style. Unquestionably, the suave rhythms of Cabell's style become monotonous, but in the main that style is deft and

James Branch Cabell—*Continued*

sensitive, as adequate an instrument for his music as one can imagine.

Cabell's distinction is not that of the great novelists, the creation of character and the designing of plot, but of a special sort deriving from his complex character of romanticist, humorist, and satirist. To the first element are due his love of the exotic, his worship of even transitory beauty, his delight in colorful remote times and places, his development of an exquisite sensuous style. But his romanticism is modified by his powers in the direction of humor and satire. His range in comedy is wide: he has the subtler humors, sarcasm and irony; he has the cruder humors of farce and burlesque. His most notorious form of humor is innuendo, a lewd suggestion beneath the surface meaning. This easiest of the forms of humor Cabell overdoes, and thereby cheapens his reputation. As a satirist almost nothing escapes his disillusioning touch. He concerns himself, not with the surfaces of our mechanical world, but with its ideals,—religion, morality, patriotism, love. But the most constant undertone of his romanticism is irony. If one side of Cabell's shield bears the device, Romance, the reverse reads, Irony.

The somewhat monotonous repetition of Cabell's ideas will condemn much of his work to oblivion, but *Jurgen* (1919) and *Figures of Earth* (1921) are almost certain to retain their attractiveness as apologues of the adventures of the human animal through an alluring if not quite satisfying universe.

Willa Cather

Somewhat more doubtfully, Willa Cather (q. v.) and Sherwood Anderson may be included among the new masters of the American novel. The doubt arises from the fact that both Miss Cather and Mr. Anderson are somewhat ill at ease in the presence of the novel-form, and both seem to be unhappily limited to the material of their own observation by a meager endowment of genuinely creative imagination.

Miss Cather finds her material in the life of the pioneer, the valiant spirit who adventures dangerously in life or in art. Her curiosity and sympathy have made use of the opportunities offered by her early life in Nebraska to study the lives and characters of the Teutonic and Slavic stocks who were carving homes and livelihoods for themselves out of the prairie. Later, both in the Southwest and in the East, she turned almost inevitably to the artistic personalities whose lives have always seemed to her more worth recording than those of the compact citizen or the vulgarized peasant on Main Street. She has always responded to her favorite subjects with a sweeping imaginative appreciation of the humbly heroic, with a freshness of observation and an insight that make her peasants and her artists singularly alive and unliterary. She has brought a deep admiration to the women whose serene and enduring stability has served them well on the frontier of physical and artistic life, and her Ántonia Shimerda and Thea Kronborg are compelling embodiments of the spirits of such women. In her view of things Miss Cather is steadily on the side of beauty and simplicity and sturdy devotion, and against shoddiness, duplicity, and vulgarity in high or low circles.

In the treatment of her material Miss Cather shows unwearied conscientiousness as to form and finish. Her style is lucid, fresh, observant. It is touched steadily with poetic sensitiveness. It has the simplicity of first-rate work, but it is the simplicity of art and not of nature. Miss Cather is still concerned with the finding of a novel-form adequate to her purpose. If she has tended to move away from the conventional novel, it may be, as Mr. Van Doren suggests, under the stimulus of her desire to find "the precise form for the representation of a memorable character." At any rate, she has seen fit to dispense very largely with plot, to avoid in the main the big scene, and to build her novel out of only that material which is relevant to the creation of significant character. Her whole art has steadily eliminated the unimportant detail, and, in *My Mortal Enemy* (1926), the sparseness of matter and the resolute abhorrence of the novelistic make one wonder whether she is suffering a diminution of creative energy or is following her own right artistic road.

Sherwood Anderson

Though Sherwood Anderson (q. v.) has done more satisfactory work in the short story [1] than in the novel-form, it is desirable to consider him briefly in this connection. As Miss Cather has devoted much of her work to the interpretation of the European peasant on American soil, so Anderson has concerned himself by and large with the American peasant. On the surface, Anderson's peasant is drab, inexpressive, and apparently insignificant. But Anderson believes that such simple people are important, and by his intuition and imagination he is able to penetrate the dull surface of their lives, and to reveal the intense emotion underneath. For the fates of such inarticulate people Anderson has something of that encompassing pity which among the Russians Dostoievsky and more particularly Gorki displayed.

For this material Anderson has had considerable difficulty in finding a form that is suitable and significant. He barely succeeds in managing a number of characters, or in working those characters into an effective pattern. At the best, he is able to juggle only two or three, and aside from these figures, the secondary characters of his novels are treated very incidentally. For instance, the story of the old harness-maker in *Poor White* (1920) is hardly an integral part of that novel. Anderson also finds it difficult to keep to his subject, the development of character or narrative. He permits himself digressions; he introduces little essays on American life and character.

Anderson has deliberately worked out a style of his own, a departure from the conventional trend of successful and popular literature. In the simplicity of his sentence-struc-

[1] See below, p. 40.

ture, the frequency of his *and*-sentences, the avoidance of literary diction, his style is closer to the level of American colloquial language than that of any current novelist. But it is lifted above the merely colloquial by his fine sense of rhythm, his sensitive use of repetition, and his suggestive use of even familiar words and phrases.

A probable weakness in Anderson is the fact that his material seems limited in the main to his own experience, and confined to his own reaction to life. Since the publication of his autobiography, *A Story-Teller's Story* (1924), it has been possible to observe how frequently he has thrown the veil of fiction over actual character and incident. The Judge of the autobiography appears as a minor character in several novels and under various names. Anderson's father, who has played a great part in his psychic development, appears as Windy McPherson's father and in other disguises as well. Anderson's heroes, moreover, are variations on the theme of his own introverted personality, most sensitively projected in the hero of *Poor White*. They tend to pass through much the same experiences: in nearly every novel of Anderson's, the hero runs away almost without warning, usually from his wife. Suffering vaguely from dissatisfaction with the universe, he goes off in a blundering quest for the meaning of life or the solution of his personal problem. Sometimes the hero's quest ends in a woman, as in *Dark Laughter* (1925), and sometimes, as in *Marching Men* (1917), in an idea. But despite the limitations of Anderson's imagination and of his technique, the total effect of his work is of the emergence of as veritably American a figure as has appeared since Whitman.

JOURNEYMEN: TARKINGTON, CHURCHILL, GLASGOW, HERGESHEIMER, LEWIS

Booth Tarkington

For range and variety of work, Booth Tarkington (q. v.) deserves the foremost position among those who are a little lower than the masters. He has tried his hand at several kinds and manners. He has willingly assisted in preparing for the stage some of his more popular novels, *Monsieur Beaucaire* and *Seventeen*, and he has written directly for the stage a series of light pieces, of which the most successful was *Clarence* (1921). Aside from *Monsieur Beaucaire* (1900), a not undistinguished contribution to the lively but passing vogue of the historical novel, his major work has been in the humorous representation of adolescence and in a semi-serious treatment of the novel of purpose. In *Penrod* (1914) and *Seventeen* (1916), he delighted a vast audience with faithful but somewhat superficial studies of boyhood and adolescence, much less searching than Mark Twain's. In such moralistic fictions as *The Gentleman from Indiana* (1899) and the better documented *Turmoil* (1915) and *The Magnificent Ambersons* (1918), while exhibiting a surface realism, he succumbed to the temptation to flatter American notions as to the all-conquering power of uprightness, and to supply a happy dénouement for the solace of the average reader. Perhaps Tarkington's best work is in a vein of subdued and honest realism which reflects lower middle-class life in Middle Western cities, without the incursion of inappropriate humor and sentimentality. *Alice Adams* (1921) is as honest a piece of work as has come from his rapid pen.

Winston Churchill

A somewhat more difficult problem is offered by the case of Winston Churchill (q. v.), who has followed the trends of

Winston Churchill—*Continued*

literary fashion with a devotion and seriousness which have been inadequately rewarded by artistic distinction. His early work at the turn of the century was in the mode of the historical romance; *Richard Carvel* (1899) and *The Crisis* (1901) are perhaps the most readable of the novels produced during that quickly fading phase. Later, with the serious social zeal which characterized the thoughtful liberal decade just before the War, Churchill turned to social and controversial subjects with the same high purpose and vigor that he had shown in his own political activity. To the attack on abuses in religious, social, and economic life he devoted himself with the absorption of a convert, and the novels that resulted from his passionate study and thought provoked many a controversy of a nature inevitably unliterary. Mr. Churchill's chief political novels were *Coniston* (1906) and *Mr. Crewe's Career* (1908); his religious novel, *The Inside of the Cup* (1913) aroused the most bitter discussion, especially in the pulpits; and in *The Dwelling Place of Light* (1917) he did his duty by the then popular industrial-problem novel. As he has now arrived at the dignity of a collected edition, it would seem that his work is well-nigh finished.

Since Mr. Churchill's intentions have always been honorable, his equivocal reputation is to be attributed to a basic mediocrity of mind and art. To the somewhat sceptical post-war period, Churchill's mind seems simple and naïve. He is always on the right side, but he is there uncritically and ingenuously. Churchill's mind has much of the obvious simplicity of Roosevelt's, a quality more serviceable to a man of action than to a man of letters. Moreover, he has rarely captured the note of life in his handling of character, or distinction of style, unless perhaps in the vein of the now outmoded historical novel.

Ellen Glasgow

Of the women who have a substantial amount of work and an established reputation to their credit, Ellen Glasgow has been most alert to changing styles in the matter and form

19

Ellen Glasgow—*Continued*

of fiction, and the most successful in adapting herself to the new modes. Herself a Virginian, she might easily have persisted in the Southern tradition of local color sentimentally applied, but she escaped a dangerous provinciality by practising with meticulous honesty the semi-historical novel, in *The Battle-ground* (1902) and *The Deliverance* (1904). It was perhaps inevitable that Miss Glasgow should have been caught up in the wave of liberalism which was so influential in the work of Winston Churchill. In such novels as *Virginia* (1913) and *Life and Gabriella* (1916), Miss Glasgow, while remaining true to her native material, ventured upon problems of conduct and character that outraged the self-conscious gentility of her native state. To the somewhat severer realism of the post-war period she has contributed such notable pieces of work as *Barren Ground* (1925) and *The Romantic Comedians* (1926).

Joseph Hergesheimer

Two writers, Joseph Hergesheimer (q. v.) and Sinclair Lewis, whose literary début coincided with the beginning of the Great War (1914), have achieved sufficient distinction to warrant separate consideration here. Since their work is as unlike as possible, their importance must be decided on quite distinct grounds. Hergesheimer has devoted himself to the period-novel with a success that is little less than astonishing. He is an antiquarian and interior decorator turned novelist. He has an unflagging passion for the decorative, and it is natural that life in his novels should sometimes be crushed out by bric-à-brac. In the carrying out of his chosen purpose, the setting down of "the colors and scents and emotions of existence," he is apt to bury the emotions under colors and scents. He is too intent on the line of the gesture to consider the meaning of the gesture. Hergesheimer's most important work, in *Java Head* (1919) and *The Three Black Pennys* (1917), is the re-creation of periods in American history the sheer picturesqueness of

Joseph Hergesheimer—*Continued*

which we are inclined to forget. In his attempts to treat modern life as decoration, he creates an unquestionable but lifeless beauty in *Linda Condon* (1919), and in *Cytherea* (1922) an implausible and grotesque love-story, crowned with a burningly vivid death-scene. If his novels are sometimes as stuffy as an antique-shop or as overdone as a decorator's studio, it is because Mr. Hergesheimer's literary taste leans to the rococo rather than to the classical.

Sinclair Lewis

After the uneventful publication of a half-dozen novels, of which *Our Mr. Wrenn* (1914) was the first, Sinclair Lewis (q. v.) won nation-wide celebrity with *Main Street* (1920), and has contrived to keep himself in the public eye ever since. Lewis belongs at once to the school of painstaking realism and to the Menckenite group of critics of American folk-ways. His work demands attention, then, both for its realism and for its satirical treatment of American characters and ideas. His realistic powers are unquestioned; he has a phenomenal memory, or equally phenomenal industry for the amassing of the details that build up as plausible a picture of small-town and small-city life as the realistic movement in America has produced. The first hundred pages of *Babbitt* (1922), which render unsparingly the minutest details of the realtor's day, are a masterpiece of malicious microscopic reporting. With the clothes, the houses, the habits, the ideas, of his victims Lewis is inexhaustibly familiar, and his monuments of detail would be wearisome, were they not cemented with satire. Like most satirists, Lewis has been accused of producing merely destructive criticism. He dislikes the provinciality of the average small town, the jargon and the muddleheadedness of the small-business man, the chicanery and vileness which have occasionally cloaked themselves in religion. If Lewis's criticism is in the main negative, his case does not differ from that of most of the satirists from Juvenal to Anatole France. If Lewis's animus leads, as in the case of *Elmer Gantry* (1927), to grotesque exaggeration, he is again accompanied by those many moralists who have driven their points home with a bludgeon. In proportion as Lewis's subjects are perennial human weaknesses, his works may abide; in all probability, however, his excessively realistic method will weary readers in a period when realism is not dominant. Of grace and elegance he is quite innocent, but force and massiveness are his notable possessions.

DOMINANT TRENDS: ROMANCE
The Historical Novel
While the dominant trend of novel-writing during the last generation has been in the direction of realism, there has been a steady and sometimes marked countercurrent of romance of a more or less specious nature. The first and most noteworthy expression of the spirit of romance was the outburst of historical novel-writing in the decade from 1895 to 1905. Inspired by the examples of Stevenson in *Kidnapped* (1886) and Rider Haggard in *She* (1887) and *King Solomon's Mines*, and stimulated further by the wide popularity of Anthony Hope's *The Prisoner of Zenda* and *Rupert of Hentzau*, the American fictionists turned to their task with a zest and industry that in many instances were abundantly rewarded. To this prodigious activity we owe the still memorable and in some cases still readable instances of S. Weir Mitchell's *Hugh Wynne* (1897), Charles Major's *When Knighthood Was in Flower* (1898)—a great popular success both as a novel and as a play—and Mary Johnston's *To Have and To Hold* (1899), which she followed up by a long series of novels of the same type but with an increasing attention to accurate detail. To this same movement belong Winston Churchill's *Richard Carvel* (1899) and *The Crisis* (1901), Henry Harland's graceful and sophisticated *Cardinal's Snuff Box* (1901), George Barr McCutcheon's popular but meretricious *Graustark* (1901), and Owen Wister's skilful and honest *Virginian* (1902). But this tide of lively romance was being met by a sturdy wave of realism, and the historical novel almost immediately faded into obscurity.

The Novel of Primitive Adventure
Since the end of the vogue of historical romance, the romantic spirit has cropped out in a host of novels of primitive

The Novel of Primitive Adventure—*Continued*

life, where adventure begins before breakfast, where heroes are always handsome and valorous, and where the villain combines lust and violence with a tendency to be overcome by the young hero in a terrific fight in the next to the last chapter. If the novel of primitive adventure has not won the attention or the respect of seasoned readers, it is because its practitioners have contented themselves with the utmost conventionality in plot and character, a style which renders natural or human beauty with ecstatic banality, and a moral issue with the simplicity of an elementary Sunday-school lesson. The favorite *milieux* for these romances of adventure have been the American West, Alaska, the Canadian Northwest, and recently the South Seas, first popularized by the travel books of Frederick O'Brien. Jack London exploited the fresh material of Alaska, James Oliver Curwood made the Canadian Northwest his own particular stamping ground, and Zane Grey has celebrated the American West in *Riders of the Purple Sage* (1912) and *The Light of Western Stars* (1914).

The Sentimental Novel

By far the most popular disguise in which the spirit of romance lurks is the sentimental novel, which with its frank appeal to tearful feminine readers has won its authors some of the most colossal successes in the history of the novel. John Fox, Jr., infused enough sentimentality into his treatment of the life of the mountain whites to raise *The Little Shepherd of Kingdom Come* (1903) and *The Trail of the Lonesome Pine* (1908) above the narrow popularity of mere local color writing. But it remained for Gene Stratton-Porter in *Freckles* (1903), *A Girl of the Limberlost* (1912), and *Laddie* (1913), to sound the depths of a sentimental attitude toward nature and character, to the unending delight of an immense audience. Even beyond her success has been that of Harold Bell Wright, who discovered early, in *That Printer of Udell's* (1903), a magic formula composed judiciously of the inevit-

The Sentimental Novel—*Continued*

able ingredients of picturesque setting, homespun nobility
and ignobility in desperate conflict, an obvious moral tone,
and a completely hackneyed style. His *Shepherd of the Hills*
(1907) and *The Winning of Barbara Worth* (1191) bid fair
to be for some time the "classics" of popular sentimental
fiction. On a somewhat higher plane is the work of Joseph C.
Lincoln, whose specialty, the quaintly eccentric characters
of Cape Cod, is handled with a telling combination of humor
and sentiment.

DOMINANT TRENDS: REALISM

The main trend of serious novel-writing, despite the exceptions just noted, has been realistic, and it is possible to distinguish several phases of realism which overlap and interweave, but which for purposes of clarity may be discussed separately. The first phase is the passage from a gentle to a strenuous use of local color; the second is the rather brief appearance of a conscientiously brutal realism in the work of Stephen Crane, Ambrose Bierce, Frank Norris, and Jack London; the third is the combination of realistic method with a social purpose, noticeable particularly in the decade or so before the War, and the fourth, the current phase of disillusioned realism exhibited by a group of post-war writers.

The local color writer after the Civil War settled down to a sentimental-humorous exploitation of provincial eccentricities or a conventionalization of both character and situation that ended too often in picturesque sterility. The limitations of the type may be suggested by the self-conscious charm of F. Hopkinson Smith's *Colonel Carter of Cartersville* (1891) and by the exquisite but fragile art of Sarah Orne Jewett (1849–1909). It remained for more robust spirits to raise provincial material to the level of national significance through a resolute facing of the economic and social facts beneath the picturesque surface. As early as 1880, in *The Grandissimes*, George Washington Cable had brought a sense of satire to bear upon the narrowness and affectation of decaying Louisiana society, and in 1883 E. W. Howe had written his bare and unlovely *Story of a Country Town*. Less than a decade later, Hamlin Garland exposed courageously the hardships and deprivations involved in the pioneering life of the Middle West, in *Main-Travelled Roads* (1891) and

26

Prairie Folks (1893). In New England, where local color writing was a flourishing cult, Mary E. Wilkins Freeman, in *A New England Nun* (1891) and in *Pembroke* (1894), brought a sterner note to the tradition of quaint humors.

But the courage of the later local colorists was presently to be outdone by several deliberately red-blooded writers who exceeded their predecessors in violence and brutality as well as in honesty and frankness. Of the group consisting of Stephen Crane (1871–1900), Frank Norris (1870–1902), and Jack London (1876–1916), the work of Stephen Crane seems to be of greatest absolute and historical interest. He combined a poetically sensitive observation and an unfashionable creed of unqualified realism that make him seem a creature born out of his time. In his novels, *Maggie* (1893) and *The Red Badge of Courage* (1895), he essayed subjects or methods which all his contemporaries left cautiously alone. Probably no war-novel written in English before 1914 equals Crane's in unflinching fidelity to fact and in verisimilitude. The interest in his work manifested by such diverse writers as Henry James and Joseph Conrad only strengthens one's confidence that in Crane's untimely death a real talent was lost. A somewhat more wilfully masculine writer was Frank Norris, whose lifespan coincided almost exactly with Crane's and whose work is only slightly less promising. The somewhat grandiose conceptions that underlie such novels as *The Octopus* (1901) and *The Pit* (1903) do not diminish one's admiration of Norris's attempt to treat American subjects in an epic vein. If he erred in his somewhat hysterical over-stressing of the elemental and the red-blooded, it was a natural protest against the namby-pamby quality of much American fiction before and since. The final member of the group, Jack London, lived long enough to pass beyond the limits of his early red-blooded period, and to cast in his lot with the literature of social protest that during the last decade of his life was to engage the efforts of the more important realists in America. But neither his contributions to the literature of radicalism nor his thinly disguised auto-biographical fictions, *Martin Eden* (1909), and *John Barley-corn* (1913), seem so important or so skilful as the earlier *Sea Wolf* (1904) and *The Call of the Wild* (1903)—one of the best animal novels written in our time. London illustrates better than any other member of the group the exaggerated virility, the almost pathological brutality, which was the logical conclusion of this trend.

London also serves as a convenient link with the next phase of realistic writing, the novel of purpose or the problem-novel. It was by no means a new form, since it had been used sensationally by Harriet Beecher Stowe in *Uncle Tom's Cabin*, and was a popular Victorian mode in the hands of Dickens, Charles Reade, and Charles Kingsley. But the rising tide of liberalism, which was presently to crash against the sea-wall of the Great War, found expression not only in Jack London, but also in Upton Sinclair, in some of the women realists to be considered later, and, after the onset of the War, in Ernest Poole and Charles Norris. London's contributions to the literature of social protest reveal the carelessness and unevenness of his work more clearly than do his novels of primitive adventure. Upton Sinclair (q. v.), who rode in on the crest of the muckraking movement with his sensational novel *The Jungle* (1906), has persevered in his radicalism, and in book after book of quasi-fiction and inflammatory exposition, attributes the evils of industry, art, and education to an incredibly ingenious monster named Capitalism. His preachments would be more convincing if one did not suspect him of monomania.

Ernest Poole (q. v.), who assisted Upton Sinclair in gathering material for *The Jungle*, is an example of the radical produced by the colleges and universities after the turn of the century, who worked off his moral indignation in literature, journalism, social service, or labor-union activities. Poole's first success was *The Harbor* (1915), and he has gone on steadily with somewhat heavy humorless problem-novels.

Charles Norris (q. v.), the brother of Frank, has recently contributed ponderous but not particularly inspired examples of this type in *Salt* (1918) and *Brass* (1921), while his wife, Kathleen (q. v.), with more talent, combines considerable fidelity to human nature with a studiously conservative view of social problems.

A word may be said here concerning the more or less realistic work of a group of women-novelists. Of them, Mrs. Margaret Deland (q. v.) is the most experienced. Her most successful work has been the exploitation, in her Old Chester books, of her familiarity with western Pennsylvania. When, under the influence of a passing literary mode, she has attempted the problem-novel, in *The Awakening of Helena Ritchie* (1906) and *The Iron Woman* (1911), she has achieved no particular distinction. Dorothy Canfield Fisher (q. v.) has been somewhat more successful in adapting herself, now to the study of Vermont austerities, and now to the novel of purpose, in *The Bent Twig* (1915) and *The Brimming Cup* (1921). In the latter type she combines her views, especially of the relationships of parents and children, with a sound realistic method. Zona Gale (q. v.), who first attained popularity in the vein of sentimental local color writing applied to Wisconsin village life, won, in *Miss Lulu Bett* (1921) and *Mister Pitt* (1925) a freedom from sentiment by her cultivation of the spirit of irony.

The realism of the post-war period has been marked by a definite note of protest, not so much against the industrial system as against the stubborn conventionalities of the middle class and the sentimental delusions dear to the heart of the great American public. Immediately after the War there was a distinct revolt against conventionality, apparent in the Greenwich Village movement and in the revival of the theory of art for art's sake. Though this movement showed itself more particularly in poetry and the plastic arts and in the establishment of numerous magazines of revolt, its influence on the novel may be suggested by the work of

Floyd Dell (q. v.), especially in *Moon-Calf* (1920) and *The Briary Bush* (1921). A more determined revolt against conventional decencies is evident in the brilliant but morbid fiction of Evelyn Scott (q. v.), who in *The Narrow House* (1921) and *Narcissus* (1922) pointed a deliberate finger at the least attractive traits and habits of human beings. Mrs. Scott's work seems to show the influence of psychoanalysis on an exacerbated sensitiveness.

It was inevitable that there should be a distinct reaction from the high mood and lofty purposes stimulated by the War. In somewhat the spirit of Barbusse's *Under Fire*, John Dos Passos (q. v.) in *Three Soldiers* (1921) revealed, to the distress of the professional patriots, some of the unattractive phases of our international military adventure. He has persisted in his rebelliousness in his experimental novel, *Manhattan Transfer* (1925), and in his equally unconventional play, *The Garbage Man* (1926). Of the disillusioned realists, Ernest Hemingway (q. v.) seems the most promising; not only in his shorter pieces and in his Sherwood Anderson parody, *The Torrents of Spring*, but in *The Sun Also Rises* (1926), his brilliant first novel, he reveals an unparalleled skill in reflecting the surfaces of life and in suggesting its desperate futilities.

LITERARY BYPATHS: FANTASY, SOPHISTICATION, POETIC PROSE

Several groups of writers are attempting to escape the restrictions of an exclusive allegiance to either realism or romance. The dealers in fantasy work in a mode alien to the average reader but attractive to a small sensitive audience. The most successful has been Donn Byrne, who out-Irishes the professional Irishman in the somewhat calculated charms of *Messer Marco Polo* (1921) and *Blind Raftery* (1924). Notable contributions to this minor type have been made by the popular columnists, Christopher Morley (q. v.), and Heywood Broun, the former with *Where the Blue Begins* (1922) and *Thunder on the Left* (1925), and the latter with *Gandle Follows His Nose*.

Of the sophisticated novel of the type established by Thomas Love Peacock, revived brilliantly by Norman Douglas, and carried on by Aldous Huxley, the American novel shows few examples. Carl Van Vechten (q. v.) has worked this vein with the most success, in *Peter Whiffle* and *The Blind Bow-Boy*, though he lacks the intellectual force of Huxley and the suave graces of Douglas. A young adherent to this type is Thornton Wilder, whose *Cabala* and *The Bridge of San Luis Rey* are distinguished work in this restricted genre.

Finally, a number of young poets have turned out novels naturally infused with poetic fineness and a devotion to beauty. Of this group the most distinguished is perhaps H. D. (q. v.), whose tales in *Palimpsest* (1926) preserve her chiselled and polished artistry. Here too, belong Stephen Vincent Benét (q. v.), whose "young man" novel, *The Beginning of Wisdom*, attracted favorable attention in 1921, Elizabeth Madox Roberts (q. v.), who handled Kentucky folk-material in *The Time of Man* and *My Heart and My Flesh* with due regard for the spirits of truth and beauty, and Glenway Wescott (q. v.), whose *Apple of the Eye*, a somberly poetic handling of Wisconsin life, prepared an eager audience for the greater sweep of *The Grandmothers*. The most faithful of the poets to poetic prose was Elinor Wylie (q. v.), whose novels, though highly artificial, have the exquisite and complex beauties of lace or chased metal.

THE SHORT STORY
Characteristics

No one can glance over the literary production of the last generation without becoming aware of the ubiquity of the short story, its general excellence, and its occasional distinction.

Its ubiquity probably finds its cause in the conditions of publication in America rather than in any essential urge of the creative spirit to express itself in this particular literary form, though some critics maintain that the concentration, the intensity, the "punch" of the short story are in close harmony with the American temperament. At any rate, the tremendous production and consumption of short stories in this country have been stimulated by the omnipresent and protean magazine. Given the magazine, it was inevitable that editors should seek for, and readers should learn to look for, fiction more manageable and more satisfying than the continued story, the novel printed in installments.

No less apparent than the ubiquity of the short story is its general excellence. The standardized American short story is a creditable product of a highly organized industry. Nothing demonstrates more clearly the fact that the writing of short stories is an industry and not an art, than the numerous manuals of short story technique which began appearing about 1910, the establishment of short story courses in colleges and universities, and the teaching of the fundamentals of the trade by correspondence. From such circumstances standardization was bound to come. Indeed, the outstanding weakness of the American short story is its standardization, its conformity to a conventionalized notion of exactly what a short story should be. It is obvious that such a process is bound for aesthetic sterility, however profitable it may be financially.

Characteristics—*Continued*

The hope of the short story would then seem to be the achievement of distinction within the rigid limits of the established form or outside the conventions of subject matter and technique. It is in the work of those who are striving to present fresh material or devise new forms that the vital examples are to be sought. A hasty survey of the short story of the last thirty-five years will assure us that over against thousands of machine-made products, can be set good work in one or the other of the directions mentioned.

The Emergence of the Short Story [1]

Though short stories in great numbers had been written throughout the nineteenth century, it was only at the end of the eighties that critics became conscious that the short story was a distinct literary form with "laws" and principles of its own. Hitherto, despite the growing influence of Poe's theory and practice, and a dim consciousness of what was happening to the short story in France, the short story had been regarded as a fragment of a novel and viewed with good-natured contempt as the sort of thing a writer might produce before he set about the serious business of writing a novel. The credit for defining the short story belongs to Brander Matthews, who signalized his "discovery" by hyphenating the term and expounding its laws. A fairly wide critical discussion of the new form developed, quickened in all probability by the sensational success of Frank R. Stockton's *The Lady or the Tiger?* (1884), which perhaps more than any other single story focussed the attention of readers and critics on the possibilities of the form.

Henry James

But the rather brittle fantastic work of Stockton is overshadowed by the more substantial work of Henry James,

[1] For some of the material of this sketch, I am indebted to Professor F. L. Pattee's invaluable *Development of the American Short Story* (Harper, 1923).

Henry James—*Continued*

who brought out five volumes in the following decade. After not a little imitation of the older forms, James worked out a technique which was probably more fastidious and exacting than any except Poe's. A scrupulous unity, a concentration on a moral dilemma, a deliberate and severe exclusion of non-essentials, a cautious and precise building up of emotion and action to the crucial situation—such were the technical precepts which James handed on to his admirers. He treated the short story with the same dignity and respect that he showed the novel, and his attitude was contagious. For though James lies somewhat outside the center of our immediate interest, his influence is pertinent to our account.

The Nineties: Bunner, Bierce, Crane

The increasing seriousness with which the short story was regarded is evident in the conscious experimentation of H. C. Bunner and his friend, Brander Matthews, in their joint volume, *In Partnership* (1884). Furthermore, in Bunner's *Made in France* (1893) there was an attempt to adapt French material and technique to American ways of thought and life. But Bunner did not content himself with experiment; he worked out his own little form, the brief swift pointed sketches in *Short Sixes* (1890) and *More Short Sixes* (1894).

Likewise to the nineties belongs the work but not the later fame of those vivid talents, Ambrose Bierce and Stephen Crane. The mordant bitterness and *diablerie* of Bierce worked itself out not only in epigrams, but also in the studies in stark horror of *In the Midst of Life* (1891) and *Can Such Things Be?* (1893), which entitle him to his own niche in the chamber of literary tortures. Bierce has recently become the center of a minor cult, and his influence is of considerable importance in counteracting the conventions cramping the short story. Stephen Crane met with wider welcome from both his fellow craftsmen and the public in his own day, but the revival of interest in his work is due not only to his steadily unromantic war-novel, *The Red Badge of Courage* (1895),

but also to his studious avoidance of the sentimental and the
lucid precision of his observation and imagination in *The
Open Boat* (1898) and *Whilomville Stories* (1900).

Transitional: Hamlin Garland, Alice Brown, Mary E. Wilkins Freeman

At this point we may well consider the work of Hamlin
Garland, Alice Brown, and Mary E. Wilkins Freeman, since
the beginnings of their long literary careers belong to the
nineties.

The work of Hamlin Garland (q. v.) was in tune with the
growing realism of the decade. Brought up under the harsh
conditions of prairie life but freed from them, Garland set
out deliberately to reveal the hardships and limitations of
life in the West, and aside from his recent autobiographical
writing, *A Son of the Middle Border* (1917), his most significant
work is to be found in such early collections as *Main-Travelled
Roads* (1891) and *Prairie Folks* (1893).

Inheritors of the strong tradition of local color in New
England fiction, Alice Brown (q. v.) and Mary E. Wilkins
Freeman (q. v.) have worked steadily for many years in the
rich deposits of tradition and custom in that section of the
country. Mrs. Freeman's work veritably begins with *A
Humble Romance* (1887) and *A New England Nun* (1891),
and though the bulk of her writing falls within the first decade
of the new century, its characteristics had been pretty definitely established before 1900. Less intent on the picturesque
aspects of New England life than Sarah Orne Jewett, Mrs.
Freeman has exploited the long decline of the provincial
temperament with frankness as well as tenderness. Always
a meticulous craftsman, she has produced volume after
volume of authentic portraits of a fading civilization. The
new and invigorating elements in the New England situation she has not been interested in treating. Although Alice
Brown has not been so singularly devoted to the short story
as Mrs. Freeman, she too has remained faithful to the sub-

jects and attitudes that were represented in *Meadow-Grass* (1895) and *Tiverton Tales* (1899). She too has expended upon her material that painstaking observation, that feminine clarity of vision, to which New England fiction owes such a debt. Both these women are utterly remote from the popular exploitation of New England oddities that endears the work of Joseph C. Lincoln to an uncritical generation.

Journalists: Richard Harding Davis, Jack London, O. Henry

Richard Harding Davis (1864–1916) devoted almost thirty years to incessant journalistic and literary activities, but he may be considered with two popular authors who, under the influence of Kipling's tremendous new reputation, annexed the short story to the domain of journalism in the first decade of the century. Kipling had revealed new sources of literary material, and given the style of the short story a new sharpness and vigor; he had, moreover, in his earliest and best known work, demonstrated the maximum effect that could be attained within the limits of space prescribed by the daily newspaper.

Davis's short stories suffer inevitably from the haste enforced upon him by his lively and multifarious activities. They have a superficial glibness and effectiveness—something of the self-confidence and assertiveness of Davis himself. They are lacking in depth and insight, however, and are as distinctly dated as the Gibson girl and the broadshouldered and somewhat vacuous Gibson man. If anything of the Davis tradition persists, it is probably to be found in the standardized narrative of the upstanding young American, cheeky and irrepressible, who overcomes almost automatically the obstacles that lie between himself and fortune.

Somewhat less conventional but equally astounding in amount is the contribution of Jack London, the lines of

whose work were fixed pretty definitely before 1910. London's
significance is to be seen, not in any innovations in form or
technique, but in the conquering of new domains of action
and emotion for the short story. London became a specialist
in the primitive and the brutal, in the lives of animals and
men under harsh conditions of life on the edges of civilization. At his best, he utilized this material with extremely
vivid sensory effect, and with eloquent appeal to the eternal
delight in elemental conflict. His later work, done under
the stimulus of huge rewards from editors and publishers,
suffered inevitably from exaggerated violence and cheap
sensationalism. His reputation lives on chiefly in Germany
and Russia, where the falsity of his high coloring is not
corrected by any precise information about "primitive"
America. His influence survives in no reputable writer, but
rather in those accounts of the struggles of excessively stal-
wart heroes in tropical or frigid settings which continue to
thrill the unadventurous.

The sensational success of O. Henry (William Sydney
Porter, 1862–1910) is confined almost exactly to the limits
of the first decade of the century. His vast reputation in
the ten years before and after his death makes it difficult to
estimate with accuracy the value of his work. Done, for
the most part, in circumstances that gave no opportunity
for revision, the mass of his work shows great skill in noting
and recording the surfaces of life, especially in the New York
of his time, and facility in the use of a formula that almost
never failed in its immediate effect. Like the other journalists, O. Henry is disappointingly lacking in depth and
richness, and his vaunted surprise-endings are bound to be
more effective on the first than on the fifth reading. To his
credit it must be said that his understanding of city types of
the lower order and his description of their habits and their
jargon are yet unequalled. It is to be regretted that almost
every page of his writing is marred by cheap effects, by gross
errors in taste, and by the devices of the unscrupulous vaude-

villean. Through his brilliant exploitation of its superficial attractions, O. Henry has probably done the short story more harm than good.

The James Tradition: Wharton and Gerould

The lofty tradition of Henry James has been carried on by two avowed disciples, Edith Wharton (q. v.) and Katherine Fullerton Gerould (q. v.). In point of view, in temperament, and in artistry they affirm their allegiance and their discipleship. Mrs. Wharton's contribution to the novel has already been considered, and little need be said here as to the major characteristics of her work. In the short story and the tale (for which like her master she has an evident predilection), she has manifested her temperamental aloofness and irony, her cosmopolitan experience and culture, and the unfailing seriousness of her craftsmanship. Like the master, both Mrs. Wharton and Mrs. Gerould are occasionally driven to the treatment of bizarre moral dilemmas that are too remote from ordinary experience to be significant. The more limited work of Mrs. Gerould reveals a like devotion to the traditional technique, and if it is less satisfying than Mrs. Wharton's, the explanation may be found in the rigidity of her ethical conceptions and a slight Pharisaism in her nature.

The War and After: Cather, Anderson, Steele, Hemingway

To distinguish the work of a few from the legions of competent short story writers of the present time may be invidious. But of the artists whose work in the short story has attracted attention since the War, those named above seem the most promising. Miss Cather should perhaps be regarded as novelist rather than short story writer, but her exquisite sense of form, her sensitive exposition of moral and aesthetic problems in *Youth and the Bright Medusa* (1920) and her tendency, as in *My Mortal Enemy* (1926), to a strict elimination of the non-essential justify her inclusion here.

39

The War and After—*Continued*

The work of Sherwood Anderson in the short story is important for its fundamentally experimental nature. He has deliberately thrown over the form, the substance, and the style of the conventional American short story. Instead of using the form that states a problem, develops it, and solves it, Anderson cultivates the fluidity of the ordinary oral narrative. His style, too, is consciously shaped on the speech of the people he knows best, and at times reproduces its diction, its grammar, and its rhythm with perfect fidelity. In the main he finds his material in the psychic lives of the inexpressive and ineffective old American stock in little midwestern towns. Though his naïve mysticism and his persistent intuition sometimes land him in bathos, *Winesburg, Ohio* (1919) is perhaps as searching a study of American life as any made in fiction in our time.

Less inclined to innovations in material and technique is Wilbur Daniel Steele (q. v.), whose devotion to the short story has had noteworthy results. He has taken the conventional form and treated it with such pains and ingenuity that he has made it seem fresh and vigorous. His bent is towards the terrible and the horrifying, and within the limits of his own interest his work is well-nigh distinguished. Its form and finish proceed from an aesthetic conscience less sullied than that exhibited in his novels, where he is unwilling to carry tragic situations through to their inevitable conclusions.

In very recent years, the most interesting newcomer is Ernest Hemingway (q. v.). The bulk of his work is still too slight to warrant more than an extremely tentative estimate. His post-war weariness and disillusionment reflect perfectly the current state of mind. The boldness with which he has discarded the conventional technique, and the brilliance of his surfaces, especially his descriptions and his amazingly authentic dialogue, make him a man worth watching. His mood and the mood of his public are bound to alter, but the vividness of his representation will remain.

The War and After—*Continued*

It would be unjust to end this sketch of the American short story without at least mentioning the colorful picturesqueness of the work of Konrad Bercovici (q. v.), the drab mid-western realism of Ruth Suckow (q. v.), the expert photographic accuracy of Ring Lardner's (q. v.) superficial studies of superficial New York types, or the exquisite style and unconventional form of the stories of Conrad Aiken.

POETRY [1]

Introduction

The search for the beginning of contemporary poetry is more quickly rewarded than a similar quest for the beginning of the contemporary American novel. We have been able to find no sharp break between the novel of the nineteenth and the novel of the twentieth century, although such books as *The Red Badge of Courage* (1895) and *Sister Carrie* (1900) were significant milestones. In the case of poetry, it is possible to distinguish the sharp emergence of a movement shortly after 1910, initiating an extremely prolific period raging with controversies, and lasting from 1914 to 1920. Since the latter date, the dust of the tumult has gradually settled, the results of the movement have become clear, and the whole affair takes on an historical aspect. Poetry may almost be said to have fallen back again into the polite but unexciting state in which we find it at the end of the century.

The End of Victorianism

If the new spirit was slow to make itself felt in the field of poetry, it cannot be because the old spirit was so vigorous. In fact it might be argued that poetry was so weak and flaccid that it seemed hopeless to attempt its revival. American poetry has always felt itself to be in the shadow of the great English tradition, and no years illustrate the habitual dependence of American poetasters upon their English models better than the closing years of the old and the early years of the new century. Unfortunately, the Tennysonian in-

[1] For parts of the organization and some of the facts in this section, I am indebted to Louis Untermeyer's indispensable *American Poetry Since 1900* (1922) and *Modern American Poetry* (1925; Harcourt, Brace).

42

fluence made itself felt in the direction of sweetness and polite morality rather than in the direction of his high artistry. Poetry seemed to be getting steadily thinner and sweeter. It was usually an anaemic imitation that deserved no more attention than it got, at the tail-ends of elegant magazine pages. It is sufficient to mention such names as Thomas Bailey Aldrich (1836-1907), Edward Rowland Sill (1841-87), and Richard Watson Gilder (1844-1909), to suggest the essentially Victorian quality of American verse in the latter part of the nineteenth century.

Traditionalists

To be sure there were exceptions to the dead level of smooth and insipid performance. James Whitcomb Riley (1849-1916) caught in numerous volumes something of the surfaces and the slighter emotions of rural life in Indiana, and by his judicious admixture of humor and sentiment with a diction that was not offensively poetic he won an intense local and a strong national following. But Riley remains a superior newspaper versifier whom a sense of humor and a taste for local color preserve from the limbo of the unnoticed and forgotten. Riley wrote innumerable delightful verses, but not a single real poem. More significance is to be found in the interrupted work of Richard Hovey (1864-1900) and the sustained work of William Vaughn Moody (1869-1910). Richard Hovey lives by reason of a few spirited songs that ring with a masculine vigor unwonted in the poetry of his period. Moody is the more impressive figure both in aim and in accomplishment. His was a real and substantial gift aroused to fiery expression by his quick sense of social injustice and national short-sightedness. His conception of the poet's function was Miltonic, and in such splendid poems as "Gloucester Moors" and "An Ode in Time of Hesitation," in his largely conceived poetic dramas, he belongs with the soothsayers among the poets. His genuine poetic powers allied with his responsiveness to a world in which he wished to play a noble part make him the most distinguished figure at the beginning of the contemporary period.

Before we turn to the tumult and shouting over the "new" poetry, we should notice that traditional poetry has not been altogether neglected in a revolutionary age. The work of women like Anna Hempstead Branch and Lizette Woodworth Reese (q. v.) is perfectly conventional in technique, but is made fresh and beautiful by its conscientious artistry and its fastidious eschewing of the time-worn and hackneyed elements in the great tradition. In the midst of a confusion now almost allayed, these poets have maintained their serene and lovely ways.

Rise of the New Poetry

The limitations of space make it impossible to discuss the sources of the quickening spirit in the field of poetry. It is, however, possible to suggest several influences: the renewed interest in Walt Whitman at home and abroad—a revival due to an increasing awareness of his unique poetic and personal character, his successful representation of at least a kind of Americanism; the outburst of experimental poetic activities, especially in France; and the contagious examples of a few enthusiasts who thought that it was quite time to take poetry seriously. The most enthusiastic student of the French experiments was Miss Amy Lowell (1874–1925), whose *Six French Poets* (1915) is one of the stimulating documents in the poetic revival, and whose *Tendencies in Modern American Poetry* (1917) announced self-confidently that there were real poets living and working in America. But the one person who perhaps precipitated the epidemic of writing, reading, and publishing poetry was Miss Harriet Monroe, who founded *Poetry: A Magazine of Verse* in 1912, introduced Tagore, Lindsay, and Frost to an astonished but increasing audience, and was imitated most sincerely by the establishment of literally dozens of magazines devoted exclusively to poetry. Of these the most important turned out to be *The*

Fugitive, Contemporary Verse, The Double Dealer, and *Palms.*
The new movement was stimulated also by the attention
magazines and newspapers gave to the critical quarrels that
soon waxed furious, and presently poets began to be treated
with the same critical consideration that novelists received.
The consequence of these various influences was a tremendous
over-production of poetry, but out of the fury of creation and
distribution, a considerable number of poets have achieved distinction and a more or less assured position in this generation.

The Discussion of Poetic Material

Before discussing individual poets or groups of poets, we
may well consider the nature of the major controversies
which rent the critical heavens through something like a
decade. The dispute centered, as might be expected from
the history of previous poetic revolts, in both the material
and the form of poetry.

The first problem was that of the suitable subject matter
for poetry. On the one hand were the conventional subjects
of the poetry of the past—love, death, nature, and the great
romantic and classical stories. On the other hand were the
"blooming, buzzing, confusion" of the modern world, so
thoroughly transformed in the course of the nineteenth
century through the indirect results of the Industrial Revolution, the turmoil of modern ideas and attitudes, the shocking consequences of the transformation of the United States
from a predominantly agricultural to an industrial nation.
It is inevitable that there should have been the widest divergence of views on this subject. Some poets clung plain-
tively to the traditional material, and demonstrated occasionally that a fresh talent might illuminate a new facet of it.
Others felt that the old material might seem new if viewed
in a new way; so Robinson re-interpreted the Arthurian
legend in his own terms, and Robert Frost and Amy Lowell
found pathos and tragedy in the New England tradition.
Others eschewed entirely the ancient and honorable, and

The Discussion of Poetic Material—*Continued*

strove to raise all aspects of current American life to poetic status. Many of the attempts were grotesque, but by the time the new movement was established, the gonfalon of poetry had been planted on many new continents, and new and glorious kingdoms were rising.

The Discussion of Poetic Forms

A far bitterer conflict was waged over the form appropriate to modern poetry. It centered in the problem of free verse, and what it really amounted to was a fresh discussion of the borderline between verse and prose. It was a purely technical discussion, and that so many unpoetic people should have been stirred by it suggests the wide appeal of the movement of poetic revolt. The essential problem was not whether poetry should dispense with rhyme, though rhyme came in for its share of round abuse, but just how much rhythm was required to distinguish verse from prose. The defenders of free verse maintained that it was quite proper and timely to throw over the regular rhythms of traditional verse, and to substitute the more subtle rhythms of a form that should be more rhythmic than prose but less mechanically regular than traditional verse. It was inevitable too that there should have been an intense discussion of poetic diction and figures. The rebels were all for discarding the shopworn diction and figures of the recent poetic past, and building up a new vocabulary and set of figures for poetry. The conservatives threw up their hands or burst into polite laughter over the conscious colloquialism or the esoteric diction of the new verse, and pointed out with justice that, since the poetic word or phrase is the one that evokes the largest number of pleasurable associations or images, it is impossible to create a new poetic vocabulary over night. It remains to be seen what actual achievements have come out of the new movement, but it may be suggested that the radicals did not win so decisive a victory in the struggle over poetic form as they did in that over poetic material.

Poets of New England: Robinson and Frost

There is remarkably general agreement that Edwin Arlington Robinson (q. v.) is the greatest poet of the contemporary
period; in fact, it has been maintained that he is the greatest
poet that America has ever produced.   But a recollection of
the repeated fallibility of contemporary judgments should content us with the sufficiently notable fact that Robinson has
been given the highest rank possible among the thousand and
one poets of our time.   That he has attained this distinction is
the more remarkable in that his view of life and its values is
somber, and his technique, in the midst of the whirling confusion of the time is, in the best sense, traditional.   If his position
is deserved, it may be by reason of his singularly consistent and
impressive philosophy, his tremendous seriousness, and the
amount of distinguished poetry he has produced.   In these not
unimportant respects, he is without a rival in America today.

In a sense, Robinson represents the fag-end of the great
New England tradition.   The view he takes of life is not that
of the hopeful sturdy pioneer or that of the Brahmin satisfied
with himself and a stable world, but that of a somewhat
melancholy spectator and interpreter of the decline of an
American province.   If he is preoccupied with failures and
eccentrics, if many of his characters' destinies end in futility,
the fault is partly that of the age and partly that of his own
temperament.   Robinson is a thoughtful, inactive man,
brooding over the plight of humanity in a contrary universe,
utterly scrupulous in noting the shadows that encompass
the life of man, and profoundly intent upon what many men
make of their lives in a dangerous, if not an indifferent,
world.   The spectacle that has absorbed him unweariedly
has not left him bitter, for he has found it constantly alluring
and touching.   He has not lost a feeling of admiration and
pity for struggling mankind.   If he feels that many men are
doomed, his artistry contrives to make the tragedy seem
glorious.   But it is evident that this view of things is as far
as possible from the superficially American view of life as a
circus; it comes from the very heart of modern Puritanism.

47

The art Robinson brings to the presentation of his reading of life is singularly unified and assured. Fifteen years before the outburst of the new poetry, Robinson was practising his subdued and dignified craftsmanship. Working almost steadily within the old metrical forms, he has built for himself a style that is distinctly his own. From the beginning he has tactfully and tastefully avoided the clichés of the Victorian tradition. He utilizes in the main the almost colloquial language of a cultivated and subtle personality. Yet with these familiar elements he has contrived again and again that maximum of suggestiveness with a minimum of apparent effort that characterizes great poetry. And his humble tools have not prevented his creating veritably romantic effects. If his style has upon occasion been justly described as obscure, it is because his over-subtle mind, impatient of the obvious and direct expression, pursues indirection until some of his poems are masterpieces of suggestiveness or mazes of the incomprehensible. From this mannerism, this fastidious circumlocution, which sometimes implies the tragic and more often the ironic, he does and will suffer, for the poetry that prides itself upon its excessive difficulty may lose a reader that it should win. But it is not to be thought that Robinson's verse is arid, or barren of sensuous and emotional delights. Almost any page of *Merlin* or *Lancelot* or *Tristram* reveals passages in which he has infused the magnificent material of the Arthurian story with emotional and sensuous richness and a somber implication of brooding tragedy.

Robert Frost

If Robert Frost (q. v.) is not so sizable a figure in contemporary poetry, it can hardly be doubted that his position is equally assured. His work is far less in bulk, but it is hardly less fastidious or precious in quality. Frost's New England is actually the New England of Robinson, but the divergence in the rendition is due to the inevitable divergence between temperaments. Frost, no less than Robinson, is aware of the waning energy of contemporary New England, is no less concerned with those eccentricities of grim humor and insanity which the isolated and ingrowing life of the back-country encourages. But on humble natural objects and activities Frost sets a somewhat higher value, and a sense of humor, which takes the place of Robinson's acrid wit, preserves him from the deepening gloom of Robinson's world. If he has drawn, with exquisite insight, the shadows of the New England scene, he has also written of its natural and human beauties with contagious delight and an exalted sense of human courage and aspiration.

The poets are alike in their avoidance of the conventionally poetic. Frost's diction comes even closer than Robinson's to the language of common speech, closer to Wordsworth's ideal of poetic diction. Not only is his diction colloquial, but the intrinsic rhythm of his verse is the rhythm of slow New England speech. Even more severely than Robinson has he eliminated poetic ornament, and if his blank verse is as fine as any written in our time, it is because of the sensitive poetic spirit working itself out in apparently unpoetic materials. If his work contains almost no failures and a large number of memorable successes, it is that his distinguished capacity for self-criticism requires the utmost sincerity and artistry in any work that is to meet the public eye. His is not the Americanism of New York, of the vigorous unlovely Middle West, of the overpowering Rockies; but it is genuine Americanism nevertheless.

Amy Lowell's similar heritage and her frequent use of New England material would seem to demand her consideration in this connection. But her work was so various, her influence and inspiration so distinctly national rather than provincial, that it seems more suitable to consider her later with the imagists, although to be sure she refuses to stay quietly in any category.

The Mid-Western Poets: Masters, Lindsay, Sandburg

The three most notable poets of the Middle West illustrate
even more strikingly than the New Englanders whom we
have just considered, the break between the new poetry and
the old. These poets have striven to extend the subject
matter of poetry, to find legitimate subjects for poetry in
phases of the modern world neglected or avoided by the traditional poets, and they have achieved sometimes, if not
always, distinct successes with new poetic subjects or manners. But although they are alike in the boldness with which
they go forth to conquer new continents, although they
share too an unfortunate lack of discrimination between
what is good and bad in their own work, it is necessary to
study them separately and to distinguish their individual
powers and weaknesses.

Edgar Lee Masters

Edgar Lee Masters (q. v.) achieved with a single volume,
Spoon River Anthology (1915), a reputation that he has found
it difficult to sustain. It is of importance to observe that
before the appearance of this notorious volume he had already published a number of obscure and undistinguished
volumes of conventional poetry and poetic drama. But
stirred by the influence of the new poets whom Miss Monroe
was introducing to the American public and urged on by
William Marion Reedy, he turned abruptly away from his
conventional material and style, and produced a work which
seems likely to be a landmark in American poetry. For here
was the life of a small Illinois village turned inside out for
the disapprobation of a horrified world. The device of having
the dead in the village graveyard speak out their honest
epitaphs opened the way to a grim exposure of hidden sores
and diseases that conventionality had concealed even in
death. Mr. Masters's temperament or his disillusioning experience as a lawyer brought it about that the seamier side
of village life was much more apparent than the smooth,
and the boldness of his revelations quite as much as the

innovations in poetic method won the book a kind of scandalous success. Whatever one may think of its poetic quality, it is an unforgettable panorama of American village life. Its form is unrhymed but more or less cadenced prose, and the vocabulary is perhaps even below the level of our colloquial language. With this fluid medium, Mr. Masters showed himself capable upon occasion, as in "Ann Rutledge," of real poetic feeling, but more frequently the poems are nothing more than prose broken up by the printer into natural and sometimes unnatural phrasing. In his succeeding work there is an increase of prose and a decrease of the amount of poetry per volume. He has attempted a Browningesque subject and technique in *Doomsday Book*, but he has not shown a tithe of Browning's power to transmute obstinate material into something like poetry. *The New Spoon River Anthology* did not repeat the success of the original, and of late he seems to have turned away from poetry, to express in prose his memories and visions of American life.

Vachel Lindsay

Vachel Lindsay (q. v.) is on the whole a more varied and attractive figure than Masters. He has deliberately attempted to bring poetry back to the people, first by writing of subjects and in a style which might attract the untutored, and second, by taking his poetry in person to audiences in villages and colleges and on the highways that he tramps as a vendor of beauty and idealism. Like many another American, Lindsay is a prey to the Messianic delusion, but his work has suffered from the failure to criticize the ideals that he vigorously espouses. His weaker writing is to be found in his political proclamations extolling any idol that may happen to arouse his naïve idealism, and in his adolescent responses to the somewhat sickish charms of popular figures of the moving-picture and sporting worlds. But despite the unfortunate fact that Lindsay is apparently unable to distinguish between worthy and unworthy objects of admira-

Vachel Lindsay—*Continued*

tion, he has done a considerable amount of beautiful or stirring work. No poet of our time comes so near as Lindsay to being an authentic folk-poet, an expresser of the imagination of the people. Lindsay's finest achievements are such poems as "The Congo," "The Booker T. Washington Trilogy," and "King Solomon and the Queen of Sheba," in which he projects with great vigor and no little beauty of imagination what he conceives to be negro psychology. In "The Congo," perhaps his most impressive work, he has created a racial vision that is at once broad, deep, and powerful. In as dissimilar poems as "General Booth" and "The Chinese Nightingale" he has also demonstrated his control over strong and subtle rhythms and his insight into minds alien to his own. If his weaknesses are only too apparent in his doggerel verse and his cheap but doubtless sincere enthusiasms, his restoration of the art of speaking poetry, his command in verse and voice of a range of movements and rhythms, make him a particularly beguiling figure in American contemporary folk-culture, if not in American poetry.

Carl Sandburg

Carl Sandburg (q. v.) is a more conscious and critical craftsman than either of his Illinois *confrères*. With a varied experience in manual labor, with a somewhat sustained contact with the cruder aspects of life in Chicago, he naturally manifests in his verse the untraditional and the unacademic. He is probably a more discriminating personality than either Masters or Lindsay, and the brutality and crudeness which are at first so apparent in his work are deliberate gestures of a sensitive and tender soul. If the language in which Sandburg writes is authentically colloquial, it is a very different colloquialism from that of Robert Frost. The language of Sandburg's brutal poems is that of stevedores and truck-drivers, and not the language of the literate Middle West. In presenting the coarse and cruel sides of modern life, he uses harsh, ugly words, and we might suspect him of a native insensitiveness if it were not that his enthusiasm for the natural and fine and strong shines out of poem after poem. The cruder poems have their intended shocking effect, but their poetic value is extremely questionable. It is in the exquisite repetitions of his delicate if colloquial cadences, in his feeling for the prairies and inviolate natural loveliness, that his best notes are heard. Of the three poets of this group, there seems little doubt that more of Sandburg will survive the devouring flames of Time.

Lyric Notes: Teasdale, Wylie, Millay

For those readers who ask first of poetry that it should sing itself into their memories, the new movement has furnished distinctly memorable examples. Now and again numbers of new poets have struck out lyrical notes from their instruments. For instance, Joyce Kilmer's "Trees" and Alan Seeger's "I Have a Rendezvous with Death" have through their own merit and tragic circumstance become contemporary classics. There are likewise numbers of accomplished living male singers, such as the Benét brothers (q. v.), Witter Bynner (q. v.), John Hall Wheelock (q. v.), and Orrick Johns (q. v.), but the surest notes come from the well-trained voices of women, and among the many feminine voices those of Sara Teasdale, Elinor Wylie, and Edna St. Vincent Millay are most clearly distinguished. They are eminently individual, but equally at ease with the difficult technique of song.

Sara Teasdale (q. v.) is perhaps the most conventionally feminine of these singers, but her sensitive expression of the feminine temperament has an openness and frankness that were rare in the writing of American women before the present generation, and remind one of the outspoken utterances of Mrs. Browning and Christina Rossetti. Miss Teasdale has perfected, in volume after volume, her control of an apparently simple lyric form until again and again she attains the perfect expression of her emotion. The emotion becomes

somewhat monotonous, but within its limits her work has
the perfection and delicate grace of a miniature.

The attitude and ideas of Elinor Wylie (q. v.) were somewhat less conventionally feminine. A hard, jewel-like
nature, she reflected the world coldly and glitteringly. If
her essentially reticent personality discouraged affection or
boisterous enthusiasm, her artistry was like a sword, intri-
cately carved, magnificently polished, and terribly effective.
The world she lived in was far from the familiar domestic
world of Sara Teasdale: it was black and white, snow and ice,
metallic and gleaming. But within the cold form burned a
high, proud heart, and a rebellious spirit beat itself into
concentrated and exquisitely finished poetry. Mrs. Wylie's
work was too aristocratic to achieve popularity, but it is
bound to contribute permanently to the delight of the discriminating.

Edna St. Vincent Millay (q. v.) has perhaps won the widest
popularity and the most general admiration of any of the
contemporary poets without an obvious sacrifice of integrity.
So spontaneous is her outcry, so accomplished her technique,
that she would seem to be the most sure of a modest immortality. Her work has an evenness of which some of the
noteworthy have been incapable, and an approachability
and amiability that make her a more exact expression of the
modern American spirit than such distinguished workmen
as Robert Frost and Edwin Arlington Robinson. Although
her output has not been large, it is sufficient to illustrate her
development and her range of power. Her *Renascence*, an
expression of adolescent mystical ecstacy, has been somewhat feverishly admired and overpraised. Her next volume,
A Few Figs from Thistles (1920), was in the current mode of
flippant Bohemianism. It was only in *Second April* (1921)
that she showed a satisfying maturity, free from adolescent
naïveté or sophistication. Her best work expresses her own
singularly honest confrontation of the impermanence of
love, her delight in the physical and mental features of life

along the New England coast, and an artistic and intellectual
eminence in the practice of the sonnet that promises much
for her maturer writing.

The Imagists: Amy Lowell, John Gould Fletcher, Conrad Aiken, H. D.

One of the most exciting moments in the history of contemporary poetry was the publication of the imagist manifesto in *Some Imagist Poets*, a volume edited by Amy Lowell
in 1915, and followed by others with the same title in 1916
and 1917. The credit for launching the imagist movement
belongs, however, to Ezra Pound (q. v.), who in 1914 had
persuaded kindred spirits to express themselves in *Des
Imagistes*. The major principles of the imagist creed may be
stated thus: (1) to use the language of common speech but
to employ the exact word; (2) to create new rhythms as the
expression of new moods; (3) to allow absolute freedom in
the choice of subject; (4) to present an image, not vague
generalities; (5) to produce poetry that is hard and clear;
(6) to aim at concentration, since concentration is the very
essence of poetry. It is obvious that these purposes were in a
measure provoked by the threadbare mannerisms of post-
Victorian verse; it is also obvious that something new in the
way of poetry might be achieved under this system, but that
to confine poetry to images was to circumscribe it unduly.
Although the imagist manifesto created tremendous excitement and stimulated the most violent critical and aesthetic
discussions, the imagists themselves soon broke away from
their arbitrary creed and associations, and went their own
artistic or inartistic ways. But the imagists' gesture was the
signal for the opening of the free-verse controversy which was
to have such conspicuous if harmless effects during the
next half-dozen years. It was also to make the way ready
for experiments of a boldness of which the imagists never
dreamed.

In the forefront of the imagist conflict was Miss Amy

The Imagists—*Continued*

Lowell (q. v.), and no better general could have been selected. With great energy, enthusiasm, and resourcefulness, she engaged in one critical combat after another, wrote poems to illustrate her theories, made her American companions aware of French experiments through her *Six French Poets* (1915), designated among her colleagues those most deserving of praise (*Tendencies in Modern American Poetry*) (1917), and discussed and read the new poetry for an astonished and sometimes amused world. Of her critical work, it is enough to say that it was invigorating if not particularly discriminating, since, like other propagandists, she emitted judgments which time has tested sadly. It is of more importance to estimate her poetic significance. Miss Lowell did not long content herself with the restrictions of the imagist creed. She experimented in various directions under French and Oriental influence. She adapted for American use "polyphonic prose," which uses metre, *vers libre*, assonance, alliteration, and repetition at will, and with it created some of her finest effects. She showed again and again a sensitive use of the free-verse form, as well as a command over the most regular technique.

If the final impression left by Miss Lowell's work is unequal to the energy and enthusiasm that created it, the reason may be found in the limitations of her temperament: her excess of intelligence, her defects in emotion, and her hypersensitiveness to sensory experience. Much of her work is deficient in feeling; more of her work dazzles by its incessantly vivid auditory and visual images. Her best work is found in free-verse passages where emotion directs the storm of imagery, and in historical panoramas such as "Gates as Keys," "The Bronze Horses," and "The Hammers," which have been somewhat overshadowed by quantities of strained and mediocre work. Despite the obvious weaknesses of her achievement, her vitality, enthusiasm, and sheer intelligence are impressive.

The early work of John Gould Fletcher (q. v.) illustrates

the weaknesses intrinsic in a strict application of the imagist creed. The most memorable parts of his early work are the eleven color symphonies in *Goblins and Pagodas* (1916). These remarkable sequences of beautiful images are a practical demonstration of the inability of the mind to live by images alone. It is not enough to string images on the thread of a color; the reader demands the added interest of emotion or thought or action. But Fletcher has been wise enough to abandon the extreme imagist creed, and, although his extended residence abroad has taken his work out of the American current, his later writing shows a gain in coherence, simplicity, and depth.

Conrad Aiken's brief connection with the imagist movement may justify his consideration in this connection. His work has suffered from the domination of a theory, but he has at least been faithful to it after his fashion. Beginning his work under the influence of Masefield and the school of brutality, he turned quickly to a solitary devotion to the creation in words of the effects of music. To this end, it was necessary to minimize the coherent significance of his lines and to emphasize the sound-values, to attempt the flowing repetitious developments of symphonic writing. The effects he obtained in this direction are beyond those attained by any other poet of our time, and if he has not been awarded the attention he deserves, it is perhaps because his concentration on a single function of poetry has deprived his work of another interest, or more probably because his preoccupation with psychoanalysis and with the débris of his own unconscious mind has wearied readers with the recurrence of motifs, a mournful mistiness, and the reek of somewhat decadent emotions.

Of the American members of the original imagist group, only one has kept the faith, only one has demonstrated the possibilities in the method none too accurately described in the imagist manifesto. H. D. 's (q. v.) early *Sea Garden* (1916) showed the odd and sometimes strained conceits of

57

experimentation, but in *Hymen* (1921) she wrought the method to the expression of intense feeling while still keeping almost strictly to pure imagery. The images are in the main the sensory aspects of the classic world seen by a fresh modern eye; out of these alien elements H. D. has devised a highly colored and polished medium that implies but does not render emotion. The figures of Greek legend and story start her imagination working most brilliantly, and her early interpretations of the Hippolytus story have resulted in an imagistic drama, *Hippolytus Temporizes* (1927). Like most of her contemporaries, H. D. reverts upon occasion, as in her masque *Hymen*, to conventional forms, but her favorite vehicle is unrhymed lines in subtle combinations of rhythm. Though too exacting for most readers, her work probably exemplifies the ultimate possibilities of the imagistic method.

The Radicals: Pound, Kreymborg, Bodenheim

With some diffidence one turns away from work, which if somewhat doctrinaire is at least comprehensible, toward the waste lands, if not the deserts, of contemporary poetic adventure. The radicals form a group not by reason of their allegiance to a defined creed like the imagistic manifesto, but by reason of their independent and radical experiments with either poetic material or method or both. The relation between them is emotional, not logical.

Of the group, Ezra Pound (q. v.) and Kreymborg are important both as creative artists and as organizers. To Pound, already settled in England, belongs the credit for organizing the first imagist group, the direction of which passed almost immediately in this country into the capable hands of Amy Lowell. To Pound also belongs the credit for a deal of energetic if not always highly persuasive propaganda for new methods in poetry. But the question of ultimate importance is the quality of his poetry, which reflects a strangely alluring but irritating personality. That personality is over-intellectual, overstuffed with odds and

The Radicals: Pound, Kreymborg, Bodenheim—*Continued*
ends of esoteric and undigested learning, witty, adroit, ego-
tistic, and deeply intent on shocking the poetic *bourgeoisie*.
Whether or not the personality which Pound's poetry projects is his own or a creation of his imagination, it dominates
and qualifies the significance of his writing. Capable at best
of a discordant satiric music, he is all too willing to waste his
wits and befuddle his readers by such deliberate mystifica-
tion as the outrageously Browningesque *Cantos*. His seems
a wilful and regrettable failure to devote his real powers to
the fundamental problem of communication.

In contrast to Pound, Alfred Kreymborg (q. v.) is perhaps
less important as a leader and more important as a poet.
He it was who brought together numbers of ill-assorted
poetasters, chiefly experimenters in free verse and worse,
under the banner of "Others." From his hand three anthologies appeared under this name in 1916, 1917, and 1919.
Then the real talents in the group had made a footing for
themselves in the poetry magazines, and the pretentious
fakes had faded into blessed silence. Kreymborg himself
is a witty troubadour with the eyes and heart of a quasi-
naïve child. His earlier technique had about it a primitive
puppet-like quality, and his best effects are in the somewhat
suspect pathos and sentimentality of a world of manikins.
Usually his wry smile saves him from childishness. Like
a perennial adolescent, he continued to contrive poetic plays
for the puppets of his dream-theatre until, suddenly realizing
that he had become of age, he wrote in *Troubadour* (1925)
of himself and the poetic movement as he had seen it. Then
to the consternation of some, he was almost the first of the
radicals to turn back to the confines of regular verse, and of
late has cultivated the austere sonnet-form with distinct
success.

Maxwell Bodenheim (q. v.) deserves mention for the
courage with which he has gone his solitary way despite
misunderstanding and ridicule. Whether Bodenheim's work
is poetry or not, the reader must decide for himself. In it

The Radicals: Pound, Kreymborg, Bodenheim—*Continued*

one senses an acute perception, a horror of the banal, an almost frantic search for novelty. The acrid, sardonic quality in Bodenheim's work may be a feature of his creative personality or an excessive protest against the cloying sentiment of the Anglo-Saxon. There is little beauty in Bodenheim's poetic achievement, but it shows an original if somewhat perverse individuality. He lives on the border between intelligent radicalism and conscious or unconscious nihilism.

The Nihilists: T. S. Eliot, E. E. Cummings, Marianne Moore, William Carlos Williams

In a poetic Siberia beyond the limits of respectable or semi-respectable poetic society, dwell a band of nihilists whose vociferous mutual admirations compel brief attention. The conscientiously radical *Dial* gives these poets a shelter and a rostrum, although it could hardly continue to provide them if the value of its prose were as doubtful as that of its poetry. The idol of the nihilists has for some years been T. S. Eliot (q. v.), who early in 1927 indicated his complete severance from all things obviously American by becoming a British subject. His work has caused perhaps the most bitter and inconclusive of recent poetic debates. Aside from the justly admired studies in frustration in "Portrait of a Lady" and "The Love Song of J. Alfred Prufrock," his rather meager poetic output is marked by wilful dissonances in tone and feeling and startling incoherence in thought and substance. Of this type, the masterpiece is the violently assailed and admired *Waste Land* (1922). The apologists for this poem contend that it expresses perfectly the disintegration of modern consciousness, the world-weariness of the post-war generation. It is more likely that it is the scattered remains of a poetic mind, odds and ends from what Edmund Wilson calls "the ragbag of the soul."

Of the later nihilists, E. E. Cummings (q. v.) demands brief notice. A fresh poetic outlook, a novel twist of the imagination, a genuine sensibility, heightened perhaps by his unhappy war-experience, equip him for noteworthy poetic work. But private devotion to freakishness or a somewhat childish desire to attract attention at any cost drives him to distort his perfectly creditable lines by preposterous printing devices. The judicious must regret that such self-conscious posturing keeps the freshness of his visions from winning the admiration it deserves. Cummings errs in forgetting that poetry is for the ear, and not for the overworked modern eye.

Other adherents of the *Dial* group are William Carlos Williams (q. v.) and Marianne Moore (q. v.), since 1926 co-editor of the magazine. Williams's style has about it something of the deliberate freakishness of Bodenheim's; moreover, his imagination apparently works in extremely unconventional channels. Much of his work seems intent merely on exhibiting the outrageous combinations of words an ingenious mind can contrive. At the lowest scale of what is usually regarded as poetry stands the work of Marianne Moore. Miss Moore has a mind, but she puts it to very bad use in her unintelligible enthusiasm for those of her cult. Her "poems" can hardly be regarded as more than shrewd critical observations on life and letters. The uneven lengths into which she cuts them and the style in which they are phrased fail to give them even the minimum essentials of what has been considered poetry in any age. She is a portent of the exhaustion of the new poetry movement.

Conclusion: The Negro Poets; Folk Poetry

If the new poetry, so fertile and flourishing and turbulent in its earlier stages, seems to have come to equilibrium again, if certain of its figures seem to have attained that treacherous immortality which a generation is only too willing to confer upon its favorites, if publishers have returned to the conventional opinion that a book of poems is a poor risk, it is not necessary to conclude that the making of good poetry

Conclusion: The Negro Poets; Folk Poetry—*Continued*

has come to an end in these states. Possibly the most interesting recent development is the recrudescence of poetic activity among the educated American negroes. There had been evidence of great interest in poetic material connected with negro life in such poems as Ridgely Torrence's "The Blackbird" and William Ellery Leonard's "The Lynching Bee," and Hervey Allen and Du Bose Heyward's *Carolina Chansons*. Among the negroes, the delightful but sentimental work of Paul Lawrence Dunbar was only the prelude to a widespread poetic activity on the part of the "new" negro, who with education and improved social position found in great Northern negro centers of New York and Chicago material and an audience for poetic expression. Much of the poetry in James Weldon Johnson's *American Negro Poetry* (1922) and *Caroling Dusk*, edited by Countee Cullen (1927), is indistinguishable from other American poetry, and no better and no worse than the run of magazine verse. But a sharpened race-consciousness, a new pride in the racial past, a sense of the artistic potentialities of their people, speaks out of the work of Johnson himself, Countee Cullen (q. v.), and many another less individual figure.

Finally, there should be mentioned the activities not only of negroes but of white poets in collecting and recording American folk-songs and ballads. Stimulated by such pioneers as Cecil Sharp and Louise Pound, numerous collectors, trained and untrained, have been scouring the country for old songs fading in the memories of the aged. Furthermore, the recording of such songs for the phonographs is an enterprise of more significance perhaps for the future than for the present. Of the many collections now available, the most noteworthy are Cecil Sharp's *Folk Songs of the Appalachian Highlands*, Natalie Curtis Burlin's *The Indians' Book*, George W. Cronyn's *The Path on the Rainbow*, Howard Brockway and Lorraine Wyman's *Lonesome Tunes*, James Weldon Johnson's two books of *American Negro Spirituals*,

Conclusion: The Negro Poets; Folk Poetry—*Continued*
John J. Niles's *Singing Soldiers*, and Sandburg's *American Songbag*.

If the myth of the Greek giant who received strength from contact with the earth has any meaning for modern poets, the next renewal of American poetry may come from the stimulus of the traditional songs of our countryside.

THE DRAMA [1]

Causes of the Dramatic Revival

The drama of almost the first fifteen years of the twentieth century shared with the drama of most of the preceding century the unhappy distinction of being almost entirely negligible as literature. This prevalent condition is only partially explicable, but certain determining circumstances may be sought in the low level of theatrical taste in the period, in the unconditioned control of the theatre by avowedly commercial producers, and in the persistent and syco-phantic dependence, even after the passage of the inter-national dramatic copyright act, of American producers on the sensationally successful dramas of England, France, and Germany. These conditions either stimulated native playwrights like Clyde Fitch to imitate foreign models, or failed to supply a "serious" dramatist like Augustus Thomas with an adequately critical atmosphere for his "intellectual" dramas.

If these conditions have been modified, it is interesting to seek the causes for the change. By and large, the change in the quality of the American drama is to be seen as a reflection of a change that began to appear in the European drama in the late eighties. It has become customary to date the beginning of the contemporary European drama from the establishment of the "free stages" in Paris and Berlin in 1887 and 1889 respectively. The hearing for serious drama which these and similar enterprises afforded went far to stimulate a wide dramatic activity on the part of some of the

[1] In this section, the dates are those of production. These for the most part agree with those given in A. H. Quinn's useful *History of the American Drama from the Civil War to the Present Day* (Harper, 1927).

best minds of the Continent and Great Britain. It is not possible to study here in detail the gradual infiltration of this modern drama into America. It is enough to suggest that a revival of drama in America had to await the formation of just such groups as appeared in Europe at the end of the eighties. Further, over and beyond the very notable influences and activities of the art-theatres should be mentioned the development of the little theatre movement, which has among other purposes that of furnishing intelligent dramatic fare to communities poorly served by the commercial theatre. Hundreds of these little theatres came into existence, and although many of them were transitory and inept, they served to develop audiences with some semblance of good taste, and in some instances have become sound and significant community theatres. Of a dozen such ventures, the Cleveland Playhouse and the Pasadena Playhouse are notable instances. Further, there has developed since the opening of the Harvard Workshop by George Pierce Baker in 1905 an epidemic of play-writing and play-producing courses in colleges, and the founding of the Drama School of the Carnegie Institute of Technology in 1914 by Thomas Wood Stevens has been followed by the creation of numberless schools of theatre-arts both in and apart from regular educational institutions. It is a rather striking circumstance that most of the important work in the current American drama has been done by people who have come into contact with one or another of those energizing agencies: the art theatre, the little theatre, or the university theatre.

The Dead Past: Clyde Fitch, Augustus Thomas, David Belasco

The pride of the drama in the twenty-year period beginning with 1890 is without question the prolific Clyde Fitch. He busied himself with making adaptations of some thirty-six French and German comedies and farces, and in the composition of twenty-one original plays. He achieved both at home

The Dead Past—*Continued*

and abroad a not inconsiderable reputation and fortune. That he had valuable gifts for the service of the drama may be admitted: keen observation of manners, of language, of costume and setting, a feeling for startling theatrical effects, a sensitive perception of feminine psychology, and a flair for dramatic construction. If his work seems quite outmoded and artificial, the reasons are not only the limitations of the theatre in which he was working, but more especially the limitations of his own personality. Fitch's personality was superficial, he lacked seriousness and depth, his men are usually incredible, and his meticulous rendition of surfaces, while it may in the future give his works a quaint documentary value, at present gives them a pitifully old-fashioned air. Only one play of his, *The Truth* (1906), seems to get far enough under the surface to have a more than historical interest. When in *The City* (1909) he strove to create masculine characters and the gripping scenes of strong drama, he lapsed into grotesque melodrama.

On the whole, however, Fitch's record is perhaps as commendable as that of any of the commercial dramatists of the period. Augustus Thomas, when he was content to combine the elements of reliable melodrama with a somewhat superficial study of local color, wrought in such pieces as *Alabama* (1891), *In Mizzoura* (1893), and *Arizona* (1899) telling and picturesque if utterly specious creations. When, with the growing seriousness of the period, he took upon himself the mission of the thesis-dramatist, he betrayed in *The Witching Hour* (1907) and *As A Man Thinks* (1911) his incapacity for lucid or distinguished thought and his infirm handling of character. Only once, in *The Copperhead* (1918), did he produce a play which by its searching psychological revelation and its impressive dramatic situation is memorable and effective.

Similarly the service of David Belasco to the American drama has not been commensurate with the high standards he has set himself and other American producers in realistic

setting, costuming, and stage-business. Aside from his innumerable adaptations of shrewdly selected foreign plays,
his own vein has been the romantic play in settings that
offered lavish opportunities to his distinguished pictorial
talents. With John Luther Long, he exploited Oriental
material in *Madame Butterfly* (1900) and *The Darling of the
Gods* (1902); alone or in collaboration he turned to the picturesque West for highly colored material and characters in
The Girl of the Golden West (1905) and *The Rose of the Rancho*
(1906). Once, in *The Return of Peter Grimm* (1911), he
wrote tenderly and skilfully of the theme of communication
with the dead, and his artistry and that of the actor David
Warfield made it perhaps his most memorable contribution
to the American theatre.

Transition: Moody, Peabody, MacKaye

In the midst of the prolific but intrinsically unimportant
dramatic writing of Fitch, Belasco, and Thomas, there
appear sporadic attempts to unite drama and literature
again. Most of these attempts are only tentative, but they
point the way to the lively revival that the drama is now
undergoing. One of these efforts at serious drama was
William Vaughn Moody's attempt to treat American material realistically. The result was the highly successful
Great Divide (1906) and the even more distinguished but un-
successful *Faith Healer* (1909). Both these plays are notable
for the devoted attention to characterization and for the
fidelity with which scene and business are imagined, and
plausible language is rendered. If the first play has lost its
effectiveness, the reason, it may be suggested, is the incessant use, in trashy melodrama and completely uncon-
vincing moving-pictures, of the theme which Moody treated
with psychological honesty. *The Faith Healer*, a study in
the religious psychology of humble people, remains one of
the authentic American dramas of the contemporary period.

The work of Josephine Preston Peabody (q. v.) was ob-

Transition: Moody, Peabody, MacKaye—*Continued*

viously anachronistic. Her attempts to revive the poetic drama, while praiseworthy, were bound to meet with defeat in a realistic or only superficially romantic period. *Marlowe* and *The Piper* (1910) were her most successful plays.

Of much more consequence has been the varied dramatic activity of Percy MacKaye (q. v.), whose father Steele MacKaye was a courageous visionary in the theatre of the later nineteenth century. MacKaye's work is the product of a highly conscious determination to raise the standard of American dramatic fare, and it has suffered not a little from this "uplift" element. Aside from the early poetic dramas on hackneyed old-world themes, such as *Jeanne d'Arc* (1906) and *Sappho and Phaon* (1907), the major part of his work has been the utilization of American historical and contemporary material in the form of masques and plays. His Puritan play, *The Scarecrow* (1910), is perhaps the most important of the earlier plays in this group, *Caliban* (1916) his most elaborate masque, and *This Fine-Pretty World* (1923) his noteworthy if somewhat too dialectal contribution to the folk-drama to be considered below.

The Living Present: Eugene O'Neill, Sidney Howard, George Kelly

The one figure of national and international importance that has arisen in the American drama of the contemporary period is, of course, Eugene O'Neill (q. v.). His achievement must be considered in the light of his own life and of his contacts in literature. O'Neill was brought up in the atmosphere of the theatre, for his father was James O'Neill, identified in the American mind with the character of Monte Cristo. Up to the age of twenty-four, when he turned to the writing of plays, his life was richer in its contacts with crude realities than the life of any other dramatist of our time. An engineering expedition to Central America, four voyages as a sailor to South America, South Africa, and England, furnished him with the strong colorful material from which some of his early plays were drawn. But the purely literary influences on O'Neill must not be overlooked, although he himself is inclined to make light of them. There are traces in his work of the influences of such diverse forces as Strindberg, Wedekind, and current German expressionism. Moreover, his conception of character has been shaped by the dynamic psychology of Freud. Finally, O'Neill's mind has assimilated some of the views of American life promulgated by his admirers and sponsors, Mencken and Nathan.

The work of O'Neill is so complex in nature that it is not easy to classify his plays according to conventional critical distinctions. He has occasionally written in the vein of pure realism and pure romance, but his most characteristic and successful pieces are those in which realism and romance are blended, and his most interesting plays are those which are experimental in material or technique. The poet in O'Neill seems to prevent his remaining absolutely faithful to the demands of pure realism. Even in the early sea-plays, which in some respects are brutally realistic, there is exoticism of setting and atmosphere, and the romantic appeal of violent, if not melodramatic, action. In such bitterly realistic plays as *The Straw* (1921) and *Diff'rent* (1920), in the Strindbergian war of love and hate of *Welded* (1924), one feels that a vital part of the playwright's temperament has been suppressed, and the consequence is a lack of poise, an excessive emphasis on warped characters. On the other hand, in so romantic a play as *The Fountain* (1925), when he relinquishes his strong grasp on reality the result is enfeebled drama, and the poetic flights of *Marco Millions* (1927) do not dominate, but suffer from, the banality of its Menckenite satire.

The most satisfying of O'Neill's plays are those in which the realistic and romantic trends combine and reënforce each other. Even *Beyond the Horizon* (1920), his first success in the commercial theater, is written on two distinct levels— the sharp realistic life of a decaying New England farm, and the imaginative life of the brother whom chance condemns

69

The Living Present—*Continued*

to inhabit it. The transition from one level to another is not easy; the interaction of a romantic spirit and a realistic environment is somewhat amateurishly presented; the slow deterioration of the characters is jerkily pictured in a play singularly devoid of action. *Anna Christie* (1921) shows an increase in artistry. The development of something like romance out of a basically sordid situation is managed with considerable adroitness, and though the redemption of the heroine narrowly escapes sentimentality, the only superficially "happy" ending is truer to life than to fiction. The most expert and powerful blend of the realistic and the poetic is *Desire Under the Elms* (1924), possibly the greatest tragedy that has come out of the last generation in America. The coarse ugly stuff of the plot is transmuted by O'Neill's imagination into great and powerful beauty, and what might have been a crude newspaper item becomes high tragedy. Nowhere else, except perhaps in *Strange Interlude* (1928), has O'Neill created so many vital distinct individuals; nowhere else have the relationships been conveyed with such truth and subtlety. In the style too O'Neill has achieved a prose which, while faithfully colloquial, responds rhythmically to the waves of energy that flow through this drama.

But the spirit of O'Neill is an uneasy one. He cannot remain satisfied with the form or the content of the conventional drama of any period. His most fascinating work is that in which he attempts far-reaching innovations. *The Emperor Jones* (1920) and *The Hairy Ape* (1922) are practically monodramas, broken into short scenes without grouping into acts. The first represents the breakdown of a negroid mentality under the stress of fear and fatigue. The collapse is indicated not only by the monologues of the central figure but by the hallucinations which O'Neill represents by stage tableaux. *The Hairy Ape* shows the influence of German expressionism in the articulateness arbitrarily conferred upon the inarticulate hero, and in the representation of the hero's distorted view of the world by the masked characters.

The influence is seen further in *All God's Chilluns Got Wings* (1924), where, although the dialogue and action are attuned to the highest standard of modern psychological drama, the increasing distortion of the scenery parallels the distortion of the characters' minds. Up to the present, O'Neill's most elaborate experiments are the dramas *The Great God Brown* (1926) and *Strange Interlude* (1928). In the first, the complicated use of masks to distinguish the real self from its social aspect was effective up to the point where the assumption of one personality by another made the rest of the drama frankly incomprehensible. In *Strange Interlude* the major innovations are the extension of the drama to nine acts and the revival and extension of the aside. Both these devices are daring, and are justified only if O'Neill creates effects that could not otherwise be secured. At the moment, it seems probable that the experiment has resulted in O'Neill's deepest reading of life and character.

In O'Neill weakness and strength are curiously interwoven. The most striking weaknesses are a lack of self-criticism, so that he is not saved from extravagances of realism or romanticism, a growing tendency to regard the drama as a medium for thought rather than an embodiment of thought in human conduct and character, and a superb scorn for the limitations of the drama as a form and of the theatre as a medium. His very great powers are certainly his style, which is in turn rich and earthy and intuitive and illuminating, his deep probing into the motivation and the dynamics of character, his power at evoking psychic conflicts, and the romantic glamor that invests his reading and projection of life.

Sidney Howard (q. v.) is perhaps as interesting as any of the young playwrights at work in America. His work is far less in amount than O'Neill's, but his attitude toward it and certain technical powers make him distinctly worth watching. After the respectful reception of his poetic drama *Swords* and a period of adaptation of plays chiefly from the French, Howard found mature expression in *They Knew What*

They Wanted (1924), a play which uses the California setting skilfully and involves three sound characters whom Howard permits to work out their destiny in terms of their own temperaments and not in terms of conventional morality. In *Lucky Sam McCarver* (1925) he relinquished the interest of plot to study the successive states in the relationship of two diverse characters in a marriage of convenience. The one is a rough and ready self-made man, the other a somewhat tarnished remnant of an aristocratic tradition. Again Howard respects the integrity of his characters completely, and the consequence is an absorbing if somewhat undramatic piece. His successful pot-boiler, *Ned McCobb's Daughter*, is of far less importance than the serious *Silver Cord* (1926), where he dramatized powerfully and maliciously the plight of sons dominated by an unscrupulous mother. Though he has driven the point home too violently, especially in the scientific tirade that states the thesis of the play, it is perhaps his most powerful piece up to the present time.

Howard has a high respect for the dignity of drama; he has developed a splendid technique. His disillusionment frees him from the conventional lies of our time. He has an absorbed interest in character and a deep concern for the preservation of its integrity. He is, moreover, unwilling to make a telling point at the expense of truth to life or character, a temptation to which most American dramatists succumb sooner or later.

George Kelly (q. v.) has evolved sufficiently from the vaudeville stage of his career to warrant critical attention. His considerable experience with vaudeville sketches and vaudeville audiences led him to mar his earlier plays, *The Torch-Bearers* and *The Show-Off*, with the repeated popping of "wise-cracks" entirely out of tone with comedy that attempts to approximate realism. This unfortunate tendency to overemphasis and his proneness to get a laugh at any cost, are disappearing from his later work, and such plays as *Craig's Wife* (1925) and *Daisy Mayme* (1926) are perhaps as faith-

The Living Present—*Continued*

fully realistic and honest in characterization as any domestic comedies of the period. The artist in Kelly promises to subdue the vaudevillean.

Types of Comedy

If the contemporary American drama has not produced any permanently distinguished comedy, it has brought to light a very considerable amount of comedy of some distinction in various kinds. There have been interesting examples of fairly high social comedy. Langdon Mitchell's *The New York Idea* (1906) is a forerunner of such clever if somewhat loquacious comedies as Jesse Lynch Williams's *Why Marry?* (1917) and *Why Not?* (1922). Rachel Crothers has practised many kinds of drama, but though she has served her turn at melodrama in *The Three of Us* (1906) or inclined to the comedy of sentiment in *Old Lady 31* (1916), *A Little Journey* (1918), and *39 East* (1919), she has attained in *Nice People* (1920), *Mary the Third* (1923), and *Expressing Willie* (1924) the wit, the grace, and occasionally the satiric bias almost inseparable from the true comedy of manners.

But the dominant trend in comedy seems toward the realistic, or the satirical wherein realism and fantasy are sometimes effectively combined. The possibilities for quiet comedy in the everyday lives of middle-class Americans were illustrated most happily in Frank Craven's *The First Year* (1920), an adroit study of bourgeois surfaces and the hearts beneath, a comedy so successful that it inspired Craven and others less inventive, to write numerous imitations of it. One of the imitations, somewhat more subdued and relentless than Craven's humor will permit, is Maxwell Anderson's *Saturday's Children* (1927), his first success since the sensation caused by the bitterly humorous war-play, *What Price Glory?* (1924), in which he collaborated with Laurence Stallings. To this vein also belongs the significant writing of Gilbert Emery, who represented the post-war disillusionment ironically in *The Hero* (1921), and in *Tarnish* (1923)

73

Types of Comedy—*Continued*

applied his faculty for honesty and irony to the emotional adventures of the bourgeois male.

But the comic spirit ill sustains the manner of subdued realism or naturalism, and it has quickly allied itself with the satiric spirit, which has touched many kinds of literary activity since the Great War. The pseudo-historical vein, the somewhat cynical treatment of hitherto idealized or romanticized figures of history or legend, has been worked by Philip Moeller (q. v.) in *Five Somewhat Historical Plays*, *Madame Sand*, and *Molière*, and has recently been resorted to by Robert E. Sherwood in the widely popular *Road to Rome*. It has proved more fruitful, however, to attack with the spirit of satire the shortcomings and the pretensions of the American caught in the web of industrialism, and some of the best comedy of the period has sprung from this source. Elmer Rice pointed the way in his somewhat derivative *Adding Machine* (1923), and J. P. McEvoy hit off the manners and the mind of the petty-business man and his family in *The Potters*. To the exposure of the conventionalization, the mechanization, of American society two young newspaper men, George Kaufman (q. v.) and Marc Connelly (q. v.), have devoted their considerable talents of enlightened observation and parody. Their most important works are *Dulcy* (1921), a dramatic portrait of a moronic female, *To the Ladies* (1922), noted for its satirical treatment of the social enterprises of business men, and above all *Beggar on Horseback* (1924), which, despite its origin in a German comedy, has been worked over into a thoroughgoing satire of business organization in America, the *nouveaux riches*, and the standards of a commercialized art and life. In *The Wisdom Tooth* (1926) Connelly combines skilfully a vein of wistful sentiment and a satire of the deadening effect of business on the individual. Satiric comedy seems likely to continue to find rich material in a prosperous and materialistic, highly standardized and over-organized society.

Pioneers: Folk-Drama and Expressionism

Noteworthy eddies in the contemporary drama are supplied by the effort on the part of authors to incorporate new material in dramatic form or to extend the effects of the drama by modifying the form itself. A product of the first impulse is the folk-drama that is being written wherever attempts have been made to develop a local drama through the media of little or university theatres. The particularly productive centers have been Wisconsin, under the inspiration of Thomas H. Dickinson, Texas, in connection with the Little Theatre at Dallas, and North Carolina, where Frederick Koch is an energizing force. Most of the work is, of course, of merely local interest, but out of the work in North Carolina have come the dramas of Paul Green (q. v.), who with his play *In Abraham's Bosom* won the Pulitzer prize in 1927. Green's plays are further significant in that several of them use negro material, and so are connected indirectly with the new movement of the negro in the arts.

Other dramatists, connected with the commercial theatre, have found it desirable to use folk-material. Hatcher Hughes in *Hell-bent fer Heaven* (1924) and *Ruint* (1925) was unable to muster the requisite technique for the effective shaping of his poor-white subject matter, though the former was awarded the Pulitzer prize in 1924. Lulu Vollmer has similarly contributed a number of mountain-white dramas of which *Sun-Up* (1923) has met with success not only at home but abroad. More drama using local material seems almost bound to come out of the movement to develop dramatic centers independent of the New York octopus, though it must be admitted that New York is eager to use anything of proved excellence from the provinces.

The attempt to find new forms of the drama to express new ideas has arisen in part under the influence of German expressionism and Russian constructivism, and in part from a legitimate weariness with the conventional forms of drama. Unfortunately, the ideas of the experimental playwrights seem limited to the somewhat stereotyped creed of H. L.

75

Pioneers: Folk-Drama and Expressionism—*Continued*
Mencken, and do not gain from a chaotic treatment of settings, speech, and structure. From the rather unified group composed of John Howard Lawson (q. v.), John Dos Passos (q. v.), Em Jo Basshe, and Francis Farogoh, the most noteworthy plays have been Lawson's *Roger Bloomer* and *Processional*. Dos Passos's *The Garbage Man* and Basshe's *Earth* seem deliberately and self-consciously nihilistic and actually sterile. But at least they point the way to a modification in the form of drama in response to the complexity of modern city-life and to the influence of the moving-picture, which should regard itself as a pictorial rather than a dramatic art.

Conclusion

On the whole there seems to be no reason to believe that the contemporary drama is already showing such signs of exhaustion as the even more brilliant British drama and American poetry show. America has the best equipped theatres in the world with the exception of Germany; we are evolving trained and stratified audiences; and though the provinces are still unfurnished with proper dramatic fare, the means to satisfy them seem to be at hand.

THE INFORMAL ESSAY

Introduction

During the period which we have been considering the informal or familiar essay has not proved a very popular type with either readers or authors. A reason for the decline of this form from the distinguished position which it occupied in the nineteenth century may perhaps be found in the usurping of its position by essays of a somewhat more formal and expository nature, devoted to the discussion of controversial social or sociological or political problems which were brought to light by the liberal movements before the war and by the disturbances of the war and the post-war period. Moreover, the material which was formerly pressed into the mould of the informal essay now tends to be dissipated in the "columns" and syndicated features of the great city-newspapers and in the unshaped and fragmentary comments of literary editors of the monthly magazines. Moreover, in the weeklies, space is too precious to furnish the leisurely personal essay a frequent refuge. However, certain names have become associated principally or incidentally with this attractive literary type.

The Nature Essay

With the flora and fauna of half a continent to observe and study and record, it is rather astonishing that the nature essay has not been more widely cultivated. To be sure, carefully rendered studies of the American scene have furnished settings for various types of novels and short stories, especially those of the local color variety. Stewart Edward White has made perhaps the most distinguished use of such resources in his novels and tales of life in the wilder parts of America, and popular novelists such as Zane Grey

and Harold Bell Wright paint the western background
vividly rather than accurately. Ernest Thompson Seton
(q. v.) may be mentioned as perhaps the most indefatigable
exploiter of material from wild life, but naturally his painstaking stories of animal activities have few of the qualities
we associate with the essay.

John Burroughs (q. v.) found the nature essay the form
most suitable for the expression of his searching, devoted
study of nature in America. Beginning with *Wake Robin*
(1871), he issued with regularity volume after volume of
sensitive and precise nature studies. Inevitably he evolved
his own rich and deep philosophical interpretation of the
phenomena he lovingly studied; and his broadly grounded
and capacious idealism make him a noteworthy figure of the
type of Thoreau or Emerson. In recent years, another trained
naturalist has stepped forward to take the place left vacant
by Burroughs. William Beebe (q. v.) combines the utmost
scientific accuracy with a style that is extremely rich in
sensory values and an enthusiasm which makes his study of
even forbidding subjects fascinating. In *Jungle Peace* (1918)
and *Edge of the Jungle* (1921) he established himself as one
of the best stylists of our time, and exhibited artistic powers
equaled by few American scientists and few professional
literary men.

Distinctly less professional in their interest in nature are
Dallas Lore Sharp (q. v.) and Henry Van Dyke (q. v.). Of
the many varied literary enterprises of Van Dyke, perhaps
none are so satisfying as his early informal sketches of American and Canadian scenes. Sensitive, urbane, pungently
humorous, they evoke at once winsome visions of woods and
streams, and a gracious cultivated personality. Professor
Sharp's work arises from his prolonged and intense study of
the New England world in which he has spent his life, rather
than, as in the case of Van Dyke, the delicate enthusiasms
of a city man on a rural or arboreal holiday. With characteristic economy, he has put to effective use the natural phe-

nomena observable from his doorstep. He gives his subject
the devotion that requires scrupulous honesty of the lover;
he attains geniality without sentimentality, and shrewdness
and humor without meanness or extravagance.

The Personal Essay

A suggestion of a certain poverty, a certain thinness of our
cultural soil, may arise from the contemplation of the very
few writers who have used the essay to express their own
personalities, their own individual points of view. The
widespread process of standardization of education, reading,
and sports has undoubtedly had its effect in leveling those
individual whims, ideas, and tastes that constitute much of
the attraction of the informal essay.

Directly in the tradition of Oliver Wendell Holmes is the
substantial output of Samuel McChord Crothers (q. v.). He
has studied the great essayists, and does not think it ignoble
to imitate them. His point of view is that of an amiable
conservative whose sense of humor and tolerance of essentially human foibles prevent that automatic rejection of
novelty to which conservative natures are prone. Scholarly,
cultivated, endlessly urbane, Dr. Crothers seems to be the
last gentleman to write with ease of the doings of the well-
bred or almost well-bred.

Less flexible and more shrill than Dr. Crothers are the
voices of Agnes Repplier (q. v.) and Katherine Fullerton
Gerould (q. v.). Both stubborn fundamentalists, they defend
the traditional in manners and morals with intelligence, and
assail the unseemly and the novel with acerbity. Miss Repplier's work is more ample in volume and more attractive
in manner than that of Mrs. Gerould. The former has a
sharp tongue, a nimble pen, and an unequalled faculty for
tremendously apt quotation. Her taste is more impeccable
than Mrs. Gerould's, and the purely literary attractions of
her work are more apparent. Mrs. Gerould is the least
attractive of the Brahmins. Her inferior sense of humor and

the arrogance and complacency of her point of view make her defense of the old order much less persuasive than Miss Repplier's.

Columnists: Morley, Strunsky, Don Marquis, Broun

The amplification of the newspaper under the pressure of modern high-powered advertising has forced upon it the acquisition of other features besides news and editorial comment. The increasing impersonality of journalism has therefore enhanced the value of writers who have the faculty for exploiting and exhibiting their personalities for the delectation of millions of readers. The defects of such journalistic writing are obvious. The conditions of its publication limit its extent severely, and force upon the author hurried and excessive production. They also allow an inadequate time for the replenishing of the personality exhausted by the constant drain of production. The success of this type of essayist is likely to depend almost entirely upon the personality he projects, and the vigor with which he projects it. Here we cannot expect grace and refinement of execution.

Of the many practitioners in this kind, Christopher Morley (q. v.) has the widest reputation. His hearty masculine tastes, his intense if not particularly sensitive literary enthusiasms, his facile if not profound acquaintance with the literary and social tradition of England, above all his familiar if somewhat elephantine playfulness, have made him the most popular of American essayists. His fellow journalists have not been so successful in projecting the personality they imagine themselves to possess. Simeon Strunsky, earlier than the others in the field, specialized in the lighter sides of life in New York apartment-houses, but has long since exhausted his original verve and freshness. The best work of Don Marquis has been in the direction of gentle satire: in Hermione and her fellow yearners for better things and in the vivid figure of the Old Soak he has illuminated American shortcomings with considerable adroitness and

Columnists—*Continued*

vivacity. The most intimate of the columnists is Heywood Broun, the results of whose exhibitionism are at first diverting and at last wearisome. His weakness is the inevitable superficiality that incessant productivity induces. His strength lies in his apparently ingenuous frankness and in the sincerity of his liberal convictions. It is to be regretted that the American public's voracity should compel promising personalities to waste themselves in incessant and consequently unreasoned and imperfect expression.

THE NEW BIOGRAPHY

The Vogue of Biography

One of the most startling features of American literature in the last decade has been the amount, the high quality, and the popularity of literary biography. After the event it is easy to indicate at least some of the underlying causes of the revival of this genre, although probably something must be set down to an arbitrary change in the taste of the reading public and more to the essentially imitative habits of both readers and writers in a country where even literary recreation tends to become standardized.

One of the major reasons which may be suggested is the perception that the Great War rather than the close of the century marked very definitely the end of an epoch for both Europe and the United States, and that the time was ripe for a revaluation of the great figures of the past. Indeed, the most characteristic note of the new biography is the insistence on the right of the author to disregard the traditional view of the subject of his biography, and arrive, after a reconsideration of all the evidence, at a fresh estimate. This movement, there is no doubt, has been encouraged and stimulated by the influence of H. L. Mencken (q. v.), who stirs the unregenerate to a delighted admiration by slinging mud at the effigies of national heroes. In other words, some of the element of reaction apparent in the new biography is normal and inevitable, and some of it is abnormal. At its worst the new biography tends to deepen the shadows wilfully and to smudge the high-lights of our ancestral portraits.

An almost equally influential motive in the new biography is the appreciation of the weapon suddenly thrust into the hands of biographical students by that most controversial branch of contemporary psychological investigation, psychoanalysis. The epoch-making work of Freud, Jung, and Adler, and of their American disciples, threw a new if uncertain light upon the problems of character-formation and motivation. It was inevitable that almost every problematical figure in the national history or literature should be submitted to the relentless scrutiny of the professional or amateur psychoanalyst. It was also inevitable that a great deal of shoddy and superficial work and a little very good work should result. But to the process of evaluation, the new psychology brings a method which makes possible a more searching and illuminating study of personality than has been possible before. In too many instances, an unfortunate emphasis has been put upon weaknesses or petty abnormalities of character and conduct, but in the main the tendency is the humanization of our heroes.

The Founders: Bradford and Strachey

A legitimate claim to be the father of the new biography may be maintained by Gamaliel Bradford (q. v.), who has been the most persistent practitioner in this kind. As early as 1895 he displayed his interest in this field in his *Types of American Character*, but it was not until 1914, with *Confederate Portraits*, that his period of real activity here began. Working at first under the influence of Sainte-Beuve, he developed his own theory of "psychography," the purpose of which should be the drawing, after prolonged study, of a psychological portrait of the character under examination. A painstaking and sensitive workman, he has turned out gallery after gallery of essentially American portraits. If his work has been less distinctive or influential than he hoped, the reason is to be sought in his inability to escape altogether from the burden of the diluted Puritanism of the nineteenth century, the genteel manners of the *Atlantic Monthly*, and a not unlimited insight. If the younger biographers have turned to the Englishman, Lytton Strachey, rather than to Bradford as a master, another reason may be

The Founders: Bradford and Strachey—*Continued*

found in Bradford's slightly anaemic style in contrast to Strachey's excessively brilliant manner of expression.

There is no doubt that the publication of *Eminent Victorians* (1918) and *Queen Victoria* (1921) is the most specific influence on the manner and method of the new biography. Here youthful aspirants found a congeries of qualities which might be more or less successfully imitated: a profound distaste for the preceding century, an impersonality and a disillusionment which seem French rather than English or American, a fondness for the picturesque and the sprightly detail, a style which is conscious and hard, ironical and barbed, and a feeling for structure which belongs to the novelist rather than the biographer. Here was a model far indeed from the stodgy factual *Life and Letters* which rose like an ill-conceived memorial to many a nineteenth century mediocrity. If the new biographers approximate only a few of Strachey's virtues, there is no reason for surprise.

Heroes: National and International

It is noteworthy that the new biographers have in general been chary of attacking the major figures in our national history. Aside from Bradford's well-tempered *Lee, the American*, Washington is the only great figure yet treated on the new terms. W. E. Woodward, whose specialty is the "debunking" of American life, submitted Washington to the process in 1926, and Rupert Hughes (q. v.) has embarked on a more elaborate reconstruction of this traditional figure, with the avowed intent of replacing the somewhat innocuous tradition with a human being. To this task he has already devoted two volumes (1926–28), which have met with rather less narrow-minded misunderstanding than was expected, or than he perhaps desired. Aside from R. F. Dibble's studies of Dewey, Hill, and Hamilton in *Strenuous Americans* (1923) and Miss Rourke's study of Greeley in *Trumpets of Jubilee*, our political and economic figureheads have thus far escaped thoroughgoing treatment. An exceptional case is that

Heroes: National and International—*Continued*

of Katharine Anthony, who with her *Catherine the Great* (1925) has gone far afield for a subject, and returned victorious. Dibble's *Mohammed* is another instance of the application of the new method to an ancient and reputable figure.

Religious Heroes

It is not unnatural that the figures that to this generation sum up the religious phenomena of the nineteenth century in America should have received frequent and irreverent treatment at the hands of the new biographers. In 1927 appeared Constance Mayfield Rourke's shrewd and subtle studies of the Beecher Stowes, Frances Willard, and Henry Ward Beecher, the most famous cleric of the period; and the same year offered the most bitterly debated example of the new method, Paxton Hibben's *Henry Ward Beecher: An American Portrait*. There is no opportunity here to discuss the accuracy of Hibben's portrait; it may be designated, however, as the most striking instance up to the present of the denigration of a sainted figure.

Literary Heroes

Here we are admittedly on the edges of, or within the confines of, a variety of criticism, but it may be well to mention certain works which emphasize the biographical rather than the critical approach. Earliest in the field was Katharine Anthony with her *Margaret Fuller: A Psychological Biography* (1920). In 1923 came Thomas Beer's *Stephen Crane: A Study in American Letters*, where the emphasis is perhaps sociological rather than biographical, since it attempts to study Crane's relation to the creative and critical activities of his time. Poe, of course, was one of the most suitable subjects for the new approach, and Krutch's *Edgar Allan Poe: A Study in Genius* (1926) and Hervey Allen's more elaborate and more problematical *Israfel* (1926) are perhaps the most daring interpretations of personality and aesthetic activity in the light of the new psychology.

Folk-Figures

In the earlier part of the period we have been considering, the nineteenth century seemed still too new and familiar to be picturesque. As the century advances, however, a veritable rage for national heirlooms has developed, and our folk heroes have been refurbished to satisfy the appetite for "quaint" American antiques. The most popular has proved to be our first great showman, P. T. Barnum. First attracting the attention of R. F. Dibble in *Strenuous Americans* (1925), he received further treatment in M. R. Werner's *Barnum* (1923) and in Miss Rourke's *Trumpets of Jubilee* (1927). Werner has also contributed a study of *Brigham Young* (1925), and Mr. Dibble continued his researches among strenuous Americans with *John L. Sullivan* (1925). The passion for the picturesque past has even manifested itself in a rehabilitation of our famous criminals. Mr. Dibble's sketch of *Jesse James* (1923) has been followed by a full-length biography of *Billy the Kid*, and other latterday Robin Hoods have achieved the sanctification of official biographies which tend to satisfy the national appetite for courageous criminality.

CRITICISM

Vogue of Criticism

Even more striking than the sudden popularity of biography have been the widespread activity in criticism and the lively discussion of the status of criticism in America. A brief survey of the kinds and qualities of contemporary criticism convinces one that criticism during the last twenty years is as significant a feature of American literary activity as the novel or poetry.

The evidence for the increasing interest in criticism is to be found in the increasing space that criticism has been allotted by newspapers such as the *New York Times* and the *New York Evening Post*, the founding of the *Saturday Review of Literature* (1924), and the development of critical groups around the standards of such weeklies as the *New Republic* and the *Nation*. Such monthly magazines, too, as the *Atlantic* and *Harper's*, have found it advisable to give more space than formerly to reviews of current books; the *Dial* as a monthly has attracted one of the most brilliant groups of current critics, and the *Yale Review*, reconstructed as a quarterly in 1911, has become a distinguished organ of critical practice.

Noteworthy evidence of an abiding interest in critical theory and practice may also be seen in the publication of volumes of collected reviews, such as Mencken's *Prejudices*, Sherman's *On Contemporary Literature*, *Americans*, and *Critical Woodcuts*, and Van Wyck Brooks's *America's Coming-of-Age* and *Letters and Leadership*. Considerations of the function and status of criticism in America are to be found in the *New Republic* pamphlet, *On American Books*, and in anthologies of criticisms and reviews, such as Lewisohn's widely read *A Book of Modern Criticism* (1919), Bowman's

87

Vogue of Criticism—*Continued*
Contemporary American Criticism (1926), and W. A. Drake's
American Criticism, 1926—a selection of significant reviews
of the year.

An attempt to plot the maze of critical theory and practice
is fraught with dangers, since no animals are more touchy
than critics, but the attempt must be made even though
later explorers revise our knowledge and construct new trails.
The enterprise is the more hazardous since each critic is
inclined to think that however uncertain his practice may be,
his theory is stout and dependable. It is, moreover, not in-
frequent that theory and practice fail strikingly to agree.
The most useful guide in the matter of theory is George E.
Woodberry (q. v.), who in *The Appreciation of Literature*
(1907) and *Two Phases of Criticism* (1914) furnishes a bal-
anced analysis of various critical approaches to literature.

Aesthetic Criticism—the Classicists: Brownell, Babbitt, More

The aesthetic critic, in theory, is concerned primarily with
the work of art as a work of art, and not as a sociological or
psychological document. His purpose is on the one hand
appreciation, and on the other, evaluation or appraisal.
The critics of this school are to be distinguished from one
another, however, by the standard by which they measure or
estimate the value of the work in question. The classical
critic of the aesthetic variety must, as Mr. Babbitt says,
"rate creation with reference to some standard set both
above his own temperament and that of the creator. . . .
He will begin to have taste only when he refers the creative
expression and his impression of it to some standard that
is set above both." That standard he finds in the great
works of the past, preferably in the Greek and Roman classics
as his imagination distorts them, but also in admittedly
great works in the English or Continental tradition. The
weakness of the classical point of view is that it tends to
reduce art to a static and ultimately sterile imitation of

ancient masterpieces, and does not provide for the essentially
dynamic and protean nature of the creative impulse. The
strength of the classic position is that it offers a refuge from
the aesthetic solipsism of individual whim and fancy.

The theory of classical criticism has been most elaborately
stated by the somewhat pontifical W. C. Brownell (q. v.).
His exegesis of critical procedure is the most elaborate and
systematic. It is to be regretted that Mr. Brownell's critical
practice has confined itself to such relatively established
figures as Americans in the great traditions and the Victorian prose-writers, and has withheld itself from the treacherous ground of criticism of contemporaries. Irving Babbitt
(q. v.) has proved a much more doughty and influential de-
fendant of classicism and assailant of what he imagines
romanticism to be. The effects of his immense learning and
his brilliance as a controversialist are negated to a degree
by his identification of romanticism with all that is in his
eyes aesthetically and ethically evil. His work betrays a dis-
concerting absence of the balance and restraint of the classicism to which he professes allegiance, and in the violence of
his anti-romantic obsession it is possible to see that even he
has not been able completely to exorcise the devil of the
romantic spirit. Paul Elmer More (q. v.) is a less spectacular
exponent of the classical attitude. Perhaps no other American critic has applied so uniformly and so steadily his
aesthetic and ethical principles to such a variety of literary
phenomena. The limitations of his achievement are the
limitations of his own temperament and theory. These are
a rigidly Puritanical conception of life, a touch of aesthetic
Pharisaism, and a style that imitates but does not equal
that of his master, Matthew Arnold.

Aesthetic Criticism—the Impressionists: Huneker, Na-
than

Still within the aesthetic fold, but at quite the opposite
end from the classical group, are the impressionistic critics.

Aesthetic Criticism—the Impressionists—*Continued*

Alike concerned chiefly with the artistic value of the work under inspection, the impressionist finds the standard of judgment within himself, at worst among his sensations, at best in the region of his often exquisite taste. "To have sensations in the presence of a work of art and to express them, that is the function of Criticism for the impressionistic critic"—such is Spingarn's statement of the creed. At its worst, impressionistic criticism may become "the record of a momentary shiver across a single set of possible degenerate nerves." [1] At its best, this critic may "realize the manifold charms the work of art has gathered unto itself from all sources and . . . interpret this *charm* imaginatively to the men of his own day and generation." [2]

Despite the allurements of this critical theory, very little notable criticism has resulted from its application in America. The most distinguished of its practitioners is perhaps the late James Huneker (q. v.). Equipped with a fairly sensitive apparatus of response, and informed somewhat superficially of current European artistic phenomena, he became a sort of critical press-agent for new and striking figures at home and abroad. The weaknesses of his method are the essentially uncritical facility of his ecstacies and enthusiasms, the superficiality of his information, and his affected and mannered style.

In so far as writing about the drama is criticism and not mere reviewing, it usually shares in America the nature of impressionistic criticism. George Jean Nathan (q. v.) is probably the most widely known critic of the current drama. His concern is so steadily with such eminently uncritical matters as shocking the conventional, exhibiting his knowledge of out of the way and unimportant European dramatic activities, and snubbing all his associates concerned with the drama, that the amount of purely critical activity is amazingly slight. But his concern with the drama is certainly aesthetic rather than sociological, and the standard by

[1] Lewis E. Gates, *Atlantic Monthly*, July, 1900.　　　[2] *Ibid.*

which he measures it is the highly individual and arbitrary
one of his own taste, sustained by his persuasion that any
American drama is bound to be a pallid imitation of a third-
rate European product, and that any American drama that
vilifies American life is a good one. Most distressing of all
is his atrocious style, apparently modeled on the critical
advertising of Huneker, but distended by journalese.

Aesthetic Criticism—the Creative Critics: Spingarn, Aiken, the " Dial " Critics

The brand of criticism first advertised by Joel E. Spingarn
under the provocative title, *Creative Criticism*, comes near-
est in theory and practice to the essential ideal of the aesthetic
position. Mr. Spingarn's slashing lecture on "The New
Criticism" (delivered in 1910 and printed in 1913) attempted
to dispose of all the older methods of criticism and to substitute his own system based upon the aesthetics of Croce.
This high-handed assault on the established procedure may
very well be regarded as the beginning of the revival of interest in the discussion of critical theories. The Spingarn
adaptation of the Crocean system involves a prolonged concentration of the critic upon the work of art in isolation, a
contemplation which has its finest result when the identification of the critic and the work is most complete. Whatever
may be the validity of the underlying aesthetics, the procedure is actually a refurbishing of the method of abstracting
the work under consideration from its historical setting and
relationships, and considering it as absolutely as possible.
This critical method has been stated most clearly by T. S.
Eliot (q. v.) in his distinguished little book, *The Sacred Wood*
(1920): "It is part of his [the critic's] business to see literature
steadily and to see it whole; and this is eminently to see it
not as consecrated by time, but to see it beyond time; to see
the best work of our time and the best work of twenty-five
hundred years ago with the same eyes." It is noteworthy
that the emphasis of this type of critic is upon essentially

Aesthetic Criticism—the Creative Critics—Continued

aesthetic qualities, and the standard of judgment becomes a work of art timeless and ideal in the Platonic sense.

If we look about for an application of the Crocean-Spingarn theory, we shall not find it in the work of Spingarn himself, since he is preëminently theorist and not practitioner. The practice is to be found, rather, in the critical activity of the young men at present associated with the *Dial*. In the work of such critics as Conrad Aiken, Cuthbert Wright, and Kenneth Burke we shall find the best examples of the profound concern with pure aesthetic qualities, the complete divorce of art from time and from life, that the ideal aesthetic theory proposes. As we shall see, this criticism, while distinguished and disinterested, is not the sort that has proved most appealing or natural to the American temper.

Historical Criticism—the Academic Critics: Canby, Van Doren, Boynton, Pattee

The type of criticism that it is convenient to call historical is concerned with the work of art as one of a series of works of art. The historical critic is prone to view the work in question in relation to the literary period that produced it, and to the type of which it is a conventional or an unconventional illustration. Since in such criticism the time-sense is highly developed, it is natural that minds that have been submitted to prolonged academic training should find themselves most at home in this type of criticism. The particular value of this method is that it relates the art of the present to the great tradition; it utilizes as a basis of judgment of the new and novel the obvious value of the established masters, the knowledge of what has been done. Its weakness is that it is inclined to be timorous in its study of the unconventional and novel, and to identify aesthetic virtue with conformity to the traditional. The chief exponents of this attitude and method are academic critics such as Henry S. Canby, Frederick L. Pattee, Percy Holmes Boynton, and Carl Van Doren.

Sociological Criticism

By far the commonest approach to the study of literature in America is one that may be designated as sociological. However antagonistic the views of the members of this group, (and no other group is so contentious and abusive), the common factor in their attitudes is the conviction that literature is to be judged in relation to life, as a representation of life. The object of this criticism is to estimate and interpret the work as a more or less imperfect representation of what the critic believes life in America is or should be. The concern, then, is obviously not with literature as art, but with literature as mirrored experience. It is inevitable, therefore, that the most significant element in the activity of such a critic is the particular conception he holds of what life in America is or what it ought to be. It is on the basis of these varying conceptions that critics of this school can best be arranged.

Sociological Criticism—Conservative: Sherman

Although Stuart Sherman's (q. v.) critical attitude was conditioned by both his classical and his historical predilections, the major clue to his position and his significance is his conception of American life. Of American life he held perfectly rigid views: Americanism to him meant the illusory Puritan tradition unmodified by a consideration of what that tradition had become. He refused to acknowledge as Americanism the "vulgar and selfish and good-humored and sensual and impudent" life of these times, and to him literature which represented such life with fidelity was not literature at all. It was such infatuation with a static and unhistorical state of mind that led him to insist that literature in America must express its "profound moral idealism," even when that idealism had ceased to exist. The strength of Sherman's work lies in his faithfulness to an unpopular tradition, his wide acquaintance with the Anglo-Saxon past, and his adroit controversial tactics. Its weakness lies in the dry-rot at its heart, the peculiarly dead object of its allegiance,

93

Sociological Criticism—Conservative—*Continued*

the essentially moralistic basis of its judgment, and the diluted Arnoldesque style that Sherman steadfastly cultivated.

Sociological Criticism—Liberal: Bourne, Brooks, Lewisohn, Lovett

The liberal conception of life is dynamic rather than static. It is inclined to stress the weaknesses and deficiencies of the current régime, and to look forward with enthusiasm to a world made better by numerous and diverse reforms. It is the attitude of the sensitive social-conscious, the unconventional, the nonconformist. It may involve allegiance to a specific program of reform or to a vaguely conceived free and creative existence wherein the stifling pressure of bourgeois respectability is relieved. The critic of this type is prone to applaud literature that celebrates unconventional ways of thinking and living, literature that furnishes channels for his own unrestrained day-dreaming about a less inhibited world.

Here belongs in the main the work of the critics who espouse the gentle liberalism of the *New Republic* or the somewhat more daring political attitudes of the *Nation*. Here belongs the brilliant work of the lamented Randolph Bourne (1886–1918), the extinction of whose cutting ironic mind was the greatest loss to criticism in our generation. In this category is to be placed the work of such notable critics as Van Wyck Brooks (q. v.), Ludwig Lewisohn (q. v.), and Robert Morss Lovett (q. v.). The earliest critical writing of these men resounds with denunciations of the conditions of life in America that do not make for a free play of the creative impulse in life and art. As literary criticism, such work shows the inevitable weakness—the tendency to discover literary excellence in works that express the ideas dearest to the critic. It is at its best when it stresses the inevitable connection between life and letters, and points out elements in both that are not apparent to the blind spots of conservatism.

Sociological Criticism—Radical: Sinclair and Calverton

Upton Sinclair (q. v.) and V. F. Calverton are radicals in widely varying senses. Mr. Sinclair is a political radical; Mr. Calverton is a radical in critical theory. Interestingly enough, the results for criticism are much the same. If the devil in Mr. Babbitt's universe is named Romanticism, the devil in Mr. Sinclair's universe is named Capitalism. In both cases, the identification has become an obsession that destroys the validity of the gentlemen's judgment. Mr. Sinclair believes that the spirit of capitalism exerts its influence with incredible subtlety and adroitness, and ultimately subjugates most writers in America, however free they may think themselves to be. There is no doubt that the enormous prices that are the reward for giving the editor and the unenlightened public what they want do influence the career and the literary production of many writers. Mr. Sinclair's devil is, however, too insidious and resourceful: he has swathed Mr. Sinclair in veils of illusions, and one can no longer be sure that he has really seen what he says he has seen. To this valiant if wrong-headed spirit, the ideal writing is naturally the literature of violent social protest, even though it be devoid of literary merit.

Mr. Calverton pushes the theory underlying the sociological attitude to its ultimate extremity. He maintains not only that literature represents life, but that it is a function of the social order, and is to be understood only as a product of economic forces. Like every theorist, Mr. Calverton believes that he is a Messiah. He is apparently unaware of the fact that he is stating in simplified form the nineteenth century theory of Hippolyte Taine. Despite the extremity of the attitude, it is a point of view that must be considered, and such studies in contemporary social history as Thomas Beer's *The Mauve Decade* or Mark Sullivan's *Our Times* illustrate in general the tendency Mr. Calverton pontifically expounds.

Sociological Criticism: H. L. Mencken

H. L. Mencken (q. v.) has stated his conception of the function of the critic in a way that illuminates his own procedure. The critic, he writes, "is trying to arrest and challenge a sufficient body of readers, to make them pay attention to him, to impress them with the charm and novelty of his ideas, to provoke in them an agreeable (or shocked) awareness of him, and he is trying to achieve thereby for his own inner ego the grateful feeling of a function performed, a tension relieved. . . . " But there can be no doubt that Mr. Mencken is primarily concerned with the relationship between art and life rather than with art in and by itself, even though it is not easy to assign him to the conservative, the radical, or the liberal category, since his own views are in a confused and contradictory condition.

Mr. Mencken's view of American life may best be built up from a catalogue of his intense likes and dislikes. He hates democracy, though it offers him a pleasant opportunity to contemplate his own superiority. His attitude toward women combines a distaste for their essentially feminine attributes with an admiration for their ingenuity in getting what they want in a man-made world. He hates the ways and means of the middle class, its ideas of comfort and culture, its standardized language and manners, its religious narrowness, and its tendency to enlarge its own egotism by forming supposedly exclusive groups with esoteric titles and costumes. Accordingly, the literature which he admires is practically confined to works that represent American life as unlovely and mean or works that expose the particular aspects of life in America of which he disapproves.

It is difficult to come to any satisfying conclusion as to the nature of Mr. Mencken's influence. That it has been enormous since the founding of the *American Mercury* goes without saying. That it has not been an unmixed good or evil is also apparent to anyone who is not completely prejudiced. To the good may be attributed his sponsoring of such important writers as Sinclair Lewis, Sher-

Sociological Criticism: H. L. Mencken—*Continued*

wood Anderson, Willa Cather, and Theodore Dreiser (whose fame is primarily due to Mencken's steadfast advertising). On this side of the ledger belongs also his influence in the exploiting of unfamiliar but significant aspects of the American scene or American thought, American folk-ways as they express themselves in folk-song, whether white or colored, such honest if uninspired pictures of western life as those of Ruth Suckow, and the picturesque habits and language of tramps, circus-followers, and criminals of various kinds. On the other hand, his influence on style has been thoroughly bad. His cheap, tasteless, and drum-thumping effects are only too easy to imitate. What is more serious is that his turning outward of the seamy side of American character and life encourages young writers and readers in the belief that decency and graciousness are no longer existent or desirable in either life or letters. But there are signs that with the increasingly mechanical application and expression of his views, his influence is waning with all except the callow and the superficial.

Biographical Criticism: Brooks, Krutch, Holloway, Allen

There has never been a time when critics have forgotten the obvious fact that the nature of the artist conditions his creations no less than does the multifold influence of his social and literary environment. But, while the biographical approach to criticism is not altogether new, it has received a tremendous impetus from the enormous activity in various kinds of psychology. The chief interest of the biographical or psychological critic is in explaining why a particular man created works of a particular nature and manner. The new weapons have proved so sharp as to be dangerous. Van Wyck Brooks's (q. v.) first use of them in *The Ordeal of Mark Twain* (1920) proved well-nigh disastrous. In *The Pilgrimage of Henry James* (1925), however, he used them with greater sureness and subtlety. Though there is a temptation to force the new theory for more than it is worth, the

Biographical Criticism—*Continued*

work in this direction—on the borderline, to be sure, between biography and criticism—is increasingly assured and persuasive. We may instance such achievements as the works of Krutch (q. v.) and Hervey Allen (q. v.) on Poe, and Emory Holloway's *Walt Whitman.*

CONCLUSION

If no literary work of the past generation can be hailed as unquestionably great, no American need be ashamed of either the quality or the quantity of the literary production of the period. The novel has held its own as the type most popular and attractive with both writers and readers. The poetic renaissance, though it has definitely died down, was brilliant and fruitful for more than a decade. In the drama there are plenty of signs of widespread interest in sound American work both within and without the commercial theatre, although O'Neill seems to stand alone in the amount and the distinction of his work. If the informal essay has been only casually cultivated, the material which in another period might have taken this shape has worked itself out in the scattered writings of columnists and hard-working literary journalists. In both biography and criticism, the output has been large in quantity and impressive in quality. For the future, hope seems justified in the light of the improvement of taste of the general reading public, in the vigor and variety of publication of both magazines and books, and in the stimulus that authors must receive from the existence of intelligent and appreciative criticism.

CONTEMPORARY AMERICAN LITERATURE

George Ade—humorist, dramatist.

Born at Kentland, Indiana, 1866. B. S., Purdue University, 1887. Newspaper work at Lafayette, Indiana, 1887–90. On the *Chicago Record*, 1890–1900. Trustee of Purdue, 1908–15. Promotor of Ross-Ade Stadium, Purdue, 1923–24.

Although some of his earlier plays were highly successful, his reputation rests chiefly upon his humorous fables of modern life, couched in carefully devised slang.

BIBLIOGRAPHY

Plays
    The Sultan of Sulu. 1903. (Musical comedy libretto.)
    Marse Covington. 1918.
    Speaking to Father. 1923.
    The Mayor and the Manicure. 1923.
    Nettie. 1923.
    The County Chairman. 1924.
    The College Widow. 1924.
    Just Out of College. 1924.
    Father and the Boys. 1924.

Novels and Short Stories
    Artie. 1896. (Dramatized.)
    Pink Marsh. 1897.
    Doc' Horne. 1899.
    Circus Day. 1903.
    In Babel. 1903.
    The Slim Princess. 1907.
    Bang! Bang! 1928.

Fables
    Fables in Slang. 1900.
    More Fables. 1900.

George Ade—*Continued*
Forty Modern Fables. 1901.
The Girl Proposition. 1902.
People You Know. 1903.
Breaking into Society. 1904.
True Bills. 1904.
Knocking the Neighbors. 1912.
Ade's Fables. 1914.
Hand-Made Fables. 1920.

Essays
Single Blessedness. 1922.

Humorous Travel Sketches
In Pastures New. 1906.

For list of unpublished plays, see Who's Who in America; *for bibliography, including privately printed works, see* The Publishers' Weekly, *Feb. 24, 1923.*

STUDIES AND REVIEWS

Dickinson. (P. N. A. T.)
Hind. (M. A. I.)
Moses.
Van Doren. (M. M.)

Am. M., 73 ('11): 71 (portrait), 73.

Bookm., 51 ('20): 568; 54 ('21): 116 (portrait).
Bost. Trans., Nov. 4, 1922: 2.
N. Y. Times, Jan. 14, 1923: 2.
No. Am., 176 ('03): 739 (Howells).
Rev., 2 ('20): 461.

Conrad (Potter) Aiken—poet, critic, short story writer.
Born at Savannah, Georgia, 1889. A. B., Harvard, 1911. Has lived abroad, in England and Italy.

SUGGESTIONS FOR READING
1. A good introduction to Mr. Aiken's verse is his own explanation of his theory in *Poetry*, 14 ('19); 152ff. To readers to whom this is not accessible, the following extracts may furnish some clue as to his aim and method:

What I had from the outset been somewhat doubtfully hankering for was some way of getting contrapuntal effects in poetry—the effects of contrasting and conflicting tones and themes, a kind of underlying

Conrad (Potter) Aiken—*Continued*

simultaneity in dissimilarity. It seemed to me that by using a large medium, dividing it into several main parts, and subdividing these parts into short movements in various veins and forms, this was rendered possible. I do not wish to press the musical analogies too closely. I am aware that the word symphony, as a musical term, has a very definite meaning, and I am aware that it is only with considerable license that I use the term for such poems as *Senlin* or *Forslin*, which have three and five parts respectively, and do not in any orthodox way develop their themes. But the effect obtained is, very roughly speaking, that of the symphony, or symphonic poem. Granted that one has chosen a theme—or been chosen by a theme!—which will permit rapid changes of tone, which will not insist on a tone too static, it will be seen that there is no limit to the variety of effects obtainable: for not only can one use all the simpler poetic tones . . . ; but, since one is using them as parts of a larger design, one can also obtain novel effects by placing them in juxtaposition as consecutive movements. . . .

All this, I must emphasize, is no less a matter of emotional tone than of form; the two things cannot well be separated. For such symphonic effects one employs what one might term emotion-mass with just as deliberate a regard for its position in the total design as one would employ a variation of form. One should regard this or that emotional theme as a musical unit having such-and-such a tone-quality, and use it only when that particular tone-quality is wanted. Here I flatly give myself away as being in reality in quest of a sort of absolute poetry, a poetry in which the intention is not so much to arouse an emotion merely, or to persuade of a reality, as to employ such emotion or sense of reality (tangentially struck) with the same cool detachment with which a composer employs notes or chords. Not content to present emotions or things or sensations for their own sakes—as is the case with most poetry—this method takes only the most delicately evocative aspects of them, makes of them a keyboard, and plays upon them a music of which the chief characteristic is its elusiveness, its fleetingness, and its richness in the shimmering overtones of hint and suggestion. Such a poetry, in other words, will not so much present an idea as use its resonance.

2. An interesting comparison may be made between the work of Mr. Aiken, and that of Mr. T. S. Eliot (q. v.), of whom he is an admirer.

3. Another interesting study is the influence of Freud upon the poetry of Mr. Aiken.

4. Study the influence of James Joyce's *Ulysses* on Mr. Aiken's experimental novel, *Blue Voyage*.

Conrad (Potter) Aiken—*Continued*

BIBLIOGRAPHY

Poems
    Earth Triumphant. 1914.
    Turns and Movies. 1916.
    The Jig of Forslin. 1916.
    Nocturne of Remembered Spring. 1917.
    The Charnel Rose, Senlin. 1918.
    The House of Dust. 1920.
    Punch: The Immortal Liar. 1921.
    Priapus and the Pool. 1922. (Enl. ed., 1925.)
    Modern American Poets. London, 1922. New York, 1927.
    The Pilgrimage of Festus. 1923.
    American Poetry, 1671–1928. 1929. (Editor.)

Novels
    Blue Voyage. 1927.

Short Stories
    Bring! Bring! 1925.
    Costumes by Eros. 1928.

Critical Essays
    Scepticisms. 1919.

STUDIES AND REVIEWS

Untermeyer, L. (A. P.)

Ath., 2 ('19): 798, 840; 1 ('20): 10.
Bookm., 47 ('18): 269; 51 ('20): 194; 53 ('21): 547.
Bost. Trans., Nov. 17, 1923: 7.
Cal. Mod. Lett., 2 ('25): 68.
Chapbook, 1–2, May, 1920: 26.
Crit., 3 ('24–'25): 583.
Dial, 64 ('18): 291 (J. G. Fletcher); 66 ('19): 558 (J. G. Fletcher); 68 ('20): 491; 70 ('21): 343, 700; 73 ('22): 563; 79 ('25): 507.
Egoist, 5 ('18): 60.
Lit. Rev., Apr. 23, 1921: 4; Dec. 12, 1925: 2.

Lond. Times, Apr. 23, 1925: 282; May 26, 1927: 372.
Nation, 111 ('20): 509; 117 ('23): 271; 125 ('27): 257.
N. Repub., 28 ('21): 139; 43 ('25): 242; 51 ('27): 316.
N. Y. Times, May 7, 1922: 12; July 24, 1927: 2.
Poetry, 9 ('16): 99; 10 ('17): 162; 13 ('18): 102; 14 ('19): 152; 15 ('20): 283; 17 ('21): 220; 22 ('23): 53.
Sat. Rev., 143 ('27): 947.
Sat. Rev. of Lit., 1 ('25): 851.

See also Book Review Digest, 1919, 1920.

Zoë Akins—dramatist.

Born at Humansville, Missouri, 1886. Educated privately and at seminaries. Began literary work as contributor to *Reedy's Mirror*. Her work shows the influence of English and Continental social drama.

BIBLIOGRAPHY

Poems
Interpretations. 1912.

Plays
Papa. 1913.
Déclassée: Daddy's Gone A-Hunting: and Greatness. 1923. (The last produced under title The Texas Nightingale.)

Novels
Cake Upon the Waters. 1919.

For list of unpublished plays, see Who's Who in America.

STUDIES AND REVIEWS

Dickinson. (P. N. A. T.)   Nathan, G. J. Materia Critica. 1924.

(William) Hervey Allen—poet and biographer.

Born at Pittsburgh, Pennsylvania, 1889. U. S. Naval Academy, 1910–11; B. Sc., University of Pittsburgh, 1915. Studied at Harvard, 1920–22. Member of Department of English, Columbia University, since 1924. Has had military experience in Mexico and France.

BIBLIOGRAPHY

Poems
Ballads of the Border. El Paso, 1916.
Wampum and Old Gold. 1921.
The Bride of Huitzil. 1922.
Carolina Chansons. 1922. (With Du Bose Heyward.)
The Blindman. 1923.
Earth Moods. 1925.
Christmas Epithalamium. 1925.
Songs for Annette. 1929.

(William) Hervey Allen—*Continued*

Novels
  Toward the Flame. 1926.

Biography
  Israfel. 1926.
  Poe's Brother. 1926. (Joint editor with Thomas Ollive Mabbott.)

STUDIES AND REVIEWS

Booklist, 23 ('27): 269.
Bost. Trans., Dec. 18, 1926: 4.
Dial, 71 ('21): 716.
Double-Dealer, 5 ('23): 178.
Ind., 118 ('27): 106.
Lit. Digest, I. B. R., Sept., 1925:
  658.
Manchester Guardian, 16 ('27):
  13.
Nation, 121 ('25): 145.

N. Repub., 50 ('27): supp. 340.
N. Y. Herald-Tribune, Apr. 26,
  1926: 7.
N. Y. Times, May 31, 1925: 11;
  Apr. 11, 1926: 6; Dec. 5, 1926:
  1.
Poetry, 22 ('23): 89.
Sat. Rev. of Lit., 2 ('25): 444.
Springfield Repub., Oct. 23, 1921:
  11a.

James Lane Allen—novelist.

Born near Lexington, Kentucky, 1849, of Scotch-Irish Revolutionary ancestry. A. B., A. M., Transylvania University; and honorary higher degrees. Taught in various schools and colleges. After 1886 gave his time entirely to writing. Nature-lover. Described the Kentucky life that he knew intimately. Died Feb. 18, 1925.

BIBLIOGRAPHY

  A Kentucky Cardinal. 1895.
  The Choir Invisible. 1897. (Dramatized, 1899.)
  The Mettle of the Pasture. 1903.
  For complete bibliography, see Who's Who in America, 1925.

Maxwell Anderson—dramatist.

Born at Atlantic, Pennsylvania, 1888. B. A., Notre Dame University; M. A., Stanford University. Taught English at

Maxwell Anderson—*Continued*

Stanford. Worked on various San Francisco newspapers. One of the founders and editor of *Measure, A Journal of Poetry*. Editorial writer, *New York World*, 1921.

BIBLIOGRAPHY

Poems
  You Who Have Dreams. 1925.

Plays
  Three American Plays. 1926. (What Price Glory? First Flight. The Buccaneer.) (With Laurence Stallings.)
  Saturday's Children. 1927.
  Gods of the Lightning, and Outside Looking In. 1928. (With Harold Hickerson.)

STUDIES AND REVIEWS

Cent., 113 ('26): 255.
Lond. Times, Nov. 3, 1927: 784.
Poetry, 27 ('25): 337.
Sat. Rev. of Lit., 3 ('26): 417.

Sherwood Anderson—short story writer, novelist.

Born at Camden, Ohio, 1876. Of Scotch-Irish ancestry. Father a journeyman harness-maker. Public school education. At the age of sixteen or seventeen came to Chicago and worked four or five years as a laborer. Soldier in the Spanish-American War. Later, in the advertising business.

In 1921, received the prize of $2,000 offered by the *Dial* to further the work of the American author considered to be most promising.

SUGGESTIONS FOR READING

  1. The autobiographical element in Mr. Anderson's work is marked and should never be forgotten in judging his work. The conventional element is easily discoverable as patched on, particularly in the long books.

  2. To realize the qualities that make some critics regard Mr. Anderson as perhaps our most promising novelist, ex-

107

Sherwood Anderson—*Continued*

amples should be noted of the following qualities which he possesses to a striking degree: (1) independence of literary traditions and methods; (2) a keen eye for details; (3) a passionate desire to interpret life; (4) a strong sense of the value of individual lives of little seeming importance.

3. Are Mr. Anderson's defects due to the limitations of his experience, or do you notice certain temperamental defects which he is not likely to outgrow?

4. Mr. Anderson's experiments in form are interesting to study. Compare the prosiness of his verse with his efforts to use poetic cadence in *The Triumph of the Egg*. Does it suggest to you the possibility of developing a form intermediate between prose and free verse?

5. Is Mr. Anderson more successful as a novelist or as a short story writer? Why?

6. Study the characters in *Winesburg, Ohio*, in the light of the psychology of Freud and Jung.

BIBLIOGRAPHY

Poems
　　Mid-American Chants. 1918.
　　A New Testament. 1927.

Novels
　　Windy McPherson's Son. 1916. Rev. ed., 1921.
　　Marching Men. 1917.
　　Poor White. 1920.
　　Many Marriages. 1923.
　　Dark Laughter. 1925.
　　Tar. 1926.

Short Stories
　　Winesburg, Ohio. 1919.
　　The Triumph of the Egg. 1921.
　　Horses and Men. 1923.

Essays and Sketches
　　The Modern Writer. 1925.
　　Sherwood Anderson's Notebook. 1926.

Autobiography
　　A Story-Teller's Story. 1924.

STUDIES AND REVIEWS

Baldwin.

Beach.

Boynton. (M. C. A.)

Calverton.

Chase, C. B. Sherwood Anderson. 1927.

Drake.

Fagin, N. B. Phenomenon of Sherwood Anderson. 1927.

Farrar.

Hackett. (H.)

Hansen.

Karsner.

Michaud.

Sherman. (C. W.)

Spratling, W. P. Sherwood Anderson and Other Famous Creoles. 1926.

Van Doren. (C. A. N.)

——. (A. B. L.)

Whipple.

Am. Merc., 1 ('24): 252.

Bookm., 45 ('17): 302 (portrait); 307.

Bost. Trans., Oct. 10, 1925: 4; May 29, 1926: 5; Dec. 11, 1926: 4.

Cal. Mod. Lett., 1 ('25): 480.

Dial, 72 ('22): 29, 79 (Lovett); 74 ('23): 400; 79 ('25): 510.

Freeman, 2 ('21): 403; 4 ('21): 281 (Colum); 8 ('23): 307.

Ind., 115 ('25): 302.

Lit. Digest, I. B. R. Dec., 1924: 15; Nov., 1925: 805.

Lit. Rev., Nov. 26, 1921: 200; Feb. 24, 1923: 483; Dec. 8, 1923: 333; July 9, 1927: 8.

Nation, 119 ('24): 640; 121 ('25): 626.

N. Repub., 9 ('17): 333; 24 ('20): 330; 28 ('21): 383; 34 (Apr. 11, '23): supp. 6; 40 ('24): 255; 44 ('25): 233.

N. Y. Herald-Tribune, Nov. 21, 1926: 1 (R. West).

N. Y. Times, Feb. 25, 1923: 10; Nov. 25, 1923: 7; Oct. 12, 1924: 6; Sept. 20, 1925: 9; May 9, 1926: 2; Nov. 21, 1926: 2; June 12, 1927: 9 (portrait).

N. Y. World, June 19, 1927: 8m.

No. Am., 224 ('27): 140.

Poetry, 12 ('18): 155.

Sat. Rev. of Lit., 1 ('24): 200; 2 ('25): 191.

Mary Raymond Shipman Andrews—short story writer, novelist.

Mrs. William Shankland Andrews. Born at Mobile, Alabama. Moved to Lexington, Kentucky, and lived there to 1880.

BIBLIOGRAPHY

Poems

Crosses of War. 1918.

Mary Raymond Shipman Andrews—*Continued*

Novels
The Marshal. 1912.
August First. 1915. (With Roy Irving Murray.)

Short Stories and Tales
Vive l'Empereur. 1902.
A Kidnapped Colony. 1903.
* The Perfect Tribute. 1906.
A Good Samaritan. 1906.
The Militants. 1907.
Better Treasure. 1908.
The Enchanted Forest. 1909.
* The Lifted Bandage. 1910.
The Courage of the Commonplace. 1911.
The Counsel Assigned. 1912.
The Eternal Masculine. 1913.
The Three Things. 1915.
The Eternal Feminine. 1916.
Old Glory. 1916.
Her Country. 1918.
Joy in the Morning. 1919.
His Soul Goes Marching On. 1922.
Yellow Butterflies. 1922.
Passing the Torch. 1924.
Pontifex Maximus. 1925.

Biography
A Lost Commander: Florence Nightingale. 1929.

STUDIES AND REVIEWS

Bookm., 27 ('08): 155.
Bost. Trans., Apr. 22, 1922: 6.
Nation, 85 ('07): 58.

N. Y. Times, May 10, 1925: 19.

See also Book Review Digest, 1912, 1915, 1919.

Gertrude Franklin Atherton—novelist.

Mrs. George H. Bowen Atherton. Born at San Francisco, 1857. Great-grandniece of Benjamin Franklin. Educated in private schools. Has lived much abroad. Made Chevalier of (French) Legion of Honor, 1925.

Mrs. Atherton's work is very uneven, but is interesting

Gertrude Franklin Atherton—*Continued*
as reflecting different aspects of social and political life in
this country.

BIBLIOGRAPHY

American Wives and English Husbands.   1898.   (Revised edition,
    1919; under the title Transplanted.)
Senator North.   1900.
The Conqueror.   1902.
Perch of the Devil.   1914.
Black Oxen.   1923.
The Immortal Marriage.   1927.
For complete bibliography, see Who's Who in America.

STUDIES AND REVIEWS

Cooper.

Courtney, W. L.   The Feminine
    Note in Fiction.   1904.

Halsey.   (Women.)

Harkins.   (Women.)

Overton.   (O. W. N.)

Underwood.

Am. Merc., 6 ('25): 249.

Bookm., 12 ('01): 541, 542 (por-
    trait); 30 ('09): 356.

Bost. Trans., Jan. 29, 1921: 8;
    Feb. 8, 1922: 6; Sept. 2, 1925: 6.

Classical Philology, 22 ('27): 332.

Forum, 58 ('17): 585.

Lit. Digest, I. B. R.   Oct., 1925:
    730.

Lit. Rev., Jan. 29, 1921: 3; Feb.
    25, 1922: 447; Jan. 27, 1923: 411.

Lond. Times, Feb. 17, 1921: 106;
    July 7, 1927: 470.

N. Y. Times, Jan. 30, 1921: 2;
    Feb. 5, 1922: 6; Jan. 21, 1923:
    14; Aug. 30, 1925: 14; Apr. 24,
    1927: 2.

Spec., 126 ('21): 816.

Mary Hunter Austin—novelist, dramatist.
Mrs. Stafford W. Austin.   Born at Carlinville, Illinois,
1868.   At the age of nineteen went to live in California.
B. S., Blackburn University, 1888.   Lived on the edge of the
Mohave Desert, where she is said to have worked like an
Indian woman, housekeeping and gardening.   Studied the
desert, its form, its weather, its lights, its plants.   Also
studied Indian lore extensively, contributing the chapter on
Aboriginal Literature to the *Cambridge History of American
Literature* (IV [Later National Literature, III], 610ff.).

Mary Hunter Austin—*Continued*

BIBLIOGRAPHY

Poems
  Outland. London, 1910. (Under pseud., Gordon Stairs.) New
    York, 1919.

Plays
 * The Arrow Maker. 1911.

Novels
  Isidro. 1905.
  Santa Lucia. 1908.
 * A Woman of Genius. 1912. (Rev. ed., 1917.)
  The Green Bough. 1913.
  The Lovely Lady. 1913.
  The Ford. 1917.
  No. 26 Jayne Street. 1920.

Short Stories
 * The Basket Woman. 1904.
  Lost Borders. 1909.
  The Trail Book. 1918.

Essays and Studies
  The Land of Little Rain. 1903.
  The Flock. 1906.
  Christ in Italy. 1912.
  California. 1914. (Repr. 1927 as The Lands of the Sun.)
  Love and the Soul Maker. 1914.
  The Young Woman Citizen. 1918.
  The American Rhythm. 1923.
  The Land of Journeys' Ending. 1924.
  Everyman's Genius. 1925.
  Children Sing in the Far West. 1928.

Biography and Religion
  The Man Jesus. 1915. (Rev. ed., 1925, as A Small-Town Man.)

STUDIES AND REVIEWS

Farrar.
Overton. (O. W. N.)

Am. Mag., 72 ('11): 178 (portrait).
Bookm., 35 ('12): 586 (portrait);
  65 ('27): 712.

Bost. Trans., May 12, 1923: 3.
Cur. Lit., 53 ('12): 698 (portrait).
Freeman, 1 ('20): 311.
Lit. Digest, I. B. R. Dec., 1924:
  42.
Lit. Rev., Nov. 3, 1923: 204.
Nation, 116 ('23): 472.

Mary Hunter Austin—*Continued*

N. Repub., 24 ('20): 151; 35 ('23): 23; 43 ('25): 53; 52 ('27): 51.
N. Y. Times, May 3, 1925: 14.
Rev., 3 ('20): 73.

Sat. Rev. of Lit., 2 ('26): 494.
Springfield Repub., Aug. 16, 1925: 7a.

Irving Babbitt—critic.

Born at Dayton, Ohio, 1865. A. B., Harvard, 1889; A. M., 1893. Member of the French Department at Harvard, 1894—. Has edited Taine, Renan, and Voltaire.

BIBLIOGRAPHY

Critical Essays and Studies
Literature and the American College. 1908.
The New Laokoön. 1910.
The Masters of Modern French Criticism. 1912.
Rousseau and Romanticism. 1919.
Democracy and Leadership. 1924.

STUDIES AND REVIEWS

Crit., 3 ('24–'25): 129; N. Crit., 4 ('26): 494.
Lond. Times, Sept. 4, 1924: 531.
Nation, 119 ('24): 293.
N. Repub., 40 ('24): 49.

N. Y. Times, June 15, 1924: 4 (S. Strunsky).
Sat. Rev. of Lit., 1 ('24): 162.
Spec., 133 ('24): 563.

Irving (Addison) Bacheller—novelist.

Born at Pierpont, New York, 1859. B. S., St. Lawrence University, 1882; M. S., 1892. Various honorary degrees. For years a journalist in New York.

His outstanding books are:
Eben Holden. 1900.
A Man for the Ages. 1919. (Lincoln, the hero.)

For bibliography, see Who's Who in America.

Irving (Addison) Bacheller—*Continued*

STUDIES AND REVIEWS

Bost. Trans., May 29, 1923: 4; Feb. 28, 1925: 3.
Lit. Digest, Aug. 19, 1922: 55.
Lit. Digest, I. B. R. Aug., 1923: 28; Apr., 1925: 328.
Lit. Rev., July 29, 1922: 835; Feb. 28, 1925: 6.
N. Y. Herald-Tribune, Mar. 27, 1927: 13.

N. Y. Times, Dec. 5, 1920: 18; July 16, 1922: 15; Mar. 13, 1927: 8.
Sat. Rev. of Lit., 1 ('25): 555; 3 ('27): 678.

See also Book Review Digest, 1919.

Ray Stannard Baker (David Grayson)—man of letters.

Born at Lansing, Michigan, 1870. B. S., Michigan Agricultural College, 1889. Studied law and literature at University of Michigan; LL. D., 1917. On the *Chicago Record*, 1892–97. Managing editor of McClure's Syndicate, 1897–98, and associate editor of *McClure's Magazine*, 1899–1905. On the *American Magazine*, 1906–15. Director of Press Bureau of the American Commission to Negotiate Peace at Paris, 1919.

His studies of country life under the pseudonym David Grayson are widely popular.

BIBLIOGRAPHY

Novel
    Hempfield. 1915.

Familiar Essays
    Adventures in Contentment. 1907.
    Adventures in Friendship. 1910.
    The Friendly Road. 1913.
    Great Possessions. 1917.
    Adventures in Understanding. 1925.
    A Day of Pleasant Bread. 1926.

Historical and Biographical Studies
    Woodrow Wilson and World Settlement. 1922.
    The Public Papers of Woodrow Wilson. 1925–26. (Joint editor with Professor William E. Dodd.)
    Life and Letters of Woodrow Wilson. 1927– . Vols. I–II.

Ray Stannard Baker (David Grayson)—*Continued*

Studies and Reviews

Acad., 86 ('14): 137.
Am. M., Nov., 1914: 38.
Bookm., 43 ('16): 1 (portrait), 394.
Bookm. (Lond.), 39 ('11): 290; 47 ('14): 107.
Lit. Rev., Nov. 26, 1927: 12.

McClure's, 24 ('04): 108, 110 (portrait).
N. Y. Times, Oct. 11, 1925: 2.
N. Y. World, Nov. 27, 1927: 10m.
Sat. Rev. of Lit., 2 ('25): 443.

(Charles) William Beebe—nature writer.

Born at Brooklyn, New York, 1877. B. S., Columbia, 1898; post-graduate work, 1898–99. Honorary Curator of Ornithology, New York Zoölogical Society since 1899; Director of the British Guiana Zoölogical Station. Has traveled extensively in Asia, South America, and Mexico, especially, for purposes of observation. Author of many technical works.

Suggestions for Reading

1. Although Mr. Beebe is preëminently an ornithologist, he belongs to literature by reason of the volumes of nature studies listed below. A comparison of his books with those of the English ornithologist, W. H. Hudson (cf. Manly and Rickert, *Contemporary British Literature*) is illuminative of the merits of both.

2. Another interesting comparison may be made between Mr. Beebe's descriptions of the jungle in *Jungle Peace* and H. M. Tomlinson's in *Sea and Jungle* (cf. Manly and Rickert, *op. cit.*).

3. An analysis of the appeal to the different senses brings out one of the main sources of Mr. Beebe's charm as a writer.

4. Read aloud several fine passages to observe the prose rhythms.

Bibliography

Description and Travel
Two Bird-Lovers in Mexico. 1905.
Our Search for a Wilderness. 1910. (With Mrs. Beebe.)

(Charles) William Beebe—*Continued*

Tropical Wild Life in British Guiana. 1917. (With G. Inness Hartley and Paul Griswold Howes.)
Galapagos, World's End. 1924.
The Arcturus Adventure. 1926. (With Ruth Rose.)

Nature Studies and Essays

The Log of the Sun. 1906.
Jungle Peace. 1918.
A Monograph of the Pheasants. London, 1918–22. (Repr. as Pheasants, Their Lives and Homes. 1926.)
Edge of the Jungle. 1921.
Jungle Days. 1925.
Pheasant Jungles. 1927.
Beneath Tropic Seas. 1928.

STUDIES AND REVIEWS

Bost. Trans., July 18, 1925: 2.
Ind., 115 ('25): 162; 116 ('26): 695.
Lit. Digest, I. B. R. Mar., 1924: 268; Aug., 1925: 574.
Lit. Rev., Mar. 15, 1924: 592; Apr. 2, 1927: 4.
Lond. Times, Apr. 17, 1924: 235; Nov. 5, 1925: 733.
Nation, 106 ('18): 213; 114 ('22): 47; 118 ('24): Apr. 16, supp. 443.
Nation and Ath., 35 ('24): 124.
N. Repub., 54 ('28): 393.
N. State., 29 ('27): supp. xiv.

N. Y. Herald-Tribune, May 30, 1926: 1.
N. Y. Times, Dec. 18, 1921: 7; Feb. 24, 1924: 1; July 5, 1925: 3; May 23, 1926: 1; Jan. 30, 1927: 6; Apr. 17, 1927: 5.
Science, n. s. 50 ('19): 473.
Spec., 95 ('05): 1128.
Yale Rev., n. s. 14 ('24): 171.

See also Book Review Digest, 1918, 1921.

Thomas Beer—novelist, essayist.

Born in Council Bluffs, Iowa, 1889. B. A., Yale, 1911. Student in law at Columbia, 1911–13. Served in World War as first lieutenant.

BIBLIOGRAPHY

Novels

The Fair Rewards. 1922.
Sandoval. 1924.
The Road to Heaven. 1928.

Thomas Beer—*Continued*

Biography and Criticism
Stephen Crane. 1923.

Sociological and Literary Study
The Mauve Decade. 1926.

STUDIES AND REVIEWS

Baldwin.
Boyd. (P. R. I.)

Am. Merc., 8 ('26): 383.
Bookm., 58 ('23): 470.
Bost. Trans., Mar. 22, 1922: 5;
Dec. 1, 1923: 5; June 12, 1926:
3.
Ind., 116 ('26): 552, 581 (E.
Boyd).

Lit. Rev., Mar. 11, 1922: 483;
May 1, 1926: 1.
Nation, 119 ('24): 125; 126 ('28):
646.
N. Repub., 37 ('24): 153.
N. Y. Herald-Tribune, Apr. 26,
1926: 1.
N. Y. Times, Dec. 30, 1923: 8;
May 25, 1924: 9; Apr. 25, 1926:
3; June 20, 1926: 4.

(John) Barry Benefield—novelist.

Born at Jefferson, Texas. Educated at State University,
Austin. Did newspaper work with *Dallas News* and *New
York Times*. Worked at advertising for a time, and then
turned to magazine fiction.

BIBLIOGRAPHY

Novels
The Chicken-Wagon Family. 1925.
Bugles in the Night. 1927.
A Little Clown Lost. 1928.

Short Stories
Short Turns. 1926.

STUDIES AND REVIEWS

Bost. Trans., Sept. 12, 1925: 3;
Sept. 29, 1926: 4.
Lit. Digest, I. B. R. Oct., 1925:
744.

N. Y. Herald-Tribune, Sept. 9,
1928: 14.
N. Y. Times, Aug. 29, 1926: 6.
Sat. Rev. of Lit., 2 ('25): 362.

Stephen Vincent Benét—poet, novelist.

Born at Bethlehem, Pennsylvania, 1898; brother of William Rose Benét (q. v.). B. A., Yale, 1919; M. A., 1920.

Mr. Benét's work at once attracted attention by its qualities of exuberance and fancy. In 1921 he shared with Carl Sandburg (q. v.) the prize of the Poetry Society of America.

BIBLIOGRAPHY

Poems

Five Men and Pompey. 1915.
Young Adventure. 1918.
Heavens and Earth. 1920.
The Ballad of William Sycamore, 1790–1880. 1923.
King David. 1923.
Tiger Joy. 1925.
John Brown's Body. 1928.

Novels

The Beginning of Wisdom. 1921.
Young People's Pride. 1922.
Jean Huguenot. 1923.
Spanish Bayonet. 1926.

STUDIES AND REVIEWS

Maynard.
Untermeyer. (A. P.)

Bookm., 54 ('21): 394.
Bost. Trans., Sept. 20, 1922: 4; Oct. 20, 1923: 4; Apr. 3, 1926: 5; Aug. 11, 1928: 1.
Dial, 71 ('21): 599.
Lit. Rev., Nov. 5, 1921: 143; Sept. 30, 1922: 4; Nov. 17, 1923: 256.

N. Repub., 56 ('28): 52.
N. Y. Times, Oct. 23, 1921: 16; Sept. 20, 1925: 12.
Poetry, 16 ('20): 53; 20 ('22): 340.
Sat. Rev. of Lit., 2 ('25): 428.

See also Book Review Digest, 1919, 1920, 1921.

William Rose Benét—poet.

Born at Fort Hamilton, New York Harbor, 1886. Ph. B., Sheffield Scientific School, Yale, 1907. Free-lance writer in California, 1907–11. Reader for the *Century Magazine*, 1911–

William Rose Benét—*Continued*

18. In 1920, associate editor of the *Literary Review* of the *New York Evening Post*.

M. A. (Hon.), Yale, 1921. Married Elinor Wylie (q. v.), 1923. Associate editor of the *Saturday Review of Literature* since May, 1924.

Mr. Benét's verse has attracted attention for its pictorial imagination, vigorous rhythms, and grotesque and lively fancy.

BIBLIOGRAPHY

Poems
Merchants from Cathay. 1913.
The Falconer of God. 1914.
The Great White Wall. 1916.
The Burglar of the Zodiac. 1918.
Perpetual Light. 1919.
Moons of Grandeur. 1920.
Poems for Youth. 1925. (Compiler.)
Man Possessed. 1927. (Selected Poems.)

Novel
The First Person Singular. 1922.

Essays and Sketches
The East I Know, by Paul Claudel. 1914. (Translator with Teresa Frances Benét.)
Saturday Papers. 1921. (With Henry Seidel Canby and Amy Loveman.)
Wild Goslings. 1927. (Includes poems.)

STUDIES AND REVIEWS

Aiken.
Farrar.
Maynard.
Untermeyer. (A. P.)
—— (N. E. A. P.)
Wilkinson. (N. V.)

Bookm., 53 ('21): 168.
Bost. Trans., May 13, 1922: 7.
Dial, 56 ('14): 67.

Lit. Rev., June 3, 1922: 669.
Nation, 114 ('22): 724.
N. Y. Times, Feb. 27, 1927: 2.
Poetry, 5 ('14): 91; 9 ('17): 322; 15 ('19): 48.
Sat. Rev. of Lit., 3 ('26): 273.

See also Book Review Digest, 1914, 1917, 1918, 1920.

Konrad Bercovici—story writer.

Born in Roumania, 1882. Educated privately. Came to the United States in 1916.

BIBLIOGRAPHY

Novels
　Costa's Daughter.　1923.
　The Marriage Guest.　1925.
　The Volga Boatman.　1926.

Short Stories
　Dust of New York.　1919.
　Ghitza.　1921.
　Murdo.　1923.　(Pub. London, 1923, as Love and the Gypsy.)
　Iliana.　1924.
　Best Short Stories of the World.　1925.　(Editor.)
　Singing Winds.　1926.
　Peasants.　1928.

Sociological and Descriptive Essays
　Crimes of Charity.　1917.
　Around the World in New York.　1924.
　On New Shores.　1925.
　Story of the Gypsies.　1928.
　Nights Abroad.　1928.

Biography
　Alexander: A Romantic Biography.　1928.

STUDIES AND REVIEWS

Karsner.

Bookm., 60 ('24): 341.
Bost. Trans., Apr. 9, 1924: 4; Oct. 10, 1925: 3.
Dial, 71 ('21): 711.
Lit. Digest, I. B. R.　Dec., 1925: 43.
Lit. Rev., Nov. 19, 1921: 183; Apr. 26, 1924: 709.

N. Y. Herald-Tribune, Apr. 1, 1928: 18.
N. Y. Times, Apr. 1, 1923: 19; Sept. 7, 1924: 9; Oct. 5, 1924: 10; Dec. 27, 1925: 23; Mar. 4, 1928: 13.
Sat. Rev. of Lit., 1 ('24): 181.

See also Book Review Digest, 1917, 1919.

Edwin (August) Björkman—critic.

Born at Stockholm, Sweden, 1866. Educated in Stockholm high school. Clerk, actor, and journalist in Sweden, 1881–91. Came to America in 1891. On staffs of St. Paul and Minneapolis papers, 1892–97; on the *New York Sun* and *New York Times*, 1897–1905. On the editorial staff of the *New York Evening Post*, 1906. Department editor of the *World's Work* and editor of the *Modern Drama Series*, 1912—. Editor and translator of many plays and novels.

BIBLIOGRAPHY

Novels
    The Soul of a Child. 1922.
    Gates of Life. 1923.

Essays and Studies
    Is There Anything New Under the Sun? 1911.
    Voices of Tomorrow. 1913.
    The Search for Atlantis. 1927.
    Thomas Burke: A Critical Appreciation. 1927.

Aphorisms
    Gleams. 1912.

STUDIES AND REVIEWS

Bost. Trans., March 31, 1923: 2.
Cur. Op., 55 ('13): 190 (portrait).
Freeman, 5 ('22): 521.
Lit. Rev., Apr. 21, 1923: 620.
Nation, 114 ('22): 601.

N. Y. Times, Mar. 12, 1922: 11; Apr. 1, 1923: 22.

See also Book Review Digest, 1913.

Maxwell Bodenheim—poet.

Born at Natchez, Mississippi, 1892. Grammar school education. Served in the U. S. Army, 1910–13. Studied law and art in Chicago. Both poetry and prose reveal a brilliant, independent, rebellious temperament.

Maxwell Bodenheim—*Continued*

BIBLIOGRAPHY

Poems
Minna and Myself. 1918. (Includes two plays in verse; one with Ben Hecht.)
Advice. 1920.
Introducing Irony. 1922.
Against This Age. 1923.
The Sardonic Arm. 1923.
Returning to Emotion. 1927.
King of Spain. 1928.

Novels
Blackguard. 1923.
Crazy Man. 1924.
Replenishing Jessica. 1925.
Ninth Avenue. 1926.
Georgie May. 1928.
Sixty Seconds. 1929.

STUDIES AND REVIEWS

Monroe.
Untermeyer. (A. P.)

Bookm., 24 ('28): 67.
Dial, 66 ('19): 356; 69 ('20): 645.
Lit. Rev., June 30, 1928: 8.

N. Y. Times, June 10, 1928: 8.
Poetry, 13 ('19): 342.
Sat. Rev. of Lit., 5 ('28): 52.

See also Book Review Digest, 1920, 1921.

James Boyd—novelist.

Born in Dauphin County, Pennsylvania, 1888. Graduated at Hill School, Pottstown, Pennsylvania, 1906; A. B., Princeton, 1910; Trinity College, Cambridge University, 1912. Served with A. E. F. in France.

BIBLIOGRAPHY

Novels
Drums. London, 1925. New York, 1926.
Marching On. 1927.

James Boyd—*Continued*

STUDIES AND REVIEWS

Bost. Trans., Apr. 15, 1925: 4.
Lit. Digest, I. B. R. May, 1925: 400.
Lit. Rev., May 14, 1927: 5.
Lond. Times, Oct. 22, 1925: 700.

N. Y. Times, Apr. 5, 1925: 14; May 1, 1927: 4 (portrait).
Sat. Rev. of Lit., 1 ('25): 687; 3 ('27): 860.

Thomas (Alexander) Boyd—novelist.

Born at Defiance, Ohio, 1898. Educated in public schools. Served with the Marine Corps, 1917–19.

BIBLIOGRAPHY

Novels
    Through the Wheat. 1923.
    The Dark Cloud. 1924.
    Samuel Drummond. 1925.
    Shadow of the Long Knives. 1928.
    Simon Girty. 1928.

Short Stories
    Points of Honor. 1925.

STUDIES AND REVIEWS

Bost. Trans., May 9, 1925: 4; Oct. 17, 1925: 5.
Dial, 75 ('23): 93.
Lit. Rev., May 26, 1923: 715.
Nation, 117 ('23): 66.

N. Y. Times, Apr. 29, 1923: 14; Sept. 7, 1924: 8; Mar. 22, 1925: 9; Aug. 30, 1925: 8; June 10, 1928: 8.
Sat. Rev. of Lit., 1 ('24–'25): 140, 764; 2 ('25): 312.

Gamaliel Bradford—man of letters.

Born at Boston, 1863. Studied at Harvard, 1882; no degree, because of ill health. Has confined his attention almost entirely to literature since 1886. Specializes in character portraits.

Gamaliel Bradford—*Continued*

BIBLIOGRAPHY

Poems
    A Pageant of Life. 1904.
    A Prophet of Joy. 1920.
    Shadow Verses. 1920.

Play
    Unmade in Heaven. 1917.

Novels
    The Private Tutor. 1904.
    Between Two Masters. 1906.
    Matthew Porter. 1908.

Critical Essays
    A Naturalist of Souls. 1917. (Rev. ed., 1926.)

Biographical and Psychological Studies
    Types of American Character. 1895.
    Lee the American. 1912.
    Confederate Portraits. 1914.
    Union Portraits. 1916.
    Portraits of Women. 1916.
    Portraits of American Women. 1919.
    American Portraits. 1922.
    Damaged Souls. 1923.
    The Soul of Samuel Pepys. 1924.
    Bare Souls. 1924.
    Wives. 1925.
    Darwin. 1926.
    D. L. Moody. 1927.
    As God Made Them. 1929.

Autobiography
    Life and I. 1928.

STUDIES AND REVIEWS

Beach.

Bookm., 41 ('15): 586 (portrait only); 52 ('20): 170; 57 ('23): 548.

Bost. Trans., Feb. 9, 1921: 4; Mar. 25, 1922: 5; May 19, 1923: 5; Apr. 12, 1924: 3; Oct. 4, 1924: 3; Oct. 3, 1925: 5; May 22, 1926: 3; Nov. 6, 1926: 4.

Freeman, 5 ('22): 47; 7 ('23): 358.

Lit. Digest, I. B. R. June, 1924: 522; Dec., 1924: 11.

Lit. Rev., Apr. 8, 1922: 562; June 9, 1923: 746 (Mencken); May

Gamaliel Bradford—*Continued*

10, 1924: 740; Oct. 25, 1924: 4;
Oct. 24, 1925: 4; Nov. 13, 1926:
6.

Lond. Times, Oct. 11, 1923: 666;
Sept. 25, 1924: 592; Oct. 22,
1925: 686.

Nation, 117 ('23): 196.

N. Repub., 9 ('16): supp. 3; 31
('22): 53; 36 ('23): 184.

N. Y. Herald-Tribune, Oct. 17,
1926: 1; Feb. 26, 1928: 1.

N. Y. Times, May 20, 1923: 4;

Apr. 27, 1924: 5; Oct. 12, 1924:
1; Oct. 11, 1925: 1; Oct. 31,
1926: 5; Nov. 6, 1927: 5; Mar.
18, 1928: 5.

Outlook, 134 ('23): 334; 141 ('25):
526.

Sat. Rev. of Lit., 4 ('27): 570.

Springfield Repub., Oct. 17, 1926:
7.

See also Book Review Digest,
1916, 1920.

Louis Bromfield—novelist.

Born at Mansfield, Ohio, 1898. Educated at Cornell University and Columbia University, honorary B. A. on account of war service. Served with American ambulance, attached to French Army, 1917–19. Awarded Croix de Guerre. His *Early Autumn* was awarded the Pulitzer novel prize in 1927.

BIBLIOGRAPHY

Novels

The Green Bay Tree. 1924. (Dramatized as The House of Women.)
Possession. 1925.
Early Autumn. 1926. ·
A Good Woman. 1927.
The Strange Case of Miss Annie Spragg. 1928.

STUDIES AND REVIEWS

Baldwin.

Atlan. (Bookshelf), Nov., 1927.

Bost. Trans., Oct. 24, 1925: 4;
Oct. 30, 1926: 4.

Lit. Digest, I. B. R. May, 1924:
474.

Lit. Rev., May 3, 1924: 719;
Oct. 17, 1925: 2.

Lond. Times, Sept. 18, 1924: 574.

Nation, 119 ('24): 78; 122 ('26):
66; 127 ('28): 374.

N. Y. Herald-Tribune, Oct. 17,
1926: 7.

N. Y. Times, Mar. 30, 1924: 5;
Oct. 4, 1925: 8; Oct. 17, 1926:
4; July 31, 1927: 5.

Sat. Rev. of Lit., 2 ('25): 403.

Charles S(tephen) Brooks—essayist.

Born at Cleveland, Ohio, 1878. A. B., Yale, 1900. Head of The Brooks Co., printers. Deeply interested in Cleveland Playhouse.

BIBLIOGRAPHY

Plays
   Frightful Plays! 1922.
   Luca Sarto. 1924.

Historical Novel
   Luca Sarto. 1920.

Essays
   Journeys to Bagdad. 1915.
   There's Pippins and Cheese to Come. 1917.
   Chimney-Pot Papers. 1919.
   Hints to Pilgrims. 1921.
   Like Summer's Cloud. 1925.

Description and Travel
   Wind in the South. 1924.
   A Thread of English Road. 1924.
   Roundabout to Canterbury. 1926.
   Roads to the North. 1928.

STUDIES AND REVIEWS

Bookm., 47 ('18): 439 (portrait).
Bost. Trans., May 14, 1924: 4; Nov. 1, 1924: 5; Apr. 25, 1925: 2.
Lit. Digest, I. B. R. June, 1924: 517.
Lit. Rev., June 29, 1921: 3; Nov. 11, 1922: 196.
Nation, 109 ('19): 178.

N. Y. Times, Apr. 26, 1925: 13.
Rev., 2 ('20): 463.
Sat. Rev. of Lit., 3 ('26): 232.
Springfield Repub., Apr. 17, 1925: 10.

See also Book Review Digest, 1916, 1917, 1919, 1920.

Van Wyck Brooks—critic.

Born at Plainfield, New Jersey, 1886. A. B., Harvard, 1907. Taught at Leland Stanford, 1911–13. With the Century Company, 1915–18. Associate editor of the *Freeman*, 1920–24.

Van Wyck Brooks—*Continued*

BIBLIOGRAPHY

Social Studies and Essays
  The Wine of the Puritans. 1909.
  America's Coming-of-Age. 1915.
  Letters and Leadership. 1918.

Biographical and Critical Studies
  John Addington Symonds. 1914.
  The World of H. G. Wells. 1915.
  The Ordeal of Mark Twain. 1920.
  The History of a Literary Radical, by Randolph Silliman Bourne.
    1920. (Editor.)
  The Pilgrimage of Henry James. 1925.
  Emerson and Others. 1927.
  The American Caravan. 1927. (Joint editor with Lewis Mumford,
    Alfred Kreymborg, and Paul Rosenfeld.)

STUDIES AND REVIEWS

Beach.
Boynton. (S. C. A.)
Drake.

Bookm., 41 ('15): 130, 132 (por-
  trait); 52 ('21): 333.
Bost. Trans., May 16, 1925: 5.
Commonweal, 1 ('25): 719.
Dial, 69 ('20): 293; 79 ('25): 235.
Forum, 78 ('27): 313.
Ind., 114 ('25): 448.

Lit. Digest, I. B. R. July, 1925:
  521.
Lit. Rev., May 9, 1925: 6; Apr.
  23, 1927: 2.
Nation, 121 ('25): 191.
N. Y. Times, Apr. 19, 1925: 4;
  Apr. 3, 1927: 2.
Sat. Rev. of Lit., 1 ('25): 701; 4
  ('27): 52.

See also Book Review Digest,
  1914, 1915, 1918, 1920.

Alice Brown—short story writer, novelist, dramatist.
Born on a farm near Hampton Falls, New Hampshire,
1857. Graduated from Robinson Seminary, Exeter, New
Hampshire, 1876. Lived on a farm many years and loves
outdoor life. Many years on staff of *Youth's Companion.*
  Her stories of New England life should be compared with
those of Sarah Orne Jewett and Mary Wilkins Freeman

Alice Brown—*Continued*

(q. v.). In 1915 she won the Winthrop Ames $10,000 prize for her play, *Children of Earth.*

BIBLIOGRAPHY

Poems
   The Road to Castaly. 1896. (Repr. with additions, 1917.)
   Ellen Prior. 1923.

Plays
   Joint Owners in Spain. 1914.
 * Children of Earth. 1915.
   One-Act Plays. 1921.
   Charles Lamb. 1924.

Novels
   Fools of Nature. 1887.
   The Day of His Youth. 1897.
   King's End. 1901. (First appeared as April Showers.)
   Margaret Warrener. 1901.
   The Mannerings. 1903.
   Judgment. 1903.
   Paradise. 1905.
   The Court of Love. 1906.
   Rose MacLeod. 1908.
   The Story of Thyrza. 1909.
   John Winterbourne's Family. 1910.
   The Secret of the Clan. 1912.
   My Love and I. 1912. (Under the pseud., Martin Redfield.)
   Robin Hood's Barn. 1913.
   The Prisoner. 1916.
   Bromley Neighborhood. 1917.
   The Black Drop. 1919.
   The Wind between the Worlds. 1920.
   Old Crow. 1922.
   The Mysteries of Ann. 1925.
   Dear Old Templeton. 1927.

Short Stories
 * Meadow-Grass. 1895.
 * Tiverton Tales. 1899.
   High Noon. 1904.
   The County Road. 1906.
   Country Neighbors. 1910.
   The One-Footed Fairy. 1911.

Alice Brown—*Continued*
Vanishing Points. 1913.
The Flying Teuton. 1918.
Homespun and Gold. 1920.

Biography
Mercy Warren. 1896.
Louise Imogen Guiney. 1921.

Travel
By Oak and Thorn. 1896.

Critical Studies
Robert Louis Stevenson. 1895. (With Louise Imogen Guiney.)

STUDIES AND REVIEWS

Overton. (O. W. N.)
Farrar.
Pattee.
Rittenhouse.
Williams.

Acad., 76 ('09): 110.
Atlan., 98 ('06): 55.
Bost. Trans., Oct. 29, 1921: 8; Oct. 6, 1923: 5; Feb. 11, 1925: 6; Apr. 11, 1925: 4.
Cur. Op., 57 ('14): 28 (portrait).

Lit. Digest, 48 ('14): 1435.
Lit. Rev., Dec. 3, 1921: 221; Nov. 25, 1922: 239; Oct. 13, 1923: 128.
N. Y. Times, Oct. 15, 1922: 18; Nov. 18, 1923: 6; Jan. 25, 1925: 16; Apr. 19, 1925: 24.
Outlook, 123 ('19): 514 (portrait).
Sat. Rev. of Lit., 1 ('25): 687.
Spec., 102 ('09): 785.

W(illiam) C(rary) Brownell—critic.
Born at New York City, 1851. A. B., Amherst, 1871; L. H. D., 1896; LL. D., 1916; Litt. D., Columbia, 1910. On staff of the *Nation*, 1879–81. For thirty-eight years a literary adviser of Charles Scribner's Sons. Died in 1928.

BIBLIOGRAPHY

Critical Essays and Studies
French Traits. 1889. (Enl. ed., 1901.)
French Art. 1892.
Victorian Prose Masters. 1901.
American Prose Masters. 1909.

W(illiam) C(rary) Brownell—*Continued*
Criticism. 1914.
Standards. 1917.
The Genius of Style. 1924.
Democratic Distinction in America. 1927.
The Spirit of Society. 1927.

STUDIES AND REVIEWS

Sherman. (P. V.)
——. (C. W.)

Dial, 78 ('25): 228.
Nation, 120 ('25): 152; 126 ('28): 164.

N. Repub., 42 ('25): 162; 56 ('28): 204.
N. Y. Times, Mar. 15, 1925: 5 (R. Le Gallienne).
Sat. Rev. of Lit., 1 ('25): 508.
Springfield Repub., Feb. 8, 1925: 7a.

(Frank) Gelett Burgess—humorist.
Born at Boston, Massachusetts, 1866. B. S., Massachusetts Institute of Technology, 1887. Associate editor of the *Wave*, 1894–95; editor of the *Lark*, 1895–97. Inventor of the "Goops" and of "Bromide." The humor of his illustrations contributes greatly to the success of his writing.

BIBLIOGRAPHY

Goops and How to Be Them. 1900.
Are You a Bromide? 1907.
The Cave Man. 1911. (Play.)
Have You an Educated Heart? 1923.
The Purple Cow. 1923. (Play.)
For complete bibliography, see Who's Who in America.

Frances (Eliza) Hodgson Burnett—novelist.
Mrs. Stephen Townsend. Born at Manchester, England, 1849, but went to live at Knoxville, Tennessee, 1865. She began to write for magazines in 1867. Died Oct. 29, 1924.

Frances (Eliza) Hodgson Burnett—*Continued*

BIBLIOGRAPHY

Plays

Esmeralda. 1881. (Dramatization of her story, in collaboration with William H. Gillette.)

Little Lord Fauntleroy. 1889.

The Little Princess. 1911. (Dramatization of Sara Crewe.)

Novels

* That Lass o' Lowrie's. 1877. (Dramatized.)

Haworth's. 1879.

Louisiana. 1880.

A Fair Barbarian. 1881.

Through One Administration. 1883.

A Lady of Quality. 1896. (Dramatized in collaboration with Stephen Townsend.)

The Dawn of a To-morrow. 1896. (Dramatized.)

His Grace of Osmonde. 1897.

In Connection with the De Willoughby Claim. 1899. (Dramatized as That Man and I.)

The Making of a Marchioness. 1901.

The Methods of Lady Walderhurst. 1901. (Combined with the previous novel under the title, Emily Fox-Seton.)

The Shuttle. 1907.

The Secret Garden. 1911.

* T. Tembarom. 1913.

The Lost Prince. 1915.

The Head of the House of Coombe. 1922.

Robin. 1922.

Tales and Short Stories

Esmeralda. 1877. (See also *Plays*.)

Dolly. 1877. (Serialized as Dorothea; later known as Vagabondia.)

Surly Tim. 1877.

Pretty Polly Pemberton. 1877.

Theo. 1877.

A Quiet Life. 1878.

Kathleen. 1878.

Lindsay's Luck. 1878.

Our Neighbor Opposite. 1878.

Miss Crespigny. 1878.

Natalie. 1879.

Jarl's Daughter. 1879. (Enl. ed., 1883.)

* Little Lord Fauntleroy. 1886. (Dramatized by Mr. Seebohm, also by the author.)

Frances (Eliza) Hodgson Burnett—*Continued*

Editha's Burglar. 1886. (Dramatized by Augustus Thomas.)
Miss Defarge. 1888.
Sara Crewe. 1888. (Dramatized under the title, The Little Princess.
Rev. and republished under the title of the play. 1905.)
The Pretty Sister of José. 1889. (Dramatized.)
Little Saint Elizabeth. 1890.
Earlier Stories. 1891. (Reprints.)
Giovanni and the Other. 1892.
Piccino. 1894.
Two Little Pilgrims' Progress. 1895.
In the Closed Room. 1904.
The Closed Door. 1906.
The Land of the Blue Flower. 1909.
The Little Hunchback Zia. 1916.
The White People. 1917.

Essays

My Robin. 1912.
In the Garden. 1925.

Autobiography

The One I Knew Best of All. 1893.

For partial list of unpublished plays, see Quinn, Hist. of Amer. Drama,
II, 272; *also* Who's Who in America.

Studies and Reviews

Burnett, V. Romantick Lady.
   1927.
Halsey. (Women.)
Harkins. (Women.)
Hind. (M. A. I.)
Overton.

Am. M., 70 ('10): 748 (portrait).
Bookm., 20 ('04): 276 (portrait).
Cur. Lit., 37 ('04): 321 (portrait).

See also Book Review Digest,
   1915–17.

John Burroughs—nature-writer, essayist, poet.

Born at Roxbury, New York, 1837. Academy education,
with honorary higher degrees. Taught for about eight years;
clerk in the Treasury, 1864–73; national bank examiner,
1873–84. From 1874 lived on a farm, after 1884 dividing his
time between market-gardening and literature. He died in
1921.

John Burroughs—*Continued*

Mr. Burroughs's cottage in the woods not far from West Park, New York, appropriately called "Slabsides," has become famous, and an effort is being made to keep it for the nation.

Mr. Burroughs continued to write and publish to the time of his death. A collected edition of his works was published in 1922.

BIBLIOGRAPHY

Poems
  Songs of Nature. 1901. (Editor.)
  Bird and Bough. 1906.
  Waiting. 1910. (A poem and two letters.)

Nature Studies and Essays
  Wake-Robin. 1871.
  Winter Sunshine. 1875.
  Birds and Poets. 1877.
  Locusts and Wild Honey. 1879.
  Pepacton. 1881.
  Fresh Fields. 1884.
  Signs and Seasons. 1886.
  Riverby. 1894.
  Squirrels and Other Fur-Bearers. 1900.
  Far and Near. 1904.
  Ways of Nature. 1905.
  Camping and Tramping with Roosevelt. 1907.
  Leaf and Tendril. 1908.
  Time and Change. 1912.
  Under the Apple-Trees. 1916.
  Field and Study. 1919.
  Under the Maples. 1921.
  Birds. 1922. (Ed. by Robert J. Cole.)
  Sharp Eyes and Other Papers. 1926.

Biographical and Critical Studies and Essays
  Notes on Walt Whitman. 1867.
  Indoor Studies. 1889.
  Whitman. 1896.
  John James Audubon. 1902.
  Literary Values. 1902.
  The Last Harvest. 1922.

John Burroughs—*Continued*

Philosophical and Religious Studies and Essays
The Light of Day. 1900.
The Summit of the Years. 1913.
The Breath of Life. 1915.
Accepting the Universe. 1920.

Autobiography and Letters
My Boyhood. 1922. (With a conclusion by Julian Burroughs.)
John Burroughs and Ludella Peck. 1925.
The Life and Letters of John Burroughs. 1925. (Ed. by Clara Barrus.)

STUDIES AND REVIEWS

Barrus, Clara. Our Friend John Burroughs. 1914.
——. John Burroughs. Boy and Man. 1920.
——. Life and Letters of John Burroughs. 1925.
De Loach, R. J. H. Rambles with John Burroughs. 1912.
Halsey.
Hind. (M. A. I.)
James, Henry. Views and Reviews. 1908.
Kennedy, W. S. The Real John Burroughs. 1924.
Sharp, Dallas Lore. The Seer of Slabsides. 1921.
Van Doren. (R. C.)
Wade, M. H. Real Americans. 1922.

Atlan., 106 ('10): 631; 128 ('21): 517.

Bookm., 49 ('19): 389; 55 ('22): 524.
Bost. Trans., Nov. 26, 1921: 8.
Cent., 63 ('02): 860 (poem by Edwin Markham to Burroughs); 80 ('10): 521; 101 ('21): 619; 102 ('21): 731 (Hamlin Garland).
Crit., 47 ('05): 101 (portraits).
Cur. Op., 70 ('21): 644 (portrait), 667; 71 ('21): 74.
Dial, 32 ('02): 7.
Edin. R., 208 ('08): 343.
Lit. Rev., Apr. 22, 1922: 600.
Liv. Age, 248 ('06): 188 (W. H. Hudson).
Nation, 112 ('21): 89, 531.
N. Repub., 26 ('21): 186; 31 ('22): 52.
N. Y. Times, Dec. 17, 1922: 9.
No. Am., 214 ('21): 177; 216 ('22): 712.
Rev. 4 ('21): 338.

(Maxwell) Struthers Burt—novelist, short story writer.

Born at Philadelphia, Pennsylvania, 1882. A. B., Princeton, 1904. Studied at Merton College, Oxford, 1906. Began

(Maxwell) Struthers Burt—*Continued*
as reporter, *Philadelphia Times;* later, instructor in English,
Princeton. Cattle-ranching business, Wyoming, since 1908;
partner Bar B. C. Ranch. Served as private, Air Service,
U. S. Army, 1918.

Poems
    In the High Hills. 1914.
    Songs and Portraits. 1920.
    When I Grew Up to Middle Age. 1925.

Novels
    The Interpreter's House. 1924.
    The Delectable Mountains. 1927.

Short Stories
    John O'May. 1918.
    Chance Encounters. 1921.
    They Could not Sleep. 1928.

Autobiography
    The Diary of a Dude-Wrangler. 1924.

Essays
    The Other Side. 1928.

Baldwin.
Williams.

Bost. Trans., Mar. 8, 1924: 3;
Jan. 29, 1927: 4.
Lit. Digest, I. B. R. May,
1924: 429.
Lit. Rev., Oct. 15, 1921: 90; Mar.
1, 1924: 555.

Nation, 125 ('27): 67.
N. Repub., 54 ('28): 354.
N. Y. Times, Feb. 17, 1924: 8;
Sept. 28, 1924: 5; Jan. 23, 1927:
9; June 17, 1928: 2.
Outlook, 141 ('25): 674.
Sat. Rev. of Lit., 3 ('27): 546.
Springfield Repub., Dec. 27, 1925:
7a.

Witter Bynner—poet, dramatist.
    Born at Brooklyn, New York, 1881. A. B., Harvard, 1902.
Assistant editor of *McClure's Magazine*, 1902–06. Literary

Witter Bynner—*Continued*

adviser to various publishing companies. Has recently traveled in the Orient. Under the pseudonyms Emanuel Morgan and Anne Knish, Bynner and Arthur Davison Ficke (q. v.) wrote *Spectra*, a burlesque of modern tendencies in poetry, which some critics took seriously. Actively interested in encouraging young poets.

BIBLIOGRAPHY

Poems
  An Ode to Harvard. 1907. (Repr. 1917 and 1925 under title Young Harvard.)
  The New World. 1915.
  Spectra. 1916. (Under pseud. Emanuel Morgan. With Arthur Davison Ficke.)
  Grenstone Poems. 1917. (Enl. ed., 1926.)
  A Canticle of Praise. 1918. (Priv. ptd.)
  The Beloved Stranger. 1919.
  A Canticle of Pan. 1920.
  Pins for Wings. 1920. (Under pseud. Emanuel Morgan.)
  A Book of Love, by Charles Vildrac. 1923. (Translator.)
  Caravan. 1925.

Plays
  Tiger. 1913.
  The Little King. 1914.
  Iphigenia in Tauris, by Euripides. 1915. (Translator.)
  A Book of Plays. 1922. (Reprints Tiger and The Little King.)
  Cake, an Indulgence. 1926.

STUDIES AND REVIEWS

Boynton. (S. C. A.)
Cook.
Untermeyer. (A. P.)

Acad., 86 ('14): 687.
Bookm., 47 ('18): 394.
Dial, 67 ('19): 302.
Forum, 55 ('16): 675.
Freeman, 1 ('20): 476; 3 ('21): 286.
Lit. Rev., Dec. 31, 1920: 10; Jan. 2, 1926: 4.

Nation, 109 ('19): 440.
N. Repub., 9 ('16): supp. 13. (Review of Spectra, Bynner.)
N. Y. Times, Oct. 11, 1925: 6.
Poetry, 7 ('15): 147; 12 ('18): 169; 15 ('20): 281; 22 ('23): 158; 27 ('26): 331.

See also Book Review Digest, 1914, 1920, 1921.

James Branch Cabell—novelist, critic.

Born at Richmond, Virginia, 1879, of an old Southern family. A. B., William and Mary College, 1898, where he taught French and Greek, 1896–97. Newspaper work from 1899–1901. Since then he has devoted his time almost entirely to the study and writing of literature. His study of genealogy and history has an important bearing upon his creative work.

Suggestions for Reading

1. Before reading Mr. Cabell's stories, read his *Beyond Life*, which explains his theory of romance. He maintains that art should be based on the dream of life as it should be, not as it is; that enduring literature is not "reportorial work;" that there is vital falsity in being true to life because "facts out of relation to the rest of life become lies," and that art therefore "must become more or less an allegory."

2. Mr. Cabell's fiction falls into two divisions:

    (1) Romances of the middle ages.

    (2) Comedies of present-day Virginia.

Both elements are found in *The Cream of the Jest* (cf. Du Maurier's *Peter Ibbetson*). The romances illustrate different aspects of his theory of chivalry; the modern comedies, his theory of gallantry (cf. *Beyond Life*).

3. In his romances he has created an imaginary province of France, the people of which bear names and use idioms drawn from widely diverse and incongruous sources. His effort to create mediaeval atmosphere by the use of archaisms does not preclude modern idiom and slang. Through all this work, elaborate pretense of non-existent sources of the tales and frequent allusions to fictitious authors are a part of the method. After reading some of these stories, consider the following criticism from the *London Times* quoted by Mr. Cabell himself at the end of *Beyond Life:* "It requires a nicer touch than Mr. Cabell's, to reproduce the atmosphere of the Middle Ages . . . the artifice is more apparent than the art. . . . "

James Branch Cabell—*Continued*

4. An interesting study is to isolate the authors for whom Mr. Cabell expresses particular admiration and those for whom he expresses contempt in *Beyond Life* and to deduce from his attitudes his peculiar literary qualities.

5. Mr. Cabell's style is notable for the elaboration of its rhythm, its careful avoidance of clichés, its preference for rare, archaic words, and its allusiveness. Consider it from the point of view of sincerity, simplicity, clarity, and charm. Does it intensify or dull your interest in what he has to say?

6. In summing up Mr. Cabell's work, consider the following:

(1) Has he a definite philosophy?

(2) Has he a genuine sense of character or do his characters repeat the same personality?

(3) Is he a sincere artist or "a self-conscious attitudinizer"?

(4) Is he likely ever to hold the high place in American literature which by some critics is denied him today? If so, on what basis?

BIBLIOGRAPHY

Poems

From the Hidden Way. 1916.
Ballades from the Hidden Way. 1928.

Play

The Jewel Merchants. 1921.

Novels

The Eagle's Shadow. 1904. (Rev. ed., 1923.)
The Cords of Vanity. 1909. (Rev. ed., 1920.)
The Soul of Melicent. 1913. (Rev. ed., 1920 as Domnei.)
The Rivet in Grandfather's Neck. 1915. (Rev. slightly, 1922.)
The Cream of the Jest. 1917. (Rev. ed., 1922.)
Jurgen. 1919. (Enl. ed., London, 1921.)
Figures of Earth. 1921.
The High Place. 1923.
The Silver Stallion. 1926.
Something About Eve. 1927.
The White Robe. 1928.

James Branch Cabell—*Continued*

Short Stories
    The Line of Love. 1905. (Enl. ed., 1921.)
    Gallantry. 1907. (Rev. ed., 1922.)
    Chivalry. 1909. (Rev. and enl. ed., 1921.)
    The Certain Hour. 1916.
    The Music from Behind the Moon. 1926.

Miscellaneous Essays and Sketches
    Beyond Life. 1919.
    The Judging of Jurgen. 1920.
    Jurgen and the Censor. 1920.
    Joseph Hergesheimer. 1921.
    Taboo. 1921.
    The Lineage of Lichfield. 1922.
    Straws and Prayer-Books. 1924.

Works on Genealogy
    Branchiana. 1907.
    Branch of Abingdon. 1911.
    The Majors and Their Marriages. 1915.

STUDIES AND REVIEWS

Baldwin.
Beach.
Boyd. (P. R. I.)
Boynton. (S. C. A.)
Bregenzer, B. M., and S. Loveman, ed. Round-Table in Poictesme: A Symposium. 1924.
Farrar.
Holt, Guy. A Bibliography of the Writings of J. B. Cabell. 1924.
Karsner.
McNeill, W. A. Cabellian Harmonics. 1928.
Mencken, H. L. James Branch Cabell. 1927.
Michaud.
Starrett.
Van Doren. (A. B. L.)
——. (A. N.)
——. (C. R. N.)

——. James Branch Cabell. 1925.
Walpole, Hugh. The Art of James Branch Cabell. 1920. (Rev. ed., 1927.)
Williams.

Am. Merc. 1 ('24): 504.
Ath., 1919, 2: 1339 (Aiken).
Bookm., 52 ('20): 200; 66 ('27): 211.
Bost. Trans., Apr. 6, 1921: 4; Dec. 31, 1924: 4; May 1, 1926: 2; Oct. 23, 1926: 4.
Commonweal, 1 ('25): 355.
Cur. Op., 66 ('19): 254; 70 ('21): 537; 73 ('25): 340. (Portraits.)
Dial, 64 ('18): 392; 66 ('19): 225; 76 ('24): 363.
Freeman, 3 ('21): 186.
Lit. Digest, I. B. R. Nov., 1924: 860.

James Branch Cabell—*Continued*

Lit. Rev., Apr. 23, 1921: 3; Nov. 29, 1924: 3.

Lond. Times, Mar. 24, 1921: 191.

Nation, 111 ('20): 343; 112 ('21): 914 (C. Van Doren); 113 ('21): 664; 115 ('22): 377; 119 ('24): 470; 122 ('26): 559; 125 ('27): 386.

N. Repub., 26 ('21): 187; 38 ('24): 157; 41 ('24): 151; 53 ('27) 52.

N. Y. Herald-Tribune, May 9, 1926: 1.

N. Y. Times, Feb. 13, 1921: 3; Mar. 6, 1921: 22; Oct. 19, 1924: 11; Apr. 25, 1926: 2; Oct. 3, 1926: 2.

Sat. Rev. of Lit., 2 ('26): 769.

Abraham Cahan—novelist.

Of Lithuanian-Jewish ancestry. Born at Vilna, Russia, 1860. Came to the United States in 1882. Became editor of the *Arbeiter Zeitung*, 1891, and of the *Jewish Daily Forward*, 1897. A journalist who has done most of his work in Yiddish, but who has also written one remarkable novel in English: *The Rise of David Levinsky*, 1917.

For bibliography, see Who's Who in America.

Henry Seidel Canby—editor.

Born at Wilmington, Delaware, 1878; Ph. B., Yale, 1899; Ph. D., 1905. Member of the English Department at Yale, 1900– . Assistant editor, *Yale Review*, 1911–20; editor, *Literary Review* (New York Evening Post), 1920–24; editor, *Saturday Review of Literature*, 1924– . Author of numerous textbooks.

BIBLIOGRAPHY

Novel

> Our House. 1919.

Essays

> College Sons and College Fathers. 1915.
> Education by Violence. 1919.
> War Aims and Peace Ideals. 1919. (Prose and verse. Joint editor with Tucker Brooke.)

Henry Seidel Canby—*Continued*

Everyday Americans. 1920.
Saturday Papers. 1921. (With William Rose Benét and Amy Loveman.)
Definitions. 1922. Second Series, 1924.
Harper Essays. 1927. (Editor.)
American Estimates. 1929.

STUDIES AND REVIEWS

Farrar.

Bost. Trans., Oct. 8, 1924: 4.
Lit. Rev., Sept. 23, 1923: 45.

Nation, 115 ('22): 339.
No. Am., 216 ('22): 715.
Sat. Rev. of Lit., 3 ('26): 3.

Dorothy Canfield. *See* Dorothy Canfield Fisher.

(William) Bliss Carman—poet.

Born at Fredericton, New Brunswick, Canada, 1861. His ancestors lived in Connecticut at the time of the Revolution. A. B., University of New Brunswick, 1881; A. M., 1884. Studied at the University of Edinburgh, 1882–83, and at Harvard, 1886–88. Studied law two years. LL.D., University of New Brunswick, 1906. Came to live in the United States, 1889. Has been teacher, editor, and civil engineer.

In collaboration with Mary Perry King, Mr. Carman has produced several poem-dances (*Daughters of Dawn*, 1913, and *Earth Deities*, 1914), which it is interesting to compare with Mr. Lindsay's development of the poem-game.

Mr. Carman's most admired work is to be found in the *Vagabondia* volumes, in three of which he collaborated with Richard Hovey (1894, 1896, 1900). His *Collected Poems* were published in 1905, and his *Echoes from Vagabondia*, 1912. Among his more recent books are *April Airs*, 1916, and *Far Horizons*, 1925.

For full bibliography, see Who's Who in America.

Willa (Sibert) Cather—novelist, short story writer.

Born at Winchester, Virginia, 1876. A. B., University of Nebraska, 1895; Litt. D., 1917. Litt. D., University of Michigan, 1924. On staff of *Pittsburgh Daily Leader*, 1897–1901. Associate editor of *McClure's Magazine*, 1906–12.

One of Ours was awarded the Pulitzer novel-prize in 1923.

SUGGESTIONS FOR READING

1. Miss Cather's special field is the pioneer life of immigrants in the Middle West. Points to be considered are: (1) her realism; (2) her detachment or objectivity; (3) her sympathy.

2. In what other respects does she stand out among the leading women novelists of today?

3. What is the value of her material?

4. Compare her studies with those of Cahan (q. v.) and Cournos (q. v.).

5. Are Miss Cather's novels really "novels," or are they series of short stories loosely connected? See in particular *The Professor's House* and *My Mortal Enemy*.

BIBLIOGRAPHY

Poems
  April Twilights. 1903. (Enl. ed., 1923.)

Novels
  Alexander's Bridge. 1912.
  O Pioneers! 1913.
  The Song of the Lark. 1915.
  My Ántonia. 1918.
  One of Ours. 1922.
  A Lost Lady. 1923.
  The Professor's House. 1925.
  My Mortal Enemy. 1926.
  Death Comes for the Archbishop. 1927.

Short Stories
  The Troll Garden. 1905.
  Youth and the Bright Medusa. 1920.
  Best Stories of Sarah Orne Jewett. 1925. (Editor.)

Willa (Sibert) Cather—*Continued*

STUDIES AND REVIEWS

Boynton. (S. C. A.)
Hazard, L. L. The Frontier in American Literature. 1927.
Michaud.
Overton. (O. W. N.)
Sergeant.
Sherman. (C. W.)
Squire.
Van Doren. (A. B. L.)
——. (C. A. N.)
Whipple.

Atlan. (Bookshelf), 132 ('23): supp. V, 12.
Bookm., 21 ('05): 456; 27 ('08): 152; 53 ('21): 212. (Portraits.)
Bost. Trans., Sept. 13, 1922: 4; Sept. 16, 1925: 6; Sept. 10, 1927: 6.
Commonweal, 3 ('25–'26): 108; 5 ('27): 499.
Dial, 73 ('22): 438.
Ind., 109 ('22): 279; 111 ('23): 198.

Lit. Rev., Sept. 16, 1922: 21–23 (S. Lewis); July 8, 1923: 860 (W. R. Benét); Sept. 5, 1925: 1.
Lond. Merc., 10 ('24): 658; 13 ('25–'26): 211, 516.
Lond. Times, June 20, 1921: 403; Nov. 19, 1925: 770.
Nation, 113 ('21): 92; 115 ('22): supp. 388; 117 ('23): 610; 121 ('25): 336; 123 ('26): 484; 125 ('27): 390.
N. Repub., 25 ('21): 233; 52 ('27): 266.
N. Y. Herald-Tribune, Oct. 24, 1926: 3.
N. Y. Times, Sept. 10, 1922: 14 (D. Canfield); Sept. 6, 1925: 8; Oct. 24, 1926: 2.
Poetry, 22 ('23): 221.
Sat. Rev. of Lit., 2 ('25): 151.

See also Book Review Digest, 1915, 1918, 1920.

Winston Churchill—novelist.

Born at St. Louis, 1871. Graduate of U. S. Naval Academy, 1894. Honorary higher degrees. Member of New Hampshire Legislature 1903, 1905. Fought boss and corporation control and was barely defeated for governor of the state, 1908. Lives at Cornish, New Hampshire.

BIBLIOGRAPHY

Plays
The Title-Mart. 1905.
Dr. Jonathan. 1919.

Novels
The Celebrity. 1898.
Richard Carvel. 1899. (Dramatized.)

Winston Churchill—*Continued*

The Crisis. 1901. (Dramatized.)
Mr. Keegan's Elopement. 1903.
The Crossing. 1904.
Coniston. 1906.
Mr. Crewe's Career. 1908.
A Modern Chronicle. 1910.
The Inside of the Cup. 1913.
A Far Country. 1915.
The Dwelling-Place of Light. 1917.

Descriptive Sketches and Essays
A Traveller in War-Time. 1918.

STUDIES AND REVIEWS

Baldwin.
Cooper.
Hackett.
Harkins.
Underwood.
Van Doren. (C. A. N.)

Bookm., 31 ('10): 246 (portrait);
41 ('15): 607.
Bookm. (Lond.), 34 ('08): 152
(portrait).
Collier's, 52 ('13): Dec. 27: 5 (portrait).
Cur. Lit., 27 ('00): 108; 52 ('12):
196 (portrait).

Cur. Op. 55 ('13): 341 (portrait).
Ind., 53 ('01): 2097; 61 ('06): 96.
(Portraits.)
Lit. Digest, 47 ('13): 250, 426,
1278.
Nation, 112 ('21): 619 (C. Van
Doren).
Outlook, 90 ('08): 93.
R. of Rs., 24 ('01): 588; 30 ('04):
123; 34 ('06): 142; 37 ('08): 763;
48 ('13): 46; 58 ('18): 328. (Por-
traits.)
Spec., 93 ('04): 124.
World's Work, 17 ('08): 10959
(portrait), 11016.

(Charles) Badger Clark—poet.
Born in Iowa, 1883. Deals with cowboy life.

BIBLIOGRAPHY

Poems
Sun and Saddle Leather. 1915.
Grass Grown Trails. 1917.

Short Stories
Spike. 1923.

Irvin S(hrewsbury) Cobb—short story writer, humorist, dramatist.

Born at Paducah, Kentucky, 1876. His reputation is built upon his stories of Kentucky life and his humorous criticisms of contemporary manners.

For complete bibliography, see Who's Who in America.

BIBLIOGRAPHY

Roughing It De Luxe. 1914.
Paths of Glory. 1915.
Old Judge Priest. 1915.
Speaking of Operations—. 1916.
The Life of the Party. 1919.
Oh, Well, You Know How Women Are! 1919.
Some United States. 1927.

STUDIES AND REVIEWS

Overton. (A. O. D.)
Newman, F. G. Story of Irvin S. Cobb. 1926.
Williams.

Bost. Trans., July 23, 1921: 5; May 12, 1923: 3; July 28, 1923: 4; Mar. 28, 1925: 10; June 13, 1925: 4; Aug. 11, 1926: 6.

Lit. Digest, May, 1923: 26.
Lit. Rev., Mar. 14, 1925: 3.
N. Y. Herald-Tribune, Sept. 12, 1926: 19.
N. Y. Times, May 14, 1922: 14; July 30, 1922: 19; July 22, 1923: 14; Mar. 1, 1925: 9; June 14, 1925: 13; July 25, 1926: 9.
Sat. Rev. of Lit., 2 ('25): 162.

Will Levington Comfort—novelist.

Born at Kalamazoo, Michigan, 1878. His work consists mainly of romances of Oriental adventure. His book, *Child and Country*, 1916, is on education.

For complete bibliography, see Who's Who in America.

BIBLIOGRAPHY

Trooper Tales. 1899.
Routledge Rides Alone. 1910.
Fate Knocks at the Door. 1912.
The Road of Living Men. 1913.
Red Fleece. 1915.
This Man's World. 1921.
Samadhi. 1927.

Will Levington Comfort—*Continued*

STUDIES AND REVIEWS

Bost. Trans., June 9, 1923: 5; Oct. 22, 1927: 6.

Lit. Rev., Nov. 5, 1921: 152; Dec. 5, 1925: 3.

N. Y. Times, Jan. 8, 1922: 28; Apr. 29, 1923: 24.

See also Book Review Digest, 1916.

Grace (Walcott) Hazard Conkling—poet.

Mrs. Roscoe Platt Conkling. Born at New York City, 1878. Graduate of Smith College, 1899. Studied music and languages at the University of Heidelberg, 1902–03, and in Paris, 1903–04. Lived also in Mexico. Has taught in various schools, and since 1914 has been a teacher of English at Smith College, where she has roused much interest in poetry. Mother of Hilda Conkling (q. v.).

BIBLIOGRAPHY

Poems
Afternoons of April. 1915.
Wilderness Songs. 1920.
Ship's Log. 1924.
Flying Fish. 1926.

STUDIES AND REVIEWS

Bost. Trans., Jan. 28, 1925: 4.
Lit. Rev., Oct. 28, 1922: 145 (L. Untermeyer).
N. Y. Times, Nov. 30, 1924: 5; Dec. 7, 1924: 7.

Poetry, 7 ('15): 152; 22 ('23): 93, 97; 27 ('25): 52; 29 ('27): 281.
Springfield Repub., Oct. 29, 1922' 7a.

See also Book Review Digest, 1915, 1920.

Hilda Conkling—poet.

Born at Catskill-on-Hudson, New York, 1910, daughter of Grace Hazard Conkling (q. v.). She began to talk her

Hilda Conkling—*Continued*

poems to her mother at the age of four. Her mother took them down without change, merely arranging the line divisions. Her earliest expression was in the form of a chant to an imaginary companion to whom she gave the name "Mary Cobweb" (cf. *Poetry*, 14 ['19]: 344).

Hilda Conkling's name is included in this list, not because her poems are remarkable for a child, but because they show actual achievement and the highest quality of imagination.

BIBLIOGRAPHY

Poems
Poems by a Little Girl. 1920.
Shoes of the Wind. 1922.
Silverhorn. 1924. (Selections from two previous volumes.)

STUDIES AND REVIEWS

Untermeyer. (A. P.)

Bookm., 51 ('20): 314.
Bost. Trans., May 15, 1920: 10.
Dial, 69 ('20): 186.

Lit. Rev., Oct. 28, 1922: 145.
N. Y. Times, May 23, 1920: 272;
    Dec. 7, 1924: 7.
Poetry, 16 ('20): 222.

See also Book Review Digest, 1920.

Marc (Marcus Cook) Connelly—playwright.

Born at McKeesport, Pennsylvania, 1890. Attended Trinity Hall, Washington, Pennsylvania, 1902–07. Early experience as newspaper reporter in Pittsburgh. Contributes to magazines and has written lyrics for musical comedies.

BIBLIOGRAPHY

Plays
Dulcy. 1921. (With George S. Kaufman.)
To the Ladies. 1923. (With George S. Kaufman.)
Beggar on Horseback. 1924. (With George S. Kaufman. Suggested by Hans Sonnenstoesser's Hohlenfahrt, by Paul Apel.)
Merton of the Movies. 1925. (With George S. Kaufman, from the novel by Harry Leon Wilson.)
The Wisdom Tooth. 1927.

John Cournos—novelist.

Born near Kieff, Russia, 1881. Came to Philadelphia at the age of 10. Left school at 13. Worked himself up to position of associate editor of the magazine-supplement on a Philadelphia newspaper. Went to London in 1912. Member of Anglo-Russian Commission to Petrograd, appointed by British Government, in 1917 and 1918. Has contributed articles on literature and art to various English, Russian, and American periodicals. His studies of the immigrant in America in *The Mask*, 1919, and in *The Wall*, 1921, attracted attention. Edited with E. J. O'Brien *The Best British Short Stories*, 1922, '23, '24, '25. Also edited, *The Fifteen Finest Short Stories*, 1928. Has made many translations from the Russian.

BIBLIOGRAPHY

Poems
  In Exile. 1923.
Play
  Sport of Gods. London, 1925. (Founded upon an episode in Babel.)
Novels
  The Mask. 1919.
  The Wall. 1921.
  Babel. 1922.
  The New Candide. 1924.
  Miranda Masters. 1926.
  O'Flaherty the Great. 1927.

Biographical Sketches
  A Modern Plutarch. 1928.

STUDIES AND REVIEWS

Baldwin.

Bookm., 51 ('20): 76.
Bookm. (Lond.), 64 ('23): 103.
Bost. Trans., Sept. 17, 1921: 6; Oct. 14, 1922: 9; May 17, 1924: 4; Oct. 20, 1928: 5.
Dial, 68 ('20): 496.
Lit. Rev., July 16, 1921: 9; Sept. 30, 1922: 63.

Lond. Times, Mar. 3, 1921: 143; Dec. 4, 1924: 820.
N. Y. Herald-Tribune, July 17, 1927: 5.
N. Y. Times, July 17, 1921: 24; Sept. 17, 1922: 6; May 18, 1924: 8; June 5, 1927: 8.
Sat. Rev., 138 ('24): 636.

See also Book Review Digest, 1920, 1921.

Nathalia (Clara Ruth) Crane—poet.

Born at New York City, 1913. Of American and Spanish-Jewish ancestry. Began to write verses at the age of eight. In her ninth year had poetry accepted on its own merit by *New York Sun*. Her remarkable verse reveals the humor and grace of childhood, a sensitive response to dictionary words, and a surprising psychic subtlety.

Bibliography

Poems

The Janitor's Boy. 1924.
Lava Lane. 1925.
The Singing Crow. 1926.
Venus Invisible. 1928.

Novel

The Sunken Garden. 1926.

Studies and Reviews

Lit. Rev., June 7, 1924: 814; Nov. 14, 1925: 1; June 19, 1926: 3.

N. Y. Times, June 8, 1924: 6; Nov. 29, 1925: 2; May 16, 1926: 11.

Sat. Rev. of Lit., 2 ('25): 367; 2 ('26): 924; 3 ('28): 857.

Adelaide Crapsey—poet.

Born at Rochester, New York, 1878. A. B., Vassar, 1902. Taught English at Kemper Hall, Kenosha, Wisconsin, 1903. In 1905 studied archaeology in Rome. Instructor in poetics at Smith College, 1911; but stopped teaching because of failing health. Died at Saranac Lake, 1914.

She had begun an investigation into the structure of English verse, which she was unable to finish. Her poems were nearly all written after her breakdown in 1913, and reflect the tragic experience through which she was passing.

Some of them are written in a form of her own invention, the "cinquain" (five unrhymed lines, having two, four, six, eight, and two syllables).

Adelaide Crapsey—*Continued*

BIBLIOGRAPHY

Poems
  Verse. 1915.
Study
  A Study in English Metrics. 1918.

STUDIES AND REVIEWS

Untermeyer. (A. P.)

Bookm., 50 ('20): 498.

Poetry, 10 ('17): 316; 21 ('23): 333.

See also Book Review Digest, 1916, 1918.

Rachel Crothers—dramatist.

Born at Bloomington, Illinois, 1878. Graduate of the Illinois State Normal School, Normal, Illinois, 1892.

Miss Crothers directs her plays and sometimes acts in them.

BIBLIOGRAPHY

Plays
  Criss Cross. 1904.
  The Rector. 1905.
  A Man's World. 1915.
  The Three of Us. 1916.
  The Herfords. 1917. (*In* Quinn, Representative American Plays, under title He and She.)
  Mary the Third; Old Lady 31; A Little Journey. 1923.
  Expressing Willie; Nice People; 39 East. 1924.
  The Heart of Paddy Whack. 1925.
  Once Upon a Time. 1925.
  Six One-Act Plays. 1925.
  Mother Carey's Chickens. 1925. (With Kate Douglas Wiggin. Based on the story of the same name.)

For list of unpublished plays, see Quinn, History of American Drama, II, 276ff.; *also* Who's Who in America.

STUDIES AND REVIEWS

Dickinson. (P. N. A. T.)
Eaton, W. P. At the New
  Theatre. 1910.

Hackett.
Moses.

Samuel McChord Crothers—essayist.

Born at Oswego, Illinois, 1857. A. B., Wittenberg College, 1873; Princeton, 1874. Studied at Union Theological Seminary, 1874–77, and at Harvard Divinity School, 1881–82. Higher honorary degrees. Ordained Presbyterian minister, 1877. Pastorates in Nevada and California. Became a Unitarian, 1882. Pastor in Brattleboro, Vermont, 1882–86; in St. Paul, Minnesota, 1886–94; and of the First Church, Cambridge, since 1894. Preacher to Harvard University. Died in 1928.

Dr. Crothers's essays are rich with suave and scholarly humor, and are written in a style suggestive of Lamb's.

BIBLIOGRAPHY

Essays, Lectures, and Sermons
  Members of One Body. 1894.
  The Gentle Reader. 1903.
  The Understanding Heart. 1903.
  The Pardoner's Wallet. 1905.
  The Endless Life. 1905.
  By the Christmas Fire. 1908.
  Oliver Wendell Holmes. 1909. (Editor.)
  Among Friends. 1910.
  Humanly Speaking. 1912.
  Three Lords of Destiny. 1913.
  Meditations on Votes for Women. 1914.
  The Pleasures of an Absentee Landlord. 1916.
  The Dame School of Experience. 1920.
  Ralph Waldo Emerson. 1921.
  The Cheerful Giver. 1923.
  The Children of Dickens. 1925.
  Prayers. 1928.
  The Thought Broker. 1928.

STUDIES AND REVIEWS

Pattee.

Bookm., 32 ('11): 631.
Bost. Trans., Mar. 9, 1921: 8;
  Nov. 10, 1923: 4; Nov. 11,
  1925: 8.

Critic, 48 ('06): 200 (portrait).
Cur. Op., 63 ('17): 406 (portrait).
Lit. Rev., Apr. 16, 1921: 4; Dec.
  15, 1923: 364.
N. Y. Times, Nov. 25, 1923: 5.
So. Atlan. Q., 8 ('09): 150.

Countee Cullen—poet.

One of the most prominent of the younger negro poets.
Born at New York City, 1903. A. B., New York University,
1925; M. A., Harvard, 1926. Assistant editor of *Opportunity:
Journal of Negro Life*, 1926.

BIBLIOGRAPHY

Poems

    Color. 1925.
    Copper Sun. 1927.
    The Ballad of the Brown Girl. 1927.
    Caroling Dusk. 1927. (Editor.)

STUDIES AND REVIEWS

Bost. Trans., May 5, 1928: 5.
Lond. Times, Jan. 21, 1926: 39.
Nation, 121 ('25): 763 (B.
    Deutsch); 125 ('27): 518.
N. Repub. 52 ('27): 218.

N. Y. Herald-Tribune, Aug. 21,
    1927: 5.
N. Y. Times, Apr. 29, 1928: 12.
Poetry, 28 ('26): 50.
Springfield Repub., Jan. 17, 1926:
    7a.

E(dward) E(stlin) Cummings—poet.

Born at Cambridge, Massachusetts, 1894. A. B., Harvard, 1915; M. A., 1916. Wrote a provocative war-novel,
The Enormous Room, and attracted attention in the *Dial*
by the bizarre style and appearance of his verses. Won the
Dial award in 1926.

BIBLIOGRAPHY

Poems

    Tulips and Chimneys. 1923.
    XLI Poems. 1925.
    &. 1925. (Priv. ptd.)
    Is 5. 1926.

Play

    Him. 1927.

Novel

    The Enormous Room. 1922.

E(dward) E(stlin) Cummings—*Continued*

STUDIES AND REVIEWS

Dial, 73 ('22): 97.
Nation, 114 ('22): 691.
N. Repub., 30 ('22): 320; 45 ('25): 60; 48 ('26): 76; 52 ('27): 293.
N. Y. Herald-Tribune, Nov. 6, 1927: 2.

N. Y. Times, Dec. 9, 1923: 5; July 18, 1926: 8.
N. Y. Tribune, Nov. 25, 1923: 21; June 14, 1925: 4.
Sat. Rev. of Lit., 3 ('26): 53.

H. D. *See* Hilda Doolittle.

T(homas) A(ugustine) Daly—poet.

Born at Philadelphia, 1871. Left college without a degree. Honorary higher degrees. In 1889 became a newspaper man, and since 1891 has been connected as reviewer, editorial writer, and columnist with Philadelphia newspapers; associate editor of the *Evening Ledger*, since 1918.

Mr. Daly has written good poetry in English, but is best known for the dialect verses which he has published in the columns edited by him. His most popular verses are in the Irish and Italian dialects.

BIBLIOGRAPHY

Poems
  Canzoni. 1906.
  Carmina. 1909.
  Madrigali. 1912.
  Little Polly's Pomes. 1913.
  Songs of Wedlock. 1916.
  McAroni Ballads. 1919.
  A Little Book of American Humorous Verse. 1926. (Compiler.)
Autobiographical Story
  Herself and the Houseful. 1924.

Mary Carolyn Davies—poet.

Born at Sprague, Washington, and educated in and near Portland, Oregon. As a freshman at the University of Cali-

Mary Carolyn Davies—*Continued*

fornia, she won the Emily Chamberlin Cook prize for poetry, 1912, and also the Bohemian Club prize.

The early poems of Miss Davies express "the girl consciousness" (Kreymborg).

BIBLIOGRAPHY

Poems
The Drums in Our Street. 1918.
Youth Riding. 1919.
A Little Freckled Person. 1919.
Outdoors and Us. 1922.
Marriage Songs. 1923.
The Skyline Trail. 1924.
Penny Show. 1927.

Play
The Slave with Two Faces. 1918.

Novel
The Husband Test. 1921.

STUDIES AND REVIEWS

Bost. Trans., June 21, 1924: 6.   *See also* Book Review Digest,
N. Repub., 55 ('28): 181.   1919.

Fannie Stearns Davis —poet.

Mrs. Augustus McKinstry Gifford. Born at Cleveland, Ohio, 1884. A. B., Smith College, 1904. Taught English at Kemper Hall, Kenosha, Wisconsin, 1906–07.

BIBLIOGRAPHY

Poems
Myself and I. 1913.
Crack o' Dawn. 1915.
The Ancient Beautiful Things. 1923.

STUDIES AND REVIEWS

Bookm., 47 ('18): 388.   Poetry, 2 ('13): 225; 6 ('15): 45.
Bost. Trans., Oct. 20, 1923: 6.

Margaret(ta Wade) Deland—novelist, short story writer.

Mrs. Lorin Fuller Deland. Born at a village called Manchester, now a part of Allegheny, Pennsylvania, 1857. Educated in private schools, and studied drawing and design at Cooper Institute. Later, taught design in a girls' school in New York City.

Mrs. Deland's father was a Presbyterian and her mother an Episcopalian (cf. *John Ward, Preacher*), and her home town is the "Old Chester" of her books.

BIBLIOGRAPHY

Poems
  The Old Garden. 1886.

Novels
  * John Ward, Preacher. 1888.
  A Summer Day. 1889.
  Sidney. 1890.
  The Story of a Child. 1892.
  Philip and His Wife. 1894.
  The Awakening of Helena Richie. 1906. (Dramatized by C. Thompson. Priv. ptd. 1908.)
  The Iron Woman. 1911.
  The Rising Tide. 1916.
  The Vehement Flame. 1922.
  The Kays. 1926.

Short Stories and Tales
  Mr. Tommy Dove. 1893.
  The Wisdom of Fools. 1897.
  * Old Chester Tales. 1898. (Dramatized as Miss Maria by Maude B. Vosburgh. 1918.)
  * Dr. Lavendar's People. 1903.
  An Encore. 1907.
  R. J.'s Mother, and Some Other People. 1908.
  The Way to Peace. 1910.
  The Voice. 1912.
  Partners. 1913.
  The Hands of Esau. 1914.
  Around Old Chester. 1915.
  The Promises of Alice. 1919.
  An Old Chester Secret. 1920.
  New Friends in Old Chester. 1924.

Margaret(ta Wade) Deland—*Continued*

Essays and Sketches
   The Common Way. 1904.
   Small Things. 1919.

Travel and Description
   Florida Days. 1889.

STUDIES AND REVIEWS

Boynton. (M. C. A.)
Halsey. (Women.)
Overton. (O. W. N.)
Pattee.
Williams.

Bookm., 25 ('07): 511 (portrait).
Bost. Trans., June 21, 1922: 4;
   June 7, 1924: 3.
Cur. Op., 65 ('18): 177 (portrait).
Harp., 123 ('11): 963.
Harp. W., 50 ('06): 859, 1110
   (portraits).

Ind., 61 ('06): 336.
Lit. Rev., June 17, 1922: 735
   (Boynton); Dec. 4, 1926: 5.
Lond. Times, Dec. 9, 1926: 908.
Nation, 124 ('27): 214.
N. Y. Herald-Tribune, Dec. 26,
   1926: 3.
N. Y. Times, June 4, 1922: 1;
   May 25, 1924: 8.
Outlook, 64 ('00): 407; 84 ('06):
   730 (portrait); 99 ('11): 628.
Sat. Rev. of Lit., 3 ('27): 561.

Mazo de la Roche—novelist.

Born at Toronto, Canada, 1885. Educated privately and at the University of Toronto. Studied art. Lives in Toronto and the Ontario countryside. Her *Jalna* won the *Atlantic Monthly* prize in 1927.

BIBLIOGRAPHY

Novels
   Explorers of the Dawn. 1922.
   Possession. 1923.
   Delight. 1926.
   Jalna. 1927.

Play
   Low Life; A Comedy in One Act. 1925.
   Low Life and Other Plays. 1929.

Mazo de la Roche—*Continued*

SroundsStUDIES AND REVIEWS

Bookm., 66 ('27): 104.
Bost. Trans., Mar. 29, 1922: 4.
Canad. Mag., 60 ('22–'23): 584.
Lit. Rev., Oct. 8, 1927: 11.
Lond. Times, 26 ('27): 912.
Nation, 125 ('27): 550.
New Crit., 4 ('26): 785.

N. State, 27 ('26): 612.
N. Y. Times, May 16, 1926: 8;
 Oct. 8, 1927: 11.
Sat. Rev., 142 ('26): 156.
Sat. Rev. of Lit., 4 ('27): 196.

See also Book Review Digest, 1927.

Floyd Dell—novelist.

Born at Barry, Illinois, 1887. Left school at sixteen for factory work. Literary editor of the *Chicago Evening Post*, 1909–13. Associate editor of the *Masses*, 1914–17, the *Liberator*, 1918–24.

BIBLIOGRAPHY

Plays
The Angel Intrudes. 1918.
Sweet and Twenty. 1921.
King Arthur's Socks. 1922. (*In* Provincetown Plays. 1916.)

Novels
Moon-Calf. 1920.
The Briary-Bush. 1921.
Janet March. 1923. (Rev. ed., 1927.)
Runaway. 1925.
This Mad Ideal. 1925.
An Old Man's Folly. 1926.
An Unmarried Father. 1927.
Souvenir. 1929.

Short Stories
Love in Greenwich Village. 1926. (Includes verse.)
Daughter of the Revolution, by John Reed. 1927. (Editor.)

Essays and Studies
Women as World-Builders. 1913.
Were You Ever a Child? 1919. (Rev. ed., 1920.)
Looking at Life. 1924.
Intellectual Vagabondage. 1926.

Biography and Criticism
Upton Sinclair. 1927.

Floyd Dell—*Continued*

STUDIES AND REVIEWS

Baldwin.
Farrar.
Hansen.
Sherman. (C. W.)
Van Doren. (C. A. N.)

Atlan. (Bookshelf), 127 ('21): supp. III: 12.
Bookm., 53 ('21): 245; 66 ('27): 216.
Bost. Trans., Dec. 10, 1921: 8; Mar. 25, 1925: 4; Oct. 10, 1925: 5; July 3, 1926: 4.
Ind., 107 ('21): 237; 116 ('26): 397.
Freeman, 2 ('21): 403.
Lit. Digest, I. B. R. June, 1925: 475; Dec., 1925: 56.
Lit. Rev., Nov. 26, 1921: 199; Dec. 9, 1922: 300; May 24, 1924: 771; Mar. 21, 1925: 3; Nov. 6, 1926: 7; Oct. 8, 1927: 11.

Nation, 111 ('20): 670; 114 ('25): 19; 119 ('24): 472; 120 ('25): 436; 125 ('27): 392, supp. 652.
N. Repub., 25 ('20): 49; 29 ('21): 78; 39 ('24): 23 (Lovett).
N. Y. Herald-Tribune, Apr. 11, 1926: 4; July 27, 1926: 3.
N. Y. Times, Nov. 27, 1921: 28; Apr. 20, 1924: 14; Feb. 22, 1925: 8; Oct. 4, 1925: 8; Apr. 4, 1926: 2; May 23, 1926: 8; Oct. 24, 1926: 6; Sept. 4, 1927: 14; Oct. 30, 1927: 7.
Sat. Rev. of Lit., 1 ('25): 786; 2 ('25–'26): 210, 918.

See also Book Review Digest, 1919, 1920.

Babette Deutsch—poet, novelist.

Mrs. Avrahm Yarmolinsky. Born at New York City, 1895. A. B., Barnard, 1917. Later, worked at the School for Social Research. She attracted attention by her first volume of poems, *Banners*, 1919.

BIBLIOGRAPHY

Poems

 Banners. 1919.
 Modern Russian Poetry. 1921. (Joint editor and translator with Avrahm Yarmolinsky.)
 Contemporary German Poetry. 1923. (With Avrahm Yarmolinsky.)
 Honey Out of the Rock. 1924.
 Russian Poetry. 1927. (With Avrahm Yarmolinsky.)

Novels

 A Brittle Heaven. 1926.
 In Such a Night. 1927.

Babette Deutsch—*Continued*

STUDIES AND REVIEWS

Bost. Trans., Oct. 9, 1926: 8.
Nation, 121 ('25): 601.
N. Repub., 45 ('25): 170.
N. Y. Times, Sept. 26, 1926: 28;
  Apr. 3, 1927: 7.

Poetry, 15 ('19): 166; 28 ('26):
  102.
Sat. Rev. of Lit., 3 ('27): 947.

See also Book Review Digest, 1921.

Martin Dooley. *See* Finley Peter Dunne.

H(ilda) D(oolittle)—poet.

Mrs. Richard Aldington. Born at Bethlehem, Pennsylvania, 1886. Educated privately in Philadelphia, entered Bryn Mawr in 1904. Began a long sojourn in Europe in 1911; 1920–21, lived in California. Has lived in Switzerland.

BIBLIOGRAPHY

Poems
  Sea Garden. London, 1916. Boston, 1917.
  Hymen. 1921.
  Heliodora. 1924.
  Collected Poems of H. D. 1925.

Play
  Hippolytus Temporizes. 1927.

Tales
  Palimpsest. 1926.
  Hedylus. 1928.

STUDIES AND REVIEWS

Lowell.
Mearns, Hughes. Pamphlet Poets.
Monroe.
Sinclair, M. Fort. n. s. 121 ('27):
  329.
Untermeyer. (A. P.)

Bost. Trans., Jan. 14, 1922: 6;
  May 29, 1925: 3.

Chapbook, 2, Mar., 1920: 22.
Dial, 72 ('22): 203 (May Sinclair).
Egoist, 2 ('15): 72 (Flint); 88
  (May Sinclair).
Lit. Rev., Jan. 21, 1922: 364;
  May 23, 1925: 4.
Lond. Times, July 3, 1924: 416.
Nation, 119 ('24): 526; 121 ('25).
  211.

H(ilda) D(oolittle)—*Continued*

N. Y. Herald-Tribune, Nov. 28, 1926: 2 (B. Deutsch).
N. Y. Times, Nov. 21, 1926: 6.
Poetry, 19 ('22): 333.

Sat. Rev. of Lit., 1 ('24): 260; 3 ('26): 482.
Spec., 128 ('22): 247.

John (Roderigo) Dos Passos—novelist.

Born at Chicago, 1896. A. B., Harvard, 1916. With ambulance service in Italy and France, 1917-19. His presentation (*Three Soldiers*) of the experiences of privates in the U. S. Army during the War roused violent discussion.

BIBLIOGRAPHY

Poems
A Pushcart at the Curb. 1922.

Plays
The Garbage Man. 1926. (Produced under title, The Moon Is a Gong.)
Airways, Inc. 1928.

Novels
One Man's Initiation—1917. London, 1920. New York, 1922.
Three Soldiers. 1921.
Streets of Night. 1923.
Manhattan Transfer. 1925.

Travel and Literary Essays
Rosinante to the Road Again. 1922.
Orient Express. 1927.

Sociological Study
Facing the Chair. 1927.

STUDIES AND REVIEWS

Baldwin.
Boynton. (M. C. A.)
Lewis, S. John Dos Passos' Manhattan Transfer. 1926.

Bookm., 54 ('21): 393.
Cal. Mod. Lett., 4 ('27): 70.

Cur. Op., 71 ('21): 624 (portrait).
Dial, 71 ('21): 606; 72 ('22): 640.
Freeman, 4 ('21): 282.
Ind., 107 ('21): 16, 97.
Lit. Digest, 71 ('21): Nov. 12: 29 (portrait).
Lit. Rev., Oct. 8, 1921:

John (Roderigo) Dos Passos—*Continued*

Lond. Merc., 5 ('22): 319.
Lond. Times, Feb. 3, 1927: 74.
Nation, 113 ('21): 480.
Nation and Ath., 30 ('21): 148.
N. Repub., 28 ('21): 162; 31 ('22): 366; 51 ('27): 52.

N. Y. Times, Oct. 2, 1921: 1; June 18, 1922: 17; Dec. 17, 1922: 2; Nov. 29, 1925: 5.
Sat. Rev. of Lit., 2 ('25): 361; 3 ('27): 677.

See also Book Review Digest, 1921.

Theodore Dreiser—novelist, dramatist.

Born at Terre Haute, Indiana, 1871, of German ancestry. Educated in the public schools of Warsaw, Indiana, and at the University of Indiana. Newspaper work in Chicago and St. Louis, 1892–95. Editor of *Every Month* (literary and musical magazine), 1895–98. Editorial positions on *Mc-Clure's, Century, Cosmopolitan*, and various other magazines, finally becoming editor-in-chief of the Butterick Publications (*Delineator, Designer, New Idea, English Delineator*), 1907–10. Organized the National Child Rescue Campaign, 1907. Made official visit to Russia, 1927.

SUGGESTIONS FOR READING

1. As Mr. Dreiser is considered by many critics the novelist of biggest stature as yet produced by America, the nature and sources of his strength and of his weakness deserve careful analysis. Observe (1) that his attitude toward life and his general method are akin to Zola's; (2) that his materials are drawn from his extensive and varied experience as a journalist; (3) that these two facts are exemplified in brief in his biographical studies, *Twelve Men*, which are "human documents."

2. Note the dates of *Sister Carrie* and of *Jennie Gerhardt*, and work out Dreiser's loss and gain during the long period of silence between them.

3. *Hey, Rub-a-Dub-Dub* should be read by every student of Dreiser, for its revelation of his attitude toward humanity,

Theodore Dreiser—*Continued*

which contributes largely to the greatness of his work, and of his failure to think out a point of view, which is a fundamental weakness. Note his admission: "I am one of those curious persons who cannot make up their minds about anything."

4. With what types of material does Mr. Dreiser succeed best? Why?

5. Discuss Mr. Dreiser's style in connection with the following topics: (1) economy; (2) realism; (3) suggestion; (4) taste; (5) rhythmic beauty.

6. How far does Mr. Dreiser represent American life? Do you think his work will be for some time the best that we can do in literature?

BIBLIOGRAPHY

Poems
   Moods Cadenced and Declaimed. 1926.

Plays
   Plays of the Natural and the Supernatural. 1916.
   The Hand of the Potter. 1918.

Novels
  * Sister Carrie. 1900.
  * Jennie Gerhardt. 1911.
   The Financier. 1912. (Rev. ed., 1927.)
   The Titan. 1914.
   The "Genius." 1915.
  * An American Tragedy. 1925. (Dramatized by Patrick Kearney.)

Short Stories
   Free. 1918.
   Twelve Men. 1919.
   Chains. 1927.
   A Gallery of Women. 1928.

Description and Travel
   A Traveler at Forty. 1913.
   A Hoosier Holiday. 1916.
   The Color of a Great City. 1923.
   Dreiser Looks at Russia. 1928.

Autobiography
   A Book About Myself. 1922.

Theodore Dreiser—*Continued*

Essays

Hey, Rub-a-Dub-Dub. 1920.

See also Edward D. McDonald. Bibliography of the writings of Theodore Dreiser. 1928.

STUDIES AND REVIEWS

Baldwin.

Beach.

Boyd. (P. R. I.)

Boynton. (S. C. A.)

Drake, W. A. American Criticism. 1926.

Harris.

Hazard, L. L. The Frontier in American Literature. 1927.

Karsner.

Mencken, H. L. Prefaces. 1922.

Michaud.

Rascoe, Burton. Theodore Dreiser. 1925.

Sherman, S. P. On Contemporary Literature. 1917.

Squire.

Van Doren. (A. B. L.)

——. (C. A. N.)

Whipple.

Acad., 85 ('13): 133.

Bookm., 34 ('11): 221; 38 ('14): 673; 53 ('21): 27. (Portraits.)

Bost. Trans., Dec. 30, 1922: 4; Jan. 9, 1924: 4; Jan. 9, 1926: 3.

Cur. Lit., 53 ('12): 696 (portrait).

Cur. Op., 62 ('17): 344 (portrait); 63 ('17): 191; 66 ('19): 175.

Dial, 62 ('17): 343, 507; 80 ('26): 331.

Egoist, 3 ('16): 159.

Ind., 71 ('11): 1267 (portrait); 110 ('23): 99; 116 ('26): 166.

Lit. Digest, I. B. R. Feb., 1923: 10; Feb., 1926: 167.

Lit. Rev., Jan. 20, 1923: 369; Jan. 16, 1926: 1; May 28, 1927: 3.

Liv. Age, 331 ('26): 43.

Lond. Times, May 12, 1927: 334.

Nation, 101 ('15): 648 (Sherman); 112 ('21): 400 (C. Van Doren); 122 ('26): 152.

N. Repub., 2 ('15): supp. Apr. 17: 7; 46 ('26): 113.

N. Y. Times, Dec. 24, 1922: 14; Dec. 23, 1923: 7; Jan. 10, 1926: 1; May 15, 1927: 2.

No. Am., 207 ('18): 902.

Rev. 2 ('20): 380 (P. E. More).

Sat. Rev., 142 ('26): 522.

Sat. Rev. of Lit., 2 ('25–'26): 475 (S. Anderson).

Spec., 118 ('17): 139.

William E(dward) B(urghardt) Du Bois—journalist.

Born at Great Barrington, Massachusetts, 1868. Of negro descent but with large admixture of white blood. A. B., Fisk University, 1888; Harvard, 1890; A. M., 1891; Ph. D., 1895.

William E(dward) B(urghardt) Du Bois—*Continued*
Studied at the University of Berlin. Professor of economics
and history, Atlanta University, 1896-1910. Director of
publicity of the National Association for the Advancement
of Colored People and editor of the *Crisis*, 1910—.

Mr. Du Bois is a distinguished economist and primarily
a propagandist for the equal rights and education of the
negro, but he belongs to literature as the author of *Darkwater*.
Author of many books on negro problems. *For fuller bibliography, see* Benjamin G. Brawley, *The Negro in Literature
and Art*, 1918.

BIBLIOGRAPHY

Novel
    The Quest of the Silver Fleece. 1911.
    Dark Princess. 1928.

Sociological Essays and Sketches
    The Souls of Black Folk. 1903.
    * Darkwater. 1920. (Includes verse and short stories.)

Sociological Study
    The Gift of Black Folk. 1924.

Biography
    John Brown. 1909.

. STUDIES AND REVIEWS

Johnson, J. W. American Negro
    Poetry. 1922.
Kerlin, R. T. Negro Poets and
    Their Poems. 1923.

Am. M., 66 ('08): 61, 65 (portrait).

Lit. Digest, 65 ('20): 86.
Nation, 110 ('20): 726.
N. Repub., 22 ('20): 189.
N. Y. Times, May 13, 1928: 19.
World Today, 12 ('07): 6 (por-
trait).

Finley Peter Dunne (Martin Dooley)—humorist.
Born at Chicago, 1867. Educated in Chicago public
schools. Began newspaper work as reporter, 1885. On
Chicago Evening Post and *Chicago Times Herald*, 1892-97.

Finley Peter Dunne (Martin Dooley)—*Continued*

Editor of the *Chicago Journal*, 1897–1900. Since 1900 has lived and worked in New York.

BIBLIOGRAPHY

Humorous Essays
Mr. Dooley in Peace and in War. 1898.
Mr. Dooley in the Hearts of His Countrymen. 1899.
What Dooley Says. 1899.
Mr. Dooley's Philosophy. 1900.
Mr. Dooley's Opinions. 1901.
Observations by Mr. Dooley. 1902.
Dissertations by Mr. Dooley. 1906.
Mr. Dooley Says. 1910.
New Dooley Book. 1911.
Mr. Dooley on Making a Will. 1919.

STUDIES AND REVIEWS

Am. M., 62 ('06): 571 (portrait); 65 ('07): 173.
Bookm., 51 ('20): 674.
Cent., 63 ('01): 63 (portrait).
Cur. Lit., 38 ('05): 29 (portrait).
No. Am., 176 ('03): 743 (Howells.)
N. Repub., 20 ('19): 235.
Outlook, 123 ('19): 94 (portrait).
Spec., 90 ('03): 258; 125 ('20): 146.

Charles (Alexander) Eastman (Ohiyesa)—writer.

Born at Redwood Falls, Minnesota, 1858, of Santee Sioux ancestry, his father being a full-blooded Indian, and his mother a half-breed. B. S., Dartmouth, 1887; M. D., Boston University, 1890. Government physician, Pine Ridge Agency, 1890–93. Indian secretary, Y. M. C. A., 1894–97. Attorney for Santee Sioux at Washington, 1897–1900. Government physician, Crow Creek, South Dakota, 1900–03. Appointed to revise Sioux family names, 1903–09. U. S. Indian inspector in Coolidge administration. Resigned 1925.

BIBLIOGRAPHY

Short Stories and Tales
Red Hunters and the Animal People. 1904.
Old Indian Days. 1907.

Charles (Alexander) Eastman (Ohiyesa)—*Continued*

Sociological Studies
 The Soul of the Indian. 1911.
 The Indian Today. 1915.

Biography
 Indian Heroes and Great Chieftains. 1918

Autobiography
 Indian Boyhood. 1902.
 Indian Child Life. 1913.
 From the Deep Woods to Civilization. 1916. (Sequel to Indian
 Boyhood.)

Max (Forrester) Eastman—poet, essayist, critic.

Born at Canandaigua, New York, 1883. Both his parents
were Congregationalist preachers. A. B., Williams College,
1905. From 1907 to 1911, assistant in philosophy at Columbia. In 1911, began to give his entire time to studying and
writing about the problems of economic inequality. In 1913
became editor of the *Masses*, a periodical which voiced his
theories, and which in 1917 became the *Liberator*.

In *The Enjoyment of Poetry*, Mr. Eastman shows in an
interesting way how poetry can be made to contribute to
the enrichment of life.

BIBLIOGRAPHY

Poems
 Child of the Amazons. 1913.
 Colors of Life. 1918.

Novel
 Venture. 1928.

Critical Essays and Studies
 The Enjoyment of Poetry. 1913. (Rev. ed., 1921.)
 Journalism Versus Art. 1916.
 The Sense of Humor. 1921.

Political Studies
 Understanding Germany. 1916.
 Since Lenin Died. 1925.

Max (Forrester) Eastman—*Continued*

Marx and Lenin: the Science of Revolution. London, 1926. New York, 1928.

The Real Situation in Russia. By Leon Trotsky. 1928. (Editor.)

Biography

Leon Trotsky. 1925.

STUDIES AND REVIEWS

Hackett.
Untermeyer.

Bookm., 38 ('28): 67.
Cur. Op., 55 ('13): 126 (portrait).
Dial, 65 ('18): 611 (L. Untermeyer); 66 ('19): 146 (Giovannitti).
Harp. W., 57 ('13): 20.

Nation, 114 ('22): 373; 125 ('27): 740; 127 ('28): 159.
N. Repub., 9 ('17): 303 (Hackett).
N. State., 25 ('25): 204.
N. Y. Times, July 12, 1925: 1; Apr. 1, 1928: 4.
Poetry, 2 ('13): 140; 3 ('13): 31; 13 ('19): 322.
Survey, 30 ('13): 489.

Walter Prichard Eaton—critic, essayist.

Born at Malden, Massachusetts, 1878. A. B., Harvard, 1900. Dramatic critic on the *New York Tribune*, 1902–07, and the *New York Sun*, 1907–08, and on the *American Magazine*, 1909–18.

BIBLIOGRAPHY

Poems

Echoes and Realities. 1918.

Play

Queen Victoria. 1922. (With David Carb.)

Short Stories and Tales

The Runaway Place. 1909. (With Elise Underhill.)
The Man Who Found Christmas. 1913.
The Idyl of Twin Fires. 1915. (Rev. ed., 1924.)
The Bird House Man. 1916.

Travel and Nature Essays

Barn Doors and Byways. 1913.
Green Trails and Upland Pastures. 1917. (Rev. ed., 1925.)

167

Walter Prichard Eaton—*Continued*
In Berkshire Fields. 1920.
Skyline Camps. 1922.
A Bucolic Attitude. 1926.

Essays on Theatrical Subjects
The American Stage of Today. 1908.
At the New Theatre and Others. 1910.
Plays and Players. 1916.
The Actor's Heritage. 1924.

Familiar Essays
Penguin Persons and Peppermints. 1922.

STUDIES AND REVIEWS

Bookm., 29 ('09): 473 (portrait). Lit. Digest, 53 ('16): 1711 (portrait).

Theatre Arts Mo., 8 ('24): 790.

T(homas) S(tearns) Eliot—poet, critic.
Born at St. Louis, Missouri, 1888. A. B., Harvard, 1909; A. M., 1911. Studied at the Sorbonne, Paris, and at Merton College, Oxford. Has lived in London since 1913. In 1927 became a British subject. Editor of the *New Criterion*.

SUGGESTIONS FOR READING

1. Is Mr. Eliot's poetry derived from a keen sense of life experienced or from literature? What echoes of earlier poets do you find in his work?

2. Does the adjective *distinguished* apply to his work? What are the sources of his distinction? What evidences of fresh vision of old things do you find? of unexpected and true associations and contrasts? of a delicate sense for essential details that make a picture? of the power of suggestive condensation? of ability to get an emotional effect through irony?

3. Consider the following quotation from Mr. Eliot as illuminative of his method of work: "The contemplation

T(homas) S(tearns) Eliot—*Continued*

of the horrid or sordid by the artist is the necessary and negative aspect of the impulse toward beauty."

4. What, if any, temperamental defect is likely to interfere with his development?

BIBLIOGRAPHY

Poems

Prufrock and Other Observations. London, 1917.
Poems. London, 1919.
Ara Vos Prec. London, 1919.
Poems. 1920.
The Waste Land. 1922.
Poems, 1909–1925. London, 1925.
Journey of the Magi. London, 1927.

Critical Essays

The Sacred Wood. 1920.
Homage to John Dryden. 1924.
Shakespeare and the Stoicism of Seneca. 1927.
An Essay of Poetic Drama. 1928.
For Lancelot Andrewes. 1928.

STUDIES AND REVIEWS

Aiken.
Monroe.
Muir.
Untermeyer. (A. P.)

Ath., Feb., 20, 1920: 239; Dec. 17, 1920: 834.
Cal. Mod. Lett., 1 ('25): 242; 2 ('25): 278.
Dial, 68 ('20): 781; 70 ('21): 336.
Freeman, 1 ('20): 381; 2 ('21): 593 (Aiken); 6 ('23): 453 (L. Untermeyer).
Hound and Horn, 1 ('28): 187.
Lit. Digest, I. B. R. Apr., 1923: 46.
Lit. Rev., Jan. 20, 1923: 396.

Lond. Merc., 3 ('21): 447; 13 ('26): 547.
Lond. Times, June 12, 1919: 322; Nov. 11, 1920: 795; Sept. 20, 1923: 616.
Nation, 115 ('22): supp. Dec. 6: 614.
N. Repub., 26 ('21): 194; 33 ('23): 294.
N. State., 16 ('21): 418, 733; 22 ('23): 116.
Poetry, 10 ('17): 264; 16 ('20): 157; 17 ('21): 345.
Sat. Rev., 131 ('21): 281.

See also Book Review Digest, 1920.

John Erskine—essayist, poet, novelist.

Born at New York City, 1879. A. B., Columbia, 1900; A. M., 1901; Ph. D., 1903. Various honorary degrees and military decorations. Taught English at Amherst and Columbia. Since 1916, professor at Columbia. Co-editor of the *Cambridge History of American Literature*. Chairman of the Army Educational Commission of the A. E. F., 1918– 19. President of the Poetry Society of America, 1922.

BIBLIOGRAPHY

Poems
    Actæon. 1907.
    The Shadowed Hour. 1917.
    Collected Poems. 1907–1922. 1922.
    Sonata. 1925.

Plays and Pageants
    A Pageant of the Thirteenth Century. 1914. (With John J. Coss.)
    Hearts Enduring. 1920.

Novels
    The Private Life of Helen of Troy. 1925.
    Galahad. 1926.
    Adam and Eve. 1927.
    Penelope's Man. 1928.

Allegory
    The Enchanted Garden. 1925.

Essays
    The Moral Obligation to be Intelligent. 1915. (Enl. ed., 1921.)
    Democracy and Ideals. 1920.
    The Kinds of Poetry. 1920.
    The Literary Discipline. 1923.
    Prohibition and Christianity. 1927.
    American Character. 1927. (Reprints.)

Studies in Literature
    The Elizabethan Lyric. 1903.
    Leading American Novelists. 1910.
    Great American Writers. 1912. (With William Peterfield Trent.)
    The Delight of Great Books. 1928.

John Erskine—*Continued*

STUDIES AND REVIEWS

Robinson, H. John Erskine.
1927.

Bost. Trans., Dec. 30, 1922: 5;
Nov. 28, 1925: 5.
Dial, 70 ('21): 347.
Ind., 115 ('25): 683 (E. Boyd).
Lit. Rev., Nov. 13, 1926: 1.
N. Repub., 53 ('27): 78.

Nation, 117 ('23): 168; 120 ('25):
63; 124 ('27): 42; 125 ('27): 690.
N. Y. Times, May 6, 1923: 9;
May 31, 1925: 11; Nov. 14,
1926: 2; Nov. 20, 1927: 2; Nov.
25, 1928: 7.
Outlook, 126 ('20): 377.

See also Book Review Digest, 1920.

Edna Ferber—short story writer, novelist.

Born at Kalamazoo, Michigan, 1887. Educated in the public and high schools of Appleton, Wisconsin. Began newspaper work at seventeen as reporter on the *Appleton Daily Crescent*. Later, employed on the *Milwaukee Journal* and the *Chicago Tribune*. *So Big* was awarded the Pulitzer novel-prize in 1925.

Miss Ferber's special contribution to American literature thus far has been her studies of American women in business.

For complete bibliography, see Who's Who in America.

BIBLIOGRAPHY

Emma McChesney and Co. 1915.
The Girls. 1921.
Gigolo. 1922.
So Big. 1924.
Show Boat. 1926.
Mother Knows Best. 1927.

Arthur Davison Ficke—poet.

Born at Davenport, Iowa, 1883. A. B., Harvard, 1904. Studied at the College of Law, State University of Iowa. Taught English at State University of Iowa, 1906–07. Ad-

Arthur Davison Ficke—*Continued*

mitted to the bar, 1908. Served in France with A. E. F. Under the name Anne Knish joined Witter Bynner (q. v.). under the pseudonym Emanuel Morgan, in writing *Spectra*, Mr. Ficke's knowledge of art, especially Japanese art, has an important bearing upon his work.

BIBLIOGRAPHY

Poems

 From the Isles. Norwich, Eng. 1907.
 The Happy Princess. 1907.
 The Earth Passion. Cranleigh, Eng. 1908.
* Sonnets of a Portrait-Painter. 1914. (Enl. ed., 1922.)
 The Man on the Hilltop. 1915.
 Twelve Japanese Painters. 1915.
 Spectra. 1916. (Under the pseud. Anne Knish, with Witter Bynner.)
 An April Elegy. 1917.
 Out of Silence. 1924.
 Selected Poems. 1926.
 Christ in China. 1927.
 Mountain Against Mountain. 1929.

Plays

 The Breaking of Bonds. 1910.
 Mr. Faust. 1913. (Rev. ed., 1922.)

Art Studies

 Chats on Japanese Prints. 1915.

STUDIES AND REVIEWS

Untermeyer. (A. P.)

Forum, 55 ('16): 240, 675.
N. Repub., 40 ('24): 26.
N. Y. Herald-Tribune, Nov. 7, 1926: 18.
Poetry, 4 ('14): 29; 6 ('15): 39,

247; 10 ('17): 323; 24 ('24): 154; 29 ('27): 275.
Springfield Repub., Jan. 7, 1923: 7a.

See also Book Review Digest, 1915.

Dorothy (Dorothea Frances) Canfield (Fisher)—novelist.

Mrs. John Redwood Fisher. Born at Lawrence, Kansas, 1879. Ph. B., Ohio State University, 1899; Ph. D., Columbia, 1904. Secretary of Horace Mann School, 1902–05. Honorary

Dorothy Canfield (**Fisher**)—*Continued*

degrees from various New England colleges. Studied and traveled widely in Europe. Spent three years in France, doing war work. Translated Papini's *Life of Christ*, 1923. Has written many books on experimental education.

BIBLIOGRAPHY

Novels
Gunhild. 1907.
The Squirrel-Cage. 1912.
*The Bent Twig. 1915.
Understood Betsy. 1917.
*The Brimming Cup. 1921.
Rough-Hewn. 1922.
The Home-Maker. 1924.
Her Son's Wife. 1926.

Short Stories and Sketches
Hillsboro People. 1915. (Includes poems by Sarah Cleghorn.)
The Real Motive. 1916. (Includes poems by Sarah Cleghorn.)
Home Fires in France. 1918.
The Day of Glory. 1919.
Raw Material. 1923.
Made-to-Order Stories. 1925.

Essays
Fellow-Captains. 1916. (With Sarah Cleghorn.)
Why Stop Learning? 1927.

Study
Corneille and Racine in England. 1904.

STUDIES AND REVIEWS

Overton. (O. W. N.)
Van Doren. (C. A. N.)
Williams.

Bookm., 42 ('16): 599; 53 ('21): 453.
Bost. Trans., Sept. 1, 1923: 2; May 31, 1924: 3; Sept. 4, 1926: 2.
Dial, 65 ('18): 320.
Ind., 111 ('23): 114.
Lit. Digest, 69 ('21): June 11: 57.
Lit. Rev., Mar. 19, 1921: 3; Oct. 21, 1922: 123; June 14, 1924: 820.

Lond. Times, July 7, 1921: 435.
N. Repub., 5 ('16): 314.
N. State., 17 ('21): 444.
N. Y. Herald-Tribune, Aug. 29, 1926: 2.
N. Y. Times, Oct. 15, 1922: 2; Aug. 26, 1923: 15; May 25, 1924: 9; Aug. 29, 1926: 4.
R. of Rs., 45 ('12): 759 (portrait).
Sat. Rev. of Lit., 3 ('26): 86.

See also Book Review Digest, 1915, 1917-19, 1921.

F(rancis) Scott (Key) Fitzgerald—novelist, short story writer.

Born at St. Paul, Minnesota, 1896. Attended Princeton, 1913–17. Military service, 1917–19.

BIBLIOGRAPHY

Plays
The Vegetable. 1923.

Novels
This Side of Paradise. 1920.
The Beautiful and Damned. 1922.
The Great Gatsby. 1925. (Dramatized by Owen Davis.)

Short Stories
Flappers and Philosophers. 1920.
Tales of the Jazz Age. 1922. (Contains play.)
All the Sad Young Men. 1926.

STUDIES AND REVIEWS

Baldwin.
Boyd. (P. R. I.)
Farrar.
Van Doren. (C. A. N.)

Bookm., 55 ('22): 22.
Bost. Trans., Mar. 20, 1926: 4.
Dial, 72 ('22): 419; 79 ('25): 162.
Lit. Digest, July 15, 1922: 51.

Lit. Rev., May 2, 1925: 3.
Nation, 114 ('22): 318.
N. Repub., 30 ('22): 348.
N. Y. Times, Oct. 20, 1922: 12; Apr. 19, 1925: 9; Mar. 7, 1926: 9.
Sat. Rev. of Lit., 1 ('25): 739.

See also Book Review Digest, 1920.

John Gould Fletcher—poet, critic.

Born at Little Rock, Arkansas, 1886. Studied at Phillips Academy, Andover, Massachusetts, and at Harvard, 1903–07. Has lived in England since 1916.

SUGGESTIONS FOR READING

1. Read the prefaces to *Irradiations* and *Goblins and Pagodas* for Mr. Fletcher's theory of poetry before you read the poems themselves. Has he succeeded in making the arts of painting and music do service to poetry?

John Gould Fletcher—*Continued*

2. After reading the poems, consider the justice or injustice of Mr. Aiken's criticism: "It is a sort of absolute poetry, a poetry of detached waver and brilliance, a beautiful flowering of language alone—a parthenogenesis, as if language were fertilized by itself rather than by thought or feeling. Remove the magic of phrase and sound and there is nothing left: no thread of continuity, no thought, no story, no emotion. But the magic of phrase and sound is powerful, and it takes one into a fantastic world."

3. Do you find any poems to which the quotation given above does not apply? Are these of more or of less value than the others?

BIBLIOGRAPHY

Poems
Fire and Wine. London, 1913.
The Dominant City. London, 1913.
Fool's Gold. London, 1913.
The Book of Nature. London, 1913.
Visions of the Evening. London, 1913.
Irradiations, Sand and Spray. 1915.
Goblins and Pagodas. 1916.
Japanese Prints. 1918.
The Tree of Life. London, 1918.
Breakers and Granite. 1921.
Preludes and Symphonies. 1922. (Reprints.)
Parables. London, 1925.
Branches of Adam. London, 1926.
The Black Rock. 1928.

Biography
Paul Gauguin. 1921.
John Smith—also Pocahontas. 1928.

Translations
The Dance over Fire and Water, by Elie Faure. 1926.
Reveries of a Solitary, by Jean Jacques Rousseau. 1927.

STUDIES AND REVIEWS

Aiken.
Lowell.
Monroe.
Untermeyer. (A. P.)

Bookm., 41 ('15): 236 (portrait only).
Crit., 5 ('27): 134.
Dial, 66 ('19): 189.

John Gould Fletcher—*Continued*

Egoist, 2 ('15): 73, 79, 177 (portrait); 3 ('16): 173.
Freeman, 3 ('21): 405 (Aiken).
Lit. Rev., Apr. 16, 1921: 1; Oct. 8, 1921: 68.
Nation, 112 ('21): supp. 562; 113 ('21): supp. 416.
N. Repub., 3 ('15): 75, 154, 204; 9 ('16): supp. 11.

N. Y. Times, Mar. 13, 1921: 6; Sept. 11, 1921: 5.
Poetry, 7 ('15): 44, 88; 9 ('16): 43; 13 ('19): 340; 19 ('21): 155; 21 ('23): 270; 27 ('26): 206 (H. Monroe).
Sat. Rev., 126 ('18): 1039.

See also Book Review Digest, 1915, 1918, 1919, 1921.

John (William) Fox, Jr.—novelist.

Born in Kentucky, 1862, of a pioneer family. Pupil of James Lane Allen, whose influence on his work should be noted. Also associated in friendship with Roosevelt and with Thomas Nelson Page. War correspondent during the Spanish and Japanese wars. Died in 1919.

BIBLIOGRAPHY

Novels and Short Stories
    A Mountain Europa. 1894.
    A Cumberland Vendetta. 1895.
    "Hell-fer-Sartain." 1896.
    The Kentuckians. 1897.
    Crittenden. 1900.
* The Little Shepherd of Kingdom Come. 1903.
    Christmas Eve on Lonesome. 1904.
    A Knight of the Cumberland. 1906.
* The Trail of the Lonesome Pine. 1908.
    The Heart of the Hills. 1913.
    In Happy Valley. 1917.
    Erskine Dale, Pioneer. 1920.

Essays
    Blue-Grass and Rhododendron. 1901.

Travel and Description
    Following the Sun-Flag. 1905.

John (William) Fox, Jr.—*Continued*

STUDIES AND REVIEWS

Bookm., 32 ('10): 363.
Nation, 109 ('19): 72.
Outlook, 90 ('08): 700 (portrait).

Scrib. M., 66 ('19): 674 (portrait)
(Thomas Nelson Page).

Waldo (David) Frank—novelist.

Born at Long Branch, New Jersey, 1889. B. A., Yale, 1911; M. A., 1911. On New York newspapers, 1911-13. A founder and editor of *Seven Arts*, 1916-17. American correspondent of French magazines.

BIBLIOGRAPHY

Novels
   The Unwelcome Man. 1917.
   The Dark Mother. 1920.
   Rahab. 1922.
   City Block. 1922.
   Holiday. 1923.
   Chalk Face. 1924.

Essays and Studies
   Our America. 1919. (London, 1922, as The New America.)
   Salvos. 1924.
   The Re-Discovery of America. 1929.

Biographical Sketches
   Time Exposures. 1926. (Under pseud. Search-Light.)

Travel
   Virgin Spain. 1926.

STUDIES AND REVIEWS

Baldwin.
Munson, G. B. Waldo Frank. 1923.

Cur. Op., 68 ('20): 80 (portrait).
Dial, 62 ('17): 244 (V. W. Brooks); 70 ('21): 95; 73 ('22): 449; 75 ('23): 386; 82 ('27): 63 (S. Sitwell).
Lit. Rev., Apr. 1, 1922: 543; Oct. 18, 1924: 3; Mar. 20, 1926: 2.

N. Repub., 36 ('23): supp. Sept. 26: 12; 47 ('26): 39.
N. Y. Herald-Tribune, May 9, 1926: 6.
N. Y. Times, Dec. 16, 1923: 6; Apr. 18, 1926: 7.
Sat. Rev. of Lit., 1 ('24): 244.

See also Book Review Digest, 1917, 1919.

Mary E(leanor) Wilkins Freeman—short story writer, novelist, dramatist.

Mrs. Charles M. Freeman. Born at Randolph, Massachusetts, 1862. Educated there and at Mount Holyoke Seminary, 1874.

BIBLIOGRAPHY

Plays
   Giles Corey, Yeoman.   1893.

Novels
   Jane Field.   1893.
   Pembroke.   1894.
   Madelon.   1896.
   Jerome, A Poor Man.   1897.
   The Heart's Highway.   1900.
   The Portion of Labor.   1901.
   The Debtor.   1905.
   "Doc." Gordon.   1906.
   By the Light of the Soul.   1906.
   The Shoulders of Atlas.   1908.
   The Butterfly House.   1912.
   An Alabaster Box.   1917.   (With Florence Morse Kingsley.)

Short Stories
   The Adventures of Ann.   1886.   (Repr., 1899, under title In Colonial
      Times.)
*A Humble Romance.   1887.
*A New England Nun.   1891.
   The Pot of Gold.   1892.
   Young Lucretia.   1892.
   Comfort Pease and Her Gold Ring.   1895.
   The People of Our Neighborhood.   1898.
   Silence.   1898.
   The Jamesons.   1899.
   The Love of Parson Lord.   1900.
   The Home-Coming of Jessica.   1901.   (Includes stories by Brander
      Matthews and Robert Grant.)
   Understudies.   1901.
   Six Trees.   1903.
   The Wind in the Rose Bush.   1903.
   The Givers.   1904.
   The Fair Lavinia.   1907.
   The Winning Lady.   1909.
   The Green Door.   1910.

Mary E(leanor) Wilkins Freeman—*Continued*
The Yates Pride. 1912.
The Copy-Cat. 1914.
Edgewater People. 1918.
* The Best Stories. 1927.

Halsey. (Women.)
Harkins. (Women.)
Overton. (O. W. N.)
Pattee.
Williams.

Atlan., 83 ('99): 665.
Bk. Buyer, 8 ('91): 53 (portrait);
23 ('01): 379.

Bookm., 24 ('06): 20 (portrait).
Bost. Trans., Mar. 19, 1927: 2.
Citizen, 4 ('98): 27.
Critic, 20 ('92): 13; 22 ('93): 256
(portrait); 32 ('98): 155 (por-
traits).
Harp. W., 47 ('03): 1879; 49 ('05):
1940. (Portraits.)

Robert (Lee) Frost—poet.
Born at San Francisco, 1875. At the age of ten, he was
taken to New England, where eight generations of his fore-
fathers had lived. In 1892, he spent a few months at Dartmouth College, but, disliking college routine, decided to earn
his living, and became a millhand in Lawrence, Massachusetts. In 1897, two years after he had married, he entered
Harvard and studied there for two years; but he finally gave
up the idea of a degree and turned to various kinds of work,
teaching, shoe-making, and newspaper work. From 1900–11,
he farmed at Derry, New Hampshire, but with little success.
At the same time, he was writing and offering for publication
poems which were invariably refused. He taught English
at Derry, 1906–11, and psychology at Plymouth, 1911–12.

In 1912, he sold his farm and with his wife and four children
went to England. After offering a collection of poems to an
English publisher, he went to live in the little country town
of Beaconsfield. The poems were published in 1913, and
their merits were quickly recognized. In 1914, Mr. Frost
rented a small place at Ledbury, Gloucestershire, near the

Robert (Lee) Frost—*Continued*

English poets, Lascelles Abercrombie and W. W. Gibson. With the publication of *North of Boston* his reputation as a poet was established.

In 1915, Mr. Frost returned to America and went to live near Franconia, New Hampshire. From 1916 to 1920, and from 1923 to 1925 he taught English at Amherst College. From 1921 to 1923 he was "poet in residence" at the University of Michigan. He is now Fellow in Letters there. He was awarded the Pulitzer prize for poetry in 1924.

SUGGESTIONS FOR READING

1. Read in succession the poems concerning New England life and decide whether they seem more authentic and more valuable than the others. If so, why?

2. Is Mr. Frost's realism photographic? Consider in this connection his own statement: "There are two types of realist—the one who offers a good deal of dirt with his potato to show that it is a real one; and the one who is satisfied with the potato brushed clean. . . . To me the thing that art does for life is to strip it to form."

In view of the last sentence it is interesting to consider the kinds of details that Mr. Frost chooses for presentation and those that he omits.

3. Read several of the long poems to discover his relative strength in narrative and in dramatic presentation.

4. Examine the vocabulary for naturalness, colloquialism, and occasional extraordinary fitness of words.

5. Try to sum up briefly Mr. Frost's philosophy of life and his attitude toward nature and people.

6. What do you observe about the metrical forms, the beauty or lack of beauty in the rhythm? Do many of the poems sing?

BIBLIOGRAPHY

Poems
  A Boy's Will. London, 1913. New York, 1915.
  North of Boston. London, 1914. New York, 1915.

Robert (Lee) Frost—*Continued*

Mountain Interval. 1916.
Selected Poems. 1923. (Rev. and enl. ed., 1928.)
New Hampshire. 1923.
West-Running Brook. 1928.

Play

A Way Out. (*In* The Seven Arts. Feb., 1917.)

STUDIES AND REVIEWS

Boynton. (S. C. A.)
Farrar.
Frank, Waldo. Our America.
  1919.
Lowell, A. Robert Frost. 1917.
Maynard.
Monroe.
Munson, G. B. Robert Frost.
  1927.
Sergeant.
Squire.
Untermeyer. (A. P.)
——. (N. E. A. P.)
Van Doren. (A. B. L.)
——. (M. M.)
Weirick.
Whipple.
Wilkinson. (N. V.)
Wood.

Bookm., 45 ('17): 430 (portrait);
  47 ('18): 135; 58 ('24): 578.
Chapbook, 1–2, May, 1920: 5.
Cur. Op., 58 ('15): 427 (portrait).
Ind., 86 ('16): 283.
Lit. Digest, 66 ('20): July 17: 32
  (portrait).
Lond. Merc., 10 ('24): 317; 13
  ('25): 176 (J. Freeman).
Lond. Times, Mar. 29, 1923: 213.
Nation, 109 ('19): 713.
N. Repub., 9 ('16): 219; 12 ('17):
  109; 37 ('23): supp. Dec. 5: 24.
N. Y. Herald-Tribune, Nov. 18,
  1928: 1.
N. Y. Times, Nov. 18, 1928: 2.
Outlook, 135 ('23): 688.
Poetry, 2 ('13): 72; 5 ('14): 127;
  9 ('17): 202; 23 ('24): 328; 25
  ('24): 146 (H. Monroe).
Spec., 126 ('21): 114; 130 ('23):
  671.

Henry B(lake) Fuller—novelist, short story writer.

Born at Chicago, 1857. Educated in Chicago public schools, and at a "classical academy" in Wisconsin. In Europe, 1879–80, '83, '92, '94, '96–97. Literary editor *Chicago Post*, 1902. Editorial writer for *Chicago Record Herald*, 1910–11, and 1914; at present, reviewer for *New Republic, Nation,* and other periodicals.

Henry B(lake) Fuller—*Continued*

Suggestions for Reading

1. Compare Mr. Fuller's stories of Europe with his studies of life in Chicago. What is their relative success? What inferences do you draw?

2. Considering dates, materials, and methods, where do you place Mr. Fuller's work in the development of the American novel?

3. Read *On the Stairs* in view of *Dial*, 64 ('18): 405.

Bibliography

Poems

Lines Long and Short. 1917.

Plays

The Puppet-Booth. 1896.
The Fan, by Goldoni. 1925. (Translator.)
The Coffee House, by Goldoni. 1925. (Translator.)

Novels

The Chevalier of Pensieri-Vani. 1890. (Under pseud. Stanton Page. Rev. ed., 1892.)
The Châtelaine of La Trinité. 1892.
The Cliff-Dwellers. 1893.
With the Procession. 1895.
The Last Refuge. 1900.
On the Stairs. 1918.
Bertram Cope's Year. 1919.

Short Stories

From the Other Side. 1898.
Under the Skylights. 1901.
Waldo Trench, and Others. 1908.

Studies and Reviews

Baldwin.   Dial, 64 ('18): 405.
Farrar.   Poetry, 10 ('17): 155.

Bookm., 38 ('13): 275; 47 ('18):   *See also* Book Review Digest,
340.   1918, 1920.

Zona Gale—novelist, short story writer, dramatist.

Mrs. William Llywelyn Breese. Born at Portage, Wisconsin, 1874. B. L., University of Wisconsin, 1895; M. L., 1899. On Milwaukee papers until 1901. Later on staff of the *New York World*. *Miss Lulu Bett* was awarded the Pulitzer prize for drama in 1921.

BIBLIOGRAPHY

Poems

The Secret Way. 1921.

Plays

The Neighbors. 1920. (*In* Wisconsin Plays. 1914.)
Miss Lulu Bett. 1921. (Dramatization of the novel.)
Uncle Jimmy. 1922.
Mister Pitt. 1925. (Dramatization of Birth.)

Novels

Romance Island. 1906.
Mothers to Men. 1911.
Christmas. 1912.
Heart's Kindred. 1915.
A Daughter of the Morning. 1917.
Birth. 1918. (See Plays.)
Miss Lulu Bett. 1920. (See Plays.)
Faint Perfume. 1923.
Preface to a Life. 1926.

Short Stories

The Loves of Pelleas and Etarre. 1907.
Friendship Village. 1908.
Friendship Village Love Stories. 1909.
Neighborhood Stories. 1914.
Peace in Friendship Village. 1919.
Yellow Gentians, and Blue. 1927.

Autobiographical Sketches and Impressions

When I Was a Little Girl. 1913.
Portage, Wisconsin, and other essays. 1928.

STUDIES AND REVIEWS

Dickinson. (P. N. A. T.)   Overton. (A. O. D.)
Follett, W. Zona Gale. 1923.   Van Doren. (C. A. N.)
Michaud.

Zona Gale—*Continued*

Acad., 75 ('08): 595.

Bookm., 13 ('01): 520 (portrait); 25 ('07): 567 (portrait); 53 ('21): 123.

Bost. Trans., Apr. 4, 1923: 4; Nov. 13, 1926: 4; Oct. 11, 1927: 4.

Lit. Rev., Dec. 3, 1921: 221; Feb. 25, 1922: 451; Mar. 24, 1923: 547; May 2, 1925: 4.

Lond. Times, Nov. 17, 1921: 753.

N. Repub., 35 ('23): 47; 52 ('27): 244.

N. Y. Herald-Tribune, Nov. 7, 1926: 2; Nov. 4, 1928: 3.

N. Y. Times, Mar. 5, 1922: 6 (R. Le Gallienne); Mar. 11, 1923: 14; Oct. 9, 1927: 2.

Sat. Rev. of Lit., 3 ('26): 364.

See also Book Review Digest, 1915, 1917–19, 1920.

Hamlin Garland—short story writer, novelist.

Born on a farm near West Salem, Wisconsin, 1860, of Scotch and New England ancestry. During his boyhood his father moved first to Iowa, then to Dakota. As a boy, Mr. Garland helped his father with all the hard work of making farmland out of prairie. While still in his teens, he was able to do a man's work. His schooling was desultory, but he finished the course at Cedar Valley Seminary, Osage, Iowa, then taught, 1882–83. In 1883 he took up a claim in Dakota, but the next year went to Boston and began his career as teacher and writer. *A Daughter of the Middle Border* was awarded the Pulitzer prize for biography in 1922.

SUGGESTIONS FOR READING

1. Read the autobiographical books, *A Son of the Middle Border* and *A Daughter of the Middle Border*, to get the background of Mr. Garland's work. Then read his essays called *Crumbling Idols*, for the literary theory on which his work was created.

2. Two literary landmarks in Mr. Garland's history are: Edward Eggleston's *The Hoosier Schoolmaster* (1871), and Joseph Kirkland's *Zury: the Meanest Man in Spring County* (1887). Read these and decide how much they influenced *Main-Travelled Roads* and similar volumes of Mr. Garland's.

Hamlin Garland—*Continued*

3. Mr. Garland says that he presents farm life "not as the summer boarder or the young lady novelist sees it—but as the working farmer endures it." Find evidence of this.

4. Consider how far Mr. Garland's success depends upon the richness of his material, how far upon his philosophy of life and his honesty to his own experience, and how far upon his technical skill as a writer.

5. What are his most obvious limitations? What is the relative importance of his novels and of his short stories?

6. Consider separately: (1) his power of visualization; (2) his choice of significant detail; (3) his originality or lack of it; (4) his range in characterization; (5) his power of suggestion as over against his vividness of delineation; (6) his economy—or lack of it—in expression. Where does his main strength lie?

BIBLIOGRAPHY

Poems
  Prairie Songs. 1893.

Plays
  Under the Wheel. 1890.

Novels and Tales
  Jason Edwards. 1891.
  A Spoil of Office. 1892. (Rev. ed., 1897.)
  A Member of the Third House. 1892.
  A Little Norsk. 1892.
* Rose of Dutcher's Coolly. 1895.
  The Eagle's Heart. 1900.
  Her Mountain Lover. 1901.
  The Captain of the Gray-Horse Troop. 1902. (Dramatized by Rachel Crothers and Louise Morgan Sill.)
  Hesper. 1903.
  The Light of the Star. 1904.
  The Tyranny of the Dark. 1905.
  The Long Trail. 1907.
  Money Magic. 1907. (Repr. 1922 as Mart Haney's Mate.)
  The Shadow World. 1908.
  The Moccasin Ranch. 1909.

Hamlin Garland—*Continued*

Cavanagh, Forest Ranger. 1910.
Victor Ollnee's Discipline. 1911.
The Forester's Daughter. 1914.

Short Stories
* Main-Travelled Roads. 1891. (Enl. ed., 1899.)
* Prairie Folks. 1892. (Enl. ed., 1899.)
  Wayside Courtships. 1897.
  The Spirit of Sweetwater. 1898. (Enl. ed., 1906, under title Witch's
    Gold.)
  Other Main-Travelled Roads. 1910.
  They of the High Trails. 1916.
  The Book of the American Indian. 1923.

Autobiographical Novels and Sketches
  Boy Life on the Prairie. 1899.
* A Son of the Middle Border. 1917.
  A Daughter of the Middle Border. 1921.
  Trail-Makers of the Middle Border. 1926.
  Back Trailers from the Middle Border. 1928.

Critical Essays
  Crumbling Idols. 1894.

Biography
  Ulysses S. Grant. 1898.

Travel
  The Trail of the Goldseekers. 1899. (In prose and verse.)

STUDIES AND REVIEWS

Boynton. (S. C. A.)
Harkins.
Hazard, L. L. The Frontier in
  American Literature. 1927.
Pattee.
Van Doren. (C. A. N.)
Williams.

Arena, 34 ('05): 206.
Bookm., 31 ('10): 226, 309 (por-
  trait).
Bost. Trans., Dec. 10, 1921: 7;
  Nov. 13, 1926: 3; Nov. 24, 1928:
  4.

Cur. Lit., 53 ('12): 589.
Cur. Op., 63 ('17): 412.
Freeman, 4 ('21): 210.
Lit. Digest, 55 ('17): Sept. 15: 28
  (portrait).
Lit. Rev., Nov. 6, 1926: 3.
Lond. Times, Dec. 27, 1923: 908.
N. Y. Herald-Tribune, Oct. 24,
  1926: 25.
N. Y. Times, Oct. 14, 1923: 5.
No. Am., 196 ('12): 523.
Sat. Rev. of Lit., 3 ('26): 270.
Sewanee R., 27 ('19): 411.

Theodosia Garrison—poet.

Mrs. Frederic J. Faulks. Born at Newark, New Jersey, 1874. Educated in private schools.

Poems
   The Joy o' Life.   1909.
   The Earth Cry.   1910.
   The Dreamers.   1917.
   As the Larks Rise.   1921.

Katherine Fullerton Gerould—short story writer, novelist, essayist.

Mrs. Gordon Hall Gerould. Born at Brockton, Massachusetts, 1879. A. B., Radcliffe College, 1900; A. M., 1901. Reader in English at Bryn Mawr College, 1901–10, except 1908–09, which she spent in England and France.

SUGGESTIONS FOR READING

1. Mrs. Gerould belongs to the school of Henry James, but shows marked individuality in her themes and in her dramatic power. A comparison of some of her short stories with stories by James and by Mrs. Wharton (q. v.) is illuminating for the powers and limitations of all three.

2. Another interesting comparison is between Mrs. Gerould's stories and the collection entitled *Bliss* by the English writer, Katherine Mansfield (Mrs. J. Middleton Murry); cf. Manly and Rickert, *Contemporary British Literature*.

BIBLIOGRAPHY

Novels
   A Change of Air.   1917.
   Lost Valley.   1922.
   Conquistador.   1923.
Short Stories
   Vain Oblations.   1914.
   The Great Tradition.   1915.
   Valiant Dust.   1922.

Katherine Fullerton Gerould—*Continued*

Essays
  Modes and Morals. 1920.

Travel and Description
  Hawaii. 1916.
  The Aristocratic West. 1925.

STUDIES AND REVIEWS

Bookm., 44 ('16): 31.
Cur. Lit., 58 ('15): 353.
Lit. Digest, I. B. R. Dec., 1922: 63.
Lit. Rev., Feb. 11, 1922: 411;
  May 5, 1923: 659.
N. Repub., 22 ('20): 97.
N. Y. Times, Jan. 22, 1922: 18;
  Nov. 26, 1922: 14; Apr. 1,
  1923: 16; Dec. 20, 1925: 1.

No. Am., 211 ('20): 564; 215 ('22):
  571.
Sat. Rev. of Lit., 2 ('25): 336.
Springfield Repub., Nov. 15, 1925:
  7a.

See also Book Review Digest,
  1914–17, 1920.

Fannie Stearns Davis Gifford. *See* Fannie Stearns Davis.

Arturo Giovannitti—poet.

Born in the Abruzzi, Italy, 1884, of a family of good social standing, his father and one of his brothers being doctors, and another brother a lawyer. Educated in a local Italian college. Came to America in 1900. Worked in a coal mine. Later, studied at Union Theological Seminary. Conducted Presbyterian missions in several places.

In 1906 he became a socialist and one of the leaders of the I. W. W. During the Lawrence strikes he preached the doctrine of Syndicalism and was arrested on the charge of inciting to riot. He also organized relief work for the strikers.

On an Italian newspaper; editor of *Il Proletario*, a socialist paper. His first speech in English was made at the time of his trial and produced a powerful effect upon his audience. During his imprisonment he studied English literature and wrote poems, of which the most famous is "The Walker." His chief concern is with the submerged, and he writes from actual experience of having been "one of those who sleep in the park."

Arturo Giovannitti—*Continued*

BIBLIOGRAPHY

Poems
  Arrows in the Gale. 1914.

STUDIES AND REVIEWS

Untermeyer. (A. P.)

Atlan., 111 ('13): 853.
Cur. Op., 54 ('13): 24 (portrait).
Forum, 52 ('14): 609.

Lit. Digest, 45 ('12): 441.
Outlook, 104 ('13): 504.
Poétry, 6 ('15): 36.
Survey, 29 ('12): 163 (portrait).

Ellen (Anderson Gholson) Glasgow—novelist.

Born at Richmond, Virginia, 1874. Privately educated. Her best work deals with life in Virginia.

BIBLIOGRAPHY

Poems
  The Freeman. 1902.

Novels
  The Descendant. 1897.
  Phases of an Inferior Planet. 1898.
  The Voice of the People. 1900.
  The Battle-Ground. 1902.
  The Deliverance. 1904.
  The Wheel of Life. 1906.
  The Ancient Law. 1908.
 * The Romance of a Plain Man. 1909.
  The Miller of Old Church. 1911.
  Virginia. 1913.
  Life and Gabriella. 1916.
  The Builders. 1919.
  One Man in His Time. 1922.
 * Barren Ground. 1925.
 * The Romantic Comedians. 1926.
  Twisted Tendril. 1928.

Short Stories
  The Shadowy Third. 1923.

Ellen (Anderson Gholson) Glasgow—*Continued*

STUDIES AND REVIEWS

Cooper.
Harkins. (Women.)
Mann, D. L. Ellen Glasgow. 1927.
Overton. (O. W. N.)
Sherman. (C. W.)
Van Doren. (C. A. N.)

Bookm., 19 ('04): 14, 43; 29 ('09): 613, 619 (Portraits).
Bost. Trans., Apr. 18, 1925: 4; Sept. 18, 1926: 3.
Cur. Op., 55 ('13): 50 (portrait).
Lit. Digest, July 15, 1922: 46.
Lit. Digest, I. B. R. May, 1925: 376.

Lit. Rev., Nov. 17, 1923: 256.
Lond. Times, July 9, 1925: 462.
Nation, 120 ('25): 521.
N. Repub., 42 ('25): 271.
N. Y. Herald-Tribune, Sept. 12, 1926: 1; July 29, 1928: 9.
N. Y. Times, May 28, 1922: 2; Oct. 28, 1923: 16; Apr. 12, 1925: 2; Apr. 26, 1925: 25; Sept. 12, 1926: 5.
Outlook, 71 ('02): 213 (portrait).
Sat. Rev. of Lit., 1 ('25): 907; 3 ('26): 133.
World's Work, 5 ('02): 2793 (portrait).

Susan Glaspell—dramatist, novelist.

Formerly Mrs. George Cram Cook. Now Mrs. Norman Matson. Born at Davenport, Iowa, 1882. Ph. B., Drake University. Post-graduate work at the University of Chicago. State-house and legislative reporter for the *News* and the *Capitol*, Des Moines. Connected with the Little Theater movement through the Provincetown Players.

BIBLIOGRAPHY

Plays
Trifles. 1916.
Suppressed Desires. 1917. (With George Cram Cook. *Pub. in* Provincetown Plays. 1916.)
People; and Close the Book. 1918.
Plays. 1920. (With George Cram Cook. Pub. London, 1926, as Trifles and Six Other Short Plays.)
Inheritors. 1921.
The Verge. 1922.
Bernice. 1924.
Three Plays. 1924. (Reprints.)
The Comic Artist. 1927. (With Norman H. Matson.)

Susan Glaspell—*Continued*

Novels
The Glory of the Conquered. 1909.
The Visioning. 1911.
Fidelity. 1915.
Brook Evans. 1928.

Short Stories
Lifted Masks. 1912.

Biography
The Road to the Temple. London, 1926. New York, 1927.

STUDIES AND REVIEWS

Dickinson. (P. N. A. T.)
Van Doren. (A. B. L.)

Bookm., 33 ('11): 350, 419; 46 ('18): 700 (portraits); 65 ('27): 344.
Cur. Op., 59 ('15): 48 (portrait).
Freeman, 1 ('20): 518.
Lond. Times, May 19, 1927: 350; Apr. 19, 1928: 288.

Nation, 111 ('20): 509; 113 ('21): 708.
N. State., 28 ('27): 510.
N. Y. Herald-Tribune, Mar. 13, 1927: 1.
N. Y. Times, Mar. 13, 1927: 2.
Sat. Rev. of Lit., 3 ('27): 675.

See also Book Review Digest, 1915, 1920.

David Grayson. *See* **Ray Stannard Baker.**

Paul Green—dramatist.
Born at Lillington, North Carolina, 1894. Graduated from Buie's Creek Academy, 1914. Served with A. E. F. in France. Graduated from University of North Carolina in 1921. Graduate work there and at Columbia. Member of philosophy department, University of North Carolina. *In Abraham's Bosom* was awarded the Pulitzer prize for drama in 1927.

BIBLIOGRAPHY

Plays
In Aunt Mahaly's Cabin. 1925.
The Lord's Will. 1925.
Lonesome Road. 1926.

Paul Green—*Continued*

The Field God; and In Abraham's Bosom. 1927.
The Man Who Died at Twelve O'Clock. 1927.
In the Valley. 1928.
The House of Connelly. 1929.

Short Stories
Wide Fields. 1928.

STUDIES AND REVIEWS

Clark, Barrett H. Paul Green.
1928.
Drama, 16 ('26): 137.
Nation, 124 ('27): 510.
N. Y. Herald-Tribune, June 6,
1926: 10; May 20, 1928: 6.

N. Y. Times, Aug. 29, 1926: 2.
N. Y. World, Apr. 17, 1927: 11m.
Sat. Rev. of Lit., 3 ('27): 940; 4
('28): 780.

Hermann Hagedorn—man of letters.

Born at New York City, 1882. A. B., Harvard, 1907.
Studied at University of Berlin, 1907–08, and at Columbia,
1908–09. Instructor in English at Harvard, 1909–11. Early
interest in outdoor drama and pageantry. Much of his
recent writing has been devoted to the memory of Roosevelt.

BIBLIOGRAPHY

Poems
The Woman of Corinth. 1908.
A Troop of the Guard. 1909. (Includes a play.)
Poems and Ballads. 1912.
The Great Maze, and The Heart of Youth. 1916. (Includes a play.)
Hymn of Free Peoples Triumphant. 1918.
Ladders through the Blue. 1925.

Plays
The Silver Blade. Berlin, 1907.
The Horse Thieves. 1909. (Priv. ptd.)
Makers of Madness. 1914.
The Heart of Youth. 1915.

Novels
Faces in the Dawn. 1914.
Barbara Picks a Husband. 1918.
The Rough Riders. 1927.

Hermann Hagedorn—*Continued*

Political and Biographical Works
   That Human Being, Leonard Wood. 1920.
   Roosevelt in the Bad Lands. 1921.
   Works of Theodore Roosevelt. 1922. (Editor.)
   Roosevelt, Prophet of Unity. 1924.

STUDIES AND REVIEWS

Baldwin.

Bost. Trans., Dec. 7, 1921: 8.
N. Repub., 7 ('16): 234.
N. Y. Times, Nov. 29, 1925: 8.

Outlook, 102 ('12): 207 (portrait only); 103 ('13): 262.
Poetry, 9 ('16): 90.

See also Book Review Digest, 1913–14, 1916–21.

Frank Harris—man of letters.

Born at Galway, Ireland, 1856, but came to the United States at 1870. Naturalized. Educated at the universities of Kansas, Paris, Heidelberg, Strassburg, Göttingen, Berlin, Vienna, and Athens (no degrees). Admitted to the Kansas bar, 1875. Later, returned to Europe, became editor of the *Evening News* and *Fortnightly Review*, and secured control of the *Saturday Review*.

Mr. Harris's work belongs in a class by itself. It is valuable partly for its content, as in the case of his intimate portraits of famous men whom he has known, and partly for the force and brilliancy of the style.

BIBLIOGRAPHY

Plays
   Mr. and Mrs. Daventry. London, 1900.
   Shakespeare and His Love. London, 1910.
   Joan la Ramée. Nice, 1926.

Novels
   The Bomb. London, 1908. New York, 1909.
   Great Days. 1914.
   Love in Youth. 1916.

Frank Harris—*Continued*

Short Stories
    Elder Conklin. 1894.
    Montes the Matador. London, 1900. New York, 1910.
    Unpath'd Waters. 1913.
    The Veils of Isis. 1915.
    A Mad Love. 1920.
    Undream'd of Shores. 1924.

Biographical and Psychological Studies
    The Man Shakespeare. 1909. (Rev. ed., 1911.)
    The Women of Shakespeare. London, 1911. New York, 1912.
    * Contemporary Portraits. 1915–1923. First Series, 1915; Second
        Series, 1919; Third Series, 1920; Fourth Series, 1923.
    Oscar Wilde. 1916.
    Latest Contemporary Portraits. 1927.

Study
    England or Germany? 1915.

Autobiography
    My Life. 1925–

STUDIES AND REVIEWS

Bost. Trans., Apr. 29, 1916: 8.
Dial, 54 ('13): 237; 64 ('18): 536.
Lond. Times, Jan. 6, 1921: 7;
    Mar. 6, 1924: 142.
N. Repub., 2 ('15) supp.: 16; 14
    ('18): 269; 29 ('21): 21.
N. Y. Herald-Tribune, Oct. 9,
    1927: 2.

N. Y. Sun, Jan. 11, 1913: 12.
N. Y. Times, May 24, 1914: 242;
    Mar. 14, 1915: 90; June 1, 1924:
    8; Oct. 2, 1927: 2.
N. Y. World, June 29, 1928: 2e.
Sat. Rev., 112 ('11): 555; 137
    ('24): 62.

Ben Hecht—novelist, dramatist.

Born at New York City, 1893. Traveled much until he
was eight years old, then lived in Racine, Wisconsin, and
was educated in the Racine high school. Went to Chicago,
intending to join the Thomas Orchestra as violinist, but
instead joined the staff of the Chicago *Journal* and later
that of the *Daily News*. War correspondent in Germany.

Ben Hecht—*Continued*

BIBLIOGRAPHY

Plays

The Hero of Santa Maria. 1920. (With Kenneth Sawyer Goodman.)
The Wonder Hat. 1920. (With Kenneth Sawyer Goodman. Repr.
with other one-act plays. 1925.)
The Hand of Siva. (*In* Shay, A Treasury of Plays for Men. 1923.)
The Front Page. 1928. (With Charles MacArthur.)

Novels and Tales

Erik Dorn. 1921.
Fantazius Mallare. 1922.
Gargoyles. 1922.
The Florentine Dagger. 1923.
Humpty Dumpty. 1924.
The Kingdom of Evil. 1924.
Count Bruga. 1926.

Short Stories and Sketches

A Thousand and One Afternoons in Chicago. 1922.
Tales of Chicago Streets. 1924.
Broken Necks. 1924.

STUDIES AND REVIEWS

Baldwin.
Hansen.
Karsner.
Sherman. (C. W.)

Bost. Trans., Oct. 19, 1921: 6.
Cur. Op., 71 ('21): 644.
Dial, 71 ('21): 597; 74 ('23): 100.
Double-Dealer, 4 ('22): 292.
Freeman, 4 ('21): 282.

Forum, 71 ('24): 123.
Lit. Rev., Aug. 20, 1921: 3; Oct.
28, 1922: 143; May 22, 1926: 3.
Nation, 113 ('21): 453; 127 ('28):
207.
N. Repub., 28 ('21): 24; 56 ('28):
73.
N. Y. Times, Jan. 21, 1922: 2;
Sept. 16, 1923: 24; May 16,
1926: 7.

Ernest Hemingway—novelist.

Born at Oak Park, Illinois, 1896. Reporter on *Kansas City Star* before the war. Served on Italian front. Wounded. Croce di Guerra. Newspaperman in Europe since 1921. Has written many short stories since 1916.

Ernest Hemingway—*Continued*

BIBLIOGRAPHY

Novels
  The Sun also Rises. 1926.
Short Stories
  In Our Time. 1925.
  Men Without Women. 1927.

Parody
  The Torrents of Spring. 1926.

STUDIES AND REVIEWS

Bost. Trans., July 3, 1926: 2; Nov. 6, 1926: 2.
Cal. Mod. Lett., 4 ('27): 72.
Ind., 116 ('26): 694; 117 ('26): 594.
Nation, 125 ('27): 548.
N. Repub., 45 ('25): 22; 48 ('26); 101; 49 ('26): 142.
N. Y. Herald-Tribune, Oct. 18, 1925: 8; Oct. 31, 1926: 4; Oct. 9, 1927: 1.
N. Y. Times, June 13, 1926: 8; Oct. 16, 1927: 9.
Sat. Rev. of Lit., 3 ('26): 420; 4 ('27): 322.

Alice Corbin Henderson—poet, critic.

Mrs. William Penhallow Henderson. Born at St. Louis, Missouri. Lived many years in Santa Fé, New Mexico, which has furnished material for many of her poems. Associate editor of *Poetry*, 1912–26.

BIBLIOGRAPHY

Poems
  The Spinning Woman of the Sky. 1912.
  The New Poetry. 1917. (Enl. ed., 1923. Compiler with Harriet Monroe.)
  Red Earth. 1920.
  The Turquoise Trail. 1928. (Compiler.)

Plays for Children
  Adam's Dream. 1909.

STUDIES AND REVIEWS

Bookm., 47 ('18): 391.
Freeman, 4 ('22): 468.
Nation, 127 ('28): 298.
N. Repub., 28 ('21): 304.

Joseph Hergesheimer—novelist.

Born at Philadelphia, 1880. Educated at a Quaker school in Philadelphia and at the Pennsylvania Academy of Fine Arts.

SUGGESTIONS FOR READING

1. Collect evidence for Mr. Hergesheimer's interest in decorative settings.

2. Make a careful study of Mr. Hergesheimer's style. Study the development of mannerisms in sentence-form, phrasing, and diction.

3. Search out his most successful pieces of characterization. Attempt to discover the reasons why many of his characters do not live.

BIBLIOGRAPHY

Novels
The Lay Anthony. 1914. (Rev. ed., 1919.)
Mountain Blood. 1915. (Rev. ed., 1919.)
The Three Black Pennys. 1917.
* Java Head. 1919.
Linda Condon. 1919.
Cytherea. 1922.
The Bright Shawl. 1922.
Tol'able David. 1922.
Balisand. 1924.
Tampico. 1926.

Short Stories and Tales
Gold and Iron. 1918.
The Happy End. 1919.
Quiet Cities. 1928.

Critical Essay
Hugh Walpole. 1919.

Travel and Description
San Cristóbal de la Habana. 1920.

Autobiographical Sketches
The Presbyterian Child. 1923.
From an Old House. 1925.

History
Swords and Roses. 1929.

Joseph Hergesheimer—*Continued*

STUDIES AND REVIEWS

Baldwin.

Beach.

Björkman. Voices of Tomorrow. 1913.

Boyd. (P. R. I.)

Boynton. (M. C. A.)

Cabell, J. B. Joseph Hergesheimer. 1921.

Farrar.

Follett, W. Joseph Hergesheimer. c. 1922.

Jones, Llewellyn. Joseph Hergesheimer. 1923.

Squire.

Swire, H. L. R. Bibliography of the Works of Joseph Hergesheimer. 1922.

Van Doren. (A. B. L.)

——. (C. A. N.)

Williams.

Ath., 1919, 2: 1339 (C. Aiken).

Bookm., 50 ('19): 267 (J. B. Cabell).

Bookm. (Lond.), 58 ('20): 193 (portrait).

Bost. Trans., Jan. 18, 1922: 4; Nov. 22, 1922: 9; Sept. 27, 1924: 3; Aug. 28, 1926: 2; June 13, 1928: 2.

Dial, 66 ('19): 449; 72 ('22): 310.

Ind., 108 ('22): 86 (Boynton).

Lit. Rev., Jan. 21, 1922: 363; Oct. 14, 1922: 103; Sept. 27, 1924: 4; Sept. 18, 1926: 3.

Lond. Merc., 1 ('20): 342; 2 ('20): 498.

Lond. Times, Jan. 20, 1927: 40.

Nation, 109 ('19): 404; 112 ('21): 741 (C. Van Doren); 114 ('22): 176; 115 ('22): 553.

N. State., 20 ('22): 142 (R. West).

N. Y. Herald-Tribune, Sept. 19, 1926: 1.

N. Y. Times, Oct. 15, 1922: 1 (H. Walpole); Sept. 14, 1924: 4; Sept. 19, 1926: 5.

Sat. Rev., 128 ('19): 343.

Sat. Rev. of Lit., 1 ('24): 123; 4 ('28): 925.

Spec., 125 ('20): 371; 129 ('22): 603.

Robert Herrick—novelist.

Born at Cambridge, Massachusetts, 1868. A. B., Harvard, 1890. Taught English at the Massachusetts Institute of Technology, 1890–93, and at the University of Chicago, 1893–1923. More important for interpretation of his work are the facts that he has carefully studied modern English and Continental literatures, and that he is deeply interested in philosophy and the social sciences.

Robert Herrick—*Continued*

Novels
  The Gospel of Freedom. 1898.
  The Web of Life. 1900.
  The Real World. 1901.
* The Common Lot. 1904.
  The Memoirs of an American Citizen. 1905.
* Together. 1908.
  A Life for a Life. 1910.
  The Healer. 1911.
  One Woman's Life. 1913.
  His Great Adventure. 1913.
  Clark's Field. 1914.
  Homely Lilla. 1923.
  Waste. 1924.
  Chimes. 1926.

Short Stories and Tales
  The Man Who Wins. 1895.
  Literary Love Letters. 1896.
  Love's Dilemmas. 1898.
  Their Child. 1903.
* The Master of the Inn. 1908.
  The Conscript Mother. 1916.
  Wanderings. 1925.

Study
  The World Decision. 1916.

STUDIES AND REVIEWS

Baldwin.
Björkman, E. Voices of To-
  morrow. 1913.
Cooper.
Hansen.
Hazard, L. L. The Frontier in
  American Literature. 1927.
Mandel, L. Robert Herrick.
  1927.
Van Doren. (A. B. L.)
——. (C. A. N.)

Bookm., 20 ('04): 192, 220; 28
  ('08): 350; 38 ('13): 274. (Por-
  traits.)
Bost. Trans., Apr. 26, 1924: 1;
  May 5, 1925: 6.
Cur. Op., 54 ('13): 317 (portrait).
Dial, 56 ('14): 5; 74 ('23): 513.
Forum, 72 ('24): 429.
Lit. Rev., Feb. 10, 1923: 447; Apr.
  19, 1924: 687.
Lond. Times, Oct. 2, 1924: 610.

Robert Herrick—*Continued*

Nation, 113 ('21): 230; 118 ('24): 588; 116 ('23)· 190; 121 ('25): 388.

N. Repub., 38 ('24): 235.

N. Y. Times, Mar. 30, 1924: 9; Aug. 30, 1925: 22; May 2, 1926: 7.

N. Y. Herald-Tribune, June 6, 1926: 3.

No. Am., 189 ('09): 812 (Howells).

Outlook, 78 ('04): 862, 864 (portrait).

Sat. Rev. of Lit., 2 ('25): 135.

Du Bose Heyward—writer, lecturer.

Born at Charleston, South Carolina, 1885. Educated in the public schools. Organized the Poetry Society of South Carolina.

BIBLIOGRAPHY

Poems
Year Book of the Poetry Society of South Carolina. 1921– . (Joint editor with John Bennett and Hervey Allen.)
Carolina Chansons. 1922. (With Hervey Allen.)
Skylines and Horizons. 1924.

Novels
Porgy. 1925. (Dramatized by the author and Dorothy Hartzell Heyward, 1927.)
Angel. 1926.
Mamba's Daughters. 1928.

Plays
Porgy. 1927. (See *Novels*.)

STUDIES AND REVIEWS

Bost. Trans., Nov. 14, 1925: 6.

Double-Dealer, 5 ('23): 178; 7 ('24): 79.

Lit. Rev., Jan. 13, 1922: 379 (Canby); Oct. 3, 1925: 3; Oct. 9, 1926: 4.

N. Y. Herald-Tribune, Oct. 31, 1926: 18 (F. Newman).

N. Y. Times, Mar. 30, 1924: 7; Oct. 10, 1926: 11.

No. Am., 222 ('25): 360.

Poetry, 22 ('23): 89; 25 ('24): 164.

Sat. Rev. of Lit., 4 ('27): 251.

Sidney (Coe) Howard—dramatist.

Born at Oakland, California, 1891. A. B., University of California, 1915. Dramatic work under George Pierce Baker in "47 Workshop," Harvard, 1915–16; member editorial staff *Life*, 1919; literary editor *Life*, 1922; special investigator and feature-writer *Hearst's International Magazine*, 1923. Service with American Ambulance before 1917, and with Aviation thereafter. Married Claire Eames (actress), 1922. Was awarded Pulitzer prize in 1925 for *They Knew What They Wanted*. Has adapted many foreign plays.

BIBLIOGRAPHY

Plays
> Swords. 1921.
> Lexington. 1924.
> They Knew What They Wanted. 1925.
> Ned McCobb's Daughter. 1926.
> Lucky Sam McCarver. 1926.
> The Silver Cord. 1927.

Tales
> Three Flights Up. 1924.

Sociological Studies
> The Labor Spy. 1924. (With Robert Dunn.)
> Professional Patriots. 1927. (Joint editor with Norman Hapgood.)

For list of adaptations, see Quinn, History of American Drama. II, 303–04.

STUDIES AND REVIEWS

Lit. Rev., Mar. 5, 1927: 11. N. Y. World, Apr. 3, 1927: 13m.
N. Repub., 49 ('27): 328. Sat. Rev., 144 ('27): 394.
N. Y. Times, Nov. 2, 1924: 8. Yale Rev., n. s. 17 ('27): 175.

Rupert Hughes—man of letters.

Born at Lancaster, Missouri, 1872. A. B., Adelbert College, 1892; A. M., 1894; A. M., Yale, 1899. Editorial work with various magazines in London and New York. Author of

Rupert Hughes—*Continued*

plays, of which the most popular was *Excuse Me,* and of vaudeville songs and sketches. Director of several motion pictures.
For complete bibliography, see Who's Who in America.

BIBLIOGRAPHY

What Will People Say? 1914.
The Cup of Fury. 1919.
Souls for Sale. 1922.
George Washington. 1926. (Biography.)

James Gibbons Huneker—critic.

Born at Philadelphia, 1860. Graduate of Roth's Military
Academy, Philadelphia, 1873. Studied law five years at the
Law Academy, Philadelphia. Studied piano in Paris and
was for ten years associated with Rafael Joseffy as teacher
of piano at the National Conservatory, New York. Musical
and dramatic critic of the *New York Recorder,* 1891–95; of
the *Morning Advertiser,* 1895–97; also musical, dramatic, and
art critic of the *New York Sun.* Died in 1921.

For an understanding of Mr. Huneker's criticism, it is
well to begin with his autobiography, *Steeplejack.*

BIBLIOGRAPHY

Short Stories
Painted Veils. 1920. (Priv. ptd.)

Critical Essays and Sketches
Mezzotints in Modern Music. 1899.
Melomaniacs. 1902.
Overtones. 1904.
Iconoclasts. 1905.
Visionaries. 1905.
Egoists. 1909.
Promenades of an Impressionist. 1910.
The Pathos of Distance. 1913.
Old Fogy, His Musical Opinions and Grotesques. 1913. (Pub.
anonymously.)
Ivory Apes and Peacocks. 1915.
New Cosmopolis. 1915.

James Gibbons Huneker—*Continued*

Unicorns. 1917.
Bedouins. 1920.
Variations. 1921.

Autobiography
Steeplejack. 1920.
Letters. 1922. (Ed. by Josephine Huneker.)
Intimate Letters. 1924. (Ed. by Josephine Huneker. Priv. ptd.)

Biography and Criticism
Chopin. 1900.
Franz Liszt. 1911.

*See also the bibliography by Joseph Lawren in Benjamin De Casseres's
pamphlet entitled* James Gibbons Huneker. New York. 1925.

STUDIES AND REVIEWS

Ath., Jan. 21, 1921: 69.
Bookm., 11 ('00): 501; 21 ('05):
  79, 564; 29 ('09): 236; 31 ('10):
  241; 37 ('13): 598; 41 ('15): 246;
  53 ('21): 124. (Portraits.)
Cent., 102 ('21): 191 (Mencken).
Cur. Lit., 39 ('05): 75; 42 ('07):
  167; 47 ('09): 57. (Portraits.)
Forum, 41 ('09): 600.

Liv. Age, 309 ('21): 426.
Lond. Times, Feb. 3, 1921: 73.
N. Repub., 25 ('21): 357.
No. Am., 213 ('21): 556.
Outlook, 126 ('20): 469 (portrait);
  127 ('21): 286.
Sat. Rev., 97 ('04): 551.
Spec., 115 ('15): 879.

Fannie Hurst—short story writer, novelist.

Mrs. Jacques S. Danielson. Born at St. Louis, 1889. A.
B., Washington University, 1909; graduate work at Columbia. Finds her material in lives of women in industry and
the professions. Visited Russia, 1924.

For complete bibliography, see Who's Who in America.

BIBLIOGRAPHY

Humoresque. 1918.
Stardust. 1919.
Lummox. 1923.
Mannequin. 1926.
A President is Born. 1927.

Wallace (Admah) Irwin—humorist, novelist.

Born at Oneida, New York, 1876. Stanford University, 1896–99. Special writer on *San Francisco Examiner*, 1900. Editor of *Overland Monthly Magazine*, 1902. Burlesque writer for the Republic Theatre, San Francisco, 1903. Writer of topical verse, *New York Globe*, 1904–05. On staff of *Collier's Weekly*, 1906–07. Most characteristic material is life in California and the Japanese there.

For complete bibliography, see Who's Who in America.

BIBLIOGRAPHY

Love Sonnets of a Hoodlum. 1902.
Letters of a Japanese Schoolboy. 1909.
Suffering Husbands. 1920.
Lew Tyler's Wives. 1923.
The Golden Bed. 1924.

STUDIES AND REVIEWS

Baldwin.

Bost. Trans., Aug. 27, 1924: 6;
Mar. 10, 1926: 4.
Lit. Digest, I. B. R. Sept., 1924:
720.

Lit. Rev., Sept. 15, 1923: 45.
N. Y. Times, Jan. 16, 1921: 7;
Sept. 16, 1923: 10; Oct. 28, 1923:
3; Aug. 17, 1924: 1; Feb. 14,
1926: 9; Sept. 2, 1928: 7.
Sat. Rev. of Lit., 2 ('26): 587.

(John) Robinson Jeffers—poet.

Born at Pittsburgh, Pennsylvania, 1887. A. B., Occidental College, 1905; graduate work at Zürich and the University of Southern California.

SUGGESTIONS FOR READING

1. Mr. Jeffers has been hailed as the most powerful of the recent poets. Study the range of his subject matter and its limitations.

2. The work of this poet has a very individual technique. Study in particular his handling of metre and the nature of his vocabulary.

(John) Robinson Jeffers—*Continued*

Bibliography

Poems
Flagons and Apples. 1912.
Californians. 1916.
Tamar. 1924.
Roan Stallion, Tamar. 1925.
The Women at Point Sur. 1927.
Cawdor. 1928.

Studies and Reviews

Sterling, George. Robinson Jeffers. 1926.
Nation, 120 ('25): 268; 121 ('25): 599; 125 ('27): 88.

N. Repub., 43 ('25): 23; 51 ('27): 341.
N. Y. Times, Jan. 3, 1926: 14; Sept. 11, 1927: 5.
Sat. Rev. of Lit., 2 ('26): 492.

Orrick Johns—poet.

Born at St. Louis, Missouri, 1887. Trained as an advertising copy-writer. Won the prize of the *Lyric Year* in 1912, with his *Second Avenue*.

Bibliography

Poems
Asphalt. 1917.
Black Branches. 1920.
Wild Plum. 1926.

Novels
Blindfold. 1923.

Studies and Reviews

Untermeyer.

Bookm., 46 ('18): 578.
Dial, 62 ('17): 476.
Lit. Rev., Sept. 11, 1926: 5.

N. Y. Herald-Tribune, Nov. 7, 1926: 26.
N. Y. Times, July 15, 1923: 21.
Poetry, 11 ('17): 44; 16 ('20): 162; 29 ('27): 221.

James Weldon Johnson—editor, author.

Born at Jacksonville, Florida, 1871. A. B., Atlanta University, 1894; A. M., 1904; graduate work at Columbia, three years; Litt. D., Talladega College, Alabama, 1917. Principal of colored high school, Jacksonville, several years; admitted to Florida bar, 1897; practised in Jacksonville; went to New York City in 1901 to collaborate with brother in writing for light-opera stage. United States consul at Venezuela and Nicaragua. Now secretary of the National Association for Advancement of Colored People.

BIBLIOGRAPHY

Poems

Fifty Years. 1917.
American Negro Poetry. 1922. (Editor.)
The Book of American Negro Spirituals. 1925. (Editor with J. Rosamond Johnson and Lawrence Brown.)
The Second Book of Negro Spirituals. 1926. (Editor with J. Rosamond Johnson.)
God's Trombones. 1927.

Autobiography

The Autobiography of an Ex-Colored Man. 1912.

STUDIES AND REVIEWS

N. Repub., 53 ('28): 303.   Poetry, 30 ('27): 291.
N. Y. Times, June 19, 1927: 11;
  Oct. 16, 1927: 14.

Owen (McMahon) Johnson—novelist, short story writer.

Born at New York City, 1878. Best known for studies in college life and in the psychology of the young woman (*The Salamander*, 1913).

For complete bibliography, see Who's Who in America.

BIBLIOGRAPHY

The Eternal Boy. 1909.
The Humming Bird. 1910.

Owen (McMahon) Johnson—*Continued*

The Varmint. 1910.
Stover at Yale. 1911.
The Salamander. 1913.
Skippy Bedelle. 1923.

Mary Johnston—novelist.

Born at Buchanan, Virginia, 1870.   Uses historical material connected with colonial Virginia.
For complete bibliography, see Who's Who in America.

BIBLIOGRAPHY

To Have and To Hold. 1900.
Lewis Rand. 1908.
The Long Roll. 1911.
Cease Firing. 1912.
Croaton. 1923.

STUDIES AND REVIEWS

Farrar.
Overton. (O. W. N.)

Bost. Trans., Nov. 15, 1922: 7;
Oct. 31, 1923: 4; Nov. 15, 1924:
4; Apr. 24, 1926: 4.
Lit. Digest, I. B. R. Jan., 1923:
57; Dec., 1924: 18.
Lit. Rev., Mar. 18, 1922: 503
(W. R. Benét); Dec. 30, 1922:
347; Oct. 27, 1923: 183.

Lond. Times, June 15, 1922: 395.
N. Y. Herald-Tribune, May 2,
1926: 4.
N. Y. Times, Mar. 19, 1922: 24;
Nov. 12, 1922: 8; Oct. 28, 1923:
8; Nov. 16, 1924: 8; May 2,
1926: 11.
Sat. Rev. of Lit., 2 ('26): 786.

George S. Kaufman—playwright.

Born at Pittsburgh, Pennsylvania, 1889.   Educated in the public schools.   Conducted humorous columns in *Washington Times*, 1912-13, *N. Y. Evening Mail*, 1914-15.   On dramatic staff of *New York Herald-Tribune* and *New York Times*.   Frequent collaboration with Marc Connelly (q. v.).

George S. Kaufman—*Continued*

Suggestions for Reading

1. Make a classification of the objects of Kaufman and Connelly's satire, and consider the permanency of its interest.

2. Make a study of the different satirical methods used by these playwrights: parody, caricature, the dream, and conscious banality.

Bibliography

Plays

Dulcy. 1921. (With Marc Connelly.)

To the Ladies. 1923. (With Marc Connelly.)

Beggar on Horseback. 1924. (With Marc Connelly. Suggested by Hans Sonnenstoesser's Hohlenfahrt, by Paul Apel.)

Minick. (*From* Old Man Minick, by Edna Ferber. 1924. A dramatization by Ferber and Kaufman of the short story.)

Merton of the Movies. 1925. (With Marc Connelly. A dramatization of the novel by Harry Leon Wilson.)

The Butter and Egg Man. 1925.

If Men Played Cards as Women Do. 1926.

The Royal Family. 1928. (With Edna Ferber.)

George (Edward) Kelly—dramatist.

Born at Philadelphia, Pennsylvania, 1887. Début in juvenile rôles, New York, 1912. Appeared in one-act vaudeville sketches of own authorship for five years. Produced a succession of one-act plays of which "Finders-Keepers" was the first. In 1926 his *Craig's Wife* was awarded the Pulitzer prize for drama.

Bibliography

Plays

Finders-Keepers. 1923.

The Torch-Bearers. 1923.

The Show-Off. 1924. (Novelized by William A. Wolff. 1924.)

The Flattering Word. 1925.

Craig's Wife. 1926.

Daisy Mayme. 1927.

Behold, the Bridegroom. 1928.

George (Edward) Kelly—*Continued*

STUDIES AND REVIEWS

Dickinson. (P. N. A. T.)   N. Y. Times, Apr. 3, 1927: 13m.
                                    Sat. Rev. of Lit., 3 ('27): 940.

Harry (Hibbard) Kemp—poet.

Born at Youngstown, Ohio, 1883. Studied at the University of Kansas but took no degree. Made trip around the world, starting with twenty-five cents. Special studies of night-life in London and New York. Went all over North America as a tramp. Manager and founder of the Poets' Theatre.

BIBLIOGRAPHY

Poems
    The Thresher's Wife. 1914.
    The Cry of Youth. 1914.
    The Passing God. 1919.
    Chanteys and Ballads. 1920.
    The Sea and the Dunes. 1926.
    The Bronze Treasury. 1927. (Editor.)

Plays
    Judas. 1913.
    The Prodigal Son. 1919.
    The Love-Rogue, by Gabriel Tellez. 1923. (Translator and Adapter.)
    Boccaccio's Untold Tale. 1924.

Autobiographical Narratives
    Tramping on Life. 1922.
    More Miles. 1926.

STUDIES AND REVIEWS

Lit. Digest, I. B. R. Jan. 23, 1923: 56.
Lit. Rev., Dec. 16, 1922: 321 (L. Lewisohn).
Nation, 115 ('22): 693.
N. Y. Times, Dec. 31, 1922: 2; Apr. 27, 1924: 12; Dec. 26, 1926: 13.
Springfield Repub., Nov. 5, 1922: 7a.

Charles Rann Kennedy—dramatist.

Born at Derby, England, 1871. Largely self-educated.
Office-boy and clerk, thirteen to sixteen; lecturer and writer
to twenty-six; actor, press-agent, and miscellaneous writer
and theatrical business-manager to thirty-four. His play
The Servant in the House established his reputation. Married Edith Wynne Matthison in 1898, and acts and directs
plays with her.

BIBLIOGRAPHY

Plays
   The Servant in the House. 1908.
   The Winterfeast. 1908.
   The Terrible Meek. 1912.
   The Necessary Evil. 1913.
   The Idol-Breaker. 1914.
   The Rib of the Man. 1917.
   The Army with Banners. 1919.
   A Repertory of Plays for a Company of Three Players. 1927. (The
      Chastening, The Admiral, The Salutation.)

STUDIES AND REVIEWS

Boynton. (S. C. A.)   Atlan., 103 ('09): 73.
Dickinson. (P. N. A. T.)   Dial, 45 ('08): 36.
                               Ind., 72 ('12): 725.
Arena, 40 ('08): 18, 20 (portrait).

(Alfred) Joyce Kilmer—poet, essayist.

Born at New Brunswick, New Jersey, 1886. Of mixed
ancestry, Irish, German, English, Scotch. A. B., Rutgers,
1904; Columbia, 1906. Taught a short time, then held various editorial positions on the *Churchman*, the *Literary
Digest*, *Current Literature*, the *New York Times Sunday
Magazine*. In 1916 he was called to the faculty of the School
of Journalism, New York University, succeeding Arthur
Guiterman. Enlisted as a private in the World War and
was killed in action, 1918. His works were edited, with a
memoir, by R. C. Holliday, in 1918.

(Alfred) Joyce Kilmer—*Continued*

BIBLIOGRAPHY

Poems
Summer of Love. 1911.
Trees. 1914.
Main Street. 1917.
Dreams and Images. 1917. (Editor.)

Essays and Sketches
The Circus. 1916. (Enl. ed., 1921.)
Literature in the Making. 1917. (Compiler.)

STUDIES AND REVIEWS

Aiken.
Holliday, R. C. Joyce Kilmer. 1918.
Kilmer, Annie Kilburn. Memories of my Son, Sergeant Joyce Kilmer. 1920.

Ath., 1919, 2: 1220.
Bookm., 48 ('18): 133 (portrait).
Bookm. (Lond.), 56 ('19): 122; 57 ('19): 118.

Bost. Trans., May 14, 1921: 6.
Cath. World, 100 ('14): 301; 108 ('18): 224; 113 ('21): 681.
Lit. Digest, Sept. 7: 32 (portrait), 42.
Lit. Rev., July 9, 1921: 2.
Outlook, 120 ('18): 12, 16; 122 ('19): 467.
Poetry, 11 ('18): 281; 13 ('18): 31, 149.

Alfred Kreymborg—poet.

Born at New York City, 1883, of Danish ancestry. Educated at the Morris High School. A chess-prodigy at the age of ten, and supported himself from seventeen to twenty-five by teaching chess and playing matches. Had several years of experience as bookkeeper.

In 1914, founded and edited the *Glebe*, which issued the first anthology of free verse. In 1916, 1917, 1919, published *Others*—three anthologies of radical poets. In 1921, went to Rome to edit, in association with Harold Loeb, an international magazine of the arts called *Broom* (cf. *Dial* 70 ['21]: 606), but shortly after resigned. Joint editor of *The American Caravan*, 1927 (with Van Wyck Brooks, Lewis Mumford,

Alfred Kreymborg—*Continued*
and Paul Rosenfeld); and of *The American Caravan*, 1928
(with Mumford and Rosenfeld).

BIBLIOGRAPHY

Poems
 Mushrooms. 1916.
 Others. 1916. (Editor.)
 Others. 1917. (Editor.)
 Others for 1919. 1920. (Editor.)
 Blood of Things. 1920.
 Less Lonely. 1923.
 Scarlet and Mellow. 1926.
 Funnybone Alley. 1927. (Sketches.)
 The Lost Sail. 1928.
 Manhattan Men. 1929.

Plays
 Plays for Poem-Mimes. 1918.
 Plays for Merry Andrews. 1920.
 Puppet Plays. 1923. (Rev. ed., 1926.)
 Lima Beans. 1925. (*In* Provincetown Plays, Second Series, 1917.)
 Manikin and Minikin. 1925.
 Rocking Chairs. 1925.
 There's a Moon Tonight. 1926.

Tale
 Erna Vitek. 1914.

Studies
 Love and Life. 1908.

Autobiography
 Troubadour. 1925.

STUDIES AND REVIEWS

Aiken.
Beach.
Dickinson. (P. N. A. T.)
Monroe.
Untermeyer. (A. P.)

Ath., 1919, 2: 1003 (C. Aiken).
Bookm., 61 ('25): 90.
Bost. Trans., Apr. 4, 1925: 1.
Chapbook, 1–2, May, 1920: 30.

Dial, 66 ('19): 29; 79 ('25): 72 (W. Frank).
Lit. Rev., Sept. 15, 1923: 38; June 20, 1925: 2; Apr. 10, 1926: 7.
Lond. Times, June 14, 1928: 402.
Nation, 120 ('25): 521.
N. Repub., 42 ('25): 11 (M. Van Doren).

Alfred Kreymborg—*Continued*

N. Y. Times, Nov. 18, 1923: 6; Mar. 29, 1925: 7; Mar. 21, 1926: 6.

Poetry, 9 ('16): 51; 13 ('19): 224; 24 ('24): 269; 29 ('27): 226.

Sat. Rev., 136 ('23): 17.

Sat. Rev. of Lit., 1 ('25): 741.

See also Book Review Digest, 1916, 1920.

Joseph Wood Krutch—critic.

Born at Knoxville, Tennessee, 1893. B. A., University of Tennessee, 1915; M. A., Columbia, 1916; Ph. D., 1923. Dramatic critic and associate editor of the *Nation* since 1923. Lecturer with rank of professor at Vassar since 1924.

BIBLIOGRAPHY

Studies in Literature
  Comedy and Conscience. 1924.

Biographical and Psychological Study
  Edgar Allan Poe. 1926.

Essays
  The Modern Temper. 1929.

Ring(gold Wilmer) Lardner—humorist.

Born at Niles, Michigan, 1885. Attended Armour Institute, 1901–02. Wide experience as reporter and sportswriter in Chicago and elsewhere.

BIBLIOGRAPHY

Verse
  Bib Ballads. 1915.

Sketches and Short Stories
  You Know Me Al. 1916.
  Gullible's Travels. 1917.
  Own Your Own Home. 1917.
  Treat 'Em Rough. 1918.
  My Four Weeks in France. 1918.

Ring(gold Wilmer) Lardner—*Continued*

The Real Dope. 1918.
Regular Fellows I Have Met. 1919.
The Young Immigrunts. 1920.
Symptoms of Being 35. 1921.
The Big Town. 1921.
Say It With Oil. 1923. (*Contains* Say It With Bricks, by Nina Wilcox Putnam.)
How to Write Short Stories, with Samples. 1924.
What of It? 1925.
The Love Nest. 1926.
The Story of a Wonder Man. 1927. (A parody.)
Round Up. 1929.

STUDIES AND REVIEWS

Van Doren. (M. M.)

Am. Merc., 2 ('24): 376; 8 ('26): 254.
Bookm., 59 ('24): 601.
Bost. Trans., Apr. 17, 1926: 5; Apr. 13, 1927: 6; June 27, 1927: 4.
Dial, 77 ('24): 69.
Ind., 114 ('25): 590.
Lit. Rev., May 24, 1924: 772; Apr. 10, 1926: 3 (F. Newman); Apr. 2, 1927: 6.

Nation, 122 ('26): 584.
N. Repub., 40 ('24): 25 (R. Littell); 42 ('25): 1; 50 ('27): 178.
N. Y. Times, May 25, 1924: 16; Apr. 19, 1925: 1; Apr. 4, 1926: 5; May 2, 1926: 4; Apr. 3, 1927: 5.
N. Y. World, Apr. 3, 1927: 12m.
Sat. Rev. of Lit., 2 ('26): 700 (W. R. Benét).

John Howard Lawson—dramatist.

Belongs to the left wing of the contemporary drama. Leader of the New Playwrights' Theatre, and experimenter with dramatic forms.

BIBLIOGRAPHY

Plays
Roger Bloomer. 1923.
Processional. 1925.
Loud Speaker. 1927.
International. 1928.

Stephen (Butler) Leacock—humorist.

Born in Hampshire, England, 1869. B. A., Toronto University; Ph. D., University of Chicago. Honorary higher degrees. Head of the department of economics, McGill University. Besides essays and lectures, he has written textbooks and studies in political economy.

BIBLIOGRAPHY

Plays
"Q." 1915.

Wit and Humor
Literary Lapses. 1910.
Nonsense Novels. 1911. (Parodies.)
Sunshine Sketches of a Little Town. 1912.
Behind the Beyond. 1913.
Arcadian Adventures with the Idle Rich. 1914.
Moonbeams from the Larger Lunacy. 1915.
Further Foolishness. 1916. (Some parodies.)
Frenzied Fiction. 1918.
The Hohenzollerns in America. 1919.
Winsome Winnie. 1920. (Parodies.)
My Discovery of England. 1922.
Over the Footlights. 1923. (Parodies.)
College Days. 1923.
The Garden of Folly. 1924.
Winnowed Wisdom. 1926.
Short Circuits. 1928.

Literary Essays
Essays and Literary Studies. 1916.

Economic and Sociological Studies
Elements of Political Science. 1906. (Rev. ed., 1913. Enl. ed., 1921.)
The Unsolved Riddle of Social Justice. 1920.

STUDIES AND REVIEWS

Hind. (M. A. I.)
MacArthur, P. Stephen Leacock.
1923.

Bookm. (Lond.), 51 ('16): 39.
Bost. Trans., Aug. 16, 1922: 8;
July 28, 1923: 3; Dec. 15, 1923:

3; Aug. 23, 1924: 3; July 31,
1926: 2.
Canad. Mag., 61 ('23): 514.
Ind., 111 ('23): 94.
Lit. Dig. I. B. R., Dec., 1924: 39.
Lit. Rev., Oct. 6, 1923: 107;
July 3, 1926: 3.

Stephen (Butler) Leacock—*Continued*

Lond. Times, June 22, 1922: 409;
June 28, 1923: 438; Aug. 7, 1924:
486.
Nation, 115 ('22): 171.
Nation and Ath., 31 ('22): 537.
N. State., 21 ('23): 528.
N. Y. Times, June 18, 1922: 15;
July 29, 1923: 2; Aug. 10, 1924:
5; July 4, 1926: 16.

Sat. Rev., 133 ('22): 658.
Sat. Rev. of Lit., 1 ('24): 30; 2
('26): 884.
Spec., 129 ('22): 146.

See also Book Review Digest,
1914–17, 1919, 1920.

William Ellery Leonard—poet.

Born at Plainfield, New Jersey, 1876. A. B., Boston
University, 1898; A. M., Harvard, 1899; Ph. D., Columbia,
1904. A member of the English Department of the University of Wisconsin, since 1909.

For complete bibliography, see Who's Who in America.

BIBLIOGRAPHY

Poems
Sonnets and Poems.   1906.
The Vaunt of Man.   1912.
Poems, 1914–16.   1916.
The Lynching Bee.   1920.
Two Lives.   1925.

Translations
Fragments of Empedocles.   1908.
Lucretius.   1916.
Beowulf.   1923.

Autobiography
The Locomotive God.   1927.

STUDIES AND REVIEWS

Nation, 120 ('25): 695; 121 ('25):
546; 125 ('27): 428.
Lit. Rev., Nov. 5, 1927: 12.

N. Y. Herald-Tribune, Mar. 15,
1925: 4.
N. Y. Times, Nov. 29, 1925: 8;
Oct. 16, 1927: 5.

Sinclair Lewis—novelist.

Born at Sauk Center, Minnesota, 1885. Son of a physician. A. B., Yale, 1907. During the next ten years was a newspaper man in Connecticut, Iowa, and California, a magazine editor in Washington, D. C., and editor for New York book publishers. In more recent years, traveled extensively in the United States, living in the most diverse places, and motoring from end to end of twenty-six states. While supporting himself by short stories and experimental novels, he laid the foundation for his unusually successful *Main Street*. His first book, *Our Mr. Wrenn*, is said to contain a good deal of autobiography. *Arrowsmith* was awarded the Pulitzer novel prize in 1926, but Mr. Lewis declined it. (See *World Almanac*, 1927.)

SUGGESTIONS FOR READING

1. Do you recognize Gopher Prairie as a type? Is Mr. Lewis's picture photography, caricature, or the kind of portraiture that is art? Or to what degree do you find all these elements?

2. Is the main interest of the book in the story? in the characterization? in the satire? or in an element of propaganda?

3. What is to be said of the constructive theory of living proposed by the heroine? Is it better or worse than the standard that prevailed before she went to Gopher Prairie to live?

4. Explain the success of the book. What, if any, elements of permanent value do you find? What conspicuous defects?

5. Trace the development of Mr. Lewis from *Main Street* through *Elmer Gantry*. Has he gained or lost in skill and effectiveness?

6. Study minutely the realism of the first hundred pages of *Babbitt*.

7. Is Mr. Lewis more successful with caricature or with characterization?

Sinclair Lewis—*Continued*

BIBLIOGRAPHY

Novels

   Our Mr. Wrenn. 1914.
   The Trail of the Hawk. 1915.
   The Job. 1917.
   The Innocents. 1917.
   Free Air. 1919.
 * Main Street. 1920.
 * Babbitt. 1922.
   Arrowsmith. 1925.
   Mantrap. 1926.
   Elmer Gantry. 1927.
   Dodsworth. 1929.

Satirical Sketches

   The Man Who Knew Coolidge. 1928.

Criticism

   John Dos Passos' Manhattan Transfer. 1926.

STUDIES AND REVIEWS

Baldwin.
Boyd. (P. R. I.)
Boynton. (M. C. A.)
Farrar.
Harrison, O. Sinclair Lewis. 1927.
Hind. (M. A. I.)
Karsner.
Michaud.
Parrington, V. L. Sinclair Lewis. 1927.
Sherman, S. P. The Significance of Sinclair Lewis. 1922.
Squire.
Van Doren. (A. B. L.)
——. (C. A. N.)
Whipple.

Am. M., 91 ('21): 16 (portrait).
Am. Merc., 4 ('25): 507; 10 ('27): 506.
Atlan., 127 ('21): supp. I: 8.
Bookm., 39 ('14): 248 (portrait only); 54 ('21): 9.

Bookm. (Lond.), 65 ('24): 195.
Bost. Trans., Sept. 16, 1922: 2; Mar. 7, 1925: 5; June 5, 1926: 4.
Commonweal, 1 ('25): 427.
Dial, 78 ('25): 515.
Freeman, 2 ('20): 237; 6 ('22): 142.
Ind., 114 ('25): 302.
Lit. Digest, I. B. R. Apr., 1925: 306; June, 1926: 485.
Lit. Rev., Sept. 16, 1922: 21, 23 (C. Van Doren); Apr. 7, 1928: 13.
Liv. Age, 325 ('25): 429; 329 ('27): 381.
Lond. Merc., 13 ('26): 273.
Lond. Times, Mar. 5, 1925: 153.
Nation, 120 ('25): 359; 122 ('26): 672; 124 ('27): 291.
Nation and Ath., 32 ('22): 121.
N. Repub., 10 ('17): 234; 25 ('20): 20; 32 ('22): 152; 42 ('25): 3; 54 ('28): 302.

Sinclair Lewis—*Continued*

N. State., 20 ('22): 78 (R. West);
24 ('25): 629; 27 ('26): 418.
N. Y. Herald-Tribune, July 4,
1926: 11; Mar. 13, 1927: 1.
N. Y. Times, Sept. 24, 1922: 1 (M.
Sinclair); Mar. 8, 1925: 1;
Apr. 8, 1928: 1.
19th Cent., 101 ('27): 739.
No. Am., 216 ('22): 716.

Sat. Rev., 132 ('21): 230; 139
('25): 389.
Sat. Rev. of Lit., 1 ('25): 575
(Canby); 3 ('27): 637.
Spec., 129 ('22): 928; 134 ('25):
372.

See also Book Review Digest, 1920.

Ludwig Lewisohn—critic, novelist.

Born at Berlin, Germany, 1882. Brought to America, 1890. A. B., and A. M., College of Charleston, 1901 (Litt. D., 1914); A. M., Columbia, 1903. Editorial work and writing for magazines, 1904–10. College instructor and professor, 1910–19. Dramatic editor of the *Nation*, 1919–20, associate editor, 1920–24, now contributing editor. Traveled in Europe and Near East, 1924–25, studying the Jewish question. Editor and chief translator of the dramas of Gerhart Hauptmann.

BIBLIOGRAPHY

Dramatic Poem
A Night in Alexandria. 1910.

Novels
The Broken Snare. 1908.
Don Juan. 1923.
Roman Summer. 1927.
The Case of Mr. Crump. Paris, 1927.
The Island Within. 1928.

Critical Essays and Studies
The Modern Drama. 1915.
The Spirit of Modern German Literature. 1916.
The Poets of Modern France. 1918.
A Modern Book of Criticism. 1919. (Editor.)
Great Modern German Stories. 1919. (Editor.)
The Drama and the Stage. 1922.
The Creative Life. 1924.
Cities and Men. 1927.

Ludwig Lewisohn—*Continued*

Sociological Study
  Israel. 1925.

Biography
  Up Stream. 1922.

STUDIES AND REVIEWS

Beach.

Am. Merc., 10 ('27): 379.
Bookm., 48 ('19): 558.
Bost. Trans., May 14, 1924: 4.
Cent., 113 ('27): 766.
Lit. Digest, I. B. R. Dec., 1923:
  42; Sept., 1924: 709 (R. Le
  Gallienne).
Lit. Rev., Nov. 3, 1923: 203;
  Aug. 16, 1924: 964; May 21,
  1927: 5.

Nation, 111 ('20): 219; 114 ('22):
  434, 500; 117 ('23): 649; 122
  ('26): 420; 124 ('27): 149, 646;
  126 ('28): 452.
N. Repub., 45 ('26): 301; 54 ('28):
  398.
N. Y. Herald-Tribune, Mar. 25,
  1928: 3.
N. Y. Times, May 4, 1924: 14;
  Mar. 11, 1928: 7.
Sat. Rev. of Lit., 2 ('26): 462; 4
  ('28): 841.

See also Book Review Digest,
  1915, 1920.

Joseph C(rosby) Lincoln—novelist.
  Born at Brewster, Massachusetts, 1870. Writes of New
England types, especially sailors.
  For complete bibliography, see Who's Who in America.

BIBLIOGRAPHY

Cap'n Eri. 1904.
Mr. Pratt. 1906.
Our Village. 1909.
Shavings. 1918.
Rugged Water. 1924.
The Aristocratic Miss Brewster. 1927.

(**Nicholas**) **Vachel Lindsay**—poet.

Born at Springfield, Illinois, 1879. Educated in the public schools. Studied at Hiram College, Ohio, 1897–1900; at the Art Institute, Chicago, 1900–03, and at the New York School of Art, 1904–05. Y. M. C. A. lecturer, 1905–09. Lecturer for the Anti-Saloon League throughout central Illinois, 1909–10. Has made long pilgrimages on foot (cf. *A Handy Guide for Beggars*). In the summer of 1912 he walked from Illinois to New Mexico, distributing his poems and speaking in behalf of "The Gospel of Beauty." Has given poem recitals in both America and England.

SUGGESTIONS FOR READING

1. Read for background *A Handy Guide for Beggars* and *Adventures while Preaching the Gospel of Beauty*.

2. An important clue to Mr. Lindsay's work is suggested in his own note on reading his poems. Referring to the Greek lyrics as the type which survives in American vaudeville, where every line may be two-thirds spoken and one-third sung, he adds: "I respectfully submit these poems as experiments in which I endeavor to carry this vaudeville form back towards the old Greek presentation of the half-chanted lyric. In this case the one-third of music must be added by the instinct of the reader. . . . Big general contrasts between the main sections should be the rule of the first attempts at improvising. It is the hope of the writer that after two or three readings each line will suggest its own separate touch of melody to the reader who has become accustomed to the cadences. Let him read what he likes read, and sing what he likes sung."

In carrying out this suggestion, note that Mr. Lindsay often prints aids to expression by means of italics, capitals, spaces, and even side-notes and other notes on expression.

3. What different kinds of material appeal especially to Mr. Lindsay's imagination? How do you explain his choice and his limitations?

4. How does the missionary spirit that is so strong in him

(**Nicholas**) **Vachel Lindsay**—*Continued*

affect his poetry? Is his poetry more valuable for its singing element or for its ethical appeal? Do you discover any special originality?

5. How does his use of local material compare with that of Masters? of Frost? of Sandburg?

6. Study his rhythmic sense in different poems, the verse forms that he uses, the tendencies in rhyme, the use of refrain, of onomatopœia, of catalogues, etc.

7. Mr. Lindsay's drawings are worth study for comparison with his poems.

8. Consider Mr. Lindsay as the "poet of democracy." What is he likely to do for the people? for poetry?

BIBLIOGRAPHY

Poems

General William Booth Enters into Heaven. 1913.
The Congo. 1914.
The Chinese Nightingale. 1917.
The Daniel Jazz. 1920.
The Golden Whales of California. 1920.
Collected Poems. 1923. (Rev. ed., 1925.)
Going-to-the-Sun. 1923.
Going-to-the-Stars. 1926.
The Candle in the Cabin. 1926.
Johnny Appleseed. 1928.

Essays, Sketches, and Studies

Adventures While Preaching the Gospel of Beauty. 1914. (Autobiographical.)
The Art of the Moving Picture. 1915. (Rev. ed., 1922.)
A Handy Guide for Beggars. 1916. (Autobiographical.)
The Golden Book of Springfield. 1920.
The Litany of Washington Street. 1929.

For privately printed poems and pamphlets, see The Publishers' Weekly, Sept. 29, 1923.

STUDIES AND REVIEWS

Aiken.
Boynton. (S. C. A.)
Cook.
Davison, Edward. Some Modern Poets. 1928.
Graham, S. Tramping with a Poet in the Rockies. 1922.
Hackett.
Maynard.
Monroe.

(Nicholas) Vachel Lindsay—*Continued*

Squire.
Untermeyer. (A. P.)
Van Doren. (A. B. L.)
——. (M. M.)
Weirick.
Whipple.
Wilkinson. (P.)
Williams-Ellis.
Wood.

Am. M., 74 ('12): 422 (portrait).
Ath., 1919, 2: 1334.
Bookm., 46 ('18): 575; 47 ('18):
    125; 53 ('21): 525 (Morley).
Bookm. (Lond.), 57 ('20): 178.
Bost. Trans., Mar. 10, 1923: 4.
Cent., 102 ('21): 638.
Chapbook, 1–2, May, 1920: 19.
Cur. Lit., 50 ('11): 320.
Cur. Op., 69 ('20): 371 (portrait).
Dial, 57 ('14): 281; 70 ('21): 208;
    75 ('23): 498.

Lit. Digest, I. B. R. Aug., 1926:
    518.
Lit. Rev., July 3, 1926: 4.
Liv. Age, 307 ('20): 671.
Lond. Merc., 2 ('20): 645; 3 ('20):
    112.
Lond. Times, Feb. 24, 1921: 118;
    Sept. 9, 1926: 593.
N. Repub., 9 ('16): supp. 6
    (Hackett); 21 ('20): 321; 25
    ('21): 234 (P. Colum); 35 ('23):
    297.
N. Y. Times, July 29, 1923: 20;
    June 27, 1926: 7.
Outlook, 134 ('23): 432.
Poetry, 3 ('14): 182; 5 ('15): 296;
    11 ('18): 214; 16 ('20): 101; 17
    ('21): 262; 24 ('24): 90 (H.
    Monroe); 29 ('27): 217.
Spec., 125 ('20): 372, 604; 126
    ('21): 645.

Jack London—novelist.

Born at San Francisco, 1876. Studied at the University of California, but left college to go to the Klondike. In 1892 shipped before the mast. Went to Japan; hunted seal in Behring Sea. Tramped far and wide in the United States and Canada in 1894, for social and economic study. War-correspondent in the Russian-Japanese War. Traveled extensively. Socialist. Died in 1916.

His work is very uneven; but the following books are regarded as among his best: *The Call of the Wild* (1903), *The Sea-Wolf* (1904), *Martin Eden* (1909), and *John Barley-corn* (1913)—both autobiographical.

For an account of his life and work, see *The Book of Jack London*, by Charmian London, 1921 (cf. Freeman, 4 ['22]:

Jack London—*Continued*

407). For reviews, cf. the Book Review Digest, especially 1905–07, 1911, 1915.

For full bibliography, see Who's Who in America.

Robert Morss Lovett—man of letters.

Born at Boston, 1870. A. B., Harvard, 1892. Taught English at Harvard, 1892–93; at the University of Chicago, since 1893; professor since 1909. Editor of the *Dial*, 1919. On the staff of the *New Republic*, 1921– .

BIBLIOGRAPHY

Novels
  Richard Gresham. 1904.
  A Wingèd Victory. 1907.

Criticism
  Edith Wharton. 1925.

Plays
  Cowards. (*In* Drama 7 ['17]: 330.)

STUDIES AND REVIEWS

Drama, 7 ('17): 325.   N. Y. Times, June 7, 1925: 13.
Nation, 121 ('25): 361.

Amy Lowell—poet, critic.

Born at Brookline, Massachusetts, 1874. Sister of President Lowell of Harvard, and of Percival Lowell, the astronomer. Distantly related to James Russell Lowell. Educated at private schools. As a child, traveled extensively in Europe. Her visits to Egypt, Greece, and Turkey influenced her development. In 1902 she decided to become a poet, and spent eight years studying, without publishing a poem. Her first poem appeared in the *Atlantic*, 1910. She died in 1925.

She was a collector of Keats manuscripts and said that the

poet who influenced her most profoundly was Keats. She
also made a special study of Chinese poetry. Awarded
(posthumously) the Pulitzer prize for poetry in 1926.

SUGGESTIONS FOR READING

1. As Miss Lowell is the principal exponent of the theories
of imagism and free verse in this country, careful reading of
some of her critical papers leads to a better understanding
of her work. Especially valuable are her studies of Paul
Fort in her volume entitled *Six French Poets*, of H. D. and
John Gould Fletcher in her *Tendencies in Modern American
Poetry*, the prefaces to different volumes of her poems and to
the anthologies published under the title *Some Imagist Poets*
(1915, 1916), and her articles in the *Dial*, 64 ('18): 51ff.,
and in *Poetry*, 3 ('13): 213ff.

2. In judging her work, consider separately her poems in
regular metrical form and those in free verse. Decide which
method is better suited to her type of imagination.

3. To what extent does her inspiration come from cultural
sources—travel, literature, art, music?

4. Consider especially her presentation of "images." How
far do these seem to be derived from direct experience?
Test them by your own experience. What principles seem
to determine her choice of details? Which sense impressions—sight, sound, taste, smell, touch—does she most
frequently and successfully suggest? Note instances where
her figures of speech sharpen the imagery and others where
they seem to distort it. In what ways is the influence of
Keats perceptible in her work?

5. It is worth while to make special study of the historical
imagery of the poems in *Can Grande's Castle*.

6. Study separately her varieties of free verse and polyphonic prose (cf. her study of Paul Fort and the preface
to *Can Grande's Castle*). Choose several poems in which
you think the free-verse form is especially adapted to the
content and draw conclusions as to the problems of develop-

Amy Lowell—*Continued*

ment of this kind of verse or of its possible influence upon regular metrical forms.

7. In summing up Miss Lowell's achievement, consider the different phases of it that appear in her volumes taken in chronological order, noting the successive influences under which she has come. In what qualities does she stand out strikingly from other contemporary poets?

BIBLIOGRAPHY

Poems and Polyphonic Prose
A Dome of Many-Coloured Glass. 1912.
Sword Blades and Poppy Seed. 1914.
Men, Women and Ghosts. 1916.
Can Grande's Castle. 1918.
Pictures of the Floating World. 1919.
Legends. 1921.
Fir-Flower Tablets. 1921. (Translator with Florence Ayscough.)
A Critical Fable. 1922.
What's O'Clock? 1925.
East Wind. 1926.
Ballads for Sale. 1927.
Selected Poems. 1928. (Ed. by John Livingston Lowes.)

Critical Studies
Six French Poets. 1915.
Tendencies in Modern American Poetry. 1917.

Biography and Criticism
John Keats. 1925.

STUDIES AND REVIEWS

Aiken.
Boynton. (S. C. A.)
Cook.
Farrar.
Frank, Waldo. Our America. 1919.
Hind. (M. A. I.)
Hunt, R., and Snow, R. H. Amy Lowell. 1921.
Maynard.
Monroe.

Sargent, G. H. Amy Lowell. 1926.
Sergeant.
Untermeyer. (A. P.)
Wilkinson. (P.)
Williams-Ellis.
Wood, C. Amy Lowell. 1926.

Bost. Trans., May 21, 1921: 6; Feb. 14, 1925: 1.
Chapbook, 1–2, May, 1920: 8.

Amy Lowell—*Continued*

Crit., 5 ('27): 130.

Dial, 61 ('16): 528; 65 ('18): 346; 67 ('19): 331; 71 ('21): 222.

Egoist, 1 ('14): 422; 2 ('15): 81, 109; 3 ('16): 9.

Freeman, 4 ('21): 18 (P. Colum).

Ind., 87 ('16): 306 (portrait); 93 ('18): 294; 114 ('25): 273.

Lit. Digest, I. B. R. Mar., 1925: 232; Nov., 1925: 806 (R. Le Gallienne).

Lit. Rev., Apr. 16, 1921: 6; Sept. 26, 1925: 1.

Lond. Merc., 3 ('21): 441.

Lond. Times, Mar. 19, 1925: 177.

Nation, 113 ('21): 151; 120 ('25): 663; 121 ('25): 710 (Lola Ridge).

Nation and Ath., 36 ('25): 749.

N. Repub., 6 ('16): 178; 41 ('25): 344; 44 ('25): 183.

N. State., 24 ('25): 748.

N. Y. Herald-Tribune, Oct. 3, 1926: 3.

N. Y. Times, June 12, 1921: 19; Feb. 15, 1925: 1; June 14, 1925: 21; Sept. 6, 1925: 161; Sept. 5, 1926: 5.

No. Am., 207 ('18): 257; 214 ('21): 283; 222 ('25): 161; 223 ('26): 548.

Outlook, 140 ('25): 466.

Poetry, 6 ('15): 32; 9 ('17): 207; 10 ('17): 149; 13 ('18): 97; 15 ('20): 332; 25 ('24): 32 (H. Monroe); 26 ('25): 208 (H. Monroe); 27 ('25): 154; 29 ('26): 160.

Sat. Rev., 139 ('25): 267 (A. E. Coppard).

Sat. Rev. of Lit., 1 ('25): 521; 2 ('25): 169.

Spec., 125 ('20): 744.

Yale Rev., n. s. 11 ('21): 175; 15 ('26): 381 (J. Drinkwater).

Percy (Wallace) MacKaye—dramatist, poet.

Born at New York City, 1875. Son of Steele MacKaye, dramatist and manager. A. B., Harvard, 1897. Traveled in Europe, 1898–1900, studying at the University of Leipzig, 1899–1900. Taught in private school in New York, 1900–04. Joined the colony at Cornish, New Hampshire, 1904. Since then has been engaged chiefly in dramatic work. Appointed to first American fellowship in poetry and drama at Miami University, Ohio, 1920.

BIBLIOGRAPHY

Poems

Poems. 1909. (2d ed., 1915, under title The Sistine Eve.)
Ode on the Centenary of Abraham Lincoln. 1909.
A Garland to Sylvia. 1910.

Percy (Wallace) MacKaye—*Continued*

Uriel. 1912.
The Present Hour. 1914.
Poems and Plays. 1916.
Dogtown Common. 1921.
The Skippers of Nancy Gloucester. 1924.
The Gobbler of God. 1928.

Plays

The Canterbury Pilgrims. 1903. (See also under *Operas*.)
Fenris the Wolf. 1905.
Jeanne d'Arc. 1906.
Sappho and Phaon. 1907.
Mater. 1908.
* The Scarecrow. 1908.
Anti-Matrimony. 1910.
Tomorrow. 1912.
Yankee Fantasies. 1912. (New and rev. ed., 1928.)
A Thousand Years Ago. 1914.
The Immigrants. 1915.
Washington, the Man Who Made Us. 1919.
* This Fine-Pretty World. 1924.
Kinfolk of Robin Hood. 1924.
Kentucky Mountain Fantasies. 1928.

Operas

The Immigrants. 1915. (Music by Frederick S. Converse.)
The Canterbury Pilgrims. 1916. (Music by Reginald DeKoven.)
Sinbad, the Sailor. 1917. (Music by Frederick S. Converse.)
Rip Van Winkle. 1919. (Music by Reginald DeKoven.)

Masques and Pageant-Rituals

Sanctuary. 1914.
Saint Louis. 1914.
The New Citizenship. 1915.
Caliban by the Yellow Sands. 1916.
The Evergreen Tree. 1917.
The Roll Call. 1918. (Music by Clarence Dickinson.)
The Will of Song. 1919. (With Harry H. Barnhart.)
The Pilgrim and the Book. 1920.

Essays and Addresses

The Playhouse and the Play. 1909.
The Civic Theatre. 1912.
A Substitute for War. 1915.
Community Drama. 1917.

Percy (Wallace) MacKaye—*Continued*

Short Stories
  * Tall Tales of the Kentucky Mountains. 1926.
Biography
  Epoch: The Life of Steele MacKaye. 1927.

STUDIES AND REVIEWS

Dickinson. (P. N. A. T.)
Moses.
Van Doren. (A. B. L.)

Am. M., 71 ('10): 121 (portrait).
Atlan. (Bookshelf), 128 ('21): supp. V: 14.
Bookm., 47 ('18): 395; 63 ('26): 710.
Bost. Trans., Aug. 10, 1921: 6.
Cur. Op., 60 ('16): 408.
Harvard Grad. M., 17 ('09): 599 (portrait).
Lit. Digest, I. B. R. Mar., 1924: 310; Sept., 1926: 633.
Lit. Rev., May 10, 1924: 748; May 24, 1924: 771 (G. Bradford).

Nation, 118 ('24): 68 (C. Van Doren).
N. Y. Herald-Tribune, May 23, 1926: 6.
N. Y. Times, Sept. 4, 1921: 4; Jan. 6, 1924: 2; May 30, 1926: 1; June 24, 1928: 4; July 29, 1928: 2.
No. Am., 199 ('14): 290.
Sat. Rev. of Lit., 2 ('26): 913.
Survey, 35 ('16): 508.

See also Percy MacKaye, A Sketch of His Life, reprinted from The Twenty-Fifth Anniversary Report of the Class of 1897, Harvard College. 1922.

Archibald MacLeish—poet.

Born at Glencoe, Illinois, 1892. His first volume was published at Yale while he was still an undergraduate. Studied law, but in 1923 abandoned practice and went to live in Paris.

BIBLIOGRAPHY

Poems
  Songs for a Summer's Day. 1915.
  Tower of Ivory. 1917.
  Happy Marriage. 1924.
  Pot of Earth. 1925.
  Streets in the Moon. 1928.
  The Hamlet of A. MacLeish. 1928.
Plays
  Nobodaddy. 1926.

Archibald MacLeish—*Continued*

STUDIES AND REVIEWS

Bost. Trans., Apr. 26, 1924: 6;
    Feb. 12, 1927: 4.
Ind., 112 ('24): 233; 116 ('26): 639.
N. Y. Times, Apr. 7, 1918: 23;
    June 7, 1925: 5; Aug. 22, 1926: 9.

N. Y. Tribune, Apr. 27, 1924: 26;
    June 14, 1925: 5; Aug. 22, 1926:
    9.
Sat. Rev. of Lit., 3 ('27): 578.

John (Albert) Macy—critic and editor.

Born at Detroit, Michigan, 1877. A. B., Harvard, 1899.
Instructor in English, Harvard, 1900–01. Associate editor
of *Youth's Companion*, 1901–09. Literary editor of *Boston
Herald*, 1913–14; literary editor of *Nation*, 1922–23.

BIBLIOGRAPHY

Critical Essays and Studies
    The Spirit of American Literature. 1913.
    The Critical Game. 1922.
    The Story of the World's Literature. 1925.

Political Study
    Socialism in America. 1916.

Biography
    Story of My Life, by Helen Keller. 1903. (Editor.)
    Edgar Allan Poe. 1907.
    Walter James Dodd. 1918.

STUDIES AND REVIEWS

Bookm., 62 ('26): 608.
Bost. Trans., Oct. 28, 1925: 5.
Freeman, 6 ('22): 427.
Lit. Digest, I. B. R. Dec., 1925:
    34 (R. Le Gallienne).
Lit. Rev., Dec. 2, 1922: 261; Dec.
    5, 1925: 2.

Nation, 115 ('22): 669; 121 ('25):
    517.
N. Repub., 32 ('22): 313.
N. Y. Times, Oct. 25, 1925: 4.
Springfield Repub., Dec. 27, 1925:
    7a.

(Charles) **Edwin Markham**—poet.

Born at Oregon City, Oregon, 1852. Went to California, 1857. Worked at farming, blacksmithing, and herding cattle and sheep during boyhood. Educated at San José Normal School and at Christian College, Santa Rosa. Principal and superintendent of schools in California until 1899. Made famous by the publication of *The Man with the Hoe*.

BIBLIOGRAPHY

Poems
> The Man with the Hoe. 1899. (Enl. ed., 1899. With notes, 1900.)
> Lincoln. 1901.
> The Shoes of Happiness. 1915.
> Gates of Paradise. 1920.
> The Book of Poetry. 1926. (Compiler.)

Sociological Study
> Children in Bondage. 1914. (With Judge Ben. B. Lindsey and George Creel.)

History and Description
> The Real America in Romance. 1909-11. (Fictionized history.) (Editor.)
> California the Wonderful. 1914.

STUDIES AND REVIEWS

Arena, 27 ('02): 391; 35 ('06): 143, 146.
Bookm., 27 ('08): 267; 37 ('13): 300; 41 ('15): 397.
Cur. Lit., 29 ('00): 1, 16; 42 ('07): 317. (Portraits.)
Poetry, 6 ('15): 308.

Don(ald Robert Perry) Marquis—humorist, columnist, poet.

Born at Walnut, Illinois, 1878. Newspaper man, conductor of the column called "The Sun Dial" in the *New York Evening Sun*.

For complete bibliography, see Who's Who in America.

BIBLIOGRAPHY

> The Cruise of the Jasper B. 1916.
> Hermione. 1916.

Don(ald Robert Perry) Marquis—*Continued*

The Old Soak. 1921.
Poems and Portraits. 1922.
The Dark Hours. 1924. (Play.)
Out of the Sea. 1927. (Play.)

STUDIES AND REVIEWS

Dickinson. (P. N. A. T.)
Farrar.
Sherman. (C. W.)

Bost. Trans., Feb. 25, 1922: 6.
Cath. World, 120 ('25): 711.
Cur. Op., 67 ('19): 119.
Everybody's, 42, ('20): Jan.: 29 (portrait).
Freeman, 5 ('22): 430.
Lit. Digest, I. B. R. Sept., 1925: 659.
Lit. Rev., June 11, 1921: 3; Oct.
22, 1921: 99; Feb. 25, 1922: 448;
Dec. 16, 1922: 315; Feb. 28, 1925: 9.
Nation, 113 ('21): 624.
N. Y. Times, July 10, 1921: 14; Sept. 4, 1921: 22; Nov. 27, 1921: 2 (B. Matthews); June 11, 1922: 9; Jan. 25, 1925: 16; June 21, 1925: 4.
Outlook, 124 ('20): 289.
Sat. Rev. of Lit., 1 ('25): 726.
Springfield Repub., Oct. 27, 1921: 6; June 16, 1922: 10.

Helen R(eimensnyder) Martin—novelist.

Born at Lancaster, Pennsylvania, 1868. Writes about the Pennsylvania Dutch.

For complete bibliography, see Who's Who in America.

BIBLIOGRAPHY

Tillie, a Mennonite Maid. 1904. (Dramatized.)
Sabina. 1905.
Revolt of Anne Royle. 1908.
Crossways. 1910.
Barnabetta. 1914. (Dramatized as Erstwhile Susan.)
The Snob. 1924.
Challenged. 1925.
Ye That Judge. 1926.
Sylvia of the Minute. 1927.

STUDIES AND REVIEWS

Overton. (O. W. N.)

Edgar Lee Masters—poet.

Born at Garnett, Kansas, 1869, but brought up in Illinois. His schooling was desultory, but he read widely. Studied one year at Knox College; learned Greek, which influenced him strongly.

Studied law in his father's office at Lewiston, and practised there for a year. Then went to Chicago, where he became a successful attorney and also took an active part in politics.

Mr. Masters's fame was established by the *Spoon River Anthology*, which was suggested by the *Greek Anthology*, with which Mr. Masters had become familiar as early as 1909, through Mr. William Marion Reedy. The *Spoon River Anthology* first appeared in *Reedy's Mirror*, under the significant pseudonym, Webster Ford.

SUGGESTIONS FOR READING

1. Begin with the *Spoon River Anthology*. (Cf. the preface to *Toward the Gulf*.) How much does it owe to its model? to other literary sources? to the central Illinois environment in which the author grew up? What are its most conspicuous merits and defects? How do you explain each?

2. Test the sketches by your own experience of small-town life. Which seem to you truest to individual character and most universal in type?

3. Compare similar sketches of personalities by Edwin Arlington Robinson, which Mr. Masters had not read until after his book was published.

4. Consider how far Mr. Masters has achieved his avowed purpose "to analyze society, to satirize society, to tell a story, to expose the machinery of life, to present a working model of the big world"; to create beauty, and to depict "our sorrows and hopes, our religious failures, successes and visions, our poor little lives, rounded by a sleep, in language and figures emotionally tuned to bring all of us closer together in understanding and affection."

5. How do you explain the sudden popularity of the *Anthology?* What are its chances of becoming a classic?

Edgar Lee Masters —*Continued*

6. Read one of Mr. Masters's later volumes and compare it with the *Anthology* as to merits and defects.

7. Mr. Masters has always been a great reader. Trace, as far as you can, the influence of the following authors: Homer; the Bible; Poe; Keats; Shelley; Swinburne; Browning.

8. Draw parallels between his work and the work of (1) Edwin Arlington Robinson, q. v., (2) of Robert Frost, q. v., (3) of Vachel Lindsay, q. v., and (4) of Carl Sandburg, q. v.

9. An interesting study might be made of the effects of Mr. Masters's legal training upon his poetry.

10. Compare *Children of the Market Place* with the *Anthology* or *Domesday Book*. Is Mr. Masters more successful as poet or as novelist?

BIBLIOGRAPHY

Poems
    A Book of Verses. 1898.
    Blood of the Prophets. 1905. (Pseud., Dexter Wallace.)
 * Spoon River Anthology. 1915. (Enl. ed., 1925.)
    Songs and Satires. 1916.
    The Great Valley. 1916.
    Toward the Gulf. 1918.
    Starved Rock. 1919.
    Domesday Book. 1920.
    The Open Sea. 1921.
    The New Spoon River. 1924.
 * Selected Poems. 1925.
    Lee. 1926.
    Jack Kelso. 1928.

Plays
    Maximilian. 1902.
    The Trifler. 1908.
    Eileen. 1910.
    The Locket. 1910.
    The Bread of Idleness. 1911.

Novels
    Mitch Miller. 1920.
    Children of the Market Place. 1922.
    Skeeters Kirby. 1923. (Autobiographical.)

Edgar Lee Masters—*Continued*
The Nuptial Flight. 1923.
Mirage. 1924.
Kit O'Brien. 1927.

Political Essays
The New Star Chamber. 1904.

Biography
Levy Mayer and the New Industrial Era. 1927.

STUDIES AND REVIEWS

Aiken.
Baldwin.
Boynton. (S. C. A.)
Farrar.
Hackett.
Hansen.
Karsner.
Lowell.
Maynard.
Monroe.
Untermeyer. (A. P.)
Van Doren. (C. A. N.)
———. (A. B. L.)
Weirick.
Wilkinson. (N. V.)
———. (P.)
Wood.

Am. Merc., 2 ('24): 250.
Bookm., 41 ('15): 355 (portrait), 432; 44 ('16): 264 (Kilmer); 47 ('18): 262 (Phelps).
Bookm. (Lond.), 49 ('16): 187; 52 ('17): 153.
Bost. Trans., Mar. 29, 1922: 4; Oct. 20, 1923: 4.
Cent., 109 ('25): 430.
Chapbook, 1–2, May, 1920: 11.
Dial, 60 ('16): 415, 498; 61 ('16): 528.
Forum, 55 ('16): 109, 118, 121.
Lit. Digest, 52 ('16): 564 (portrait).

Lit. Digest, I. B. R. June, 1924: 552; Dec., 1924: 32.
Lit. Rev., May 13, 1922: 651; Aug. 4, 1923: 875; Sept. 22, 1923: 61; Sept. 27, 1924: 2.
Lond. Times, May 19, 1921: 318.
Nation, 116 ('23): 473; 117 ('23): 270; 118 ('24): 616 (L. Lewisohn); 119 ('24): 388 (M. Van Doren).
N. Repub., 20 ('19): supp. 10; 39 ('24): 138 (R. Herrick); 40 ('24): 148.
N. State., 6 ('16): 332; 7 ('16): 593; 17 ('21): 362.
N. Y. Herald-Tribune, Oct. 10, 1926: 7.
N. Y. Times, July 9, 1922: 21; Mar. 4, 1923: 14; Mar. 30, 1924: 9; Sept. 28, 1924: 6; Jan. 23, 1927: 6; May 8, 1927: 9; July 1, 1928: 5.
Poetry, 6 ('15): 145; 8 ('16): 148; 9 ('17): 202; 12 ('18): 150; 16 ('20): 151; 18 ('21): 214; 21 ('22): 154; 24 ('24): 204 (H. Monroe); 25 ('25): 273; 29 ('27): 336.
Sat. Rev. of Lit., 1 ('24): 178; 2 ('25): 443; 3 ('27): 731.
Springfield Repub., Apr. 2, 1922: 13a; Mar. 18, 1923: 7e.
Yale Rev., n. s. 10 ('21): 636.

(James) Brander Matthews—critic, man of letters.

Born at New Orleans, 1852. A. B., Columbia, 1871; LL. B., 1873; A. M., 1874. Many honorary higher degrees. Admitted to the bar in 1873, but took up writing. Professor at Columbia University since 1892. Died on March 31, 1929. *For complete bibliography*, *see* Who's Who in America.

BIBLIOGRAPHY

French Dramatists of the Nineteenth Century. 1881.
In Partnership. 1884. (With H. C. Bunner.)
Vignettes of Manhattan. 1894.
Aspects of Fiction. 1896.
The Philosophy of the Short-Story. 1901.
The Development of the Drama. 1903.
Principles of Playwriting. 1919.
Playwrights on Playmaking. 1923.

STUDIES AND REVIEWS

Farrar.
Halsey.
Sherman. (P. V.)
Williams.

Am. Rev., 1 ('23): 111.
Bk. Buyer, 22 ('21): 15 (portrait).
Bookm., 56 ('22): 222 (B. Rascoe).
Bost. Trans., Jan. 20, 1923: 5.
Forum, 39 ('08): 377; 71 ('24): 847.
Lit. Digest, I. B. R. Nov., 1923: 44; Oct., 1926: 675.

Lit. Rev., Dec. 3, 1921: 224 (H. Bradley); Oct. 21, 1922: 125; Oct. 2, 1926: 1.
Lond. Times, Oct. 18, 1923: 685.
N. Y. Herald-Tribune, Sept. 26, 1926: 4.
N. Y. Times, Oct. 2, 1921: 2 (B. Matthews); Oct. 29, 1922: 8.
Outlook, 117 ('17): 640; 144 ('26): 312.
Spec., 106 ('11): 969; 114 ('15): 686; 131 ('23): 848.
Springfield Repub., Oct. 24, 1921: 6; Sept. 25, 1926: 10.

H(enry) L(ouis) Mencken—critic, man of letters.

Born at Baltimore, Maryland, 1880, of German ancestry. Graduate of Baltimore Polytechnic, 1896. On the *Baltimore Herald*, 1903–06, *Baltimore Sun*, 1906–10, and *Evening Sun*, 1910–. Literary critic on the *Smart Set*, 1908–14; co-editor with George Jean Nathan (q. v.), 1914–23. Editor of the

H(enry) L(ouis) Mencken—*Continued*

American Mercury, 1924– ; contributing editor of the *Nation*, 1921– .

Suggestions for Reading

1. Attempt to put in order Mr. Mencken's views of democracy, the middle class, criticism, women.

2. Make a study of the weaknesses and the strength of Mr. Mencken's style. Is it a style suitable to his purpose as you understand it? Is it a style that will bear frequent re-reading?

3. Study Mr. Mencken's successive expressions of his opinions of the work of Conrad, of Willa Cather, of Sinclair Lewis, and of Theodore Dreiser.

4. Ambrose Bierce, it has been said, exerted a great influence on the literary development of Mr. Mencken. Study the similarities in their ideas and methods.

5. Analyze the adverse criticism in *Menckeniana: A Schimpflexicon.* How much of the criticism there seems just? Why?

BIBLIOGRAPHY

Poems
   Ventures into Verse. 1903.

Plays
   The Artist. 1912.
   Heliogabalus. 1920. (With George Jean Nathan.)

Critical Essays, Sketches, and Studies.
   George Bernard Shaw. 1905.
   The Philosophy of Friedrich Nietzsche. 1908.
   A Book of Burlesques. 1916.
 * A Book of Prefaces. 1917.
   Damn! A Book of Calumny. 1918. (Repub. as A Book of Calumny.)
   In Defense of Women. 1918.
   The American Language. 1919. (Rev. and enl. eds., 1921, 1923.)
   Prejudices. 1919–27. (Series includes 6 vols. to date.)
 * Selected Prejudices. 1927. (Reprints.)
   James Branch Cabell. 1927.

Sociological Essays and Sketches
   Men vs. the Man. 1910. (With Robert Rives LaMonte.)
   A Little Book in C Major. 1916. (Epigrams.)

H(enry) L(ouis) Mencken—*Continued*

* The American Credo. 1920. (Rev. and enl. ed., 1921. With George
Jean Nathan.)
Antichrist, by Friedrich Nietzsche. 1920. (Translator.)
Americana. 1925, 1926. (Editor.)
Notes on Democracy. 1926.

Travel and Description
Europe after 8:15. 1914. (With George Jean Nathan and Willard
Huntington Wright.)

STUDIES AND REVIEWS

Beach.
Boyd. (P. R. I.)
Boynton. (S. C. A.)
Calverton.
Farrar.
Frey, C. Bibliography of the
Writings of H. L. Mencken.
1924.
Goldberg, Isaac. The Man
Mencken. 1925.
Harris.
Harrison, J. B. Short View of
Menckenism in Menckenese.
1927.
Hatteras, O. A. J. Pistols for
Two. 1917.
Menckeniana: A Schimpflexicon.
1928.
Pattee.
Rascoe, Burton, and Others (Vin-
cent O'Sullivan, and F. C. Hen-
derson). H. L. Mencken: Brief
Appreciations and a Bibliog-
raphy. 1920.
Sergeant.
Sherman. (A.)
———. (C. W.)
Van Doren. (M. M.)
———. (A. B. L.)

Am. Rev., 3 ('25): 72.
Ath., 1920, 1: 10.

Bookm., 41 ('15): 46, 56; 53 ('21):
79; 54 ('22): 551; 60 ('25): 632.
(Portraits.)
Bookm. (Lond.), 64 ('23): 160.
Bost. Trans., Apr. 29, 1922: 7;
Jan. 13, 1923: 3; Dec. 4, 1926: 3.
Cur. Op., 66 ('19): 391 (portrait);
71 ('21): 360.
Dial, 68 ('20): 267.
Freeman, 1 ('20): 88; 6 ('22): 381.
Lit. Digest, I. B. R. Jan., 1925:
125.
Lit. Rev., Dec. 2, 1922: 261.
Liv. Age, 303 ('19): 798.
Lond. Merc., 6 ('22): 439.
Lond. Times, Oct. 13, 1921: 659;
Dec. 11, 1924: 844; Dec. 3, 1925:
821; Dec. 23, 1926: 946; Mar.
17, 1927: 174, 388.
Nation, 114 ('22): 430, 690; 115
('22): 441; 124 ('27): 174.
Nation and Ath., 40 ('27): 376.
N. Repub., 21 ('20): 239; 26 ('21):
191; 27 ('21): 10; 33 ('22): supp.
Nov. 29: 9.
N. State., 14 ('20): 748.
N. Y. Herald-Tribune, Oct. 24,
1926: 5; Nov. 14, 1926: 4; Jan.
2, 1927: 4.
N. Y. Times, Dec. 31, 1922: 7;
Nov. 2, 1924: 3; Nov. 21, 1926:
2; Nov. 28, 1926: 4.

H(enry) L(ouis) Mencken—*Continued*

19th Cent., 101 ('27): 117.
Sat. Rev., 132 ('21): 535; 143 ('27): 276, 355.

Sat. Rev. of Lit., 1 ('24): 297; 2 ('25): 401; 3 ('26): 413; 3 ('27): 858.

Edna St. Vincent Millay—poet, dramatist.

Mrs. Eugen Jan Boissevain. Born at Rockland, Maine, 1892. A. B., Vassar, 1917. Connected with the Provincetown Players both as dramatist and as actress.

Miss Millay's first poem, "Renascence," was published in *The Lyric Year*, 1912. She was awarded the Pulitzer prize for poetry in 1923.

SUGGESTIONS FOR READING

1. The poems need to be read aloud to give the full effect of their passion and lyric beauty.

2. Compare Miss Millay's naïveté with that of Blake. Do you find suggestions of philosophy behind it, or only emotion?

3. Does Miss Millay's later work show growth toward greatness or toward sophisticated cleverness?

4. Consider the strength and weakness of Miss Millay as a poetic dramatist.

BIBLIOGRAPHY

Poems

Renascence. 1917. (*In* The Lyric Year, 1912.)
A Few Figs from Thistles. 1920. (Enl. ed., 1921.)
Second April. 1921.
The Ballad of the Harp-Weaver. 1922.
Poems. London. 1923.
The Harp-Weaver, and Other Poems. 1923.
The Buck in the Snow. 1928.

Plays

Aria da Capo. 1921. (*In* The Chapbook, London, 1920.)
The Lamp and the Bell. 1921.
Two Slatterns and a King. 1921.
Three Plays. 1926. (Reprints.)
The King's Henchman. 1927.

Edna St. Vincent Millay—*Continued*

Humorous Dialogues and Sketches
    Distressing Dialogues. 1924. (Pseud. Nancy Boyd.)

STUDIES AND REVIEWS

Collins, Joseph. Taking the Literary Pulse. 1924.
Farrar.
Maynard.
Monroe.
Untermeyer. (A. P.)
Van Doren. (M. M.)
——. (A. B. L.)
Wilkinson. (P.)
Wood.

Bost. Trans., Jan. 9, 1924: 4.
Freeman, 1 ('20): 307; 4 ('21): 189.
Ind., 107 ('21): 194.
Lit. Rev., July 16, 1921: 3; Feb. 26, 1927: 2.
Lond. Times, Sept. 1, 1921: 567; June 26, 1924: 401.

Nation, 118 ('24): 209 (M. Van Doren); 124 ('27): 263.
Nation and Ath., 35 ('24): 118 (V. Sackville-West).
N. Y. Times, Oct. 16, 1921: 10; Dec. 23, 1923: 11; Nov. 2, 1924: 12; Mar. 20, 1927: 2.
Poetry, 13 ('18): 167; 19 ('21): 151; 24 ('24): 264 (H. Monroe); 30 ('27): 42.
Sat. Rev. of Lit., 3 ('27): 661.
Springfield Repub., Feb. 17, 1924: 7a.
Yale Rev., n. s. 14 ('24): 158 (L. Untermeyer).

See also Book Review Digest, 1918, 1921.

Meade Minnigerode—novelist, biographer.
    Born of American parents at London, England, 1887. Educated at Harrow. A. B., Yale, 1910. Representative in France of United States Shipping Board, 1917–18. Served with A. E. F., 1918–19.

BIBLIOGRAPHY

Novels
    Laughing House. 1920.
    The Big Year. 1921.
    Oh, Susanna! 1922.
    The Seven Hills. 1923.
    Cordelia Chantrell. 1926.
    Cockades. 1927.

Social Studies
    The Fabulous Forties, 1840–1850. 1924.
    Presidential Years, 1787–1860. 1928.

Meade Minnigerode—*Continued*

Biographical Sketches and Studies
Some Personal Letters of Herman Melville. 1922.
Aaron Burr. 1925. (With Samuel H. Wandell.)
Lives and Times. 1925.
Some American Ladies. 1926.
Certain Rich Men. 1927.
Memoirs of a Poor Relation. 1927.
Jefferson, Friend of France, 1793. 1928.

STUDIES AND REVIEWS

Bost. Trans., Mar. 29, 1922; 4; Mar. 21, 1925: 2; Mar. 27, 1926: 11.
Lit. Digest, I. B. R. Oct., 1923: 64; Apr., 1924: 354 (B. Matthews); Oct., 1924: 785; May, 1926: 378.
Lit. Rev., Apr. 16, 1921: 9; June 9, 1923: 752; Apr. 4, 1925: 4.
Lond. Times, Jun. 11, 1925: 401; May 27, 1926: 349.
Nation, 121 ('25): 193.

N. Repub., 39 ('24): 106.
N. Y. Herald-Tribune, Apr. 11, 1926: 6.
N. Y. Times, Mar. 19, 1922: 11; Jan. 21, 1923: 3; Aug. 26, 1923: 17; Mar. 9, 1924: 3; Mar. 22, 1925: 5; Mar. 28, 1926: 5; Sept. 5, 1926: 6; Apr. 24, 1927: 19.
Outlook, 136 ('24): 527.
Sat. Rev. of Lit., 3 ('26): 466.
Spec., 132 ('24): 881.

Phillip Moeller—dramatist.

Born at New York City, 1880. Student at Columbia, 1901–08. Studied the theatre in Europe. A founder and director of the Washington Square Players, 1914, and of the Theatre Guild. Has translated and adapted many plays.

BIBLIOGRAPHY

Plays
Helena's Husband. (*In* Washington Square Plays. 1916.)
Madame Sand. 1917.
Five Somewhat Historical Plays. 1918.
Two Blind Beggars and One Less Blind. 1918.
Molière. 1919.
Sophie. 1919.

STUDIES AND REVIEWS

Dickinson. (P. N. A. T.)

Harriet Monroe—critic, poet.

Born at Chicago, 1860. Editor of *Poetry*, 1912–. Compiler of *The New Poetry; an Anthology* (with Alice Corbin Henderson, q. v.), 1917; new and enl. ed., 1923.

For complete bibliography, see Who's Who in America.

BIBLIOGRAPHY

Poems
  Valeria. 1891.
  Commemoration Ode. 1892. (Repr. 1893, as The Columbian Ode.)
  The Passing Show. 1903. (Plays.)
  The Dance of the Seasons. 1911.
  You and I. 1914.
  The Difference. 1924.

Criticism
  Poets and Their Art. 1926.

Biography
  John Wellborn Root. 1896.

STUDIES AND REVIEWS

Hansen.

Bookm., 60 ('24): 94.
Lond. Times, Sept. 23, 1926: 628.

Nation and Ath., 40 ('26): 30.
  (R. Graves).
N. Repub., 48 ('26): 277.

Marianne Moore—poet.

Born at St. Louis, Missouri, 1887. B. A., Bryn Mawr, 1909. From 1911 to 1915 taught at the Indian School at Carlisle, Pennsylvania. Since 1919 she has worked in the New York Public Library. In 1925 she received the *Dial* award for "distinguished service to American letters." Since 1926 she has been co-editor (with Scofield Thayer) of the *Dial*.

BIBLIOGRAPHY

Poems
  Poems. London, 1921.
  Observations. 1924.

Marianne Moore—*Continued*

STUDIES AND REVIEWS

Untermeyer.   (A. P.)

Lit. Rev., Aug. 8, 1925: 4.

Nation, 120 ('25): 297.
N. Y. Times, Feb. 1, 1925: 5.
Poetry, 26 ('26): 39.

Paul Elmer More—critic, man of letters.

Born at St. Louis, 1864.   A. B., Washington University, 1887; A. M., 1892; Harvard, 1893.   Honorary higher degrees. Taught Sanskrit at Harvard, 1894–95; Sanskrit and classical literature at Bryn Mawr, 1895–97.   Literary editor of the *Independent*, 1901–03; *New York Evening Post*, 1903–09. Editor of the *Nation*, 1909–14.

BIBLIOGRAPHY

Poems
   Helena.   1890.

Novel
   The Jessica Letters.   1904.   (With Corra May Harris.)

Critical and Sociological Essays
   Shelburne Essays.   1904–21.   (Eleven vols. to date.   Since 1913
      vols. are issued under individual titles.)
   The Drift of Romanticism.   1913.   (Shelburne Essays, Series 8.)
   Aristocracy and Justice.   1915.   (Shelburne Essays, Series 9.)
   With the Wits.   1919.   (Shelburne Essays, Series 10.)
   A New England Group.   1921.   (Shelburne Essays, Series 11.)
   The Demon of the Absolute.   1928.   (New Shelburne Essays, Series 1.)

Philosophical and Religious Studies
   Nietzsche.   1912.
   Platonism.   1917.
   The Religion of Plato.   1921.
   Hellenistic Philosophies.   1923.
   The Christ of the New Testament.   1924.
   Christ the Word.   1927.

Biography
   Benjamin Franklin.   1900.

Paul Elmer More--*Continued*

Pattee.
Sherman. (A.)

Acad., 80 ('11): 353.
Ath., 1909, 1: 67; 1920, 1: 703.
Bookm. (Lond.), 44 ('13): 256;
58 ('20): 207.
Cur. Op., 55 ('13): 126.
Dial, 71 ('21): 236.
Freeman, 3 ('21): 283.
Ind., 107 ('21): 167.
Lit. Rev., Aug. 6, 1921: 4 (Canby);
Apr. 29, 1924; 629.
Lond. Times, Sept. 15, 1921: 592.
Nation, 113 ('21): 101; 114 ('22):
290.

Nation and Ath., 29 ('21): 473.
N. Repub., 26 ('21): 163.
N. Y. Times, July 10, 1921: 9;
Jan. 20, 1924: 9; June 22,
1924: 16.
No. Am., 219 ('24): 429.
Outlook, 81 ('05): 678.
Philos. R., 26 ('17): 409.
Rev., 2 ('20): 54.
Sat. Rev., 132 ('21): 323.
Sewanee R., 26 (18): 63.
Spec., 116 ('16): 632; 125 ('20):
113.
Springfield Repub., Apr. 3, 1921:
5a; June 24, 1924: 10.

Christopher (Darlington) Morley—essayist, poet, novelist. Born at Haverford, Pennsylvania, 1890. A. B., Haverford College, 1910. Rhodes Scholar at Oxford, 1910–13. Editorial staff, Doubleday, Page and Company, 1913–17; *Ladies' Home Journal*, 1917–18; *Philadelphia Evening Public Ledger*, 1918–20; *New York Evening Post*, 1920–24. Contributing editor of the *Saturday Review of Literature*.

BIBLIOGRAPHY

Poems
Songs for a Little House. 1917.
The Rocking Horse. 1919.
Hide and Seek. 1920.
Chimneysmoke. 1921.
Translations from the Chinese. 1922.
Parsons' Pleasure. 1923.
The Bowling Green. 1924. (Compiler.)
Toulemonde. 1928.

Plays
Thursday Evening. 1922.
One-Act Plays. 1924.
Good Theatre. 1926.

Christopher (Darlington) Morley—*Continued*

Novels, Tales, and Fantasies

The Eighth Sin. Oxford, 1912
Parnassus on Wheels. 1917.
The Haunted Bookshop. 1919.
Kathleen. 1920.
* Where the Blue Begins. 1922. (Dramatized by the author in collaboration with E. S. Colling. Priv. ptd. 1925.)
Pandora Lifts the Lid. 1924. (With Don Marquis.)
Two Fables from Alfred de Musset and Wilhelm Hauff. 1925. (Editor and translator.)
* Thunder on the Left. 1925.
The Arrow. 1927.
Pleased to Meet You. 1927.
I Know a Secret. 1927.

Essays and Sketches

* Shandygaff. 1918.
In the Sweet Dry and Dry. 1919. (With Bart Haley.)
* Mince Pie. 1919. (Includes poems.)
Travels in Philadelphia. 1920.
Pipefuls. 1920.
Tales from a Rolltop Desk. 1921.
Plum Pudding. 1921.
Modern Essays. 1921. Second Series, 1924. (Compiler.)
The Powder of Sympathy. 1923.
Inward Ho! 1923.
Religio Journalistici. 1924.
Hostages to Fortune. 1925. (Includes poems.)
Forty-Four Essays. 1925. (Ed. by Rollo LaVerne Lyman.)
Safety Pins. London, 1925.
The Romany Stain. 1926. (Reprinted in part as Nine Essays. 1927.)
Off the Deep End. 1928.
The Seacoast of Bohemia. 1929.

Works

The Haverford Edition. 1927. 12 v.

STUDIES AND REVIEWS

Baldwin.
Karsner.
Overton. (A. O. D.)
Van Doren. (M. M.)

Bookm., 46 ('18): 657 (portrait).

Bookm. (Lond.), 70 ('26): 212.
Bost. Trans., Dec. 3, 1921: 5;
Dec. 9, 1922: 10; June 27, 1923:
4; June 18, 1924: 4; Nov. 14,
1925: 5; July 7, 1926: 4.
Cath. World, 118 ('24): 856.

Christopher (Darlington) Morley—*Continued*

Everybody's, 42 ('20): Feb.: 29 (portrait).

Lit. Digest, I. B. R. Jan., 1926: 126.

Lit. Rev., June 25, 1921: 4; Dec. 3, 1921: 226 (H. W. Boynton); Dec. 17, 1921: 279; Oct. 14, 1922: 103 (Walpole); Dec. 1, 1923: 302; Jan. 5, 1924: 419; May 22, 1926: 2; Dec. 6, 1926: 4.

Lond. Times, Mar. 25, 1926: 234; Oct. 20, 1927: 736.

N. Y. Times, July 10, 1921: 14; May 25, 1924: 12; Nov. 29, 1925: 10; Dec. 6, 1925: 2; Aug. 1, 1926: 7; Apr. 24, 1927: 16.

Outlook, 124 ('20): 202 (portrait); 136 ('24): 193.

Sat. Rev., 141 ('26): 456.

Sat. Rev. of Lit., 2 ('25): 363; 2 ('26): 489, 767; 3 ('27): 860; 4 ('28): 844.

Springfield Repub., Dec. 26, 1921: 6; Aug. 7, 1923: 8; Nov. 29, 1925: 7a; Sept. 27, 1926: 8.

Lewis Mumford—man of letters.

Born at Flushing, Long Island, 1895. Studied at Columbia University, the College of the City of New York, and New York University. In 1918 he was a radio operator, U. S. N.; in 1919 he joined the staff of the *Dial* as associate editor; in 1920 he went to England as acting editor of the *Sociological Review*. At present, Mr. Mumford is considered one of the leading authorities on regional planning and civic architecture. Joint editor of *The American Caravan*, 1927 (with Van Wyck Brooks, Alfred Kreymborg, and Paul Rosenfeld); and of *The American Caravan*, 1928 (with Kreymborg and Rosenfeld).

BIBLIOGRAPHY

Studies

The Story of Utopias. 1922.
Sticks and Stones. 1924.
The Golden Day. 1926.

Biography

Herman Melville. 1929.

STUDIES AND REVIEWS

Bost. Trans., Jan. 5, 1927: 5.

Dial, 78 ('25): 153.

Ind., 117 ('26): 680 (E. Boyd).

Lit. Rev., Jan. 20, 1923: 397; Dec. 13, 1924: 5; Dec. 4, 1926: 1.

Lewis Mumford—*Continued*

Nation, 119 ('24): 604; 123 ('26): Dec. 1, supp. 601.

N. Repub., 33 ('22): 73 (Lovett); 41 ('24): Dec. 10, supp. 7.

N. Y. Herald-Tribune, Dec. 1, 1926: 7.

N. Y. Times, Dec. 24, 1922: 11; Sept. 21, 1924: 4; Dec. 19, 1926: 2.

Sat. Rev. of Lit., 1 ('24): 413; 3 ('27): 544.

Springfield Repub., Jan. 28, 1923: 7a.

George Jean Nathan—critic, man of letters.

Born at Fort Wayne, Indiana, 1882. A. B., Cornell, 1904. On editorial staff of the *New York Herald*, 1904–06. On the staffs of various magazines, including *Harper's Weekly*, the *Associated Sunday Magazines*, and the *Smart Set*, usually as dramatic critic, 1906–14. With James Huneker (q. v.) dramatic critic for *Puck*, 1915–16. Dramatic critic for the National Syndicate of Newspapers since 1912. Editor of the *Smart Set* (with H. L. Mencken, q. v.), 1914–23. Founder and editor (with H. L. Mencken) of the *American Mercury*, 1924–25, contributing editor, 1925– . Dramatic editor of *Judge*, 1922– .

BIBLIOGRAPHY

Plays
  Heliogabalus. 1920. (With H. L. Mencken.)
Critical Essays on the Drama
  Another Book on the Theatre. 1915.
  Bottoms Up. 1917.
  Mr. George Jean Nathan Presents. 1917.
  The Popular Theatre. 1918.
  Comedians All. 1919.
  The Theatre, the Drama, the Girls. 1921.
  The Critic and the Drama. 1922.
  The World in Falseface. 1923.
  Materia Critica. 1924.
  The House of Satan. 1926.
  Art of the Night. 1928.
Sociological Essays, Sketches, and Studies
  A Book Without a Title. 1918.
  The American Credo. 1920. (With H. L. Mencken. Rev. and enl. ed., 1921.)

George Jean Nathan—*Continued*
The Autobiography of an Attitude. 1925.
Land of the Pilgrims' Pride. 1927.
The New American Credo. 1927.

Description and Travel
Europe after 8:15. 1914. (With H. L. Mencken and Willard Huntington Wright.)

STUDIES AND REVIEWS
Boyd. (P. R. I.)
Goldberg, Isaac. The Theatre of George Jean Nathan. 1926.
Hatteras, O. A. J. Pistols for Two. 1917.

Bookm., 43 ('16): 282 (portrait only); 53 ('21): 163; 55 ('22): 64.
Bost. Trans., June 3, 1922: 4; Aug. 30, 1924: 3; Oct. 17, 1925: 4.
Cur. Op., 63 ('17): 95 (portrait).
Ind., 117 ('26): 218 (E. Boyd).
Lit. Rev., May 26, 1923: 716; Sept. 18, 1926: 2.

Liv. Age, 332 ('27): 648.
Lond. Times, May 26, 1921: 332; Oct. 13, 1927: 718.
N. Repub., 54 ('28): 277.
N. Y. Times, Feb. 6, 1921: 9 (Phelps); Feb. 4, 1923: 9; Sept. 14, 1924: 6; Aug. 29, 1926: 5.
Sat. Rev., 136 ('23): 444.
Sat. Rev. of Lit., 1 ('24): 198.
Springfield Repub., Jan. 12, 1923: 8.

See also Book Review Digest, 1919, 1920.

Robert Nathan—novelist.
Born at New York City, 1894. Educated privately in the United States and in Switzerland. Studied at Harvard. An excellent musician.

BIBLIOGRAPHY
Poems
Youth Grows Old. 1922.
The Cedar Box. 1929.

Novels
Peter Kindred. 1919.
Autumn. 1921.
The Puppet Master. 1923.
Jonah. 1925. (London, 1925, under the title Son of Amittai.)
The Fiddler in Barly. 1926.
The Woodcutter's House. 1927.
The Bishop's Wife. 1928.

Robert Nathan—*Continued*

STUDIES AND REVIEWS

Bost. Trans., Oct. 24, 1923: 4; Mar. 18, 1925: 4; Oct. 26, 1927: 2.

Lit. Rev., Oct. 15, 1921: 83; Feb. 21, 1925: 6; Dec. 11, 1926: 3.

London Times, Sept. 10, 1925: 582.

Nation, 114 ('22): 624.

N. Y. Times, Oct. 28, 1923: 7; Feb. 15, 1925: 8; Dec. 12, 1926: 38; Oct. 16, 1927: 8; Sept. 16, 1928: 6.

Rev., 2 ('20): 392.

Sat. Rev. of Lit., 1 ('25): 627; 3 ('26): 335; 5 ('28): 163.

John G(neisenau) Neihardt—poet.

Born at Sharpsburg, Illinois, 1881. Finished scientific course at Nebraska Normal College, 1897; Litt. D., University of Nebraska, 1917. Lived among the Omaha Indians, 1901–07, studying them and their folk-lore Has worked many years on an American epic cycle of pioneer life. Shared with Gladys Cromwell the prize of the Poetry Society of America, 1919. Appointed poet laureate of Nebraska by legislative act, 1921; appointed professor of poetry at the University of Nebraska, 1923.

BIBLIOGRAPHY

Poems

The Divine Enchantment. 1900.
A Bundle of Myrrh. 1907.
Man-Song. 1909.
The River and I. 1910.
The Stranger at the Gate. 1912.
The Song of Hugh Glass. 1915.
The Quest. 1916.
The Song of Three Friends. 1919.
The Poet's Pack. 1921. (Editor.)
The Song of the Indian Wars. 1925.
Collected Poems. 1926.

Plays in Verse

Two Mothers. 1921.

John G(neisenau) Neihardt)—*Continued*

Novels
  The Dawn-Builder. 1911.
  Life's Lure. 1911.
  Splendid Wayfaring. 1920. (Historical.)

Short Stories
  The Lonesome Trail. 1907.
  Indian Tales and Others. 1926.

Critical Essays
  Poetic Values. 1925.

STUDIES AND REVIEWS

House, J. T. John G. Neihardt: Man and Poet. 1920.
Bookm., 47 ('18): 395; 49 ('19): 496; 62 ('25): 88.
Bost. Trans., Dec. 4, 1915: 7; Nov. 24, 1920: 2.
Lit. Rev., Jan. 15, 1927: 9.
N. Y. Times, Nov. 8, 1914: 488; Aug. 10, 1919: 409; June 5, 1921: 6; Oct. 10, 1926: 28.
N. Y. Herald-Tribune, Sept. 20, 1925: 4; Jan. 2, 1927: 7.
Poetry, 7 ('16): 264; 17 ('20): 94.
Sat. Rev. of Lit., 2 ('25): 428; 2 ('26): 949; 4 ('27): 38.

Meredith Nicholson—novelist, man of letters.

Born at Crawfordsville, Indiana, 1866. Various honorary degrees. His reputation was established by the novel, *The House of a Thousand Candles*, 1905. He has published also several volumes of essays and studies, beginning with *The Hoosiers* (National Studies in American Letters), 1900. Note among them *The Valley of Democracy*, 1918, a characterization of the Middle West.

For complete bibliography, see Who's Who in America.

BIBLIOGRAPHY

The House of a Thousand Candles. 1905.
Port of Missing Men. 1907.
Siege of the Seven Suitors. 1910.
Otherwise Phyllis. 1913.
The Valley of Democracy. 1918. (Essays.)
Broken Barriers. 1922.

Meredith Nicholson—*Continued*
Hope of Happiness. 1923.
And They Lived Happily Ever After. 1925.
The Cavalier of Tennessee. 1928.

STUDIES AND REVIEWS

Bost. Trans., Oct. 25, 1922: 6; Nov. 14, 1923: 8; Oct. 17, 1925: 5.
Dial, 71 ('21): 604.
Freeman, 8 ('23): 263.
Lit. Rev., Nov. 19, 1921: 187; Oct. 14, 1922: 103; Oct. 27, 1923: 183.

N. Y. Herald-Tribune, July 22, 1928: 2.
N. Y. Times, Oct. 23, 1921: 25; May 14, 1922: 16; Oct. 14, 1923: 9; Oct. 4, 1925: 22.
Springfield Repub., Dec. 31, 1922: 7a.

Charles G(ilman) Norris—novelist.
Born at Chicago, 1881. Brother of Frank Norris, the novelist. Married Kathleen Thompson (cf. Kathleen Norris).

BIBLIOGRAPHY

Drama
The Rout of the Philistines. 1922. (Priv. ptd. Music by Nino Marcelli.)

Novels
The Amateur. 1916.
Salt. 1918.
Brass. 1921.
Bread. 1923.
Pig Iron. 1926.
Zelda Marsh. 1927.

STUDIES AND REVIEWS

Baldwin.

Bookm., 47 ('18): 679; 66 ('27): 105.
Bost. Trans., Aug. 24, 1921: 6; Aug. 18, 1923: 4; Mar. 6, 1926: 4.

Ind., 111 ('23): 142; 116 ('26): 334.
Lit. Digest, I. B. R. Oct., 1921: 46.
Lit. Rev., Sept. 17, 1921: 19; Sept. 15, 1923: 39; Mar. 13, 1926: 4.

Charles G(ilman) Norris—*Continued*

N. Repub., 29 ('21): 48 (Lovett); 36 ('23): 23; 52 ('27): 118.

N. Y. Herald-Tribune, Mar. 14, 1926: 1 (S. Sherman).

N. Y. Times, Sept. 25, 1921: 20;

June 19, 1923: 18; Mar. 7, 1926: 5.

Sat. Rev. of Lit., 2 ('26): 609.

See also Book Review Digest, 1918, 1921.

Kathleen (Thompson) Norris—novelist.

Born at San Francisco, 1880. Educated privately. Had experience as business woman. Married Charles Gilman Norris (q. v.), 1909.

BIBLIOGRAPHY

Plays
The Kelly Kid. 1926. (With Dan Totheroh.)

Novels and Tales
Mother. 1911.
The Rich Mrs. Burgoyne. 1912.
Saturday's Child. 1914.
The Treasure. 1914.
The Story of Julia Page. 1915.
The Heart of Rachael. 1916.
Martie, the Unconquered. 1917.
Undertow. 1917.
Josselyn's Wife. 1918.
Sisters. 1919.
Harriet and the Piper. 1920.
The Beloved Woman. 1921.
Lucretia Lombard. 1922.
Certain People of Importance. 1922.
Butterfly. 1923.
Uneducating Mary. 1923.
Rose of the World. 1924.
The Callahans and the Murphys. 1924.
Little Ships. 1925.
Hildegarde. 1926.
The Black Flemings. 1926.
Barberry Bush. 1927.
The Sea Gull. 1927.

Kathleen (Thompson) Norris—*Continued*
My Best Girl. 1927.
Beauty and the Beast. 1928.
The Foolish Virgin. 1928.

Short Stories
Poor, Dear Margaret Kirby. 1912.

Autobiography
Noon. 1925.

STUDIES AND REVIEWS

Overton. (O. W. N.)

Bookm., 34 ('11): 437; 37 ('13): 109 (portrait).
Bost. Trans., Aug. 21, 1921: 6; Apr. 1, 1922: 6; Apr. 23, 1924: 4; Oct. 1, 1924: 4; Oct. 17, 1925: 4; Mar. 24, 1926: 4; Oct. 27, 1926: 4.
Lit. Digest, Sept. 23, 1922: 60.
Lit. Digest, I. B. R. Dec., 1925: 54.
Lit. Rev., Apr. 29, 1922: 619; Aug. 19, 1922: 883; Oct. 20, 1923: 146; Aug. 23, 1924: 980; Mar. 6, 1926: 3.

N. Repub., 32 ('22): 177 (Lovett).
N. Y. Herald-Tribune, Oct. 17, 1926: 16.
N. Y. Times, Sept. 4, 1921: 23; Mar. 26, 1922: 14; Aug. 20, 1922: 7; Sept. 30, 1923: 4; Apr. 13, 1924: 8; Aug. 24, 1924: 9; Jan. 25, 1925: 6; Sept. 13, 1925: 19; Mar. 7, 1926: 9; Oct. 17, 1926: 7.
Sat. Rev. of Lit., 2 ('26): 609.

See also Book Review Digest, 1911, 1913-17.

Frederick O'Brien—travel-writer.
Born at Baltimore, Maryland, 1869. Early experiences as sailor, tramp, casual worker. Extensive journalistic and publishing experience. Has traveled widely since 1921. Mr. O'Brien's account of experiences in the Marquesas Islands created a literary fashion for the South Sea Islands.

BIBLIOGRAPHY

Description and Travel
White Shadows in the South Seas. 1919.
Mystic Isles of the South Seas. 1921.
Atolls of the Sun. 1922.

Frederick O'Brien—*Continued*

STUDIES AND REVIEWS

Beach.

Farrar.

Lit. Digest, I. B. R. Jan., 1923: 38.

Lit. Rev., Apr. 23, 1921: 5 (Canby); Jan. 13, 1923: 380.

Lond. Times, Aug. 4, 1921: 497.

Nation, 112 ('21): 898.

N. Y. Times, Apr. 17, 1921: 7; Oct. 15, 1922: 4.

Outlook, 128 ('21): 173.

Harvey (Jerrold) O'Higgins—journalist.

Born at London, Ontario, Canada, 1876. Student, University of Toronto, 1893–97. Interested in relating psychoanalysis to biography and the novel. Died Feb. 28, 1929.

BIBLIOGRAPHY

Plays (In collaboration with Harriet Ford.)
  "When a Feller Needs a Friend." 1920.
  On the Hiring Line. 1923.
  The Dummy. 1925. (Copyrighted 1913 under the title, Kidnapped.)
  Mr. Lazarus. 1926.
  Orphan Aggie. 1927.
  The Argyle Case. 1927. (Novelized by Arthur Hornblow. 1913.)
  Old P. Q. 1928.

Novels
  Don-a-Dreams. 1906.
  A Grand Army Man. 1908. (Founded on the play by David Belasco, Pauline Phelps, and Marion Short.)
  Old Clinkers. 1909.
  Julie Cane. 1924.
  Clara Barron. 1926.

Short Stories and Sketches
  The Smoke-Eaters. 1905.
  Silent Sam. 1914.
  The Adventures of Detective Barney. 1915.
  From the Life. 1919.
  Some Distinguished Americans. 1922.

Essays and Studies
  The Beast. 1910. (With Judge Ben. B. Lindsey.)
  Under the Prophet in Utah. 1911. (With Frank J. Cannon.)

Harvey (Jerrold) O'Higgins—*Continued*

The Doughboy's Religion. 1919. (With Judge Ben. B. Lindsey.)
The Secret Springs. 1920.
The American Mind in Action. 1924. (With Dr. Edward H. Reede.)

STUDIES AND REVIEWS

Bookm., 56 ('23): 756; 59 ('24): 471.
Bost. Trans., Jan. 6, 1923: 4; Oct. 11, 1924: 4; Mar. 13, 1926: 5.
Ind., 113 ('24): 76.
Lit. Digest, I. B. R. Dec., 1924: 58.
Lit. Rev., Oct. 28, 1922: 146; May 17, 1924: 756; Dec. 13, 1924: 12; Mar. 13, 1926: 3.
Lond. Times, Sept. 25, 1924: 594.
N. Repub., 40 ('24): 280.
N. Y. Times, Oct. 29, 1922: 20; May 11, 1924: 22; Oct. 12, 1924: 9; Mar. 14, 1926: 6.
Sat. Rev. of Lit., 2 ('26): 646.

Eugene (Gladstone) O'Neill—dramatist.

Born at New York City, 1888. Son of the actor, James O'Neill. Studied at Princeton, 1906–07. Much of the material used in his plays seems to be drawn from or based upon his adventurous experiences between 1907 and 1914. Actor and newspaper reporter. Spent two years at sea. In 1909 is said to have gone on a gold-prospecting expedition in Spanish Honduras (cf. *Gold*). Lived in the Argentine. Threatened tuberculosis gave him his first leisure (cf. *The Straw*). In 1914–15, he studied dramatization at Harvard. In 1918, when he married, he went to live in a deserted life-saving station near Provincetown. Associated with the Provincetown Players. He was awarded the Pulitzer prize for drama, in 1920 (*Beyond the Horizon*), 1922 (*Anna Christie*), and 1928 (*Strange Interlude*).

SUGGESTIONS FOR READING

1. What effect has Mr. O'Neill's life experience had upon the quality of his plays?

2. What evidence of originality do you find in his (1) themes, (2) background, and (3) technique?

Eugene (Gladstone) O'Neill—*Continued*

3. Consider the influence of Joseph Conrad (cf. Manly and Rickert, *Contemporary British Literature*) upon O'Neill. Read especially *The Nigger of the "Narcissus."*

4. What do you make of the fact that Mr. O'Neill has struck out in various directions instead of working a particular vein?

5. What is O'Neill trying to accomplish by means of his experiments with dramatic technique and novel dramatic material?

6. Why does O'Neill find the limits of pure realism or pure romanticism too confining?

BIBLIOGRAPHY

Plays
   Thirst, and Other One-Act Plays. 1914.
   Before Breakfast. 1916.
   Bound East for Cardiff. (*In* Provincetown Plays. First Series. 1916.)
   The Long Voyage Home. (*In* The Smart Set. Oct., 1917.)
   Ile. (*In* The Smart Set. May, 1918.)
   The Moon of the Caribbees. (*In* The Smart Set. Aug., 1918.)
 * The Moon of the Caribbees, and Six Other Plays of the Sea. 1919.
   Beyond the Horizon. 1920.
   Gold. 1920.
   Straw. 1920.
   The Emperor Jones, Diff'rent, The Straw. 1921.
   The Hairy Ape, Anna Christie, The First Man. 1922.
   The Dreamy Kid. 1925. (*First pub. in* Theatre Arts Magazine. 1920.)
   All God's Chillun Got Wings, and Welded. 1924.
 * Desire Under the Elms. 1925. (*In* Complete Works. 1924.)
   The Great God Brown, The Fountain, The Moon of the Caribbees. 1926.
   Marco Millions. 1927.
   Lazarus Laughed. 1927.
 * Strange Interlude. 1928.
   Dynamo. 1929.

Collected Editions
   The Complete Works. 1924. (Some are rev.)
   Plays. 1925– .

See also *Barrett H. Clark*, Eugene O'Neill, 1929, *and Quinn*, History of American Drama, II, 320–22.

Eugene (Gladstone) O'Neill—*Continued*

STUDIES AND REVIEWS

Boyd. (P. R. I.)

Clark, Barrett H. Eugene O'Neill. 1929.

Dickinson. (P. N. A. T.)

Hamilton.

Karsner.

Nathan, G. J. Materia Critica.

Sergeant.

Sutton, Graham. Some Contemporary Dramatists. 1925.

Van Doren. (A. B. L.)

Whipple.

Bookm., 53 ('21): 511; 54 ('22): 463.

Century, 103 ('22): 351 (portrait).

Contemp., 129 ('26): 363.

Cur. Op., 65 ('18): 159 (portrait); 68 ('20): 339.

Everybody's, 43 ('20): July: 49 (portrait).

Fortn., 119 ('23): 852 (L. Lewisohn).

Freeman, 1 ('20): 44.

Lit. Rev., July 16, 1921: 3; June 7, 1924: 806; Apr. 10, 1926: 2.

Liv. Age, 314 ('22): 856.

Lond. Merc., 15 ('26): 215.

Nation, 113 ('21): 626; 118 ('24): 376, 664 (L. Lewisohn), 743; 126 ('28): 19.

N. Repub., 25 ('21): 173; 32 ('22): 307; 39 ('24): 22; 50 ('27): 91.

N. Y. Herald-Tribune, Mar. 11, 1928: 1.

N. Y. Times, June 19, 1921: 17; Aug. 13, 1922: 7; May 15, 1927: 6 (portrait); Nov. 27, 1927: 5.

N. Y. World, May 22, 1927: 8m.

Sat. Rev. of Lit., 4 ('28): 541.

Theatre Arts Mo., 4 ('20): 286; 9 ('25): 4.

Yale Rev., n. s. 15 ('26): 789.

James Oppenheim—novelist, short story writer, poet.

Born at St. Paul, Minnesota, 1882. Two years later his family moved to New York, where he has lived ever since. Special student at Columbia, 1901–03. Has done settlement work, as assistant head-worker of the Hudson Guild Settlement. Superintendent of the Hebrew Technical School for Girls, 1904–07. In 1916–17 edited the magazine *The Seven Arts* (cf. *Poetry*, 9 ['16–'17]: 214).

SUGGESTIONS FOR READING

1. The following influences have entered largely into Oppenheim's work: Whitman, the Bible, and the theories of psychoanalysis developed by Freud and Jung. Without

James Oppenheim—*Continued*

considering these, no fair estimate of the value of his work can be reached.

2. In what respects does his poetry reflect the Oriental temperament?

3. What strength do you find in his work? what weakness?

BIBLIOGRAPHY

Poems
  Monday Morning. 1909.
  Songs for the New Age. 1914.
  War and Laughter. 1916.
  The Book of Self. 1917.
  The Solitary. 1919. (Includes a play.)
  Golden Bird. 1923.
  The Sea. 1924.

Plays
  The Pioneers. 1910.
  Night. 1918.

Novels
  Wild Oats. 1910.
  The Nine-Tenths. 1911.
  The Olympian. 1912.
  Idle Wives. 1914.
  The Beloved. 1915.

Short Stories
  Doctor Rast. 1909.
  Pay Envelopes. 1911.

Essays
  Your Hidden Powers. 1923.
  Behind Your Front. 1928.

Autobiography in Free Verse
  The Mystic Warrior. 1921.

STUDIES AND REVIEWS

Untermeyer. (A. P.)

Acad., 89 ('15): 218.
Bookm., 30 ('09): 322 (portrait only), 393; 57 ('23): 553.

Bost. Trans., May 28, 1921: 7; Mar. 17, 1923: 5.
Dial, 67 ('19): 301; 71 ('21): 232.
Lit. Rev., June 4, 1921: 6 (L. Untermeyer).

James Oppenheim—*Continued*

N. State., 6 ('16): 332.
N. Y. Times, Mar. 4, 1923: 6;
Mar. 16, 1924: 9.

Poetry, 5 ('14): 88; 11 ('18): 219;
16 ('20): 49; 20 ('22): 216; 25
('25): 333.

Martha Ostenso—novelist.

Born at Bergen, Norway, 1900. Brought as an infant to the United States. Educated in the public schools of Minnesota, Brandon (Canada) Collegiate School, University of Manitoba (1928), Columbia University (1921–22). Her novel *Wild Geese* won the *Pictorial Review* prize in 1925.

BIBLIOGRAPHY

Poems
A Far Land. 1924.

Novels
Wild Geese. 1925.
The Dark Dawn. 1926.
The Mad Carews. 1927.

STUDIES AND REVIEWS

Bookm., 62 ('25): 493; 64 ('27):
632.
Bost. Trans., Oct. 31, 1925: 3;
Nov. 13, 1926: 3.
N. Repub., 53 ('27): 144.

N. Y. Times, Oct. 18, 1925: 8;
Oct. 24, 1926: 6; Oct. 9, 1927: 6.
N. Y. Herald-Tribune, Nov. 8,
1925: 1; Oct. 9, 1927: 4.
Sat. Rev. of Lit., 3 ('26): 191; 4
('27): 197.

Anne Parrish—novelist.

Mrs. Charles Albert Corliss. Born at Colorado Springs, Colorado, 1888. Educated in private schools in Colorado and Delaware. Won the Harper prize for 1925 with *The Perennial Bachelor*.

Anne Parrish—*Continued*

Bibliography

Novels
A Pocketful of Poses. 1923.
Semi-Attached. 1924.
The Perennial Bachelor. 1925.
To-Morrow Morning. 1927.
All Kneeling. 1928.

Essays and Sketches
Lustres. 1924. (With Dillwyn Parrish.)

Studies and Reviews

Bookm., 64 ('27): 737.
N. Y. Herald-Tribune, Sept. 9,
1928: 7.
N. Y. Times, Sept. 9, 1928: 5.
Sat. Rev. of Lit., 3 ('27): 497.

Elliot H(arold) Paul—novelist.

Born at Malden, Massachusetts, 1891. Educated in the public schools and at the University of Maine, 1908–09. Served in the A. E. F.

Bibliography

Novels
Indelible. 1922.
Impromptu. 1923.
Imperturbe. 1924.

Studies and Reviews

Bost. Trans., Apr. 30, 1924: 4.
Lit. Rev., May 5, 1923: 659.
N. Y. Herald-Tribune, Apr. 15,
1923: 18.
N. Y. Times, Apr. 8, 1923: 9;
Apr. 27, 1924: 8.

Josephine Preston Peabody—poet, dramatist.

Mrs. L. S. Marks. Born at New York City, 1874. Educated at Girls' Latin School, Boston, and at Radcliffe,

Josephine Preston Peabody—*Continued*

1894–96. Instructor in English at Wellesley College, 1901–03. Her play *The Piper* obtained the Stratford-on-Avon prize in 1910. Died in 1922.

BIBLIOGRAPHY

Poems

The Wayfarers. 1898.
Fortune and Men's Eyes. 1900. (Includes a play.)
The Singing Leaves. 1903.
The Singing Man. 1911.
Harvest Moon. 1916.
Collected Poems. 1927.

Plays

Marlowe. 1901. (Rev. ed., 1905.)
Pan. 1904. (A Masque. Music by C. A. E. Harriss.)
The Piper. 1909.
The Wolf of Gubbio. 1913.
The Wings. 1914.
The Chameleon. 1917.
Portrait of Mrs. W. 1922.
Collected Plays. 1927.

Tales

Old Greek Folk-Stories Told Anew. 1897.

Autobiography

Diary and Letters. 1925. (Sel. and ed. by Christina Hopkinson Baker.)

STUDIES AND REVIEWS

Dickinson. (P. N. A. T.)
Eaton, W. P. Plays and Players. 1916.
Moses.
Rittenhouse.

Bk. Buyer, 21 ('00): 9 (portrait).
Bookm., 47 ('18): 550.
Bost. Trans., Apr. 29, 1922: 7; Nov. 21, 1925: 3.

Cut. Lit., 49 ('10): 435 (portrait).
Lit. Rev., June 24, 1922: 755.
New England M., n. s. 33 ('05): 426; 39 ('08): 236; 42 ('10): 270 (portrait).
Poetry, 9 ('17): 269.
Springfield Repub., Dec. 27, 1925: 7a.

Bliss Perry—critic.

Born at Williamstown, Massachusetts, 1860. A. B., Williams, 1881; A. M., 1883. Studied at the universities of Berlin and Strassburg. Honorary higher degrees. Professor of English at Williams College, 1886–93; at Princeton, 1893–1900. Editor of the *Atlantic Monthly*, 1899–1909. Professor of English literature at Harvard, 1907– . Harvard lecturer at University of Paris, 1909–10.

BIBLIOGRAPHY

Novels
The Broughton House. 1890.
The Plated City. 1895.

Short Stories
Salem Kittredge. 1894.
The Powers at Play. 1899.

Critical Essays and Studies
A Study of Prose Fiction. 1902. (Rev. ed., 1920.)
The Amateur Spirit. 1904.
Park-Street Papers. 1908.
The American Mind. 1912.
The American Spirit in Literature. 1918.
A Study of Poetry. 1920.
The Praise of Folly. 1923.

Familiar Essays
Pools and Ripples. 1927.

Criticism and Biography
Walt Whitman. 1906. (Rev. ed., 1908.)
John Greenleaf Whittier. 1907.
Thomas Carlyle. 1915.
Life and Letters of Henry Lee Higginson. 1921. (Editor.)
The Heart of Emerson's Journals. 1926. (Editor.)

STUDIES AND REVIEWS

Bookm., 36 ('12): 443.
Dial, 70 ('21): 347; 72 ('22): 305 (R. Herrick).
Lit. Rev., Feb. 18, 1922: 428 (Boynton); May 28, 1927: 2.
Nation, 114 ('22): 321.
N. Repub., 30 ('22): 319.
N. Y. Times, Nov. 25, 1923: 5.
Outlook, 78 ('04): 880 (portrait); 102 ('12): 648.
Spec., 110 ('13): 809.
Springfield Repub., Dec. 8, 1923: 8.

William Lyon Phelps—critic.

Born at New Haven, Connecticut, 1865. A. B., Yale, 1887; Ph. D. 1891; A. M., Harvard, 1891. Instructor in English literature at Yale, 1892–96, assistant professor of the English language and literature, 1896–1901; Lampson professor since 1901.

For complete bibliography, see Who's Who in America.

BIBLIOGRAPHY

Beginnings of the English Romantic Movement. 1893.
Essays on Modern Novelists. 1910.
Essays on Russian Novelists. 1911.
The Advance of the English Novel. 1916.
The Advance of English Poetry. 1918.
The Twentieth Century Theatre. 1918.
Essays on Modern Dramatists. 1920–21.

Ernest Poole—novelist.

Born at Chicago, 1880. A. B., Princeton, 1902. Lived in University Settlement, New York, 1902–05, studying social conditions, especially in connection with child-labor, and in the movement to fight tuberculosis. He helped Upton Sinclair (q. v.) gather stockyards material for *The Jungle.* War correspondent in Germany and France, 1914–15. As a socialist, Mr. Poole also worked for a time in Russia with the revolutionaries.

The familiarity with dockyards and dockmen, which is such a striking feature of *The Harbor,* dates back to Mr. Poole's boyhood. *His Family* was awarded the Pulitzer novel prize in 1918.

BIBLIOGRAPHY

Novels
The Voice of the Street. 1906.
* The Harbor. 1915.
His Family. 1917.
His Second Wife. 1918.
Blind. 1920.

Ernest Poole—*Continued*
Beggar's Gold. 1921.
Millions. 1922.
Danger. 1923.
The Avalanche. 1924.
The Hunter's Moon. 1925.
With Eastern Eyes. 1926.
Silent Storms. 1927.

Russian Studies, Sketches, and Tales
The Village. 1918.
"The Dark People." 1918.
The Little Dark Man. 1925.

STUDIES AND REVIEWS

Baldwin.
Van Doren. (C. A. N.)

Atlan. (Bookshelf), 127 ('21):
supp. II: 10.
Bookm., 41 ('15): 115 (portrait).
Bost. Trans., Nov. 9, 1921: 4;
Apr. 21, 1923: 4; June 14, 1924:
4.
Cur. Op., 58 ('15): 266 (portrait).
Lit. Digest, I. B. R. Aug., 1924:
673.
Lit. Rev., Dec. 17, 1921: 275;

Dec. 23, 1922: 340; June 2,
1923: 731.
N. Y. Times, Sept. 24, 1922: 14;
May 13, 1923: 13; June 8, 1924:
8; Apr. 26, 1925: 8; Oct. 4, 1925:
2; Nov. 21, 1926: 28.
Sat. Rev. of Lit., 2 ('25): 235;
3 ('26): 466.
Springfield Repub., July 8, 1923:
7a.

See also Book Review Digest, 1915,
1917, 1918, 1920.

Ezra (Loomis) Pound—poet, critic.
Born at Hailey, Idaho, 1885. Of English descent; on his
mother's side distantly related to Longfellow. Ph. B.,
Hamilton College. Fellow of the University of Pennsylvania. Traveled in Spain, in Italy, in Provence, 1906–07;
lived in Venice, London, Paris, and recently in Rapallo.
London editor of the *Little Review*, 1917–19, and foreign
correspondent of *Poetry*, 1912–19.

SUGGESTIONS FOR READING
1. Mr. Pound is an experimenter in verse, who has come
under many influences and belonged to many schools. His

Ezra (Loomis) Pound—*Continued*

work should be studied chronologically to discover these changes in interest and relationship. To be noted among the influences are: (1) the mediæval poetry of Provence; (2) the Greek poets; (3) the Latin poets of the Empire; (4) among modern French poets, Laurent Tailhade; (5) the poets of China and Japan, whom he learned to know through the manuscript notes of Ernest Fenollosa; (6) the work of the English Imagists (cf. especially the poems of T. E. Hulme, published in Mr. Pound's volume called *Ripostes* and elsewhere).

2. Consider also this from his own theory of poetry: "Poetry is a sort of inspired mathematics, which gives us equations, not for abstract figures, triangles, spheres and the like, but equations for the human emotions. If one have a mind which inclines to magic rather than science, one will prefer to speak of these equations as spells or incantations; it sounds more arcane, mysterious, recondite." Can this be related to the qualities of Mr. Pound's poetry?

3. After reading Mr. Pound's output, discuss the adequacy of the following: "When content has become for an artist merely something to inflate and display form with, then the petty serves as well as the great, the ignoble equally with the lofty, the unlovely like the beautiful, the sordid as the clean. . . . Real feeling consequently becomes rarer, and the artist descends to trivialities of observation, vagaries of assertion, or mere bravado of standards and expression— pure tilting at convention."

BIBLIOGRAPHY

Poems
A Quinzaine for This Yule. London, 1908.
A Lume Spento. Venice, 1909.
Exultations. London, 1909.
Personæ. London, 1909. (* Enl. ed., New York, 1926.)
Provença. 1910.
Canzoni. London, 1911.
Ripostes. London, 1912. Boston, 1913. (Contains poems by T. E. Hulme.)
The Sonnets and Ballate of Guido Cavalcanti. 1912. (Translator.)

Ezra (Loomis) Pound—*Continued*

Cathay. London, 1915. (Translations for the most part from the Chinese of Rihaku, from the notes of Ernest Fenollosa.)

Lustra. London, 1916. New York, 1917. (Contents vary.)

Quia Pauper Amavi. London, 1919.

The Fourth Canto. London, 1919. (Priv. ptd.)

Hugh Selwyn Mauberley. London, 1920.

* Umbra. London, 1920. (Contains translations from Guido Cavalcanti and Arnaut Daniel, and poems by T. E. Hulme.)

Poems, 1918–21. 1921.

Sixteen Cantos of Ezra Pound. Paris, 1924.

Cantos I–XVI. London, 1925.

Cantos XVII–XXVII. London, 1928.

* Selected Poems. London, 1928. (Edited by T. S. Eliot.)

Essays and Studies

The Spirit of Romance. 1910.

Certain Noble Plays of Japan. Dundrum, 1916. (Edited from the MSS. of Ernest Fenollosa.)

Twelve Dialogues of Fontenelle. London, 1917. (Translator.)

Noh—or, Accomplishment. London, 1916. (With Ernest Fenollosa.)

Pavannes and Divisions. 1918.

Instigations. 1920. (Contains an essay by Ernest Fenollosa.)

The Natural Philosophy of Love, by Rémy de Gourmont. 1922. (Translator.)

Indiscretions. London, 1923.

Antheil and the Treatise on Harmony. Paris, 1924.

Biography

Gaudier-Brzeska. London, 1916.

STUDIES AND REVIEWS

Aiken.

Monroe.

Untermeyer. (A. P.)

Acad., 81 ('11): 354.

Ath., 1911, 2: 238; 1919, 2: 1065, 1132, 1268.

Bookm., 35 ('12): 156; 46 ('18): 577.

Chapbook, 1–2, May, 1920: 22 (Fletcher).

Dial, 54 ('13): 370; 72 ('22): 87.

Egoist, 2 ('15): 71; 4 ('17): 7, 27, 44.

Eng. Rev., 2 ('09): 627.

Lit. Rev., Feb. 19, 1927: 1.

N. Repub., 16 ('18): 83; 30 ('22): 232.

N. State., 8 ('17): 332, 476.

N. Y. Times, Feb. 5, 1922: 2; Jan. 23, 1927: 21.

Poetry, 7 ('16): 249 (Sandburg); 11 ('18): 330; 14 ('19): 52; 15 ('20): 211; 16 ('20): 213; 21 ('22): 95; 26 ('25): 90 (H. Monroe); 30 ('27): 216.

(John) Herbert Quick—novelist.

Born near Steamboat Rock, Greenly County, Iowa, 1861. Reared on farm; attended country schools; engaged in teaching 1882–90, becoming principal of ward school in Mason City, Iowa, and meanwhile studying law. Admitted to Iowa bar in 1889; engaged in practice at Sioux City, 1890–1909. Editor of *Farm and Fireside*, 1909–16. Mayor of Sioux City, 1898–1900. Author of the *Fairview Idea*, 1919; and of *Vandemark's Folly*, 1922, which introduces fresh material (canalboat life) into fiction, and also contributes to the literature that deals with the opening-up of the Middle West. Died in 1925.

Studies and Reviews

Bost. Trans., Aug. 15, 1923: 6; Dec. 17, 1924: 4.
Ind., 111 ('23): 69.
Lit. Digest, I. B. R. Jan., 1925: 36; Nov., 1925: 787.
Lit. Rev., Feb. 25, 1922: 445; Sept. 15, 1923: 39.
Nation, 114 ('22): 318.
N. Repub., 31 ('22): 82; 41 ('25): 265.

N. Y. Times, Feb. 19, 1922: 5; Aug. 5, 1923: 17; Dec. 7, 1924: 8; Nov. 15, 1925: 7.
Sat. Rev. of Lit., 1 ('24): 341; 2 ('25): 293.
Springfield Repub., Oct. 14, 1923: 7a.

See also Book Review Digest, 1919, 1924.

Lizette Woodworth Reese—poet.

Born at Baltimore, 1856. Educated in private and public schools. Teacher in Baltimore high school until 1921.

Her poems, always conventional in form and limited in ideas, are admired for their simplicity, intensity of emotion, and perfection of technique.

Bibliography

Poems

A Branch of May. 1887.
A Handful of Lavender. 1891.
A Quiet Road. 1896.
A Wayside Lute. 1909.

Lizette Woodworth Reese—*Continued*

Spicewood. 1920.
Wild Cherry. 1923.
The Selected Poems. 1926.
Little Henrietta. 1927.

STUDIES AND REVIEWS

Rittenhouse.
Untermeyer. (A. P.)

Bost. Trans., Jan. 29, 1921: 9;
Mar. 29, 1924: 13.
Lit. Digest, I. B. R. July, 1924:
599
Lit. Rev., July 31, 1926: 4.

N. Repub., 48 ('26): 23.
N. Y. Herald-Tribune, July 11,
1926: 5.
Outlook, 136 ('24): 439.
Poetry, 23 ('24): 341.
Sat. Rev. of Lit., 3 ('26): 7 (P.
Colum).

Agnes Repplier—essayist.

Born at Philadelphia, 1858, of French extraction. Educated at the Sacred Heart Convent, Torresdale, Pennsylvania. Litt. D., University of Pennsylvania, 1902; Yale,
1925. Has traveled much in Europe. Roman Catholic.
Received the Laetare medal from the University of Notre
Dame, 1911.

BIBLIOGRAPHY

Essays
    Books and Men. 1888.
    Points of View. 1891.
    Essays in Miniature. 1892.
    Essays in Idleness. 1893.
    In the Dozy Hours. 1894.
    Varia. 1897.
    The Fireside Sphinx. 1901.
    Compromises. 1904.
    A Happy Half-Century. 1908.
    Americans and Others. 1912.
    Counter-Currents. 1916.
    Points of Friction. 1920.
    Under Dispute. 1924.

Description and Travel
    Philadelphia. 1898.

Agnes Repplier—*Continued*

Biography
J. William White, M. D. 1919.
Père Marquette. 1929.

Autobiography
In Our Convent Days. 1905.

STUDIES AND REVIEWS

Halsey. (Women.)
Pattee.

Critic, 47 ('05): 204 (portrait).
Lit. Digest, 48 ('14): 827 (portrait).
Lit. Digest, I. B. R. Oct., 1924: 780.

Nation, 119 ('24): 76.
N. Repub., 7 ('16): 20 (Francis Hackett).
N. State., 7 ('16): 597.
N. Y. Times, July 6, 1924: 4.
Spec., 117 ('16): 105.
Springfield Repub., July 28, 1924: 6.

Alice (Caldwell) Hegan Rice—novelist.

Mrs. Cale Young Rice. Born at Shelbyville, Kentucky, 1870. Educated in private schools. One of the founders of the Cabbage Patch Settlement House, Louisville. Uses her own experience in charity work in her books.

For complete bibliography, see Who's Who in America.

BIBLIOGRAPHY

Mrs. Wiggs of the Cabbage Patch. 1901.
Lovey Mary. 1903.
Sandy. 1905.
Captain June. 1907.
Mr. Opp. 1909.
A Romance of Billy-Goat Hill. 1912.
The Honorable Percival. 1918.
Calvary Alley. 1918.
Quin. 1921.
The Buffer. 1929.

STUDIES AND REVIEWS

Overton. (O. W. N.)

Bookm., 29 ('09): 412; 32 ('10): 369.
Bost. Trans., Sept. 14, 1921: 6.
N. Y. Times, Sept. 11, 1921: 24.

Outlook, 72 ('02): 802 (portrait); 78 ('04): 282, 286 (portrait).

See also Book Review Digest, 1905, 1907, 1909, 1912, 1918.

Cale Young Rice—poet, dramatist.

Born at Dixon, Kentucky, 1872. Married Alice Hegan Rice (q. v.).

For complete bibliography, see Who's Who in America.

BIBLIOGRAPHY

Collected Plays and Poems. 1915.
Earth and New Earth. 1916.
Wraiths and Realities. 1918.
Sea Poems. 1921.
Youth's Way. 1923.
Bitter Brew. 1925.
Selected Plays and Poems. 1926.
Stygian Freight. 1927.

STUDIES AND REVIEWS

Bookm., 47 ('18): 550 (Phelps).
Bookm., (Lond.) 64 ('23): 152; 65 ('23): 34; 68 ('25): 210; 69 ('25): 28.
Bost. Trans., Sept. 20, 1924: 5.
Lit. Rev., May 26, 1923: 723; Apr. 25, 1925: 6.
Lond. Times, May 29, 1924: 342.
N. Y. Herald-Tribune, Oct. 19, 1924: 9.
N. Y. Times, Apr. 8, 1923: 24.
Springfield Repub., Oct. 9, 1921: 9a; June 3, 1923: 7a.

Mary Roberts Rinehart—novelist.

Born at Pittsburgh, Pennsylvania, 1876. Educated in the public schools. Studied nursing. Married Dr. Stanley Marshall Rinehart in 1896. Started vogue of mystery play with *The Bat* (with Avery Hopwood), 1920.

For complete bibliography, see Who's Who in America.

BIBLIOGRAPHY

The Circular Staircase. 1908.
The Man in Lower Ten. 1909.
Amazing Adventures of Letitia Carberry. 1911.
"K." 1915.

Charles G(eorge) D(ouglas) Roberts—poet, nature-writer.
Born at Douglas, New Brunswick, 1860. Studied at the University of New Brunswick, 1876. Has been a teacher, editor, soldier. In France during the War.

Major Roberts has published many volumes of poems, besides novels and animal stories.

BIBLIOGRAPHY

Poems
Orion. 1880.
Poems. 1901.
The Book of the Rose. 1903.
New Poems. 1919.
The Sweet o' the Year. 1925.

Short Stories
The Haunters of the Silences. 1907.
Kings in Exile. 1910.
Babes of the Wild. 1912.
The Secret Trails. 1916.
Wisdom of the Wilderness. 1922.
They Who Walk in the Wild. 1924.

STUDIES AND REVIEWS

Cappon, James. Charles G. D. Roberts. (With selections, a portrait, and bibliography.)

Bookm., 49 ('19): 623.
Bost. Trans., May 29, 1923: 4.

Lit. Digest, I. B. R. Aug., 1924: 682.
Lit. Rev., Apr. 1, 1922: 543.
N. State., 23 ('24): 626.
N. Y. Times, Mar. 26, 1922: 19.

Elizabeth Madox Roberts—novelist.
Born at Perryville, Kentucky, 1885. Ph. B., University of Chicago, 1921. Received the Fiske poetry prize for the group of poems later published as *Under the Tree*. Has used her intimate knowledge of Kentucky life and speech in both verse and prose.

BIBLIOGRAPHY

Poems
In the Great Steep's Garden. 1915.
Under the Tree. 1922.

Elizabeth Madox Roberts—*Continued*

Novels
  The Time of Man. 1926.
  My Heart and My Flesh. 1927.
  Jingling in the Wind. 1928.

STUDIES AND REVIEWS

Atlan. (Bookshelf), Dec., 1927.
Lond. Times, Mar. 3, 1927: 142.
Manchester Guardian, 16 ('27): 193.

Nation, 125 ('27): 606.
N. Repub., 53 ('27): 50.
Poetry, 22 ('23): 45.

Edwin Arlington Robinson—poet.

Born at Head Tide, Maine, 1869. Educated at Gardiner, Maine, on the Kennebec River ("Tilbury Town"). Studied at Harvard, 1891–93. Struggled in various ways to make a living in New York, even working in the subway, while publishing his first poems. His *Captain Craig*, 1902, attracted the attention of Roosevelt, who gave the author a position in the New York Custom House, which he held 1905–10. Since then he has given his entire time to poetry. Has received many poetic awards, including the Pulitzer prize in 1922 (*Collected Poems*), in 1925 (*The Man Who Died Twice*), and in 1928 (*Tristram*).

SUGGESTIONS FOR READING

1. A good introduction to Mr. Robinson's work is Miss Lowell's review of his *Collected Poems*, in the *Dial*, 72 ('22): 130. Although Miss Lowell's contention that Mr. Robinson is our greatest living poet would be disputed by some critics, her article suggests many points of departure in the study of his very important contribution to American poetry.

2. Divide Mr. Robinson's work into two groups: (1) poems of which the material is based upon literature; (2) those of which it comes from his own life experience. Is it possible to say now which of these two groups has the better chance of long endurance? Can you decide how far literature

Edwin Arlington Robinson—*Continued*

has had a good effect upon Mr. Robinson's work, and how far it has lessened the value of his poetry?

3. Consider as a group the poems that grow out of Mr. Robinson's New England origin. In what ways is he characteristic of New England? Compare his work with that of Mr. Frost in this respect.

4. Compare and contrast Mr. Robinson's portraits of persons with names as titles with similar portraits in the *Spoon River Anthology*. This type of verse seems to have been developed independently by both poets.

5. An interesting study could be made of the influence on Robinson of Crabbe; another, of the influence of Hardy.

6. Another interesting study might grow out of the consideration of Robinson as a poet born twenty years too soon. How much has the temper of his work been determined by the fact that he had to wait so long for recognition?

7. What are the main features of Mr. Robinson's philosophy as suggested in the poems?

8. Can you find many poems that sing? What is to be said of the poet's mastery of rhythms?

9. After reading the best of Mr. Robinson's work, it is interesting to look up the comments of various admirers of it published on the occasion of his fiftieth birthday, in the *New York Times*, December 21, 1919, or the quotations from this article in *Poetry*, 15 ('20): 265, and to see how far your judgment bears out these extravagant statements.

10. The influence of Robinson's work on younger American poets, especially on Lindsay and Sandburg, makes an interesting study.

11. What justification is there for Robinson's treatment of the hackneyed material of Arthurian romance?

BIBLIOGRAPHY

Poems

The Torrent and the Night Before. 1896. (Priv. ptd.)
The Children of the Night. 1897.
Captain Craig. 1902. (Rev. ed., 1915.)

Edwin Arlington Robinson—*Continued*

The Town Down the River. 1910.
The Man Against the Sky. 1916.
Merlin. 1917.
The Three Taverns. 1920.
Lancelot. 1920.
Avon's Harvest. 1921.
* Collected Poems. 1921. (New eds., 1924, 1927.)
Roman Bartholow. 1923.
The Man Who Died Twice. 1924.
Dionysus in Doubt. 1925.
* Tristram. 1927.
Sonnets, 1889–1927. 1928.
Cavender's House. 1929.
Modred, A Fragment. 1929.

Plays

Van Zorn. 1914.
The Porcupine. 1915.

STUDIES AND REVIEWS

Beebe, L. M. E. A. Robinson and the Arthurian Legend. 1927.
Boynton. (S. C. A.)
Farrar.
Lowell.
Maynard.
Monroe.
Morris, L. R. The Poetry of Edwin Arlington Robinson. 1923.
Redman, Ben Ray. Edwin Arlington Robinson. 1925.
Squire.
Untermeyer. (A. P.)
Van Doren. (A. B. L.)
Van Doren, M. E. A. Robinson. 1927.
Weirick.
Whipple.
Wood.

Am. Rev., 1 ('23): 180.
Bookm., 45 ('17): 429 (portrait); 47 ('18): 551; 50 ('20): 507; 51 ('20): 457.

Bookm. (Lond.), 63 ('23): 206.
Bost. Trans., Apr. 2, 1921: 6 (Braithwaite); Apr. 21, 1923: 5; Apr. 4, 1925: 2.
Chapbook, 1–2, May, 1920: 1 (Fletcher).
Cur. Op., 72 ('22): 525.
Dial, 34 ('03): 18; 72 ('22): 130 (Amy Lowell); 77 ('24): 168.
Fortn., 86 ('06): 429; 117 ('22): 649 (J. Drinkwater).
Forum, 45 ('11): 80; 51 ('14): 305; 67 ('22): 179; 78 ('27): 312.
Freeman, 4 ('21): 43 (Aiken); 5 ('22): 141; 7 ('23): 140.
Lit. Digest, I. B. R. May, 1923: 23; Aug., 1925: 586.
Lit. Rev., Apr. 2, 1921: 6; Feb. 11, 1922: 409; June 23, 1923: 781; Apr. 4, 1925: 5.
Lond. Merc., 13 ('26): 401 (J. C. Squire).
Lond. Times, Sep. 18, 1924: 582.

Edwin Arlington Robinson—*Continued*

Nation, 75 ('02): 465; 111 ('20): 453; 112 ('21): 596; 113 ('21): 570 (C. Van Doren); 116 ('23): 700; 118 ('24): Apr. 16, supp. 445; 124 ('27): 586.

New Eng. M., 33 ('05): 425.

N. Repub., 2 ('15): 267; 7 ('16): 96 (Amy Lowell); 23 ('20): 259; 29 ('22): 311; 51 ('27): 22.

N. Y. Times, June 26, 1921: 27; Oct. 30, 1921: 6; Mar. 25, 1923: 3; Mar. 23, 1924: 10; Mar. 29, 1925: 5; May 8, 1927: 1 (portrait).

No. Am., 211 ('20): 121.

Outlook, 105 ('13): 736; 112 ('16): 786; 123 ('19): 535.

Poetry, 8 ('16): 46; 10 ('17): 211; 15 ('20): 265; 16 ('20): 217; 19 ('22): 278; 24 ('24): 96; 25 ('25): 206; 27 ('25): 40.

Sat. Rev. of Lit., 1 ('25): 741 (L. Untermeyer); 3 ('27): 839 (portrait).

Spec., 131 ('23–'24): 759, 1044.

Carl Sandburg—poet.

Born at Galesburg, Illinois, 1878, of Swedish stock. At thirteen drove a milk-wagon, and for the next six years did all kinds of rough work—as porter in a barber shop, scene-shifter, truck-handler in a brickyard, turner-apprentice in a pottery, dish-washer in hotels, harvest-hand in Kansas.

During the Spanish-American War served as private in Porto Rico.

Studied at Lombard College, Galesburg, 1898–1902, where he was captain of the basket-ball team and editor-in-chief of the college paper.

After leaving college, earned his living in various ways— as advertising manager for a department store, salesman, newspaper man, "safety first" expert. Worked also as district organizer for the Social-Democratic party of Wisconsin and was secretary to the mayor of Milwaukee, 1910–12.

In 1904 he had published a small pamphlet of poems, but his first real appearance before the public was in *Poetry*, 1914. In the same year he was awarded the Levinson prize for his "Chicago." In 1918 he shared with Margaret Widdemer the prize of the Poetry Society of America, and in 1921, with Stephen Vincent Benét (q. v.).

Carl Sandburg—*Continued*

Mr. Sandburg has a good voice and sings his poems to the accompaniment of the guitar.

Suggestions for Reading

1. In judging Mr. Sandburg's work, it is important to remember that his theory involves complete freedom from conventions of all sorts—in thinking, in metrical form, and in vocabulary. His aim seems to be to reproduce the impressions that all phases of life make upon him.

2. Consider whether his early prairie-environment had anything to do with the large scale of his imagination, the appeal to him of enormous periods of time, masses of men, and forces.

3. Do you find elements of universality in his exaggerated localisms? Do they combine to form a definite philosophy?

4. What effect do the eccentricities and crudities of form have upon you? Do you consider them an essential part of his poetic expression or blemishes that he may one day overcome?

5. Do you find elements of greatness in Mr. Sandburg's work? Do you think they are likely to outweigh his obvious defects?

6. Compare and contrast his democratic ideals with those of Lindsay.

7. Is Sandburg a realist? a materialist? What is the relation of his deliberate coarseness to his view of life?

Bibliography

Poems
Chicago Poems. 1916.
Cornhuskers. 1918.
Smoke and Steel. 1920.
Slabs of the Sunburnt West. 1922.
Selected Poems. 1926. (Ed. by Rebecca West.)
The American Songbag. 1927. (Compiler.)
Good Morning, America. 1928.

Children's Tales
Rootabaga Stories. 1922.
Rootabaga Pigeons. 1923.
The Rootabaga Country. 1929. (Reprints.)

Carl Sandburg—*Continued*

Biography

Abraham Lincoln, the Prairie Years. 1926. (Abr. ed., 1929.)

Abe Lincoln Grows Up. 1928. (First twenty-seven chapters of preceding book.)

Articles

The Chicago Race Riots. 1919.

STUDIES AND REVIEWS

Aiken.

Beach.

Boynton. (S. C. A.)

Hansen.

Karsner.

Lowell.

Maynard.

Monroe.

Sherman. (A.)

Untermeyer. (A. P.)

Van Doren. (M. M.)

——. (A. B. L.)

Weirick.

Whipple.

Wood.

Am. Merc., 8 ('26): 381.

Am. Rev., 2 ('24): 356.

Bookm., 47 ('18): 389; 52 ('21): 242, 285 (*for* 385); 53 ('21): 389 (portrait); 54 ('21): 360; 63 ('26): 86.

Bookm. (Lond.), 70 ('26): 126.

Bost. Trans., July 29, 1922: 4; Feb. 6, 1926: 2; Oct. 6, 1926: 4.

Cal. Mod. Lett., 3 ('26): 75.

Chapbook, 1–2, May, 1920: 15 (Fletcher).

Dial, 65 ('18): 263 (Untermeyer); 73 ('22): 563; 80 ('26): 513.

Edin. R., 244 ('26): 204.

Forum, 75 ('26): 632.

Ind., 116 ('26): 193; 117 ('26): 331.

Lit. Digest, I. B. R. Feb., 1926: 189.

Lit. Rev., Nov. 11, 1922: 193; Feb. 13, 1926: 1.

Liv. Age, 308 ('21): 231.

Lond. Times, July 29, 1926: 503.

Nation, 115 ('22): 96; 117 ('23): 651; 122 ('26): 149.

Nation and Ath., 39 ('26): 130.

N. Repub., 22 ('20): 98; 25 ('20): 86; 32 ('22): 26; 33 ('22): 126; 46 ('26): 116; 49 ('26): Dec. 8, supp. 86 (Untermeyer).

N. State., 27 ('26): June 5, supp. iii.

N. Y. Herald-Tribune, Feb. 7, 1926: 1 (Sherman); Feb. 21, 1926: 8; Oct. 10, 1926: 4.

N. Y. Times, June 4, 1922: 11; Feb. 14, 1926: 1; Oct. 21, 1928: 2.

No. Am., 223 ('26): 353.

Outlook, 142 ('26): 296.

Poetry, 8 ('16): 90; 13 ('18): 155; 15 ('20): 271; 17 ('21): 266; 20 ('22): 332.

Sat. Rev. of Lit., 2 ('26): 659 (J. Drinkwater); 3 ('26): 251 (Untermeyer).

Spec., 136 ('26): 911.

Yale Rev., n. s. 13 ('24): 409.

George Santayana—poet, critic.

Born at Madrid, Spain, 1863. Came to the United States, 1872. A. B., Harvard, 1886; A. M., Ph. D., 1889. In 1889 began to teach philosophy at Harvard; professor, 1907–12.

While Mr. Santayana's chief work is in philosophy, he belongs to literature by the beauty of his poems, especially his sonnets, and by the quality of his prose.

BIBLIOGRAPHY

Poems
Sonnets. 1894.
The Hermit of Carmel. 1901.
Poems. 1923.

Play
Lucifer. 1899. (Rev. ed., 1924.)

Philosophical Essays and Studies
The Sense of Beauty. 1896.
Interpretations of Poetry and Religion. 1900.
The Life of Reason. 1905–06.
Three Philosophical Poets. 1910.
Winds of Doctrine. 1913.
Egotism in German Philosophy. 1916.
Philosophical Opinion in America. 1918.
Character and Opinion in the United States. 1920.
Little Essays. 1920. (Reprints. Ed. by Logan Pearsall Smith in collaboration with the author.)
Soliloquies in England. 1922.
Skepticism and Animal Faith. 1923.
Dialogues in Limbo. 1925.
The Realm of Essence. 1927. (Bk. I of Realms of Being.)
Platonism and the Spiritual Life. 1927.

STUDIES AND REVIEWS

Cook.
Priestley.
Rittenhouse.
Untermeyer. (A. P.)
Van Doren. (M. M.)
——. (A. B. L.)
Weirick.

Acad., 79 ('10): 561.
Am. Rev., 1 ('23): 190.
Ath., 1913, 1: 353.
Bookm. (Lond.), 58 ('20): 208.
Bost. Trans., Dec. 19, 1925: 5.
Critic, 42 ('03): 129.
Cur. Op., 55 ('13): 120; 69 ('20): 860. (Portraits.)

George Santayana—*Continued*

Dial, 73 ('22): 559 (B. Russell); 75 ('23): 278.

Freeman, 7 ('23): 71, 573 (B. Russell).

Ind., 61 ('06); 335 (portrait).

Lit. Rev., Sept. 22, 1923: 62; May 21, 1927: 4.

Liv. Age, 307 ('20): 50; 308 ('21): 200; 312 ('21): 300 (J. Middleton Murry).

Lond. Merc., 2 ('20): 411 (R. Bridges); 6 ('22): 658; 8 ('23): 436.

Lond. Times, June 8, 1922: 377; May 31, 1923: 368, 546; Aug. 6, 1925: 519; May 26, 1927: 370.

Nation, 109 ('19): 12; 117 ('23): 299.

Nation and Ath., 31 ('22): 474; 37 ('25): 650.

N. Repub., 23 ('20): 221; 25 ('21): 321; 33 ('22): Nov. 29, supp. 10; 34 ('23): 102; 35 ('23): 294.

N. State., 16 ('21): 729; 19 ('22): 325; 21 ('23): 81; 29 ('27): 279.

N. Y. Times, Aug. 13, 1922, 8; Mar. 14, 1923: 11; June 3, 1923: 6; Oct. 18, 1925: 2; June 5, 1927: 2.

Outlook, 126 ('20): 729 (portrait).

Poetry, 23 ('24): 338; 24 ('24): 320 (H. Monroe).

Spec., 95 ('05): 119; 125 ('20): 239; 126 ('21): 19; 129 ('22): 144.

Lew (R.) Sarett—poet.

Born at Chicago, 1888. A. B., Beloit, 1911. Studied at Harvard, 1911–12; LL. B., University of Illinois, 1916. Woodsman and guide in the Northwest several months each year for sixteen years. Teacher of English and oratory. Since 1921, professor in Northwestern University School of Speech. Lecturer on the Canadian North and on Indian life. Sarett's *Many, Many Moons: A Book of Wilderness Poems*, 1920 (with an introduction by Carl Sandburg), is a reflection of his familiarity with Indian material. Received the Levinson prize for his poem, "The Box of God," 1921.

BIBLIOGRAPHY

Poems

Many Many Moons. 1920.
The Box of God. 1922.
Slow Smoke. 1925.

Lew (R.) Sarett—*Continued*

STUDIES AND REVIEWS

Hansen.
Monroe.
Untermeyer. (A. P.)
Wilkinson. (P).

Lit. Rev., Jan. 6, 1923: 364 (W. R. Benét).

Nation, 115 ('22): Dec. 6, supp. 624.
Poetry, 17 ('20): 158; 21 ('23): 325; 27 ('25): 88.

See also Book Review Digest, 1920.

Evelyn Scott—poet, novelist.
Mrs. Scott has lived many years in Brazil (cf. *Poetry*, 15 ['19]: 100).

BIBLIOGRAPHY

Poems
Precipitations. 1920.

Novels
The Narrow House. 1921.
Narcissus. 1922.
The Golden Door. 1925.
Migrations. 1927.

Short Stories
Ideals. 1927.

Autobiography
Escapade. 1923.

STUDIES AND REVIEWS

Bost. Trans., Mar. 26, 1921: 6; Aug. 15, 1923: 6.
Cent., 103 ('22): 520 (Canby).
Dial, 70 ('21): 591, 594; 73 ('22): 346; 75 ('23): 598.
Freeman, 3 ('21): 452.
Lit. Rev., Apr. 2, 1921: 3; June 15,

1922: 803; Sept. 8, 1923: 19; May 9, 1925: 3.
Lond. Merc., 5 ('22): 319.
Nation, 112 ('21): 20, 596; 117 ('23): 141 (L. Lewisohn); 121 ('25): 76; 124 ('27): 505.

Evelyn Scott—*Continued*

N. Repub., 28 ('21): 305 (P. Colum); 31 ('22): 283 (Lovett); 35 ('23): 363.

N. Y. Times, Mar. 13, 1921: 18 (Sinclair Lewis); May 3, 1925: 22; Apr. 10, 1927: 8.

Poetry, 17 ('21): 334.

Sat. Rev., 132 ('21): 439.

See also Book Review Digest, 1920, 1921.

Anne Douglas Sedgwick—novelist.

Mrs. Basil De Sélincourt. Born at Englewood, New Jersey, 1873. Educated at home. Left America when nine years old and has since lived abroad, chiefly in Paris and London. Studied painting for several years in Paris. Her reputation was made by *Tante*, 1911.

BIBLIOGRAPHY

Novels

The Dull Miss Archinard. 1898.
The Confounding of Camelia. 1899.
The Rescue. 1902.
Paths of Judgment. 1904.
The Shadow of Life. 1906.
A Fountain Sealed. 1907. (London, 1908, as Valerie Upton.)
Amabel Channice. 1908.
* Franklin Winslow Kane. 1910.
* Tante. 1911.
The Encounter. 1914.
The Third Window. 1920.
Adrienne Toner. 1922.
* The Little French Girl. 1924.
The Old Countess. 1927.
Dark Hester. 1929.

Short Stories

The Nest. 1913.
Christmas Roses. 1920. (London, 1920, as Autumn Crocuses.)

Biography

A Childhood in Brittany Eighty Years Ago. 1919.

Anne Douglas Sedgwick—*Continued*

STUDIES AND REVIEWS

Bookm., 34 ('12): 655.
Bost. Trans., Apr. 29, 1922: 6; Aug. 30, 1924: 1.
Dial, 52 ('12): 323.
Ind., 72 ('12): 678; 108 ('22): 565.
Lit. Digest, I. B. R. Oct., 1924: 818.
Lit. Rev., June 17, 1922: 737; Sept. 6, 1924: 3.
Lond. Merc., 5 ('22): 433; 10 ('24): 359 (J. B. Priestley).
Lond. Times, May 13, 1920: 301; Sept. 9, 1921: 581, 695; Aug. 14, 1924: 500; Apr. 7, 1927: 248.

Nation, 94 ('12): 262; 114 ('22): 653; 119 ('24): 447; 124 ('27): 376.
N. State., 15 ('20): 137; 18 ('21): 200 (R. West); 23 ('24): 648; 29 ('27): 44.
N. Y. Times, July 23, 1922: 19; Aug. 31, 1924: 12; Apr. 26, 1925: 16; Apr. 10, 1927: 7 (portrait).
Sat. Rev., 143 ('27): 638.
Sat. Rev. of Lit., 3 ('27): 711.
Spec., 125 ('21): 571; 127 ('21): 711; 133 ('24): 298.

Ernest Thompson Seton—nature writer.

Born at South Shields, England, 1860. Lived in the backwoods of Canada, 1866–70 and on the Western plains, 1882–87. Educated at the Toronto Collegiate Institute and (as artist) at the Royal Academy, London. Official naturalist to the government of Manitoba. Studied art in Paris, 1890–96. One of the illustrators of the *Century Dictionary*. Prominent in the organization of the Boy Scout movement in America. For many years kept full journals of his expeditions and observations (illustrated). These make the "most complete pictorial animal library in the world."

For complete bibliography, see Who's Who in America.

BIBLIOGRAPHY

Wild Animals I Have Known. 1898.
The Biography of a Grizzly. 1900.
Lives of the Hunted. 1901.
Woodcraft and Indian Lore. 1912.
Wild Animals at Home. 1913.
Preacher of Cedar Mountain. 1916.

Ernest Thompson Seton—*Continued*

STUDIES AND REVIEWS

Halsey.

Acad., 82 ('12): 523.
Am. M., 91 ('21): 14 (portrait).
Atlan., 91 ('03): 298.
Bookm. (Lond.), 45 ('13): 144,
  147 (portrait).

Critic, 39 ('01): 320 (portrait).
Lit. Rev., Apr. 23, 1921: 19.
Liv. Age, 232 ('02): 222.
Spec., 105 ('10): 488; 117 ('16):
  345.

Dallas Lore Sharp—nature writer.

Born at Haleyville, New Jersey, 1870. A. B., Brown, 1895; S. T. B., Boston University, 1899; Litt. D., Brown, 1917. Ordained for the Methodist Episcopal ministry, 1895. Pastor, 1896–99; librarian, 1899–1902. On staff of *Youth's Companion*, 1900–03. Has taught English in Boston University since 1902, professor since 1909.

BIBLIOGRAPHY

Nature Essays and Studies
  Wild Life Near Home. 1901.
  A Watcher in the Woods. 1903.
  Roof and Meadow. 1904.
  The Lay of the Land. 1908.
  The Face of the Fields. 1911.
  The Fall of the Year. 1911.
  Winter. 1912.
  The Spring of the Year. 1912.
  Ways of the Woods. 1912.
  Summer. 1914. (Repr. with The Fall of the Year, Winter, and The
    Spring of the Year, as The Whole Year Round. 1915.)
  Beyond the Pasture Bars. 1914.
  Where Rolls the Oregon. 1914.
  The Hills of Hingham. 1916.
  Highlands and Hollows. 1923.
  The Magical Chance. 1923.
  The Spirit of the Hive. 1925.
  Sanctuary! Sanctuary! 1926.

Dallas Lore Sharp—*Continued*

Essays on Education and Democracy
  Patrons of Democracy. 1920.
  Education in a Democracy. 1922.

Biography
  The Seer of Slabsides. 1921.

Novel
  The Better Country. 1928.

STUDIES AND REVIEWS

Bost. Trans., Dec. 1, 1923: 4.
Cur. Lit., 37 ('04): 230 (portrait).
Dial, 45 ('08): 297.
Freeman, 6 ('22): 356.
Lit. Rev., Oct. 20, 1923: 149.
N. Y. Times, Dec. 5, 1926: 2.

Springfield Repub., Nov. 27, 1921:
  11a; Oct. 22, 1923: 6.

See also Book Review Digest,
  1914, 1916.

Edward (Brewster) Sheldon—dramatist.

Born at Chicago, 1886. A. B., Harvard, 1907; A. M., 1908.
Mr. Sheldon's most successful play thus far is *Romance*,
which was played by Doris Keane for almost ten years.

BIBLIOGRAPHY

Plays
  Salvation Nell. 1908. (Priv. ptd.)
  "The Nigger." 1910.
  Egypt. 1912. (Priv. ptd.)
  The High Road. 1912. (Priv. ptd.)
  Romance. 1914. (Novelized by Acton Davies. 1913.)
  The Song of Songs. 1914. (Priv. ptd. Dramatization of *Das Hohe Lied*, by Sudermann.)
  The Garden of Paradise. 1915. (Based on "The Little Mermaid," by Hans Andersen.)
  The Boss. (*In Quinn*, Representative American Plays. 1917.)

For list of unpublished plays, see Quinn, History of American Drama, II,
  324–25.

Edward (Brewster) Sheldon—*Continued*

STUDIES AND REVIEWS

Dickinson. (P. N. A. T.)
Eaton, W. P. Plays and Players.
1916.

Eaton, W. P. At the New Theatre.
Moses. 1910.

Stuart P(ratt) Sherman—critic.

Born at Anita, Iowa, 1881. A. B., Williams, 1903; A. M., Harvard, 1904; Ph. D., 1906. Taught English at Northwestern University, 1906–11; professor at the University of Illinois, 1911–24. Associate editor of the *Cambridge History of American Literature*. Literary editor of the *New York Herald-Tribune*, 1924–27. Died in 1927.

BIBLIOGRAPHY

Critical Essays
* On Contemporary Literature. 1917.
  The Significance of Sinclair Lewis. 1922.
  Americans. 1922.
  The Genius of America. 1923.
  My Dear Cornelia. 1924.
  Points of View. 1924.
  Men of Letters of the British Isles. 1924. (With Theodore Spicer-Simson.)
  Letters to a Lady in the Country. 1925.
* Critical Woodcuts. 1926.
  The Main Stream. 1927.
  Shaping Men and Women. 1928.

Criticism and Biography
  Matthew Arnold. 1917.

STUDIES AND REVIEWS

Beach.
Boynton. (S. C. A.)
Calverton.
Farrar.
Hackett.
Van Doren. (M. M.)

Am. Rev., 1 ('23): 236.
Bookm., 57 ('23): 86; 68 ('28): 359.
Cur. Op., 64 ('18): 269 (portrait).
Freeman, 6 ('23): 477; 7 ('23): 429.
Forum, 75 ('26): 799.

Stuart P(ratt) Sherman—*Continued*

Ind., 113 ('24): 373 (E. Boyd), 457; 115 ('25): 587 (E. Boyd).

Lit. Digest, I. B. R. Mar., 1923: 23.

Lit. Rev., June 30, 1923: 800.

Nation, 116 ('23): 100, 723; 119 ('24): 641; 122 ('26): 370.

N. Repub., 33 ('23): 178; 41 ('25): 204.

N. Y. Herald-Tribune, Apr. 18, 1926: 5; Apr. 17, 1927: 3; Oct. 14, 1928: 4.

N. Y. Times, Dec. 24, 1922: 1; Apr. 15, 1923: 1; Nov. 16, 1924: 6; Apr. 11, 1926: 2; May 8, 1927: 2; Oct. 28, 1928: 9.

Sat. Rev. of Lit., 2 ('26): 881.

Springfield Repub., Feb. 15, 1923: 8; Dec. 7, 1924: 7a; Apr. 9, 1927: 10.

Yale Rev., n. s. 16 ('27): 380.

See also Book Review Digest, 1917.

Upton (Beall) Sinclair—novelist.

Born at Baltimore, Maryland, 1878. A. B., College of the City of New York, 1897. Did graduate work for four years at Columbia. Assisted in the government investigation of the Chicago stockyards, 1906 (cf. *The Jungle*). Socialist. Founded the Helicon Hall communistic colony at Englewood, New Jersey, 1906–07, and the Intercollegiate Socialist Society. Has run for various political offices on the Socialist ticket. Founder of the Civic Federation Union of California.

BIBLIOGRAPHY

Plays

Plays of Protest. 1912.
Hell. 1923.
Singing Jailbirds. 1924.
The Pot-Boiler. 1924.
Bill Porter. 1925.

Novels and Tales

A Soldier Monk. 1899. (Under pseud. Ensign Clarke Fitch, U. S. N.)
Springtime and Harvest. 1901. (Priv. ptd.)
King Midas. 1901.
Prince Hagen. 1903. (Satiric fable.)
Manassas. 1904.
* The Jungle. 1906.
A Captain of Industry. 1906.

Upton (Beall) Sinclair—*Continued*

The Overman. 1907.
The Metropolis. 1908.
The Money-Changers. 1908. (Rev. ed., 1923.)
Samuel the Seeker. 1910.
Love's Pilgrimage. 1911. (Autobiographical.)
Damaged Goods. 1913. (*Novelized from* Les Avariés, by Brieux.)
Sylvia. 1913.
Sylvia's Marriage. 1914.
King Coal. 1917.
Jimmie Higgins. 1919.
100%. 1920. (Pub. in England under title The Spy.)
They Call Me Carpenter. 1922.
The Millennium. 1924.
Oil! 1927.
Boston. 1928.

Sociological Essays and Studies
The Industrial Republic. 1907.
The Cry for Justice. 1915. (Editor.)
The Profits of Religion. 1918.
* The Brass Check. 1919. (Repr. in part as Associated Press and Labor.)
The Book of Life. 1921.
The Goose-Step. 1922.
The Goslings. 1924.
Mammonart. 1925.
Money Writes! 1927.

Autobiography
The Journal of Arthur Stirling. 1903. (Pub. anonymously.)

Books on Health
Good Health and How He Won It. 1909. (With Michael Williams.)
The Fasting Cure. 1911.

Pamphlets
Sinclair-Astor Letters. 1914.
The Crimes of the "Times." 1919.
Letters to Judd. 1926.
What's the Use of Books? 1926.
The Spokesman's Secretary. 1926.

STUDIES AND REVIEWS

Baldwin.
Brooks, V. W., Emerson and
Others. 1927.

Dell, F. Upton Sinclair. 1927.
Harris.
Karsner.

Upton (Beall) Sinclair—*Continued*

Van Doren. (A. B. L.)
——. (C. A. N.)

Am. Merc., 2 ('24): 504.
Ath., 1 ('12): 558; 2 ('12): 247.
Bookm., 23 ('06): 130, 195, 244, 584; 24 ('07): 2, 443; 61 ('25): 480. (Portraits.)
Bost. Trans., Mar. 28, 1925: 10.
Commonweal, 2 ('25): 312.
Cur. Lit., 41 ('06): 3 (portrait).
Cur. Op., 66 ('19): 386; 68 ('20): 669 (portrait).
Freeman, 4 ('21): 258, 262; 7 ('23): 332.
Ind., 57 ('04): 1133 (portrait); 62 ('07): 711; 71 ('11): 326; 114 ('25): 418.

Lit. Digest, I. B. R. May, 1925: 406.
Lit. Rev., Nov. 18, 1922: 219; Apr. 14, 1923: 602.
Nation, 113 ('21): 347; 116 ('23): Apr. 11, supp. 433; 119 ('24): 340; 124 ('27): 643; 126 ('28): 163.
N. Repub., 34 ('23): Apr. 11, supp. 8; 38 ('24): 343; 53 ('28): 227; 56 ('28): 354.
N. State., 1 ('13): 209; 21 ('23): 150.
N. Y. Times, Apr. 6, 1924: 10; Mar. 22, 1925: 12.
Rev., 4 ('21): 128.
Sewanee Rev., 31 ('23): 508.
Spec., 96 ('06): 793; 99 ('07): 231.

Elsie Singmaster—novelist.

Mrs. Harold Lewars. Born at Schuylkill Haven, Pennsylvania, 1879. A. B., Radcliffe, 1907; Litt. D., Pennsylvania College, 1916. Her novels deal with the Pennsylvania Dutch. Writer of juvenile fiction and Lutheran biography and pamphlets.

BIBLIOGRAPHY

Novels
Katy Gaumer. 1915.
Emmeline. 1916.
Basil Everman. 1920.
Ellen Levis. 1921.
Bennett Malin. 1922.
The Hidden Road. 1923.
Keller's Anna Ruth. 1926.
'Sewing Susie.' 1927.
What Everybody Wanted. 1928.

Elsie Singmaster—*Continued*

Short Stories
Gettysburg. 1913.
John Baring's House. 1920.
Bred in the Bone. 1925.

STUDIES AND REVIEWS

Bost. Trans., Feb. 9, 1921: 4; June 14, 1922: 4; June 30, 1923: 5.
Ind., 111 ('23): 68.
Lit. Digest, Aug. 19, 1922: 55.
Lit. Rev., Apr. 23, 1921: 10.
Nation, 115 ('22): 214.
N. Y. Herald-Tribune, May 30, 1926: 12.

N. Y. Times, Mar. 13, 1921: 19; June 11, 1922: 26; Apr. 4, 1926: 22.

See also Book Review Digest, 1917, 1920.

Laurence Stallings—dramatist.

Born at Macon, Georgia, 1894. Wake Forest (North Carolina) College, 1915; M. Sc., Georgetown University, 1922. Began newspaper work with *Atlanta Journal*, 1915; editor of literary column "The First Reader," *New York World*. Served with A. E. F. Awarded the Croix de Guerre.

BIBLIOGRAPHY

Plays
Three American Plays. 1926. (What Price Glory, First Flight, The Buccaneer. With Maxwell Anderson.)
Novel
Plumes. 1924.

STUDIES AND REVIEWS

Cent., 113 ('26): 255.
Ind., Oct. 18, 1924: 290.

Nation, 119 ('24): 644.
N. Repub., 40 ('24): 394.

Wilbur Daniel Steele—novelist, short story writer.

Born at Greensboro, North Carolina, 1886. A. B., University of Denver, 1907. Studied art in Boston, Paris, and

Wilbur Daniel Steele—*Continued*

New York, 1907–10. Received prizes (1919, 1921, 1925) from O. Henry Award Committee for distinguished work in the short story.

Plays
 The Giants' Stair. 1924.
 The Terrible Woman. 1925.

Novels
 Storm. 1914.
 Isles of the Blest. 1924.
 Taboo. 1925.
 Meat. 1928.

Short Stories
 Land's End. 1918.
 The Shame Dance. 1923.
 Urkey Island. 1926.
 The Man Who Saw Through Heaven. 1927.

Bookm., 46 ('18): 704 (portrait).
Bost. Trans., June 9, 1923: 4; Aug. 26, 1925: 6; June 2, 1926: 4.
Lit. Rev., June 23, 1923: 783.

N. Y. Times, June 10, 1923: 17; Sept. 13, 1925: 16; Mar. 28, 1926: 8.
Sat. Rev. of Lit., 2 ('25): 362.

See also Book Review Digest, 1918.

Gertrude Stein—poet, short story writer, novelist.

Born at Allegheny, Pennsylvania, 1874. Educated at Radcliffe College, graduating in 1897, and Johns Hopkins Medical School, 1897–1902. Has lived in Paris since 1903. A leader of the extremists in literary experimentation.

Poems
 Tender Buttons. 1914.
Plays
 Geography and Plays. 1922.

Gertrude Stein—*Continued*

Novels
The Making of Americans. 1926.

Short Stories
Three Lives. 1909.

Critical Essays
Composition as Explanation. London, 1926.
Useful Knowledge. 1928.

STUDIES AND REVIEWS

Lewis, Wyndham. Time and Western Man. 1927.
Sherman. (P. V.)

Cal. Mod. Lett., 3 ('27): 329.
Dial, 74 ('23): 408.
Lit. Rev., Aug. 11, 1923: 891.
Outlook, 134 ('23): 139.

George Sterling—poet.

Born at Sag Harbor, New York, 1869. Educated in private and public schools. About 1895 he moved to the West and lived in California until his death in 1926.

BIBLIOGRAPHY

Poems
The Testimony of the Suns. 1903.
A Wine of Wizardry. 1907.
The House of Orchids. 1911.
Beyond the Breakers. 1914.
Ode on the Opening of the Panama-Pacific International Exposition. 1915.
The Evanescent City. 1915.
The Caged Eagle. 1916.
Yosemite. 1916.
The Binding of the Beast. 1917.
Thirty-Five Sonnets. 1917. (Priv. ptd.)
Sails and Mirage. 1921.
Selected Poems. 1923.
Sonnets to Craig. 1928.

Plays and Masques
The Triumph of Bohemia. 1907. (Priv. ptd.)
Twilight of the Kings. 1918. (Priv. ptd. Lyrics only by Sterling.)

George Sterling—*Continued*
Lilith. 1919.
Rosamund. 1920.
Truth. 1923.

Biography
Robinson Jeffers. 1926.

STUDIES AND REVIEWS

Untermeyer. (A. P.)

Bost. Trans., Aug. 25, 1923: 3;
  May 12, 1926: 4.
Freeman, 7 ('23): 548.
Lit. Rev., Aug. 18, 1923: 907;
  May 22, 1926: 5.

N. Y. Times, June 10, 1923: 12;
  Aug. 22, 1926: 9.
Poetry, 7 ('16): 307.

See also Book Review Digest, 1916.

James Stevens—novelist.
Born on farm near Albia, Iowa, 1892. At fifteen took to
roads and worked in various road-camps, gaining experience
among hobo-laborers. Was a sergeant during the war.
Lives in Tacoma, Washington.

BIBLIOGRAPHY
Novels
Brawnyman. 1926. (Autobiographical.)
Mattock. 1927. (Autobiographical in part.)

Short Stories
Paul Bunyan. 1925.
Homer in the Sage Brush. 1928.

STUDIES AND REVIEWS

Bookm., 61 ('25): 473.
Lit. Digest, I. B. R. Sept., 1926:
  637.
N. Y. Times, Apr. 12, 1925: 5;
  June 13, 1926: 14; Apr. 24, 1927:
  8.

N. Y. World, Apr. 19, 1925: 6;
  June 13, 1926: 4.
Sat. Rev. of Lit., 2 ('25): 81; 3
  ('27): 959.

Simeon Strunsky—essayist, man of letters.

Born at Vitebsk, Russia, 1879. A. B., Columbia, 1900. Department editor of the *New International Encyclopedia*, 1900–06, and editorial writer for the *New York Evening Post*, 1906–20, editor, 1920–24; editorial staff, *New York Times*, 1924– .

BIBLIOGRAPHY

Novels
Professor Latimer's Progress. 1918.
King Akhnaton. 1928.

Essays and Sketches
The Patient Observer and His Friends. 1911.
Post-Impressions. 1914.
Belshazzar Court. 1914.
Sinbad and His Friends. 1921. (Satire.)

Humor
Little Journeys towards Paris. 1918.

STUDIES AND REVIEWS

Bookm., 51 ('20): 65.
Bost. Trans., Dec. 3, 1921: 6.
Cur. Op., 57 ('14): 198; 65 ('18): 51. (Portraits.)
Ind., 80 ('14): 245 (portrait).

Lit. Rev., Jan. 14, 1922: 351.
N. Y. Herald-Tribune, Sept. 2, 1928: 3.

See also Book Review Digest, 1914, 1918.

Ruth Suckow—novelist.

Born at Hawarden, Iowa, 1892. Student at Grinnell (Iowa) College, 1910–13; School of Expression, Boston, Mass., 1914–15. A. B., University of Denver, 1917. Owner and manager of The Orchard Apiary, Earlville, Iowa.

BIBLIOGRAPHY

Novels
Country People. 1924.
The Odyssey of a Nice Girl. 1925.
The Bonney Family. 1928.

Short Stories
Iowa Interiors. 1926.

Ruth Suckow—*Continued*

STUDIES AND REVIEWS

Bost. Trans., June 1, 1924: 4; Dec. 19, 1925: 6.

Lit. Rev., Oct. 23, 1926: 2.

N. Repub., 44 ('25): 336 (Lovett).

N. Y. Herald-Tribune, Oct. 3, 1926: 6; Jan. 22, 1928: 7.

N. Y. Times, June 1, 1924: 7; Nov. 8, 1925: 8; Jan. 22, 1928: 2.

Sat. Rev. of Lit., 3 ('26): 330.

(Newton) Booth Tarkington—novelist, dramatist.

Born at Indianapolis, Indiana, 1869, of French ancestry on one side. Came early under the influence of Riley, a neighbor. Educated at Phillips Exeter Academy, Purdue University, and Princeton. Honorary higher degrees. Popular at college for his singing, acting, and social talents. Began to study art but was not successful as an artist. Has written songs. Takes an active part in the social and political life of his state. Served in the Indiana legislature, 1902–03. *The Magnificent Ambersons* was awarded the Pulitzer novel prize in 1919, and *Alice Adams* in 1922.

SUGGESTIONS FOR READING

1. Consider separately Mr. Tarkington's studies of boy life (especially *Penrod*), and of adolescence (especially *Seventeen* and *Clarence*). Judged by your own experience and observation, are they presented with true knowledge and humor, or are they a farcical skimming of surface eccentricities? Compare them with Mark Twain's books about boys and with Howells's *Boy's Town*.

2. Consider separately the historical novels. Is pure romance Mr. Tarkington's field? Why or why not?

3. Consider the justice or the injustice of the following:

According to all the codes of the more serious kinds of fiction, the unwillingness—or the inability—to conduct a plot to its legitimate ending implies some weakness in the artistic character; and this weakness is Mr. Tarkington's principal defect. . . . Now this causes the more regret for the reason that he has what is next best to character in a

(Newton) Booth Tarkington—*Continued*

novelist—that is, knack. He has the knack of romance, when he wants to employ it: a light, allusive manner; a sufficient acquaintance with certain charming historical epochs and the "properties" thereto pertaining . . . ; a considerable experience in the ways of the "world"; gay colors, swift moods, the note of tender elegy. He has also the knack of satire, which he employs more frequently than romance . . . he has traveled a long way from the methods of his greener days. Why, then, does he continue to trifle with his threadbare adolescents, as if he were afraid to write candidly about his coevals? Why does he drift with the sentimental tide and make propaganda for provincial complacency?

4. In what direction lies Mr. Tarkington's future? Is he likely to become more than a popular writer? What, if any, elements of enduring value do you find in his work?

5. What "Hoosier" elements do you find in his work? Compare him with Ade, Riley, Nicholson, and with the older writers of Indiana, Edward Eggleston, and Maurice Thompson.

BIBLIOGRAPHY

Plays

The Man from Home. 1908. (Rev. and produced recently under the title, Hoosiers Abroad. With Harry Leon Wilson.)

Beauty and the Jacobin. 1912.

Mr. Antonio. (*In* Harper's Magazine, 134 ['17]: 187.)

The Gibson Upright. 1919. (With Harry Leon Wilson.)

Poldekin. (*In* McClure's Magazine, Mar.–July, 1920.)

Clarence. 1921.

The Country Cousin. 1921. (Priv. ptd. 1916 under title The Ohio Lady. With Julian Street.)

The Wren. 1922.

The Ghost Story. 1922.

The Trysting Place. 1923. (*In* The Ladies' Home Journal, Sept., 1922.)

The Intimate Strangers. 1924. (*In Cohen*, Longer Plays by American Authors, 1922, *and in* Harper's Magazine, 1922.)

Tweedles. 1924. (With Harry Leon Wilson.)

Bimbo, the Pirate. 1926.

The Travelers. 1927.

Station YYYY. 1927.

Beaucaire. (A dramatization of Monsieur Beaucaire. With Evelyn Greenleaf Sutherland. *In Pence*, Dramas by Present-Day Writers, 1927.)

(Newton) Booth Tarkington—*Continued*

Novels and Tales

   The Gentleman from Indiana. 1899.
* Monsieur Beaucaire. 1900. (See *Plays*. Also dramatized by Ethel
   Hale Freeman. 1916.)
   The Two Vanrevels. 1902.
   Cherry. 1903.
   The Conquest of Canaan. 1905.
   The Beautiful Lady. 1905.
   His Own People. 1907.
   The Guest of Quesnay. 1908.
   The Flirt. 1913.
* Penrod. 1914. (Dramatized by Edward E. Rose. 1921.)
* The Turmoil. 1915.
   Penrod and Sam. 1916.
* Seventeen. 1916. (Dramatized by Hugh Stanislaus Stange, Stannard
   Mears, and Stuart Walker. 1924.)
* The Magnificent Ambersons. 1918.
   Harlequin and Columbine. 1918.
   Ramsey Milholland. 1919.
* Alice Adams. 1921.
   Gentle Julia. 1922.
   The Midlander. 1923.
   Women. 1925.
   The Plutocrat. 1927.
   Growth. 1927. (A reprint of The Magnificent Ambersons, The Tur-
   moil, and The Midlander.)
   Claire Ambler. 1928.

Short Stories

   In the Arena. 1905.
   Beasley's Christmas Party. 1909.
   The Fascinating Stranger. 1923.

Essays

   Looking Forward. 1926.

Autobiography

   The World Does Move. 1928.

For a list of unpublished plays, see Quinn, History of American Drama,
II, 326ff.

STUDIES AND REVIEWS

Baldwin.
Boynton. (S. C. A.)

Clark, B. H. Study of the Modern Drama. 1925.

(Newton) Booth Tarkington—*Continued*

Cooper.
Dickinson. (P. N. A. T.)
—— Booth Tarkington. 1926.
Eaton, W. P. At the New Theatre. 1910.
Farrar.
Holliday, Robert C. Booth Tarkington. 1918.
Nicholson, Meredith. The Hoosiers. (National Studies in American Letters.) 1900.
Overton. (A. O. D.)
Phelps.
Sherman. (P. V.)
Van Doren. (A. B. L.)
——. (C. A. N.)
Williams.

Bookm., 21 ('05): 5; 24 ('07): 605; 42 ('16): 505, 507; 48 ('18): 493; 53 ('21): 449. (Portraits.)
Bookm., (Lond.), 55 ('19): 123 (portrait).
Bost. Trans., June 1, 1921: 4; Apr. 29, 1922: 6; May 5, 1923: 4; Jan. 19, 1924: 4; Dec. 12, 1925: 4; Dec. 29, 1926: 7; Jan. 8, 1927: 3.

Critic, 37 ('00): 396.
Cur. Lit., 30 ('01): 280.
Freeman, 4 ('21): 66.
Ind., 112 ('24): 53.
Lit. Digest, July 23, 1921: 44; July 15, 1922: 42.
Lit. Rev., May 21, 1921: 3; Dec. 31, 1921: 316; Apr. 29, 1922: 619; Apr. 21, 1923: 620; Jan. 19, 1924: 455; Jan. 8, 1927: 3.
Liv. Age, 300 ('19): 541.
Nation, 103 ('16): 330; 112 ('21): 233 (C. Van Doren); 113 ('21): 125; 118 ('24): 318; 124 ('27): 186.
N. Y. Herald-Tribune, Jan. 9, 1927: 2; Nov. 25, 1928: 21.
N. Y. Times, May 22, 1921: 22; Apr. 30, 1922: 14; Apr. 15, 1923: 22; Jan. 20, 1924: 7; Nov. 29, 1925: 5; Jan. 9, 1927: 2; Jan. 15, 1928: 5.
Outlook, 72 ('02): 817; 128 ('21): 658. (Portraits.)
Sat. Rev., 132 ('21): 491.
Sat. Rev. of Lit., 2 ('25): 403; 3 ('26): 355; 5 ('28): 393.

Sara Teasdale—poet.

Mrs. Ernst B. Filsinger. Born at St. Louis, Missouri, 1884. Educated in private schools, St. Louis. Traveled in Europe and the Near East. Received prizes from the Poetry Society of America, 1916, 1918.

Sara Teasdale's love-lyrics have been admired for their simplicity, feeling, and perfection of form.

BIBLIOGRAPHY

Poems
Sonnets to Duse. 1907.
Helen of Troy. 1911.

Sara Teasdale—*Continued*
Rivers to the Sea. 1915.
Love Songs. 1917.
The Answering Voice. 1917. (Enl. ed., 1928.) (Editor.)
Vignettes of Italy. 1919. (Songs. Music by Wintter Watts.)
Flame and Shadow. 1920.
Rainbow Gold. 1922. (Editor.)
Poems. 1923. (Reprints.)
Dark of the Moon. 1926.

STUDIES AND REVIEWS

Cook.
Maynard.
Monroe.
Untermeyer. (A. P.)
Wilkinson. (P.)

Bookm., 42 ('15): 365 (portrait), 457; 47 ('18): 392 (Phelps).
Forum, 65 ('21): 229.
Lit. Digest, July 13, 1918: 29 (portrait).

Lit. Rev., Oct. 16, 1926: 7.
N. Repub., 15 ('18): 239; 49 ('26): 48.
N. Y. Herald-Tribune, Nov. 28, 1926: 2.
N. Y. Times, Nov. 14, 1926: 4.
Poetry, 7 ('15): 148; 12 ('18): 264; 17 ('21): 272; 25 ('25): 262; 29 ('26): 157.

Eunice (Strong Hammond) Tietjens—poet.
Mrs. Cloyd Head. Born at Chicago, 1884. Married Paul Tietjens, the composer, 1904; Cloyd Head, the writer, 1920. On staff of *Poetry* since 1913. War correspondent in France, 1917–18.

Mrs. Tietjens's *Profiles from China* is based upon her experiences in China.

BIBLIOGRAPHY
Poems
Profiles from China. 1917.
Body and Raiment. 1919.
Profiles from Home. 1925.
Anthology of Oriental Poetry. 1927. (Editor.)

Eunice (Strong Hammond) Tietjens—*Continued*

Novel
  Jake. 1921.

Description and Travel
  Japan, Korea and Formosa. 1924.

STUDIES AND REVIEWS

Untermeyer. (A. P.)

N. Y. Times, May 8, 1921: 22;
  Mar. 1, 1925: 5.
Poetry, 10 ('17): 326; 15 ('20):
  272; 26 ('25): 227 (H. Monroe).

Spec., 124 ('20): 315.
Springfield Repub., Aug. 28, 1921:
  9a.

See also Book Review Digest, 1917,
  1919.

(Frederic) Ridgely Torrence—poet, dramatist.

Born at Xenia, Ohio, 1875. Educated at Miami University
and Princeton. Librarian in the Astor Library, 1897–1901,
and Lenox Library, 1901–03. Assistant editor of the *Critic*,
1903–04, and associate editor of the *Cosmopolitan*, 1906–07.

Mr. Torrence's plays for a negro theatre are worth special
study.

BIBLIOGRAPHY

Poems
  The House of a Hundred Lights. 1900.
  Hesperides. 1925.

Plays
  El Dorado. 1903.
  Abelard and Heloise. 1907.
  Granny Maumee, The Rider of Dreams, Simon the Cyrenian. 1917.

STUDIES AND REVIEWS

Dickinson. (P. N. A. T.)
Maynard.
Rittenhouse.
Wilkinson. (P.)

Atlan., 96 ('05): 712; 98 ('06): 333.
Fortn., 86 ('06): 434.

Lit. Digest, I. B. R. Aug., 1925:
  585.
N. Repub., 10 ('17): 325.
N. Y. Times, June 7, 1925: 7.
Poetry, 26 ('25): 286 (H. Monroe).
Sat. Rev. of Lit., 1 ('25): 756 (L.
  Untermeyer).

Jean Starr Untermeyer—poet.

Mrs. Louis Untermeyer. Born at Zanesville, Ohio, 1886. Educated at Putnam's Seminary, Zanesville, and at Columbia.

BIBLIOGRAPHY

Poems
    Growing Pains. 1918.
    Dreams Out of Darkness. 1921.
    Steep Ascent. 1927.

STUDIES AND REVIEWS

Untermeyer. (A. P.)   Poetry, 14 ('19): 47 (Amy Lowell).
                                         20 ('22): 220.

N. Y. Times, Nov. 27, 1921: 3 (L.   *See also* Book Review Digest, 1918.
Untermeyer).

Louis Untermeyer—poet, critic.

Born at New York City, 1885. Educated at the De Witt Clinton high school, New York. An accomplished pianist and professional designer of jewelry. In jewelry business, 1902–23. Associate editor of the *Seven Arts* (cf. *Poetry*, 9 ['16–'17]: 214). Contributing editor to the *Liberator*. Socialist.

Mr. Untermeyer's early verse was influenced by Heine, Housman, and Henley, especially the last; but he has broken away from them to an individual expression of social passion.

BIBLIOGRAPHY

Poems
    First Love. 1911.
    Challenge. 1914.
    These Times. 1917.
    Modern American Poetry. 1919. (Rev. ed., 1921, 1925.) (Editor.)
    The New Adam. 1920.
    Modern British Poetry. 1920. (Rev. ed., 1925.) (Editor.)
    Modern American and British Poetry. 1922. (Editor.)
    Roast Leviathan. 1923.

Louis **Untermeyer**—*Continued*
This Singing World. 1923. (Editor.)
Yesterday and Today. 1926. (Editor.)
Burning Bush. 1928.

Novel
Moses. 1928.

Parodies
" —— And Other Poets." 1916.
Including Horace. 1919.
Heavens! 1922.
Collected Parodies. 1926.

Critical Essays and Studies
The New Era in American Poetry. 1919.
American Poetry Since 1900. 1923. (Based on The New Era.)
Forms of Poetry. 1926.

Translations
Poems of Heinrich Heine. 1917. (Rev. ed., 1923.)
Man and the Masses, by Ernst Toller. 1924.
The Fat of the Cat, by Gottfried Keller. 1925.

STUDIES AND REVIEWS

Aiken.
Farrar.
Wilkinson. (N. V.)

Bookm., 47 ('18): 266 (Phelps).
Bost. Trans., Apr. 5, 1922: 7;
 Dec. 8, 1923: 5.
Freeman, 8 ('23): 236.
Lit. Rev., Sept. 8, 1923: 19.
Lond. Times, July 26, 1923: 507.

Nation, 115 ('22): 311.
N. Repub., 35 ('23): 338.
N. State., 18 ('21): 114.
N. Y. Times, Mar. 25, 1923: 6.
Outlook, 122 ('19): 644 (portrait).
Poetry, 4 ('14): 203; 11 ('17): 157;
 14 ('19): 159; 17 ('21): 212.
Sat. Rev., 132 ('21): 737.
Sat. Rev. of Lit., 5 ('28): 84.

Carl **Van Doren**—critic.

Born at Hope, Illinois, 1885. A. B., University of Illinois,
1907; Ph. D., Columbia, 1911. Taught English at the University of Illinois, 1907–16; assistant professor, 1914–16.
Associate in English at Columbia since 1916. Headmaster

Carl Van Doren—*Continued*

of The Brearley School, New York, 1916–19. Literary editor
of the *Nation*, 1919–22, of the *Century Magazine*, 1922–25.
Co-editor of the *Cambridge History of American Literature*.

BIBLIOGRAPHY

Novel
   The Ninth Wave. 1926.

Criticism
   The American Novel. 1921.
   Contemporary American Novelists. 1922.
   The Roving Critic. 1923.
   Many Minds. 1924.
   James Branch Cabell. 1925.
   Other Provinces. 1925.
   American and British Literature Since 1890. 1925. (With Mark
      Van Doren.)

Biography
   Thomas Love Peacock. 1911.

STUDIES AND REVIEWS

Bost. Trans., Apr. 5, 1924: 4;
   Oct. 30, 1926: 1.
Cur. Op., 71 ('21): 642.
Dial, 71 ('21): 355.
Ind., 115 ('25): 362 (E. Boyd).
Lit. Rev., Dec. 16, 1922: 317;
   June 2, 1923: 732; Apr. 12,
   1924: 665; Sept. 25, 1926: 4.
Nation, 113 ('21): 18 (Mencken);
   114 ('22): 571; 116 ('23): 574
   (R. Herrick); 118 ('24): 741;
120 ('25): 494; 121 ('25): 600;
   123 ('26): 372.
N. Repub., 29 ('21): 106; 32 ('22):
   Sept. 27, supp. 20.
N. Y. Times, Apr. 6, 1924: 7;
   Mar. 29, 1925: 11; Sept. 27,
   1925: 4; Nov. 8, 1925: 5; Oct. 3,
   1926: 8.
Outlook, 131 ('22): 312.
Sat. Rev. of Lit., 2 ('26): 492.
Yale Rev., n. s. 12 ('22): 186.

Henry Van Dyke—man of letters.

Born at Germantown, Pennsylvania, 1852. Graduate of
the Brooklyn Polytechnic Institute, 1869; A. B., Princeton,
1873, A. M., 1876; Princeton Theological Seminary, 1877;
at the University of Berlin, 1877–79. Many honorary higher

Henry Van Dyke—*Continued*

degrees and other marks of distinction. Ordained minister in the Presbyterian Church, 1879. Pastor in Newport, Rhode Island, 1879–82, and in New York, 1883–1900, 1902, 1911. Professor of English literature at Princeton University, 1900–23. American lecturer at the University of Paris, 1908–09. United States Minister to The Netherlands, 1913–17.

For full bibliography, see Who's Who in America.

BIBLIOGRAPHY

Little Rivers. 1895.
The Story of the Other Wise Man. 1896.
Fisherman's Luck. 1899.
The Ruling Passion. 1901.
The Blue Flower. 1902.
The House of Rimmon. 1908.
Collected Poems. 1911.
Camp Fires and Guide Posts. 1921.
Companionable Books. 1922.
Half-Told Tales. 1925.
Chosen Poems. 1927.

STUDIES AND REVIEWS

Halsey.

Bookm., 38 ('13): 20 (portrait).
Cent., 67 ('04): 579 (portrait).
Critic, 42 ('03): 511, 516 (portrait).

Cur. Lit., 28 ('00): 282.
Nation, 104 ('17): 54.
N. Y. Times, Sept. 11, 1921: 11.
Outlook, 99 ('11): 704.

Hendrik Willem Van Loon—man of letters.

Born at Rotterdam, Holland, 1882. A. B., Cornell, 1905; Ph. D., Munich, 1911. Associated Press correspondent in Russia during the revolution of 1906 and in various countries of Europe during the war. Lecturer on history and the history of art. Newspaper correspondent in Europe, 1914–18. Professor of history, Antioch College, 1922–23. Associate editor, *Baltimore Sun*, 1923–24.

Hendrik Willem Van Loon—*Continued*

BIBLIOGRAPHY

Historical Studies
   The Fall of the Dutch Republic. 1913.
   The Rise of the Dutch Kingdom. 1915.
   The Golden Book of the Dutch Navigators. 1916.
   A Short History of Discovery. 1917.
   History with a Match. 1917. (Juvenile.)
   Ancient Man. 1920. (Juvenile.)
   The Story of Mankind. 1921. (Juvenile.)
   The Story of the Bible. 1923. (Juvenile.)
   Tolerance. 1925.
   America. 1927.
   Man the Miracle Maker. 1928.
   Life and Times of Pieter Stuyvesant. 1928.

Satire
   The Story of Wilbur the Hat. 1925.

STUDIES AND REVIEWS

Bookm., 58 ('24): 570; 62 ('25): 342.

Bookm. (Lond.), 63 ('22): 31; 70 ('26): 259.

Bost. Trans., Nov. 14, 1923: 2; Dec. 5, 1925: 5.

Eng. Rev., 43 ('26): 251.

Forum, 73 ('25): 928; 74 ('25): 952.

Freeman, 8 ('23): 357.

Lit. Rev., Nov. 12, 1921: 165; Nov. 10, 1923: 231; Nov. 17, 1923: 254.

Nation, 113 ('21): 759; 117 ('23): 714; 120 ('25): 469 (M. Van Doren).

N. Repub., 29 ('21): 105.

N. Y. Times, Jan. 8, 1922: 14; Oct. 28, 1923: 1; Mar. 29, 1925: 7; Oct. 18, 1925: 5.

Sat. Rev. of Lit., 2 ('25): 293.

See also Book Review Digest, 1921.

Carl Van Vechten—critic, novelist.

Born at Cedar Rapids, Iowa, 1880. Ph. B., University of Chicago, 1903. Assistant music critic on *New York Times*, 1906–07, 1910–13. Paris correspondent on *Times*, 1908–09. Editor, Programme Notes for Symphony Society of New York, 1910–11. Dramatic critic, *New York Press*, 1913–14.

Carl Van Vechten—*Continued*

BIBLIOGRAPHY

Novels
  Peter Whiffle. 1922.
  The Blind Bow-Boy. 1923.
  The Tattooed Countess. 1924.
  Firecrackers. 1925.
  Nigger Heaven. 1926.
  Spider Boy. 1928.

Critical Essays
  Music after the Great War. 1915.
  Music and Bad Manners. 1916.
  Interpreters and Interpretations. 1917. (Repr. in part under title
    Interpreters. 1920.)
  The Merry-Go-Round. 1918.
  The Music of Spain. 1918.
  In the Garret. 1920.
  Red. 1925.
  Excavations. 1926. (Some reprints.)

Books on Cats
  The Tiger in the House. 1920.
  Lords of the Housetops. 1921. (Editor.)

STUDIES AND REVIEWS

Baldwin.
Cunningham, S. Bibliography of
  the Writings of Carl Van Vechten. 1924.

Bost. Trans., Sept. 1, 1923: 5;
  Sept. 19, 1925: 3; Aug. 21, 1926:
  4; Aug. 25, 1928: 2.
Dial, 75 ('23): 387.
Freeman, 6 ('22): 19.
Ind., 114 ('25): 188.
Lit. Digest, I. B. R. Oct., 1924:
  772; Apr., 1926: 300.
Lit. Rev., Aug. 25, 1923: 923;
  Aug. 16, 1924: 963; Oct. 3, 1925:
  3; Aug. 21, 1926: 3.

Lond. Times, Nov. 1, 1923: 726;
  Apr. 21, 1927: 278.
Nation, 112 ('22): 243; 114 ('22):
  569; 117 ('23): 244; 119 ('24):
  241; 121 ('25): 491.
N. Repub., 36 ('23): 259; 48 ('26):
  Sept. 29, supp. 162.
N. State., 27 ('26): 362.
N. Y. Herald-Tribune, Mar. 7,
  1926: 7; Aug. 19, 1928: 1.
N. Y. Times, July 2, 1922: 21;
  Aug. 26, 1923: 17; Jan. 10,
  1926: 5; Aug. 22, 1926: 2; Aug.
  19, 1928: 5.
Sat. Rev. of Lit., 2 ('26): 507; 3
  ('26): 153.

Stuart Walker—dramatist.

Born at Augusta, Kentucky. A. B., University of Cincinnati, 1902. Studied at the American Academy of Dramatic Arts. Play-reader, actor, and stage-manager with David Belasco, 1909-14. Originator of the Portmanteau Theatre, 1914, and since 1915 his own producer. Director of repertory company in Indianapolis, 1917-23; director of repertory company in Cincinnati, 1922-23.

BIBLIOGRAPHY

Plays
  Portmanteau Plays. 1917.
  More Portmanteau Plays. 1919.
  Portmanteau Adaptations. 1921.
  Seventeen. 1924. (Dramatized in collaboration with Hugh Stanislaus Stange and Stannard Mears from the story by Booth Tarkington.)
  The King's Great-Aunt Sits on the Floor. 1925.

STUDIES AND REVIEWS

N. Repub., 13 ('17): 222; 21 ('19): *See also* Book Review Digest, 1919. 60.

Mary S(tanbery) Watts—novelist.

Mrs. Miles Taylor Watts. Born at Delaware, Ohio, 1868. Educated at the Convent of the Sacred Heart, Cincinnati, 1881-84.

BIBLIOGRAPHY

Plays
  Three Short Plays. 1917.

Novels
  The Tenants. 1908.
 * Nathan Burke. 1910.
  The Legacy. 1911.
  Van Cleve. 1913.
 * The Rise of Jennie Cushing. 1914.
  The Rudder. 1916.

Mary S(tanbery) Watts—*Continued*
The Boardman Family. 1918.
From Father to Son. 1919.
The Noon-Mark. 1920.
The House of Rimmon. 1922.
Luther Nichols. 1923.
The Fabric of the Loom. 1924.

STUDIES AND REVIEWS

Overton. (O. W. N.)

Atlan. (Bookshelf), 127 ('21): supp. III: 14.
Bookm., 27 ('08): 157; 31 ('10): 454. (Portraits.)
Bost. Trans., Apr. 5, 1922: 6.
Cur. Op., 56 ('14): 137 (portrait).
Lit. Digest, June 10, 1922: 58.
Lit. Digest, I. B. R. Dec., 1924: 60.

Lit. Rev., Apr. 15, 1922: 579 (C. Van Doren); Oct. 20, 1923: 146.
N. Repub., 2 ('15): 152 (R. Herrick).
N. Y. Times, Apr. 2, 1922: 14; Oct. 14, 1923: 9; Oct. 19, 1924: 9.

See also Book Review Digest, 1916–20.

John V(an) A(lstyn) Weaver—poet, playwright, novelist.
Born at Charlotte, North Carolina, 1893. A. B., Hamilton College, Clinton, New York, 1914. Studied at Harvard, 1915. Assistant to book editor, *Chicago Daily News*, 1916–17, 1919–20. Literary editor, *Brooklyn Daily Eagle*, 1920–24. Married Peggy Wood (actress), 1924.

BIBLIOGRAPHY

Poems
In American. 1921.
Finders. 1923.
More "In American" Poems. 1926.
To Youth. 1928.
Plays
So That's That. 1926.
Love 'Em and Leave 'Em. 1926. (With George Abbott.)
Novels
Margey Wins the Game. 1922.
Her Knight Comes Riding. 1928.

John V(an) A(lstyn) Weaver—*Continued*

Bookm., 53 ('21): 81.
Bost. Trans., Feb. 2, 1921: 8;
  Jan. 27, 1926: 4.
Lit. Rev., Feb. 26, 1921: 6.
N. Y. Herald-Tribune, July 29,
  1928: 3.

N. Y. Times, Jan. 28, 1923: 2;
  Jan. 31, 1926: 12; July 15, 1928:
  7; Feb. 19, 1928: 12.
Poetry, 18 ('21): 162; 22 ('23):
  48.
Sat. Rev. of Lit., 5 ('28): 39.

Henry Kitchell Webster—novelist.

Born at Evanston, Illinois, 1875. Ph. M., Hamilton College, 1897. Instructor in rhetoric at Union College, 1897–98. Since then he has given his time entirely to writing novels.

BIBLIOGRAPHY

Novels

  The Short-Line War. 1899. (With Samuel Merwin.)
  The Banker and the Bear. 1900.
  Calumet "K." 1901. (With Samuel Merwin.)
  Roger Drake. 1902.
  The Duke of Cameron Avenue. 1904.
  Traitor and Loyalist. 1904.
  Comrade John. 1907. (With Samuel Merwin.)
  The Whispering Man. 1908.
  A King in Khaki. 1909.
  The Sky-Man. 1910.
  The Girl in the Other Seat. 1911.
  The Ghost Girl. 1913.
  The Butterfly. 1914.
  The Real Adventure. 1916.
  The Thoroughbred. 1917.
  An American Family. 1918.
  Mary Wollaston. 1920.
  Real Life. 1921.
  Joseph Greer and His Daughter. 1922.
  The Innocents. 1924.
  The Corbin Necklace. 1926.
  Philopena. 1927.
  The Beginners. 1927.

Henry Kitchell Webster—*Continued*
The Quartz Eye. 1928.
The Clock Strikes Two. 1928.
The Sealed Trunk. 1929.

Short Stories
The Painted Scene. 1916.
The Other Story. 1923.

STUDIES AND REVIEWS

Baldwin.

Bookm., 26 ('07): 4 (portrait only).
Everybody's, Nov., 1917: 16 (portrait).
Lit. Rev., Dec. 2, 1922: 260; Sept. 13, 1924: 3.

N. Y. Times, Nov. 5, 1922: 10; Nov. 11, 1923: 9; Sept. 14, 1924: 9.

See also Book Review Digest, 1917, 1918, 1920.

M(orris) R(obert) Werner—biographer.
Born at New York City, 1897. Student at Columbia University, 1915–17. Obituary editor, *New York Tribune*, 1919. Visited Japan and China as special correspondent for *Tribune*, 1920. With U. S. A. Med. Corps in France, 1917–19.

BIBLIOGRAPHY

Biography
Barnum. 1923.
Brigham Young. 1925.
Tammany Hall. 1928.
Bryan. 1929.

STUDIES AND REVIEWS

Bost. Trans., June 13, 1925: 4.
Freeman, 7 ('23): 228.
Ind., July 11, 1925: 51.
Lit. Digest, I. B. R. May, 1923: 8; Aug., 1925: 602.
Lit. Rev., Apr. 7, 1923: 581; July 3, 1925: 6.
Nation, 116 ('23): Apr. 11, supp. 429 (C. Van Doren).

N. Repub., 34 ('23): 274; 43 ('25): 129.
N. State., 22 ('23): Oct. 13, supp. 10; 26 ('25): 116.
N. Y. Times, Apr. 8, 1923: 3; June 14, 1925: 1.
Outlook, 140 ('25): 592.
Sat. Rev. of Lit., 1 ('25): 853.
Spec., 131 ('23): 758.

Glenway Wescott—novelist.

Born at Kewaskum, Wisconsin, 1901. Educated in public schools and University of Chicago. Has lived in New Mexico and Europe; makes his home in France.

BIBLIOGRAPHY

Novels
The Apple of the Eye. 1924.
The Grandmothers. 1927.
Short Stories
Good-Bye, Wisconsin. 1928.
Poems
The Bitterns. 1920. (Priv. ptd.)
Natives of Rock. 1925. (Decorations by Pamela Bianco.)

STUDIES AND REVIEWS

Bookm., 66 ('27): 87; 68 ('28): 220.
Bost. Trans., Nov. 29, 1924: 5.
Dial, 77 ('24): 513.
Ind., 113 ('24): 458.
Lit. Rev., Oct. 18, 1924: 6.

Nation, 119 ('24): 654; 125 ('27): 396.
N. Y. Times, Oct. 12, 1924: 8; Aug. 28, 1927: 2; Sept. 16, 1928: 2.
Sat. Rev. of Lit., 1 ('24): 320.

Edith (Newbold Jones) Wharton—novelist, short story writer.

Mrs. Edward Wharton. Born in New York City, 1862. Educated at home, but spent much time abroad when she was young. Mrs. Wharton is a society woman and a great lover of outdoors and of animals. Officer of the Legion of Honor of France, and of Order of Leopold of Belgium. *The Age of Innocence* was awarded the Pulitzer novel prize in 1921.

SUGGESTIONS FOR READING

1. Mrs. Wharton's friendship with Henry James and the derivation of her methods from his suggest an interesting comparison of the work of these two writers. For this comparison, books treating of similar material should be chosen;

Edith (Newbold Jones) Wharton—*Continued*

for example, Mrs. Wharton's *The Custom of the Country* or *Madame de Treymes* with Mr. James's *Portrait of a Lady* or *The Ambassadors*. The result will show that Mrs. Wharton, having an essentially different type of mind, has worked out an interesting set of variations of Mr. James's method.

2. Mrs. Wharton's novels of American social life should be studied and judged separately from her Italian historical novel, *The Valley of Decision*, and from her New England stories, *Ethan Frome* and *Summer*.

3. Two special phases of Mrs. Wharton's work that call for study are her management of supernatural effects in some of her short stories and her use of satire.

4. Her short stories offer a basis of comparison with those of Mrs. Gerould (q. v.), another disciple of Mr. James.

5. Has Mrs. Wharton enough originality and enough distinction to hold a permanent high place as a novelist of American manners?

6. Use the following criticisms by Mr. Carl Van Doren as the basis of a critical judgment of your own. Decide whether he is in all respects right.

From the first Mrs. Wharton's power has lain in the ability to reproduce in fiction the circumstances of a compact community in a way that illustrates the various oppressions which such communities put upon individual vagaries, whether viewed as sin, or ignorance, or folly, or merely as social impossibility.

She has always been singularly unpartisan, as if she recognized it as no duty of hers to do more for the herd or its members than to play over the spectacle of their clashes the long, cold light of her magnificent irony.

It is only in these moments of satire that Mrs. Wharton reveals much about her disposition: her impatience of stupidity and affectation and muddy confusion of mind and purpose; her dislike of dinginess; her toleration of arrogance when it is high-bred. Such qualities do not help her, for all her spare, clean movement, to achieve the march or rush of narrative; such qualities, for all her satiric pungency, do not bring her into sympathy with the sturdy or burly or homely, or with the broader aspects of comedy. . . . So great is her self-possession that she holds criticism at arm's length, somewhat as her chosen circles hold the barbarians. If she had a little less of this pride of dignity she might perhaps

Edith (Newbold Jones) Wharton—*Continued*

avoid her tendency to assign to decorum a larger power than it actually exercises, even in the societies about which she writes. . . . The illusion of reality in her work, however, almost never fails her, so alertly is her mind on the lookout to avoid vulgar or shoddy romantic elements.

BIBLIOGRAPHY

Poems

Artemis to Actæon. 1909.

Novels and Novelettes

The Touchstone. 1900. (London, under title A Gift from the Grave.)
The Valley of Decision. 1902.
Sanctuary. 1903.
* The House of Mirth. 1905.
* Madame de Treymes. 1907.
The Fruit of the Tree. 1907.
* Ethan Frome. 1911.
The Reef. 1912.
* The Custom of the Country. 1913.
Summer. 1917.
The Marne. 1918.
* The Age of Innocence. 1920. (Dramatized by Margaret Ayer Barnes.)
The Glimpses of the Moon. 1922.
A Son at the Front. 1923.
The Old Maid. 1924.
New Year's Day. 1924.
False Dawn. 1924.
The Spark. 1924.
The Mother's Recompense. 1925.
Twilight Sleep. 1927.
The Children. 1928.

Short Stories

The Greater Inclination. 1899.
Crucial Instances. 1901.
The Descent of Man. 1904.
The Hermit and the Wild Woman. 1908.
Tales of Men and Ghosts. 1910.
* Xingu. 1916.
Here and Beyond. 1926.

Travel and Description

Italian Villas and Their Gardens. 1904.
Italian Backgrounds. 1905.
A Motor-Flight through France. 1908.

Edith (Newbold Jones) Wharton—*Continued*

Fighting France, from Dunkerque to Belfort. 1915.
French Ways and Their Meaning. 1919.
In Morocco. 1920.

Critical Studies
The Writing of Fiction. 1925.

STUDIES AND REVIEWS

Björkman, E. Voices of To-morrow. 1913.
Boynton. (S. C. A.)
Cooper.
Hackett.
Halsey. (Women.)
Hind. (M. A. I.)
Lovett, Robert Morss. Edith Wharton. 1925.
Melish, L. M. Bibliography of the Collected Writings of Edith Wharton. 1925.
Michaud.
Overton. (O. W. N.) (A. O. D.)
Sedgwick, H. D. The New American Type. 1908.
Squire.
Underwood.
Van Doren. (A. B. L.)
——. (C. A. N.)
Williams.

Bookm., 33 ('11): 302 (portrait).
Bost. Trans., May 24, 1924: 4; May 2, 1925: 5; May 8, 1926: 4; May 28, 1927: 5; Sept. 1, 1928: 2.
Critic, 37 ('00): 103 (portrait), 173.
Dial, 68 ('20): 80; 73 ('22): 343.
Forum, 68 ('22): 905; 74 ('25): 154; 78 ('27): 78.
Ind., 109 ('22): 79; 111 ('23): 157.
Lit. Digest, Aug. 4, 1917: 37 (portrait).
Lit. Digest, I. B. R. Oct., 1923: 15; June, 1924: 538; Oct., 1924: 785.

Lit. Rev., Aug. 19, 1922: 883; Sept. 22, 1923: 61 (Boynton); June 7, 1924: 803; May 9, 1925: 3 (L. Bromfield).
Lond. Merc., 13 ('25): 52.
Lond. Times, Dec. 4, 1919: 710; Sept. 7, 1922: 566; Sept. 20, 1923: 618; Sept. 11, 1924: 553; June 16, 1927: 422.
Nation, 85 ('07): 514; 97 ('13): 404; 112 ('21): 40 (C. Van Doren).
N. Repub., 2 ('15): 40; 3 ('15): 20; 10 ('17): 50; 36 ('23): 105 (Lovett); 39 ('24): 77; 51 ('27): 78.
N. State., 8 ('16): 234; 19 ('22): 588 (R. West).
N. Y. Herald-Tribune, Sept. 2, 1928: 1.
N. Y. Times, July 23, 1922: 1; Sept. 9, 1923: 1; May 18, 1924: 1; Apr. 26, 1925: 7; May 2, 1926: 9; May 22, 1927: 1; Sept. 2, 1928: 2.
No. Am., 182 ('06): 840; 183 ('06): 125; 219 ('24): 139.
Outlook, 71 ('02): 209, 211 (portrait); 81 ('05): 719.
Quarterly R., 223 ('15): 182 (P. Lubbock) =Liv. Age, 284 ('15): 604.
Sat. Rev. of Lit., 1 ('24): 43; 5 ('28): 84.
Spec., 95 ('05): 470; 129 ('22): 373; 131 ('23): 514; 132 ('24): 1006.

John Hall Wheelock—poet.

Born at Far Rockaway, Long Island, 1886. A. B., Harvard, 1908; studied at the University of Göttingen, 1909; University of Berlin, 1910. With Charles Scribner's Sons since 1911.

Strongly influenced by Whitman and Henley.

BIBLIOGRAPHY

Poems
The Human Fantasy. 1911.
The Beloved Adventure. 1912.
Love and Liberation. 1913.
Dust and Light. 1919.
The Black Panther. 1922.
The Bright Doom. 1927.

STUDIES AND REVIEWS

Untermeyer. (A. P.)
Wilkinson. (P.)
Wood.

Bookm. (Lond.), 65 ('24): 315.
Bost. Trans., Sept. 30, 1922: 7.
Lit. Digest, Nov. 10, 1917: 29 (portrait).

Lit. Rev., Nov. 25, 1922: 240 (L. Untermeyer).
Nation, 115 ('22): Dec. 6, supp. 622.
N. Repub., 54 ('28): 228.
Poetry, 4 ('14): 163; 15 ('20): 343; 21 ('23): 224.

See also Book Review Digest, 1919.

Stewart Edward White—novelist, short story writer.

Born at Grand Rapids, Michigan, 1873, of pioneer ancestry. At the age of twelve, went with his father to California and for four years lived mostly in the saddle. At the age of sixteen, went to high school in Michigan, but spent much time in the woods, studying the birds and making a large collection of specimens. Ph. B., University of Michigan, 1895; A. M., 1903. Went to the Black Hills in a gold-rush, but returned poor and went to Columbia to study law, 1896–97. He was influenced by Brander Matthews to write. Made his way into literature via bookselling and reviewing. Explored

Stewart Edward White—*Continued*
in the Hudson Bay wilderness and in Africa, spent a winter
as a lumberman in a lumber camp, and finally went to the
Sierras of California to live. He is a thorough woodsman.
For complete bibliography, see Who's Who in America.

* The Blazed Trail.   1902.
  Conjuror's House.   1903.
* The Silent Places.   1904.
  Arizona Nights.   1907.
* The Rules of the Game.   1909.
  The Land of Footprints.   1912.
  Gold.   1913.
  The Gray Dawn.   1915.
  The Rose Dawn.   1920.
  The Glory Hole.   1924.
  Back of Beyond.   1927.
  Why Be a Mud Turtle?   1929.

STUDIES AND REVIEWS

Baldwin.
Overton. (A. O. D.)

Bookm., 17 ('03): 308; 31 ('10):
486; 38 ('13): 9. (Portraits.)
Bookm. (Lond.), 27 ('05): 253;
46 ('14): 31 (portrait and illustrations).
Bost. Trans., Nov. 12, 1924: 6;
June 6, 1925: 5; May 1, 1926: 1.

Lit. Rev., Sept. 30, 1922: 73;
Nov. 29, 1924: 4; Mar. 5, 1927:
8.
N. Y. Times, Sept. 3, 1922: 11;
Nov. 9, 1924: 22.
Outing, 43 ('03): 218 (portrait).
Sat. Rev. of Lit., 1 ('24): 412.
Springfield Repub., Aug. 23, 1925:
7a.

Margaret Widdemer—poet, novelist.
Mrs. Robert Haven Schauffler. Born at Doylestown,
Pennsylvania. Educated at home. Graduate of the Drexel
Institute Library School, 1909. Her first published poem,
"Factories," attracted wide attention for its humanitarian
interest. In 1918, she shared with Carl Sandburg (q. v.)

Margaret Widdemer—*Continued*

the prize of the Poetry Society of America. Her verse reflects
the attitudes and interests of the modern woman.

Poems
    Factories. 1915.
    Old Road to Paradise. 1918.
    Cross-Currents. 1921.
    A Tree With a Bird in It. 1922. (Parodies.)
    Poems, Ballads and Lyrics. 1925.
    Collected Poems. 1928.

Play
    The Singing Wood. 1926.

Novels
    I've Married Marjorie. 1920.
    The Year of Delight. 1921.
    Graven Image. 1923.
    Charis Sees It Through. 1924.
    Gallant Lady. 1926.
    More Than Wife. 1927.
    Rhinestones. 1929.

Short Stories
    The Boardwalk. 1920.
    Minister of Grace. 1922.

Untermeyer. (A. P.)

Bookm., 42 ('15): 458; 47 ('18): 392.
Bost. Trans., Dec. 17, 1921: 6; Oct. 25, 1922: 6; Nov. 25, 1922: 5.
Lit. Digest, Nov. 4, 1922: 66.
Lit. Rev., Oct. 20, 1923: 152; Sept. 27, 1924: 10.

N. Y. Times, Sept. 25, 1921: 18; Sept. 24, 1922: 20; Oct. 21, 1923: 4; Nov. 23, 1924: 16; Sept. 19, 1926: 16.
Poetry, 7 ('15): 150; 14 ('19): 273; 20 ('22): 340.
Springfield Repub., Dec. 23, 1923: 8a.

See also Book Review Digest, 1915, 1917, 1918, 1920.

Kate Douglas Wiggin—story writer.

Mrs. George C. Riggs. Born at Philadelphia, 1859. As a child, lived in New England and was educated at home, and at Abbott Academy, Andover, Massachusetts. Honorary Litt. D., Bowdoin, 1906. Studied to be a kindergarten teacher. Later, her family moved to Southern California, and she organized the first free kindergarten for poor children on the Pacific coast. Her kindergarten experience is seen in her first two books. Musician (piano and vocal); composer. She died in 1923.

For complete bibliography, see Who's Who in America.

BIBLIOGRAPHY

The Story of Patsy. 1883.
The Birds' Christmas Carol. 1887.
* Timothy's Quest. 1890.
Penelope's English Experiences. 1893.
Penelope's Progress. 1898.
* Rebecca of Sunnybrook Farm. 1903. (Dramatized, 1908.)
The Old Peabody Pew. 1907. (Dramatized, 1917.)
Mother Carey's Chickens. 1911. (Dramatized, 1915.)
Collected Works. 1917.

STUDIES AND REVIEWS

Burnett, F. Kate Douglas Wiggin. 1924.
Cooper.
Halsey. (Women.)
Harkins. (Women.)
Overton.
Smith, W. A. Kate Douglas Wiggin as Her Sister Knew Her. 1925.
Wiggin, K. D. The Girl and the Kingdom: Learning to Teach. 1915.

Bk. Buyer, 8 ('91): 285.
Bookm., 18 ('03): 4, 652; 20 ('05): 402; 25 ('07): 226, 304, 566; 32 ('10): 236; 58 ('23): 467. (Portraits.)
Bookm. (Lond.), 38 ('10): 149 (portrait); 43 ('12): 9; 66 ('24): 39.
Bost. Trans., Oct. 13, 1923: 4.
Cur. Lit., 30 ('01): 277.
Cur. Op., 76 ('24): 34.
Lamp, 29 ('05): 585.
Lit. Digest, I. B. R. Dec., 1923: 28.
Lit. Rev., Oct. 20, 1923: 147.
N. Y. Times, Nov. 4, 1923: 3.
Outlook, 75 ('03): 847 (portrait).
Springfield Repub., Oct. 21, 1923: 7.

Thornton (Niven) Wilder—novelist.

Born at Madison, Wisconsin, 1897. He spent his early years in China, where his father was Consul-General, and later prepared for college in California. He was graduated from Yale in 1920, after which he spent two years at the American Academy in Rome. His first novel, *The Cabala*, grew out of the experiences of those two years. He taught at Lawrenceville after his return from Rome and also studied at the Princeton Graduate College. Mr. Wilder was awarded the 1928 Pulitzer novel prize for *The Bridge of San Luis Rey*.

BIBLIOGRAPHY

Novels
  The Cabala. 1926.
  The Bridge of San Luis Rey. 1927.

Plays
  The Angel that Troubled the Waters. 1928.

STUDIES AND REVIEWS

Bookm., 63 ('26): 478.
Ind., 119 ('27): 608.
Lit. Rev., May 15, 1926: 5.
Nation, 125 ('27): 687.
Lit. Rev., Dec. 13, 1927: 14.

N. Y. Herald-Tribune, Nov. 18, 1928: 2.
N. Y. Times, May 9, 1926: 9; Nov. 27, 1927: 7; Nov. 18, 1928: 2.
Sat. Rev. of Lit., 4 ('27): 371.

Marguerite (Ogden Bigelow) Wilkinson—poet.

Mrs. James G. Wilkinson. Born at Halifax, Nova Scotia, 1883. Compiler of *Golden Songs of the Golden State* (California anthology), 1917, and of *New Voices* (studies in modern poetry with extensive quotations), 1919. Published several volumes of poetry. Died in January, 1928.

BIBLIOGRAPHY

  Golden Songs of the Golden State. 1917. (Compiler.)
  New Voices. 1919. (Compiler.)
  Bluestone. 1920.

Marguerite (Ogden Bigelow) Wilkinson—*Continued*
The Dingbat of Arcady. 1922.
Contemporary Poetry. 1923. (Criticism.)
The Way of the Makers. 1925. (Criticism.)
Yule Fire. 1925.
Citadels. 1926.

STUDIES AND REVIEWS

Atlan. (Bookshelf), Dec., 1921.
Forum, 74 ('25): 476.
N. Y. Times, Nov. 6, 1921: 6 (R.
  Le Gallienne); July 12, 1925: 9.

Poetry, 23 ('23): 48.
Sat. Rev. of Lit., 2 ('25): 39.
Springfield Repub., Aug. 2, 1925:
  7a.

Jesse Lynch Williams—novelist, short story writer.
Born at Sterling, Illinois, 1871. A. B., Princeton, 1892;
A. M., 1895. His play *Why Marry* was awarded the Pulitzer
prize for drama in 1918. Fellow in creative arts, University
of Michigan, 1925–26.

For complete bibliography, see Who's Who in America.

BIBLIOGRAPHY
The Stolen Story. 1899.
The Adventures of a Freshman. 1899.
New York Sketches. 1902.
The Day-Dreamer. 1906.
And So They Were Married. 1914. (Rev. ed. as Why Marry?
  1918.)
Not Wanted. 1923.
Why Not? 1924.
They Still Fall in Love. 1929.

William Carlos Williams—poet.
Born at Rutherford, New Jersey, 1883, of Dutch, Jewish,
and Basque ancestry. Educated in New York and Geneva,
Switzerland. Took his degree in medicine at the University
of Pennsylvania, 1906. Has practised medicine in Rutherford since 1910.

William Carlos Williams—*Continued*

BIBLIOGRAPHY

Poems
Poems. 1909.
The Tempers. London, 1913.
A Book of Poems. 1917.
Kora in Hell. 1920.
Sour Grapes. 1921.

Essays
The Great American Novel. Paris, 1923.
In the American Grain. 1925.

Novel
Voyage to Pagany. 1928.

STUDIES AND REVIEWS

Aiken.
Untermeyer. (A. P.)

Commonweal, 3 ('26): 446.
Dial, 72 ('22): 197.
Nation, 122 ('26): 413.
N. Repub., 46 ('26): 148 (D. H.
Lawrence).

N. Y. Herald-Tribune, Mar. 14,
1926: 7.
N. Y. Times, Feb. 7, 1926: 21.
Poetry, 17 ('21): 329; 23 ('23):
103; 24 ('24): 45.
Sat. Rev. of Lit., 2 ('25): 425.

Owen Wister—novelist.
Born at Philadelphia, 1860. A. B., Harvard, 1882; A. M.,
LL. B., 1888; honorary LL. D., University of Pennsylvania,
1907. Admitted to the Philadelphia bar, 1889. In literary
work since 1891.

BIBLIOGRAPHY

Novels
The Virginian. 1902.
Lady Baltimore. 1906.

Play
Watch Your Thirst. 1923.

Short Stories, Tales, and Sketches
The Dragon of Wantley. 1892.
Red Men and White. 1896.

320

Owen Wister—*Continued*

Lin McLean. 1898.
The Jimmyjohn Boss. 1900.
Philosophy 4. 1903.
How Doth the Simple Spelling Bee. 1907.
Mother. 1907. (First published anonymously in a volume entitled
   A House Party, 1901.)
Members of the Family. 1911.
Padre Ignacio. 1911.
Indispensable Information for Infants. 1921.
The New Swiss Family Robinson. 1922. (First published in The
   Harvard Lampoon. 1882.)
When West was West. 1928.

Political and Sociological Studies
The Pentecost of Calamity. 1915.
A Straight Deal. 1920.
Neighbors Henceforth. 1922.

Biography
Ulysses S. Grant. 1900.
The Seven Ages of Washington. 1907.

STUDIES AND REVIEWS

Baldwin.
Cooper.

Bk. Buyer, 25 ('02): 199.
Bookm., 27 ('08): 458, 465 (por-
   trait).
Bost. Trans., Dec. 16, 1922: 8.
Crit., 41 ('02): 358.

Cur. Lit., 33 ('02): 129 (portrait
   only), 238.
Dial, 59 ('15): 303.
Ind., 60 ('06): 1159 (portrait).
N. Y. Times, July 1, 1928: 7.
World's Work, 5 ('02): 2792, 2795
   (portrait).

Charles Erskine Scott Wood—poet.

Born at Erie, Pennsylvania, 1852. Graduate of U. S.
Military Academy, 1874; Ph. B., LL. B., Columbia, 1883.
Served in the U. S. Army, 1874–84, in various campaigns
against the Indians. Admitted to the bar, 1884, in Portland, Oregon, and practised until he retired, 1919. Painting,
as well as writing, an avocation.

His knowledge of the Indians and of the desert appears

Charles Erskine Scott Wood—*Continued*

in his principal work, a long poem in the manner of Whitman,
The Poet in the Desert.

BIBLIOGRAPHY

A Book of Tales. 1901.
A Masque of Love. 1904.
The Poet in the Desert. 1915.
Maia. 1916.
A Christmas Cantata. 1916.
Heavenly Discourse. 1927. (Satire.)

STUDIES AND REVIEWS

Untermeyer. (A. P.)
Wood.

Cur. Op., 59 ('15): 268.
Poetry, 6 ('15): 311.
Sunset, 28 ('12): 232 (portrait).

George Edward Woodberry—poet, critic.

Born at Beverly, Massachusetts, 1855. A. B., Harvard,
1877. Honorary higher degrees. Professor of English at
the University of Nebraska, 1877-78, 1880-82, and of com-
parative literature, Columbia, 1891-1904.

BIBLIOGRAPHY

Poems
The North Shore Watch. 1893. (Priv. ptd. 1890.)
Wild Eden. 1899.
Poems. 1903.
A Day at Castrogiovanni. 1912. (Priv. ptd.)
The Kingdom of All-Souls. 1912. (Priv. ptd.)
The Flight. 1914.
Ideal Passion. 1917. (Priv. ptd.)
The Roamer. 1920.
At Burn Side. 1927. (With Louisa Putnam Loring. Priv. ptd.)

Literary and Critical Essays and Studies
Studies in Letters and Life. 1890. (Enl. ed. 1900 under title Makers
of Literature.)
Heart of Man. 1899.
America in Literature. 1903.

George Edward Woodberry—*Continued*

The Torch. 1905. (Enl. ed., 1920.)
The Appreciation of Literature. 1907.
The Inspiration of Poetry. 1910.
Two Phases of Criticism. 1914. (Priv. ptd.)
Literary Essays. 1920.
Collected Essays. 1920–21.
Literary Memoirs of the Nineteenth Century. 1921.
Studies of a Litterateur. 1921.

Biography and Criticism
Edgar Allan Poe. 1885.
Nathaniel Hawthorne. 1902.
Swinburne. 1905.
Ralph Waldo Emerson. 1907.
Great Writers. 1907.

Description and Travel
North Africa and the Desert. 1914.
Taormina. 1926.

Study
A History of Wood-Engraving. 1883.

STUDIES AND REVIEWS

Bacon, E. M. Literary Pilgrimages. 1902.
Boynton. (S. C. A.)
Calverton.
Halsey.
Ledoux, L. V. The Poetry of George Edward Woodberry. 1917.
Rittenhouse.

Bookm., 17 ('03): 336 (portrait); 47 ('18): 549.
Cur. Lit., 33 ('02): 513; 42 ('07): 289 (portrait).
Freeman, 3 ('21): 402.
Lit. Rev., May 7, 1921: 2.
Poetry, 3 ('13): 69; 11 ('17): 103.
Rev., 4 ('21): 180, 273.

William E. Woodward—novelist, biographer.

Born at Ridge Spring, South Carolina, 1874. Graduate, South Carolina Military Academy. Associated for fifteen years with New York advertising agencies. Left the advertising business to become a banker. Was vice-president of the Industrial Finance Corporation of New York. Left the

William E. Woodward—*Continued*

banking business at the age of forty-seven to devote himself
to writing. In writing *George Washington,* Mr. Woodward
says, he has not made any effort to "show him up," but
rather has tried to humanize him.

BIBLIOGRAPHY

Novels
  Bunk. 1923.
  Lottery. 1924.
  Bread and Circuses. 1925.

Biography
  George Washington. 1926.
  Meet General Grant. 1928.

STUDIES AND REVIEWS

Bost. Trans., Jan. 7, 1925: 4;
  Oct. 30, 1926: 3; Nov. 10, 1928:
  2.
Cent., 109 ('24): 285; 113 ('27):
  379 (C. Van Doren).
Ind., 111 ('23): 172.
Lit. Rev., Sept. 29, 1923: 83.
Nation, 117 ('23): Oct. 10, supp.
  398; 119 ('24): 575; 121 ('25):
762; 123 ('26): 431; 127 ('28):
  628.
N. Y. Herald-Tribune, Oct. 10,
  1926: 1.
N. Y. Times, Nov. 16, 1924: 14;
  Nov. 29, 1925: 11; Oct. 24,
  1926: 1; Nov. 11, 1928: 1.
Sat. Rev. of Lit., 3 ('26): 415.

Elinor (Hoyt) Wylie—poet, novelist.

Mrs. William Rose Benét. Born at Somerville, New
Jersey, but Pennsylvanian in tradition. Passed her girlhood
in Washington, D. C. Lived and traveled abroad. Died
on December 16, 1928.

BIBLIOGRAPHY

Poems
  Nets to Catch the Wind. 1921.
  Black Armour. 1923.
  Trivial Breath. 1928.
  Angels and Earthly Creatures. 1929.

Elinor (Hoyt)Wylie—*Continued*

Novels
    Jennifer Lorn. 1923.
    The Venetian Glass Nephew. 1925.
    The Orphan Angel. 1926.
    Mr. Hodge and Mr. Hazard. 1928.

STUDIES AND REVIEWS

Jordan, Laurence. Elinor Wylie.
    1926.
Sergeant.
Untermeyer. (A. P.)
Wood.

Bookm., 54 ('22): 579.
Bost. Trans., Nov. 30, 1921: 9;
    Dec. 5, 1923: 8; Nov. 21, 1925:
    3.
Cent., 113 ('26): 253 (C. Van
    Doren).
Dial, 74 ('23): 625.
Freeman, 7 ('23): 452.
Lit. Rev., Aug. 4, 1923: 876;
    Nov. 27, 1926: 1.

Lond. Times, Feb. 24, 1927: 124.
Nation, 121 ('25): 465; 126 ('28):
    454; 127 ('28): 185.
N. Repub., 29 ('21): 133 (L. Un-
    termeyer); 37 ('23): Dec. 5,
    supp. 16; 44 ('25): 176; 54 ('28):
    226; 55 ('28): 286; 57 ('29): 316.
N. Y. Herald-Tribune, Oct. 31,
    1926: 1 (C. Van Doren); Mar.
    18, 1928: 1; June 24, 1928: 3.
N. Y. Times, Nov. 25, 1923: 8;
    Sept. 27, 1925: 11; Oct. 31, 1926:
    7; Mar. 24, 1928: 12.
Poetry, 23 ('24): 277.
Sat. Rev., 143 ('27): 240.
Sat. Rev. of Lit., 3 ('26): 293.

Stark Young—critic, dramatist.

Born at Como, Mississippi, 1881. A. B., University of
Mississippi; A. M., Columbia. Instructor of English, University of Mississippi, instructor of English literature and
professor of general literature, University of Texas, and
professor of English, Amherst. Editorial staff of *New Republic*, 1921–24; associate editor of *Theatre Arts Monthly*,
1921–24. Dramatic critic, *New York Times*, 1924–25; member of editorial staff, *New Republic*, 1927–

BIBLIOGRAPHY

Poems
    The Blind Man at the Window. 1906.

Stark Young—*Continued*

Plays
  Guenevere. 1906.
  Addio, Madretta and Other Plays. 1912.
  Three One-Act Plays. 1921.
  The Colonnade. 1924.
  The Saint. 1925. (Music by Macklin Marrow.)
  George Dandin, by Moliere. 1925. (Translator.)
  The Twilight Saint. 1925.
  Mandragola, by Machiavelli. 1927. (Translator.)

Novels
  Heaven Trees. 1926.
  The Torches Flare. 1928.

Critical Essays and Studies
  The Flower in the Drama. 1923.
  Glamour. 1925.
  Encaustics. 1926.
  Theatre Practice. 1926.
  The Theatre. 1927.

Travel Sketches
  The Three Fountains. 1924.

STUDIES AND REVIEWS

Bost. Trans., Apr. 14, 1923: 2; May 3, 1924: 5; Aug. 4, 1926: 6.
Lit. Rev., May 19, 1923: 699; Sept. 12, 1925: 2; Oct. 2, 1926: 4.
Lond. Times, May 22, 1924: 310.
Nation, 118 ('24): 511.
N. Repub., 43 ('25): 214.
N. Y. Herald-Tribune, Oct. 10, 1926: 16.
N. Y. Times, Aug. 21, 1921: 26; Mar. 18, 1923: 8; May 11, 1924: 13; May 31, 1925: 18; Oct. 3, 1926: 8.
No. Am., 221 ('25): 763.
Sat. Rev. of Lit., 4 ('28): 986.
Springfield Repub., Apr. 15, 1923: 7a.
Theatre Arts Mo., 9 ('25): 417.

INDEXES AND CRITICAL PERIODICALS

INDEXES

American Library Association Index to 1900..........A. L. A. I.
    Supplement, 1901–10...........................A. L. A. Supp.
Annual Literary Index, 1892–1904..................A. L. I.
    Continued as Annual Library Index, 1905–10......A. L. I.
    Continued as American Library Annual, 1911– ....A. L. A.
Dramatic Index, 1909– ....D. I.
    Published with Annual Magazine Subject Index.
Magazine Subject Index: Boston, 1908..............M. S. I.
    Continued as Annual Magazine Subject Index, 1909– A. S. I.
Poole's Index to Periodical Literature, 1802–81 ....Poole.
    Supplements, 1882–1906; 1907–08................Poole Supp.
Reader's Guide to Periodical Literature, 1900– ......R. G.
Reader's Guide Supplement, 1907–15, 1916–19........R. G. Supp.
    Continued as International Index to Periodicals,
    1921– ....I. I. P.

PERIODICALS

(The initials following the abbreviated titles of the periodicals refer to
the indexes in which they are listed.)
The Book Review Digest, 1905– , contains summaries of important
reviews in periodicals and newspapers.
Academy: London (ceased 1916)—Acad.
American Magazine: New York—Am. M.—R. G.
American Mercury: New York—Am. Merc.—R. G.; D. I.
Arena: Boston—Arena—Poole.
Athenæum: London—Ath.—A. L. I. Combined with Nation (London)
Feb. 19, 1921.
Atlantic Monthly: Boston—Atlan.—R. G.; D. I.
Bellman: Minneapolis (ceased 1919).
Book Buyer: New York—Bk. Buyer—Poole.
Booklist A. L. A.: Chicago—Booklist.
Bookman: London—Bookm. (Lond.)—D. I.; A. S. I.; I. I. P.
Bookman: New York—Bookm.—R. G.
Boston Transcript: Boston—Bost. Trans.

Calendar of Modern Letters: London (1925–27)—Cal. Mod. Lett.
Catholic World: New York—Cath. World.
Century: New York—Cent.—R. G.; D. I.
Chapbook, A Monthly Miscellany: London (1919–21).
Chautauquan: Meadville, Pa.—Chaut.—Poole.
Citizen: Philadelphia—Citiz.—Poole.
Classical Philology: Chicago—Class. Philol.—I. I. P.
Collier's National Weekly: New York—Collier's—R. G.; D. I.
Commonweal: New York (1924–).
Contemporary Review: London—Contemp.—R. G.; D. I.
Critic: New York—Critic—Poole.
Current Literature: New York. Cur. Lit.—R. G. Name changed to
    Current Opinion, 1913.
Current Opinion: New York.—Cur. Op.—R. G. Merged in Literary
    Digest, 1925.
Dial: New York—Dial—R. G.; D. I.
Double-Dealer: New Orleans.
Drama: Washington—Drama—R. G.; D. I.
Dublin Review: London—Dub. R.—A. S. I.; D. I.; I. I. P.
Edinburgh Review: Edinburgh—Edin. R.—R. G.; D. I.
Egoist. London. 1914–19.
English Review: London—Eng. Rev.—I. I. P.; D. I.; A. S. I.
Everybody's Magazine: New York—Everybody's—R. G.; D. I.
Fortnightly Review: London and New York—Fortn.—R. G.; D. I.
Forum: New York—R. G.; D. I.
Freeman: New York (1920–27).
Harper's Magazine: New York—Harp.—R. G.; D. I.
Harper's Weekly: New York—Harp. W.—R. G.
Harvard Graduates Magazine: Boston—Harv. Grad. M.—A. S. I.; I. I. P.
Independent: New York—Ind.—R. G.; D. I.
Lamp: New York—Lamp.
Literary Digest: New York—Lit. Digest.—R. G.; D. I.
Literary Digest International Book Review: New York—Lit. Digest,
    I. B. R.
Literary Review of the New York Evening Post: New York, 1921–24.—
    Lit. Rev.—R. G.
Little Review: Chicago.
Littell's Living Age: Boston—Liv. Age—R. G.; D. I. Reprints from the
    best periodicals.
London Mercury: London—Lond. Merc.—A. S. I.; I. I. P.
London Times Literary Supplement: London—Lond. Times—A. S. I.
McClure's Magazine: New York—McClure—R. G.
Manchester Guardian: Manchester, England. The best English provin-
    cial paper for reviews.
Nation: London—Nation and Ath.—D. I.; I. I. P. *See* Athenæum.

Nation: New York—Nation—R. G.; D. I.
New England Magazine: Boston—New Eng. M.—R. G.
New Republic: New York—N. Repub.—R. G.; D. I.
New Statesman: London—N. State.—I. I. P.
New York Evening Post. *See* Literary Review.
New York Herald-Tribune (Books): New York—N. Y. Herald-Tribune.
New York Times Review of Books: New York—N. Y. Times.
New York World: New York—N. Y. World.
Nineteenth Century and After: London and New York—19th Cent.—
    R. G.; D. I.
North American Review: New York—No. Am.—R. G.; D. I.
Outlook: New York—Outlook—R. G.; D. I.
Philosophical Review: New York—Phil. Rev.—I. I. P.
Poet Lore: Boston—Poet Lore—R. G.; D. I.
Poetry: Chicago—Poetry—R. G.
Quarterly Review: London and New York—Quar. Rev.—R. G.; I. I. P.
The Review: New York—Rev. Began 1919; changed its name, June,
    1920, to Weekly Review; consolidated with Independent, October,
    1921.
Review of Reviews: New York—R. of Rs.—R. G.
Saturday Review: London—Sat. Rev.—D. I.; I. I. P.
Saturday Review of Literature: New York—Sat. Rev. of Lit.—R. G.
Scribner's Magazine: New York—Scrib. M.—R. G.; D. I.
Sewanee Review: Sewanee, Tenn.—Sewanee R.—I. I. P.
Spectator: London—Spec.—D. I.; I. I. P.
Springfield Republican: Springfield, Mass.—Springfield Repub.
Sunset: New York—Sunset—R. G.
Survey: New York—Survey—R. G.
Theatre Arts Monthly: New York—Theatre Arts Mo.—R. G.; D. I.
Unpopular Review: New York, 1915-19. Continued as Unpartizan
    Review to 1921.
Weekly Review: New York—Rev. 1920-21.
Westminster Review: London—Westm. R. Ceased 1914.
World's Work: New York—World's Work—R. G.; D. I.
Yale Review: New Haven, Conn.—Yale Rev.—R. G.; D. I.

INDEX OF
ABBREVIATIONS OF BOOKS CONTAINING STUDIES

Sherman (C. W.)—Sherman, Stuart, Critical Woodcuts.
Sherman (P. V.)—Sherman, Stuart, Points of View.
Squire—Squire, J. C., Contemporary American Authors.
Starrett—Starrett, V., Buried Cæsars.
Underwood—Underwood, J. C., Literature and Insurgency.
Untermeyer (A. P.)—Untermeyer, Louis, American Poetry Since 1900.
Untermeyer—Untermeyer, Louis, The New Era in American Poetry.
Van Doren (A. B. L.)—Van Doren, Carl, American and British Literature Since 1890.
Van Doren (A. N.)—Van Doren, Carl, The American Novel.
Van Doren (C. A. N.)—Van Doren, Carl, Contemporary American Novelists.
Van Doren (M. M.)—Van Doren, Carl, Many Minds.
Van Doren (R. C.)—Van Doren, Carl, The Roving Critic.
Weirick—Weirick, Bruce, From Whitman to Sandburg in American Poetry.
Whipple—Whipple, T. K., Spokesmen.
Wilkinson (N. V.)—Wilkinson, M., New Voices.
Wilkinson (P.)—Wilkinson, M., Poetry of Our Times.
Williams—Williams, B. C., Our Short Story Writers.
Williams-Ellis—Williams-Ellis, A., An Anatomy of Poetry.
Wood—Wood, C., Poets of America.

GENERAL WORKS OF REFERENCE

I. Histories and General Discussion

Bechofer, C. E. Literary Renaissance in America. 1923.

Boynton, Percy Holmes. A History of American Literature. 1919. (Bibliographies.)

Cambridge History of American Literature, ed. by W. P. Trent, John Erskine, Stuart P. Sherman and Carl Van Doren. Vol. III–IV. 1917–21. (Bibliographies.)

Foerster, Norman. American Criticism. 1928.

Hazard, Lucy L. The Frontier in American Literature. 1927.

Macy, John. The Spirit of American Literature. 1913.

Munson, G. B. Destinations. 1928.

Pattee, Fred Lewis. A History of American Literature since 1870. 1915. (Bibliographies.)

Perry, Bliss. The American Spirit in Literature. 1918.

Stearns, Harold E. America and the Young Intellectual. 1921.

Stearns, H. E., *ed.* Civilization in the United States. 1922. (Special chapters.)

Short History of American Literature based on the Cambridge History of American Literature, ed. by W. P. Trent, John Erskine, Stuart P. Sherman and Carl Van Doren. 1922.

Sullivan, Mark. Our Times: The Turn of the Century. 1926.

—— Our Times: America Finding Herself. 1927.

Van Doren, Carl. American and British Literature since 1890. 1925.

II. Criticism of Special Authors or Phases

Beach, J. W. The Outlook for American Prose. 1926.

Boynton, Percy Holmes. Some Contemporary Americans: the Personal Equation in Literature. 1924.

Boynton, Percy Holmes. More Contemporary Americans. 1927.

Calverton, V. F. The Newer Spirit: A Sociological Criticism of Literature. 1925.

Canby, H. S. Definitions. 1922.

Canby, H. S., Benét, W. R., and Loveman, Amy. Saturday Papers. 1921.

Drake, W. A. American Criticism, 1926. 1926.

Farrar, J. The Literary Spotlight. 1924.
Green, Paul and Elizabeth L. Contemporary American Literature. 1925.
Hackett, Francis. Horizons: A Book of Criticism. 1918.
Hackett, Francis, *ed.* On American Books, 1920: Symposium by J. E. Spingarn, Padraic Colum, H. L. Mencken, Morris R. Cohen and Francis Hackett.
Karsner, David. Sixteen Authors to One. 1928.
Macy, John. The Critical Game. 1922.
Matthews, B. The Tocsin of Revolt. 1922.
Mencken, H. L. A Book of Prefaces. 1917.
—— Prejudices, First, Second, Third, Fourth, Fifth and Sixth Series. 1919–26.
Muir, Edwin. Transition.
Priestley, J. B. Figures in Modern Literature. 1924.
Sherman, S. P. Critical Woodcuts. 1926.
—— The Genius of America. 1923.
—— Points of View. 1924.
Squire, J. C., and others. Contemporary American Authors. 1928.
Starrett, V. Buried Cæsars. 1923.
Underwood, J. C. Literature and Insurgency. 1914.
Van Doren, Carl. Many Minds. 1924.
—— The Roving Critic. 1923.
Whipple, T. K. Spokesmen. 1928.

III. The Novel and the Short Story

Adams, S. H., Austin, Mary, and others. The Novel of Tomorrow and the Scope of Fiction, by Twelve American Novelists. 1922.
Baldwin, C. C. (George Gordon). Men Who Make Our Novels. 1919.
Cooper, Frederic Taber. Some American Story-Tellers. 1911.
Follett, H. T. and W. Some Modern Novelists: Appreciations and Estimates. 1918.
Follett, Wilson. The Modern Novel. 1918, 1923.
Hall, Ernest. The Satirical Element in the American Novel. 1922.
Marble, Annie Russell. A Study of the Modern Novel, British and American since 1900. 1928.
Mencken, H. L. A Book of Prefaces. 1917.
Michaud, Regis. The American Novel To-day. 1927.
O'Brien, Edward J. The Advance of the American Short Story. 1923.
Overton, Grant. Authors of the Day. 1924.
—— The Women Who Make Our Novels. 1918.
Pattee, Fred L. The Development of the American Short Story. 1923.
Phelps, William Lyon. The Advance of the English Novel. 1916.
Van Doren, Carl. The American Novel. 1921.

Van Doren, Carl. Contemporary American Novelists. 1922.
Wharton, Edith. The Writing of Fiction. 1925.
Wheeler, H. L. Contemporary Novels and Novelists: A List of References to Biographical and Critical Material. 1921.
Wilkinson, Hazel. Social Thought in American Fiction (1910–17). 1919.
Williams, Blanche C. Our Short-Story Writers. 1920.

IV. DRAMA

Andrews, Charlton. The Drama Today. 1913.
Baker, George Pierce. Dramatic Technique. 1912.
Beegle, Mary Porter, and Crawford, Jack R. Community Drama and Pageantry. 1916.
Burleigh, Louise. The Community Theatre in Theory and in Practice. 1917. (Bibliography.)
Burton, Richard. The New American Drama. 1913.
Chandler, F. W. Aspects of Modern Drama. 1914.
Cheney, Sheldon. The Art Theatre. 1917.
—— The New Movement in the Theatre. 1914.
—— The Out-of-Door Theatre. 1918.
Clark, Barrett H. The British and American Drama of Today. 1915, 1921.
—— A Study of the Modern Drama. 1925.
Dickinson, Thos. H. The Case of the American Drama. 1915.
—— The Insurgent Theatre. 1917.
—— Playwrights of the New American Theatre. 1925.
Eaton, Walter Prichard. At the New Theatre and Others. 1910.
—— Plays and Players: Leaves from a Critic's Notebook. 1916.
Goldberg, Isaac. The Drama of Transition. 1922.
Goldman, Emma. The Social Significance of the Modern Drama. 1914.
Grau, Robert. The Theatre of Science. 1914.
Hamilton, Clayton. Conversations on Contemporary Drama. 1924.
—— Problems of the Playwright. 1917.
—— Studies in Stagecraft. 1914.
Henderson, Archibald. The Changing Drama. 1914.
Lewis, B. Roland. The Technique of the One-Act Play. 1918.
Lewisohn, Ludwig. The Drama and the Stage. 1922.
—— The Modern Drama. 1915.
Macgowan, K. The Theatre of Tomorrow. 1921.
Mackay, Constance D'Arcy. The Little Theatre in the United States. 1917.
MacKaye, Percy. The Civic Theatre. 1912.
—— Community Drama. 1917.
—— The Playhouse and the Play. 1909.
Matthews, B. A Book about the Theatre. 1916.

Matthews, B. Playwrights on Playmaking and Other Studies. 1923.
Moderwell, Hiram Kelly. The Theatre of Today. 1914.
Moses, Montrose J. The American Dramatist. 1917.
Nathan, George Jean. Another Book on the Theatre. 1915.
—— The Critic and the Drama. 1922.
—— The Drama and the Stage. 1922.
—— Materia Critica. 1924.
—— The Theatre, the Drama, the Girls. 1922.
Phelps, W. L. Essays on Modern Dramatists. 1921.
—— The Twentieth Century Theatre. 1918.
Quinn, Arthur Hobson. A History of the American Drama from the Civil War to the Present Day. 1927.

V. POETRY

Aiken, Conrad. Scepticisms. Notes on Contemporary Poetry. 1919.
Austin, Mary. The American Rhythm. 1923.
Caswell, E. S. Canadian Singers and their Songs. 1920.
Cook, H. W. Our Poets of Today. 1918.
Garvin, J. W. Canadian Poets and Poetry. Stokes. 1916.
Kerlin, R. T. Negro Poets and Their Poems. 1923.
Lowell, Amy. A Critical Fable. 1922.
—— Tendencies in Modern American Poetry. 1917.
Lowes, John Livingston. Convention and Revolt in Poetry. 1919.
Maynard, Theodore. Our Best Poets, English and American. 1922.
Monroe, Harriet. Poets and their Art. 1926.
Peckham, E. H. Present-Day American Poetry. 1917.
Phelps, William Lyon. The Advance of English Poetry in the Twentieth Century. 1918.
Rittenhouse, Jessie B. The Younger American Poets. 1904.
Untermeyer, Louis. The New Era in American Poetry. 1919, 1923.
—— American Poetry since 1900. 1923.
Weirick, Bruce. From Whitman to Sandburg in American Poetry. 1924.
Wilkinson, Marguerite. New Voices. 1919.
—— The Way of the Makers. 1925.
Williams-Ellis, A. An Anatomy of Poetry. 1922.
Wood, Clement. Poets of America. 1925.

VI. BIOGRAPHICAL AND PERSONAL

Boyd, E. Portraits, Real and Imaginary. 1924.
Halsey, F. W. American Authors and Their Homes: Personal Descriptions and Interviews. 1901. (Illustrated.)
—— Women Authors of our Day in Their Homes. 1903. (Illustrated.)

Hansen, H. Midwest Portraits; a Book of Memories and Friendships.
    1923.
Harkins, E. F. Famous Authors (Men). 1901.
—— Famous Authors (Women). 1901.
Hind, Louis. Authors and I. 1921.
—— More Authors and I. 1922.
Karsner, David. Sixteen Authors to One. 1928.
Overton, Grant. Authors of the Day. 1924.

COLLECTIONS OF POETRY

Aiken, Conrad. Modern American Poets. Secker. 1922. Modern Library, 1927.

American Poetry: A Miscellany. Harcourt, Brace. 1925, 1927.

Andrews, C. E. From the Front; Trench Poetry. Appleton. 1918.

Anthology of American Humour in Verse. Duffield. 1917.

Armstrong, H. F. Book of New York Verse. Putnam. 1917.

Baker, H. C. Contemporary American Poetry. Stratford. 1928.

Benét, William Rose. Poems for Youth: An American Anthology. Dutton. 1925.

Braithwaite, W. S. Anthology of Magazine Verse and Yearbook of American Poetry. Small, Maynard. 1914–23. Brimmer. 1923—.
—— Golden Treasury of Magazine Verse. Small, Maynard. 1918.

Brown, Sharon. Poetry of Our Time. Scott, Foresman. 1928.

Carman, Bliss. Oxford Book of American Verse. Oxford University Press. 1927.

Clarke, G. H. Treasury of War Poetry. Houghton, Mifflin. First Series, 1917; Second Series, 1919.

Cook, H. W. Our Poets of Today. Moffat, Yard. 1918.

Cronyn, George W. The Path on the Rainbow (North American Indian Songs and Chants). Boni and Liveright. 1918.

Daly, T. A. A Little Book of American Humorous Verse. McKay. 1926.

Des Imagistes: 1914. Poetry Bookshop. London, 1914.

Edgar, W. C. The Bellman Book of Verse, 1906–19. Bellman Co. 1919.

Erskine, John. Contemporary Verse Anthology. Dutton. 1920. (War Poetry.)

Forbes, Anita P. Modern Verse, British and American. Holt. 1922.

Greever, G., and Bachelor, J. M. The Soul of the City: An Urban Anthology. Houghton, Mifflin. 1923.

Johnson, J. W. American Negro Poetry: An Anthology. Harcourt, Brace. 1922.

Kreymborg, Alfred. Others. Knopf. 1916, 1917, 1919.

Le Gallienne, Richard. Modern Book of American Verse. Boni and Liveright. 1919.

Methuen, Sir Algernon. An Anthology of Modern Verse. Methuen and Co. 1923.

Monroe, Harriet, and Henderson, Alice Corbin. The New Poetry. Macmillan. 1917; revised edition, 1920.

Morley, Christopher. The Bowling Green; An Anthology of Verse. Doubleday, Page. 1924.

Moult, Thomas. Best Poems of 1927, 1928. Harcourt, Brace. 1927, 1928. (British and American.)

O'Brien, Edward J. A Masque of Poets. Dodd, Mead. 1918.

Rand, Theodore H. A Treasury of Canadian Verse. E. P. Dutton. 1900.

Richards, G. M. High Tide; Songs of Joy and Vision. Houghton, Mifflin. 1918.

—— The Melody of Earth. Houghton, Mifflin. 1920. (Nature and Garden Poems from Present-Day Poets.)

—— Star Points: Songs of Joy, Faith and Promise. Houghton, Mifflin. 1921.

Rittenhouse, Jessie B. The Little Book of Modern Verse. Houghton, Mifflin. 1913–19.

—— Second Book of Modern Verse. Houghton, Mifflin. 1919.

—— Third Book of Modern Verse. Houghton, Mifflin. 1927.

Sanders, G. D., and Nelson, J. H. Chief Modern Poets of England and America. Macmillan. 1929.

Some Imagist Poets; 1915, 1916, 1917. Houghton, Mifflin. 1915–17.

Sterling, George. Continent's End; An Anthology of Contemporary California Poets. 1925.

Stork, Charles Wharton. Contemporary Verse Anthology: Favorite Poems Selected from the *Magazine of Contemporary Verse*. 1916–20. Dutton. 1920.

Untermeyer, Louis. Modern American Poetry. Harcourt, Brace. Third Revised Edition. 1925.

—— This Singing World. Harcourt, Brace. 1923.

White, N. I., and Jackson, W. C. An Anthology of Verse by American Negroes. Trinity College Press. 1924.

Wilkinson, Marguerite. Contemporary Poetry. Macmillan. 1923.

COLLECTIONS OF PLAYS

Baker, George Pierce. Harvard Plays. Brentano.
  I. 47 Workshop Plays: First Series. 1918. (Rachel L. Field, Hubert Osborne, Eugene Pillot, William L. Prosser.)
  II. Plays of the Harvard Dramatic Club: First Series. 1918. (Winifred Hawkridge, H. Brock, Rita C. Smith, K. Andrews.)
  III. Plays of the Harvard Dramatic Club: Second Series. 1919. (Louise W. Bray, E. W. Bates, F. Bishop, C. Kinkead.)
  IV. 47 Workshop Plays: Second Series. 1920. (Kenneth Raesback, Norman C. Lindau, Eleanor Holmes Hinkley, Doris F. Halnan.)
—— Modern American Plays. Harcourt, Brace. 1920. (Belasco, Sheldon, Thomas.)
Brooks, W. W. One-Act Plays by Canadian Authors. 1926.
Cohen, Helen Louise. One-Act Plays by Modern Authors. Harcourt, Brace. 1921. (MacKaye, Marks, Peabody, R. E. Rogers, Tarkington, Stark Young.)
—— Longer Plays by Modern Authors. Harcourt, Brace. 1922. (Thomas, Tarkington.)
—— More One-Act Plays by Modern Authors. Harcourt, Brace. 1927.
Cook, G. C., and Shay, F. Provincetown Plays. Stewart Kidd.
—— First Series. 1916. (Louise Bryant, Dell, O'Neill.)
—— Second Series. 1916. (Neith Boyce and Hutchins Hapgood, G. C. Cook and Susan Glaspell, John Reed.)
—— Third Series. 1917. (Neith Boyce, Kreymborg, O'Neill.)
—— Fourth Series. 1922. (Boyce and Hapgood, Cook and Glaspell, Dell, P. King, Millay, O'Neill, Oppenheim, Alice Rostetter, W. D. Steele, Wellman.)
Dickinson, Thomas H. Chief Contemporary Dramatists. Houghton, Mifflin. 1915. (MacKaye, Thomas.)
—— Second Series. 1921. (G. C. Hazelton and Benrimo, Peabody, Walter.)
—— Wisconsin Plays. Huebsch.
—— First Series. 1914. (Thomas H. Dickinson, Gale, William Ellery Leonard.)
—— Second Series. 1918. (M. Ilsley, H. M. Jones, Laura Sherry.)
—— and Crawford, J. R. Contemporary Plays. Houghton, Mifflin. 1925. (Anspacher, O'Neill, Crothers, Davis, Rice.)

Eaton, W. P.   One-Act Plays for Stage and Study.   Second Series.
    French.   1925.
47 Workshop Plays.   *See* Baker.
Harvard Dramatic Club Plays.   *See* Baker.
Knickerbocker, Edwin Van B.   Plays for Classroom Interpretation.
    Holt.   1921.
Koch, Frederick H.   Carolina Folk Plays.   Holt.
—— First Series.   1922.
—— Second Series.   1924.
—— Third Series.   1928.
Leonard, Sterling A.   The Atlantic Book of Modern Plays.   Atlantic.
    1922.
Lewis, B. Roland.   Contemporary One-Act Plays.   Scribner.   1922.
    (Bibliographies.)   (Middleton, Althea Thurston, MacKaye, Eugene
    Pillot, Bosworth Crocker, Kreymborg, Paul Green, Arthur Hop-
    kins, Jeannette Marks, Oscar M. Wolff, David Pinski, Beulah
    Bornstead.)
Mantle, Burns.   Best Plays of 1919–20 and the Year Book of Drama in
    America and succeeding volumes.   Small, Maynard.   1920–24; Dodd,
    Mead, 1925—.
Mayorga, Margaret Gardner.   Representative One-Act Plays by Ameri-
    can Authors.   Little, Brown.   1919.   (Full bibliographies.)   (Mary
    Aldis, Cook and Glaspell, Sada Cowan, Bosworth Crocker, Elva
    De Pue, Beulah Marie Dix, Hortense Flexner, Esther E. Galbraith,
    Alice Gerstenberg, Doris F. Halnan, Ben Hecht and Kenneth
    Sawyer Goodman, Phœbe Hoffman, Kreymborg, MacKaye,
    Marks, Middleton, O'Neill, Eugene Pillot, Frances Pemberton
    Spencer, Thomas Wood Stevens and Kenneth Sawyer Goodman,
    Walker, Wellman, Wilde, Oscar M. Wolff.)
More Portmanteau Plays.   Stewart Kidd.   1919.   (Stuart Walker.)
Morningside Plays.   Shay.   1917.   (Elva De Pue, Caroline Briggs, Elmer
    L. Reizenstein, Zella Macdonald.)
Moses, Montrose J.   Representative Plays by American Dramatists.
    Dutton.   1918–25.   Vol. III.   (Belasco, Thomas, Walter.)
—— Representative American Dramas.   Little, Brown.   1925.
Pierce, John Alexander.   The Masterpieces of Modern Drama, Eng-
    lish and American.   Doubleday, Page.   1915.   (Summarized and
    Quoted.)   (Thomas, Walter, MacKaye, Belasco.)
Plays for Small Stages.   Duffield.   1915.   (Mary Aldis.)
Portmanteau Plays.   Stewart Kidd.   1918.   (Stuart Walker.)
Provincetown Plays.   *See* Cook.
Quinn, A. H.   Representative American Plays.   Century.   1917.   (Croth-
    ers, MacKaye, Sheldou, Thomas.)
Shay, Frank.   Contemporary One-Act Plays of 1921.   Stewart Kidd.
    1922.

Shay, Frank. Fifty More Contemporary One-Act Plays. Appleton. 1928.

—— Plays for Strolling Mummers. Appleton. 1926.

—— A Treasury of Plays for Men. Little, Brown. 1923.

—— A Treasury of Plays for Women. Little, Brown. 1922.

Shay, Frank, and Loving, P. Fifty Contemporary One-Act Plays. Stewart Kidd. 1920.

Smith, Alice Mary. Short Plays by Representative Authors. Macmillan. 1920. (Constance D'Arcy Mackay, Mary Macmillan, Marks, Torrence, Walker.)

Stage Guild Plays and Masques. Chicago Stage Guild. 1912. (Kenneth Sawyer Goodman, Thomas Wood Stevens.)

Thomas, Augustus. One-Act Plays for Stage and Study. French. 1925.

Washington Square Plays. Drama League Series. Doubleday, Page. 1916. (Lewis Beach, Alice Gerstenberg, Edward Goodman, Moeller.)

Wilde, Percival. One-Act Plays for Stage and Study. Third Series. French. 1927.

Wisconsin Plays. *See* Dickinson.

BIBLIOGRAPHIES OF SHORT PLAYS

Boston Public Library. One-Act Plays in English. 1900–20.
Brown University Library. Plays of Today. 1921. (100 of the best modern dramas.)
Chicago Public Library. Actable One-Act Plays. 1916.
University of Utah. The One-Act Play in Colleges and High Schools. 1920.
Worcester, Massachusetts, Free Public Library. Selected List of One-Act Plays. 1921.
Boynton, Percy H. History of American Literature. 1919.
Cheney, Sheldon. The Art Theatre. 1917. (Appendix.)
Clapp, John Mantel. Plays for Amateurs. 1915. (Drama League of America.)
Clark, Barrett H. How to Produce Amateur Plays. 1917.
Dickinson, Thomas H. The Insurgent Theatre. 1917. (Appendix.)
Drummond, A. M. Fifty One-Act Plays. 1915. (*Quarterly Journal of Public Speaking*, I, 234.)
—— One-Act Plays for Schools and Colleges. 1918. (*Education*, IV, 372.)
Firkins, Ina Ten Eyck. Index to Plays: 1800–1926. 1927.
Goldstone, G. A. One-Act Plays. 1926–27.
Johnson, Gertrude Elizabeth. Choosing a Play. 1920.
Logasa, Hannah, and Ver Nooy, Winifred. An Index to One-Act Plays. 1924.
Lewis, B. Roland. Contemporary One-Act Plays. 1922.
Mackay, Constance D'Arcy. The Little Theatre in the United States. 1917. (Appendix.)
Mayorga, Margaret Gardner. Representative One-Act Plays by American Authors. 1919.
Plays for Amateurs; a Selected List Prepared by the Little Theatre Department of the New York Drama League. 1921.
Riley, Alice C. D. The One-Act Play Study-Course. (*Drama League Monthly*, Feb.-Apr., 1918.)
Shay, Frank. One Thousand and One Plays for the Little Theatre. 1923.
—— Plays and Books of the Little Theatre. 1921.
Thomas, Augustus. One-Act Plays for Stage and Study. 1925.

COLLECTIONS OF SHORT STORIES

Aces. Putnam. 1924.

Brewster, Dorothy. Book of Modern Short Stories. Macmillan. 1928.

Clark, B. H., and Lieber, M. Great Short Stories of the World. Mc-
Bride. 1925.

Gerould, G. H. Types of the Contemporary Short Story. Harper. 1927.

Heydrick, B. A. Americans All. Harcourt, Brace. 1920.

Howells, W. D. Great Modern American Stories. Boni and Liveright.
1920. (Does not include much recent work.)

Laselle, Mary Augusta. Short Stories of the New America. Holt. 1919.

Law, F. H. Modern Short Stories. Century. 1918.

Lieber, M., and Clark, B. H. Great Stories of All Nations. Brentano.
1927.

More Aces. Putnam. 1925.

O'Brien, Edward J. H. Best Short Stories for 1915, 1916, etc. Small,
Maynard, 1916–1925; Dodd, Mead, 1926– .

Pence, Raymond W. Short Stories by Present-Day Authors. 1922.

Ramsay, Robert L. Short Stories of America. Houghton, Mifflin. 1921.

Thomas, Charles Swain. Atlantic Narratives. Atlantic. 1918.

Trumps. Putnam. 1926.

Wells, Carolyn. American Mystery Stories. Oxford University Press.
1927.

—— American Detective Stories. Oxford University Press. 1927.

Wick, Jean. The Stories Editors Buy and Why. Small, Maynard. 1921.

Williams, Blanche Colton. Our Short-Story Writers. Moffat, Yard.
1920.

—— Best American Stories. 1919–24. Doubleday. 1926.

343

COLLECTIONS OF ESSAYS

Bowman, J. C. Contemporary American Criticism. Holt. 1926.
Brown, Sharon. Essays of Our Time. Scott, Foresman. 1928.
Criticism in America; Its Function and Status. Harcourt, Brace. 1924.
Farrar, John. The Bookman Anthology of Essays. Doran. 1923.
Hastings, W. T. Contemporary Essays. Houghton, Mifflin. 1928.
Kilmer, Joyce. Literature in the Making. Harper, 1917.
Lewisohn, Ludwig. A Modern Book of Criticism. Modern Library. 1919.
McCullough, B. W., and Burgum, E. B. A Book of Modern Essays. Scribner. 1926.
Morley, Christopher. Modern Essays. Harcourt, Brace. 1921.
—— Modern Essays, Second Series. Harcourt, Brace. 1924.
Tanner, W. M. Essays and Essay-Writing. Atlantic. 1917.

CLASSIFIED INDEXES

Since the authors appear in the body of the book in alphabetical order, page references have been omitted in these indexes.

I. POETS

Masters, Edgar Lee
Mencken, H. L.
Millay, Edna St. Vincent
Monroe, Harriet
Moore, Marianne
Morgan, Emanuel (*See* Bynner)
Morley, Christopher
Nathan, Robert
Neihardt, John G.
Nicholson, Meredith
Oppenheim, James
Ostenso, Martha
Peabody, Josephine Preston
Pound, Ezra
Reese, Lizette Woodward
Rice, Cale Young
Roberts, Charles G. D.
Roberts, Elizabeth Madox
Robinson, Edwin Arlington
Sandburg, Carl
Santayana, George
Sarett, Lew R.

Scott, Evelyn
Stein, Gertrude
Sterling, George
Teasdale, Sara
Tietjens, Eunice
Torrence, Ridgely
Untermeyer, Jean Starr
Untermeyer, Louis
Van Dyke, Henry
Weaver, John V. A.
Wescott, Glenway
Wharton, Edith
Wheelock, John Hall
Widdemer, Margaret
Wiggin, Kate Douglas
Wilkinson, Marguerite
Williams, William Carlos
Wood, C. E. S.
Woodberry, George Edward
Wylie, Elinor
Young, Stark

SUPPLEMENTARY LIST OF POETS

(With name of anthology where poems may be found.)

Adams, Franklin P. Untermeyer
Adams, Lêonie. Untermeyer
Aldis, Mary. Monroe. Others, 1916
Arensberg, W. C. Monroe.
Auslander, Joseph. Untermeyer
Barrett, Wilton Agnew. Monroe
Beach, Joseph Warren. Monroe
Branch, Anna Hempstead. Untermeyer
Britten, Rollo. Monroe
Brody, Alter. Untermeyer
Brown, Robert Carleton. Others, 1916
Burr, Amelia Josephine. Untermeyer
Burton, Richard. Untermeyer

Cannell, Skipwith. Monroe. Others, 1916, 1917
Carnevale, Emanuele. Others, 1919
Cleghorn, Sarah. Untermeyer
Crane, Hart.
Cromwell, Gladys. Monroe
Curran, Edwin. Untermeyer
Davidson, Donald.
Dillon, George.
Dodd, Lee Wilson. Monroe
D'Orge, Jeanne. Others, 1917, 1919
Dresbach, Glen Ward. Monroe
Driscoll, Louise. Monroe
Dudley, Dorothy. Monroe
Dudley, Helen. Monroe
Evans, Donald. Others, 1919
Flanner, Hildegarde. Monroe

346

Frank, Florence Kiper. Monroe
Gilman, Charlotte. P. S. Untermeyer
Glaenzer, Richard Butler. Monroe
Gorman, Herbert S. Untermeyer
Gould, Wallace. Others, 1919
Gregg, Frances. Others, 1916
Groff, Alice. Others, 1916
Guiney, Louise Imogen. Untermeyer
Hartley, Marsden. Others, 1916
Hartpence, Alanson. Others, 1916
Helton, Roy. Untermeyer
Herford, Oliver. Untermeyer
Hoffenstein, Samuel.
Holley, Horace. Monroe. Others, 1916
Hoyt, Helen. Monroe. Others, 1916, 1917
Hughes, Langston.
Iris, Scharmel. Monroe
Jennings, Leslie Nelson. Untermeyer
Johnson, Fenton. Others, 1919
Kilmer, Aline. Monroe
Knibbs, H. H. Untermeyer
Lee, Agnes. Monroe
Lee, Muna. Monroe
Leseman, Maurice. Monroe
Long, Haniel. Monroe
Long, Lily A. Others, 1919
Loy, Mina. Others, 1916, 1917, 1919
McCarthy, John Russell. Others, 1916
McClure, John. Others, 1916
McKay, Claude. Untermeyer
Michelson, Max. Monroe. Others, 1919
Morton, David. Untermeyer
Noguchi, Yone. Monroe
Norton, Grace Fallon. Monroe
North, Jessica.
O'Brien, Edward J. Others, 1917
O'Neil, David. Others, 1917

O'Sheel, Shaemas. Untermeyer
Parker, Dorothy.
Piper, Edwin Ford. Untermeyer
Ramos, Edward. Others, 1916
Ransom, John Crowe.
Ray, Man. Others, 1916
Reed, John. Monroe
Reyher, Ferdinand. Others, 1916
Ridge, Lola. Untermeyer
Riding, Laura.
Robinson, Edwin Meade. Untermeyer
Rodker, John. Others, 1916, 1917
Sainsbury, Hester. Others, 1916
Sanborn, Pitts. Others, 1916
Sanborn, Robert Alden. Others, 1916, 1917, 1919
Saphier, William. Others, 1919
Seeger, Alan.
Seiffert, Marjorie Allen. Others, 1919
Shanafelt, Clara. Monroe
Shaw, Frances. Monroe
Simpson, William. Monroe
Skinner, Constance Lindsay. Monroe
Speyer, Leonora. Monroe
Stevens, Wallace. Untermeyer
Strobel, Marion. Monroe
Syrian, Alan. Monroe
Taggard, Genevieve. Monroe
Thomas, Edith M. Untermeyer
Towne, Charles Hanson. Monroe
Turbyfill, Mark. Monroe
Upward, Allen. Monroe
Wattles, Willard. Untermeyer
Welles, Winifred. Untermeyer
White, Hervey. Monroe
Wilkinson, Florence. Monroe
Winters, Yvor. Monroe
Wolff, Adolph. Others, 1916
Wyatt, Edith. Monroe
Zaturensky, Marya. Monroe
Zorach, Marguerite. Others, 1916
Zorach, William. Others, 1916

II. Dramatists

Ade, George
Akins, Zoë
Anderson, Maxwell
Brooks, Chas. S.
Brown, Alice
Burgess, Gelett
Burnett, Frances Hodgson
Bynner, Witter
Cabell, James Branch
Churchill, Winston
Cobb, Irvin S.
Connelly, Marc
Cournos, John
Crothers, Rachel
Cummings, E. E.
D., H. (*See* Doolittle)
Davies, Mary Carolyn
De la Roche, Mazo
Dell, Floyd
Dos Passos, John
Dreiser, Theodore
Eaton, Walter Prichard
Ferber, Edna
Ficke, Arthur Davison
Fitzgerald, F. Scott
Frost, Robert
Fuller, Henry B.
Gale, Zona
Glaspell, Susan
Hagedorn, Hermann, Jr.
Harris, Frank
Hecht, Ben
Hergesheimer, Joseph
Heyward, Du Bose
Howard, Sidney
Hughes, Rupert
Johnson, Owen
Kaufman, George S.

Kelly, George
Kemp, Harry
Kennedy, Charles Rann
Kreymborg, Alfred
Lawson, John Howard
MacKaye, Percy
MacLeish, Archibald
Marquis, Don
Masters, Edgar Lee
Matthews, Brander
Mencken, H. L.
Millay, Edna St. Vincent
Moeller, Philip
Morley, Christopher
Nathan, George Jean
Neihardt, John G.
Norris, Charles A.
Norris, Kathleen
O'Higgins, Harvey
O'Neill, Eugene
Oppenheim, James
Peabody, Josephine Preston
Rice, Cale Young
Rinehart, Mary Roberts
Robinson, Edwin Arlington
Sheldon, Edward
Sinclair, Upton
Stallings, Laurence
Steele, Wilbur Daniel
Stein, Gertrude
Sterling, George
Tarkington, Booth
Torrence, Ridgely
Walker, Stuart
Weaver, John V. A.
Williams, Jesse Lynch
Wood, Charles E. S.
Young, Stark

III. Novelists

Ade, George
Aiken, Conrad
Akins, Zoë
Allen, Hervey
Allen, James Lane
Anderson, Sherwood
Andrews, Mary Raymond Shipman
Atherton, Gertrude
Austin, Mary
Bacheller, Irving
Baker, Ray Stannard
Beer, Thomas
Benefield, Barry
Benét, Stephen Vincent
Benét, William Rose
Bercovici, Konrad
Björkman, Edwin
Bodenheim, Maxwell
Boyd, James
Boyd, Thomas
Bromfield, Louis
Brown, Alice
Burnett, Frances Hodgson
Burt, Struthers
Cabell, James Branch
Cahan, Abraham
Cather, Willa
Churchill, Winston
Clark, Badger
Cobb, Irvin S.
Comfort, Will Levington
Cournos, John
Crane, Nathalia
D., H. (*See* Doolittle)
Davies, Mary Carolyn
Deland, Margaret
De la Roche, Mazo
Dell, Floyd

Deutsch, Babette
Dos Passos, John
Dreiser, Theodore
Du Bois, William E. B.
Eastman, Max
Erskine, John
Ferber, Edna
Fisher, Dorothy Canfield
Fitzgerald, F. Scott
Fox, John, Jr.
Frank, Waldo
Freeman, Mary E. Wilkins
Fuller, Henry B.
Gale, Zona
Garland, Hamlin
Gerould, Katherine Fullerton
Glasgow, Ellen
Glaspell, Susan
Grayson, David (*See* Baker)
Hagedorn, Hermann, Jr.
Harris, Frank
Hecht, Ben
Hemingway, Ernest
Hergesheimer, Joseph
Herrick, Robert
Heyward, Du Bose
Hughes, Rupert
Hurst, Fannie
Irwin, Wallace
Johns, Orrick
Johnson, Owen
Johnston, Mary
Kreymborg, Alfred
Lewis, Sinclair
Lewisohn, Ludwig
Lincoln, Joseph C.
London, Jack
Lovett, Robert Morss
Martin, Helen R.

Masters, Edgar Lee
Minnigerode, Meade
Morley, Christopher
Nathan, Robert
Neihardt, John G.
Nicholson, Meredith
Norris, Charles G.
Norris, Kathleen
O'Higgins, Harvey
Oppenheim, James
Ostenso, Martha
Parrish, Anne
Paul, Elliot H.
Perry, Bliss
Poole, Ernest
Quick, Herbert
Rice, Alice Hegan
Rice, Cale Young
Rinehart, Mary Roberts
Roberts, Charles G. D.
Roberts, Elizabeth Madox
Scott, Evelyn
Sedgwick, Anne Douglas
Sharp, Dallas
Sinclair, Upton

Singmaster, Elsie
Stallings, Laurence
Steele, Wilbur Daniel
Stein, Gertrude
Stevens, James
Strunsky, Simeon
Suckow, Ruth
Tarkington, Booth
Tietjens, Eunice
Untermeyer, Louis
Van Vechten, Carl
Watts, Mary S.
Webster, Henry Kitchell
Wescott, Glenway
Wharton, Edith
White, Stewart Edward
Widdemer, Margaret
Wiggin, Kate Douglas
Wilder, Thornton
Williams, Jesse Lynch
Wister, Owen
Woodward, W. E.
Wylie, Elinor
Young, Stark

IV. Short Story Writers

Ade, George
Aiken, Conrad
Allen, James Lane
Anderson, Sherwood
Andrews, Mary Raymond Shipman
Austin, Mary
Benefield, Barry
Bercovici, Konrad
Boyd, Thomas
Brown, Alice
Burgess, Gelett
Burnett, Frances Hodgson
Burt, Struthers
Cabell, James Branch
Cahan, Abraham
Cather, Willa
Cobb, Irvin S.
Comfort, Will Levington
Deland, Margaret
Dell, Floyd
Dreiser, Theodore
Eastman, Charles Alexander
Ferber, Edna
Fisher, Dorothy Canfield
Fitzgerald, F. Scott
Fox, John, Jr.
Freeman, Mary E. Wilkins
Fuller, Henry B.
Gale, Zona
Garland, Hamlin
Gerould, Katharine Fullerton
Glasgow, Ellen
Glaspell, Susan
Harris, Frank
Hecht, Ben
Hemingway, Ernest
Hergesheimer, Joseph
Herrick, Robert

Hughes, Rupert
Huneker, James Gibbons
Hurst, Fannie
Irwin, Wallace
Johnson, Owen
Johnston, Mary
Lardner, Ring
Lincoln, Joseph C.
London, Jack
Marquis, Don
Martin, Helen Reimensnyder
Matthews, Brander
Morley, Christopher
Nicholson, Meredith
Norris, Kathleen
O'Higgins, Harvey
Oppenheim, James
Perry, Bliss
Rice, Alice Hegan
Rice, Cale Young
Rinehart, Mary Roberts
Scott, Evelyn
Sedgwick, Anne Douglas
Singmaster, Elsie
Steele, Wilbur Daniel
Stein, Gertrude
Stevens, James
Suckow, Ruth
Tarkington, Booth
Van Dyke, Henry
Webster, Henry Kitchell
Wharton, Edith
White, Stewart Edward
Widdemer, Margaret
Wiggin, Kate Douglas
Williams, Jesse Lynch
Wister, Owen
Wood, C. E. S.

V. ESSAYISTS

Ade, George
Anderson, Sherwood
Austin, Mary
Baker, Ray Stannard
Beebe, William
Björkman, Edwin
Bradford, Gamaliel
Brooks, Charles S.
Burroughs, John
Burt, Struthers
Canby, Henry Seidel
Cabell, James Branch
Carman, Bliss
Crothers, Samuel McChord
Dell, Floyd
Du Bois, William E. B.
Eastman, Max
Eaton, Walter Prichard
Eliot, T. S.
Erskine, John
Fisher, Dorothy Canfield
Frank, Waldo
Gerould, Katherine Fullerton
Grayson, David (*See* Baker)
Harris, Frank
Huneker, James Gibbons

Leacock, Stephen B.
Lewisohn, Ludwig
MacKaye, Percy
Marquis, Don
Matthews, Brander
Mencken, H. L.
More, Paul Elmer
Morley, Christopher
Nathan, George Jean
Nicholson, Meredith
Oppenheim, James
Parrish, Anne
Perry, Bliss
Phelps, William Lyon
Pound, Ezra
Repplier, Agnes
Santayana, George
Sharp, Dallas Lore
Sinclair, Upton
Stein, Gertrude
Strunsky, Simeon
Van Dyke, Henry
Van Vechten, Carl
Woodberry, George Edward
Young, Stark

VI. Critics

Aiken, Conrad
Babbitt, Irving
Beer, Thomas
Björkman, Edwin
Brooks, Van Wyck
Brownell, W. C.
Cabell, James Branch
Canby, Henry Seidel
Deutsch, Babette
Eastman, Max
Eaton, Walter Prichard
Eliot, T. S.
Erskine, John
Huneker, James Gibbons
Krutch, Joseph Wood
Lewisohn, Ludwig
Lovett, Robert Morss
Lowell, Amy
Macy, John

Matthews, Brander
Mencken, H. L.
More, Paul Elmer
Mumford, Lewis
Nathan, George Jean
Perry, Bliss
Phelps, William Lyon
Pound, Ezra
Santayana, George
Sherman, Stuart P.
Stein, Gertrude
Untermeyer, Louis
Van Doren, Carl
Van Dyke, Henry
Van Vechten, Carl
Wharton, Edith
Wilkinson, Marguerite
Woodberry, George Edward
Young, Stark

VII. Writers on Country Life, Nature, and Travel

Allen, James Lane
Baker, Ray Stannard
Beebe, William
Burroughs, John
Deland, Margaret
Dos Passos, John
Dreiser, Theodore
Eaton, Walter Prichard
Fox, John, Jr.
Frank, Waldo
Garland, Hamlin
Gerould, Katherine Fullerton
Grayson, David (*See* Baker)
Hergesheimer, Joseph

Mencken, H. L.
O'Brien, Frederick
Phelps, William Lyon
Quick, Herbert
Repplier, Agnes
Rinehart, Mary Roberts
Roberts, Charles G. D.
Seton, Ernest Thompson
Sharp, Dallas Lore
Van Dyke, Henry
Wharton, Edith
White, Stewart Edward
Young, Stark

VIII. Humorists

Ade, George
Bacheller, Irving
Boyd, Nancy (*See* Millay)
Burgess, Gelett
Cobb, Irvin S.
Dunne, Finley Peter
Irwin, Wallace

Lardner, Ring
Leacock, Stephen B.
Marquis, Don
Millay, Edna St. Vincent
Strunsky, Simeon
Van Loon, Hendrik Willem

IX. WRITERS OF BIOGRAPHY, AUTOBIOGRAPHY, HISTORY

Allen, Hervey
Anderson, Sherwood
Atherton, Gertrude
Austin, Mary
Baker, Ray Stannard
Bradford, Gamaliel
Brooks, Charles S.
Brooks, Van Wyck
Brown, Alice
Burnett, Frances Hodgson
Burroughs, John
Comfort, Will Levington
Dell, Floyd
Dreiser, Theodore
Du Bois, William E. B.
Eastman, Charles Alexander
Eastman, Max
Fletcher, John Gould
Frank, Waldo
Gale, Zona
Garland, Hamlin
Glaspell, Susan
Hagedorn, Hermann, Jr.
Harris, Frank
Hughes, Rupert
Huneker, James Gibbons
Johnson, James Weldon
Kemp, Harry
Kreymborg, Alfred
Krutch, Joseph Wood

Leacock, Stephen
Leonard, William Ellery
Lewisohn, Ludwig
Lindsay, Vachel
London, Jack
Lowell, Amy
Macy, John
Markham, Edwin
Masters, Edgar Lee
Mencken, H. L.
Minnigerode, Meade
More, Paul Elmer
Norris, Kathleen
Perry, Bliss
Pound, Ezra
Quick, Herbert
Repplier, Agnes
Sandburg, Carl
Scott, Evelyn
Sharp, Dallas Lore
Sherman, Stuart P.
Sinclair, Upton
Sterling, George
Stevens, James
Van Loon, Hendrik Willem
Werner, M. R.
White, Stewart Edward
Wiggin, Kate Douglas
Woodward, W. E.

X. Subject Index (Including Background)

This list is not complete but merely suggestive. Titles are given only in cases where the books might not be readily identified. Some special information is also given in parenthesis.

AFRICA
White, Stewart Edward

ALASKA
Beach, Rex
London, Jack

ANIMALS. *See* Nature.

ARIZONA
White, Stewart Edward

ART AND ARTISTS
Ficke, Arthur Davison (Japanese)
James, Henry
Norris, Charles G. (The Amateur)

BOSTON
Dos Passos, John
Howells, W. D.
James, Henry
Sinclair, Upton

BUSINESS AND PROFESSIONS
Cahan, Abraham (The Rise of David Levinsky)
Dreiser, Theodore (The Financier, The Titan)
Ferber, Edna
Herrick, Robert
Howells, William Dean (The Rise of Silas Lapham, The Quality of Mercy)
Hurst, Fannie

BUSINESS, PROFESSIONS—*Cont'd*
Kaufman, George, and Marc Connelly
Lewis, Sinclair (Arrowsmith, Babbitt)
Norris, Charles G. (Pig Iron)
Norris, Kathleen
Tarkington, Booth (The Turmoil)

CALIFORNIA
Atherton, Gertrude
Austin, Mary
Howard, Sidney
Irwin, Wallace (Japanese)
Lindsay, Vachel
Markham, Edwin
Sterling, George
White, Stewart Edward

CANADA
Curwood, James Oliver
De La Roche, Mazo
Roberts, Charles G. D.

CAPITAL AND LABOR
Anderson, Sherwood (Marching Men)
Atherton, Gertrude (Perch of the Devil)
Lawson, John Howard (Processional)
Markham, Edwin
Sinclair, Upton (The Jungle, Jimmy Higgins, King Coal)

357

358

359

IMMIGRANTS
  Cahan, Abraham (Lithuanian)
  Cather, Willa (Bohemian)
  Cournos, John (Russian)
  Daly, T. A. (Irish, Italian)
  MacKaye, Percy (The Immi-
    grants)

INDIANA
  Ade, George
  Nicholson, Meredith
  Riley, James Whitcomb
  Tarkington, Booth

INDIANS
  Austin, Mary
  Eastman, Charles A.
  Garland, Hamlin (The Captain
    of the Gray Horse Troop)
  Neihardt, John G.
  Sarett, Lew R.
  Wister, Owen (Red Men and
    White)
  Wood, C. E. S.

INTERNATIONAL SCENES
  Atherton, Gertrude (The Aris-
    tocrats, American Wives and
    English Husbands)
  Bromfield, Louis (The Green
    Bay Tree)
  Burnett, Frances Hodgson
  Hemingway, Ernest (The Sun
    Also Rises)
  Howells, William Dean
  James, Henry
  Wharton, Edith

IOWA
  Garland, Hamlin
  Poole, Ernest (Silent Storms)
  Quick, Herbert
  Suckow, Ruth
  Van Vechten, Carl (The Tat-
    tooed Countess)

IRISH
  Daly, T. A.
  Dunne, Finley Peter

ITALY AND ITALIANS
  Bromfield, Louis (The Strange
    Case of Miss Annie Spragg)
  Daly, T. A.
  Fuller, Henry B.
  Howells, William Dean (A Fore-
    gone Conclusion)
  James, Henry (Roderick Hud-
    son, Daisy Miller, The Por-
    trait of a Lady, The Wings
    of a Dove, The Aspern Papers,
    etc.)
  Lewisohn, Ludwig (Roman
    Summer)
  Wharton, Edith (The Valley
    of Decision)
  Wilder, Thornton (The Cabala)

JAPANESE
  Irwin, Wallace (in California)

JEWS
  Cahan, Abraham
  Ferber, Edna (Fanny Herself)
  Hurst, Fannie
  Lewisohn, Ludwig

JOURNALISM
  Cournos, John (The Wall)
  Hecht, Ben (The Front Page)
  Howells, William Dean (A Haz-
    ard of New Fortunes, The
    World of Chance)

KENTUCKY
  Allen, James Lane
  Cobb, Irvin S.
  Fox, John, Jr.
  MacKaye, Percy
  Rice, Alice Hegan
  Roberts, Elizabeth Madox

MARRIAGE
Anderson, Maxwell (Saturday's Children)
Barry, Philip (Paris-Bound)
Churchill, Winston (A Modern Chronicle)
Deland, Margaret
Dell, Floyd (The Briary Bush)
Fisher, Dorothy Canfield (The Brimming Cup)
Herrick, Robert (Together)
Hughes, Rupert
Irwin, Wallace
Norris, Charles G. (Brass)
Norris, Kathleen
Poole, Ernest (His Second Wife)
Webster, Henry Kitchell (Thoroughbred)
Wharton, Edith (The Children)
Widdemer, Margaret (I've Married Marjorie)
Williams, Jesse Lynch (And So They Were Married)

MIDDLE WEST
Anderson, Sherwood
Cather, Willa
Gale, Zona
Garland, Hamlin
Hurst, Fannie (A President is Born)
Lewis, Sinclair
Lindsay, Vachel
Masters, Edgar Lee
Neihardt, John G.
Quick, Herbert
Sandburg, Carl

MONTANA
Atherton, Gertrude (Perch of the Devil—Butte)

NATURE
Beebe, William
Burroughs, John
Eaton, Walter Prichard

NATURE—*Cont'd*
London, Jack
Roberts, Charles G. D.
Seton, Ernest Thompson
Sharp, Dallas Lore
White, Stewart Edward

NEBRASKA
Cather, Willa

NEGROES
Burnett, Frances Hodgson
Cullen, Countee
Du Bois, William B.
Green, Paul
Heyward, Du Bose
Howells, William Dean (An Imperative Duty)
Johnson, James Weldon
King, Grace
Lindsay, Vachel (The Congo)
O'Neill, Eugene (The Emperor Jones, All God's Chilluns)
Page, Thomas Nelson
Sheldon, Edward (The Nigger)
Torrence, Ridgely (Plays for a Negro Theatre)
Van Vechten, Carl

NEW ENGLAND
Brown, Alice
Eaton, Walter Prichard
Freeman, Mary Wilkins
Frost, Robert
Hergesheimer, Joseph (Java Head)
Howard, Sidney (Ned McCobb's Daughter)
Howells, William Dean
Lincoln, Joseph (Cape Cod)
Millay, Edna St. Vincent
Nathan, Robert
O'Neill, Eugene (Beyond the Horizon, Desire Under the Elms)
Robinson, Edwin Arlington
Sharp, Dallas Lore

361

NEW ENGLAND—*Cont'd*
  Wharton, Edith (Ethan Frome, Summer)
  Wiggin, Kate Douglas

NEW MEXICO
  Cather, Willa (Death Comes for the Archbishop)
  Henderson, Alice Corbin

NEW ORLEANS
  Cable, George W.

NEW YORK
  Bercovici, Konrad (The Dust of New York)
  Bodenheim, Maxwell (Ninth Avenue)
  Dos Passos, John (Manhattan Transfer)
  Howells, William Dean (A Hazard of New Fortunes, The World of Chance)
  Hurst, Fannie
  James, Henry (Washington Square)
  Lardner, Ring
  Poole, Ernest (The Harbor)
  Strunsky, Simeon
  Weaver, John U. A.
  Wharton, Edith (The Age of Innocence)

NONSENSE
  Ade, George
  Burgess, Gelett
  Cobb, Irvin S.
  Lardner, Ring
  Leacock, Stephen
  Marquis, Don

OHIO
  Anderson, Sherwood
  Howells, William Dean (The Leatherwood God, The New Leaf Mills)
  Watts, Mary S.

ORIENT
  Benét, William Rose (The Great White Wall)
  Comfort, Will Levington
  Lindsay, Vachel (The Chinese Nightingale)
  Lowell, Amy (Fir-Flower Tablets)
  O'Neill, Eugene (Marco Millions)
  Pound, Ezra
  Tietjens, Eunice

PARIS
  Bromfield, Louis (The Green Bay Tree)
  Wharton, Edith (Madame de Treymes)
  Van Vechten, Carl (Peter Whiffle)

PENNSYLVANIA
  Deland, Margaret (Allegheny)
  Hergesheimer, Joseph
  Kelly, George
  Martin, Helen R. (Dutch)
  Singmaster, Elsie (Dutch)

PHILOSOPHY (popular)
  Baker, Ray Stannard (David Grayson)
  Brooks, Charles S.
  Crothers, Samuel McChord
  Fisher, Dorothy Canfield, and Cleghorn, Sarah (Fellow-Captains)
  Morley, Christopher
  Van Dyke, Henry

PIONEERS
  Cather, Willa (O Pioneers, My Ántonia)
  Neihardt, John G.

WOMEN (PSYCHOLOGY OF)—*Cont'd*

Erskine, John (The Private Life of Helen of Troy)

Ferber, Edna (The Girls)

Fisher, Dorothy Canfield

Gale, Zona (Miss Lulu Bett)

Hergesheimer, Joseph (Linda Condon)

Howard, Sidney (The Silver Cord)

Johnson, Owen (The Salamander, Virtuous Wives)

Kelly, George (Craig's Wife)

Lewis, Sinclair (Dodsworth)

Norris, Charles G. (Zelda Marsh)

Norris, Kathleen

Parrish, Anne (To-Morrow Morning, All Kneeling)

Tarkington, Booth (Alice Adams, Gentle Julia, Claire Ambler)

Teasdale, Sara

Watts, Mary S. (The Rise of Jennie Cushing)

YOUTH (PSYCHOLOGY OF)

Allen, James Lane (A Summer in Arcady, The Kentucky Warbler)

Anderson, Sherwood

Björkman, Edwin (The Soul of a Child)

Davies, Mary Carolyn

Dell, Floyd

Fitzgerald, F. Scott

Hecht, Ben

James, Henry (The Awkward Age)

Lawson, J. H. (Roger Bloomer)

Nathan, Robert (Peter Kindred)

Norris, Charles G. (Salt)

Paul, Elliot H.

Sherman, Stuart P. (My Dear Cornelia)

Tarkington, Booth (Seventeen, Clarence)

Widdemer, Margaret (The Boardwalk)

XI. Authors Grouped According to Place of Birth

In some cases information as to birthplace could not be obtained.

ALABAMA
Andrews, Mary Raymond Shipman

ARKANSAS
Fletcher, John Gould

CALIFORNIA
Atherton, Gertrude
Frost, Robert
Howard, Sidney
London, Jack
Norris, Charles G.
Norris, Kathleen

COLORADO
Parrish, Anne

CONNECTICUT
Phelps, William Lyon

DELAWARE
Canby, Henry Seidel

FLORIDA
Johnson, James Weldon

GEORGIA
Aiken, Conrad
Stallings, Laurence

IDAHO
Pound, Ezra

ILLINOIS
Austin, Mary
Crothers, Rachel
Crothers, Samuel McChord
Dell, Floyd

ILLINOIS—Cont'd
Dos Passos, John (Chicago)
Dunne, Finley Peter (Chicago)
Fuller, Henry B. (Chicago)
Hemingway, Ernest
Lindsay, Vachel
MacLeish, Archibald
Marquis, Don
Monroe, Harriet (Chicago)
Neihardt, John G.
Norris, Charles (Chicago)
Poole, Ernest (Chicago)
Sandburg, Carl
Sarett, Lew (Chicago)
Sheldon, Edward
Tietjens, Eunice (Chicago)
Van Doren, Carl
Webster, Henry Kitchell
Williams, Jesse Lynch

INDIANA
Ade, George
Dreiser, Theodore
Nathan, George Jean
Nicholson, Meredith
Tarkington, Booth (Indianapolis)

IOWA
Beer, Thomas
Clark, Badger
Ficke, Arthur Davison
Glaspell, Susan
Quick, Herbert
Sherman, Stuart Pratt
Stevens, James
Suckow, Ruth
Van Vechten, Carl

KANSAS
Fisher, Dorothy Canfield
Masters, Edgar Lee

KENTUCKY
Allen, James Lane
Cobb, Irvin S.
Fox, John, Jr.
Rice, Alice Hegan
Rice, Cale Young
Roberts, Elizabeth Madox
Walker, Stuart

LOUISIANA
Matthews, Brander

MAINE
Millay, Edna St. Vincent
Robinson, Edwin Arlington

MARYLAND
Mencken, H. L. (Baltimore)
O'Brien, Frederick (Baltimore)
Reese, Lizette Woodworth
Sinclair, Upton (Baltimore)

MASSACHUSETTS
Bradford, Gamaliel (Boston)
Burgess, Gelett (Boston)
Cummings, Edward E.
Du Bois, William E. B.
Eaton, Walter Prichard
Freeman, Mary E. Wilkins
Gerould, Katherine Fullerton
Herrick, Robert (Cambridge)
Lincoln, Joseph C.
Lovett, Robert Morss (Boston)
Lowell, Amy
Paul, Elliot H.
Perry, Bliss
Woodberry, George Edward

MICHIGAN
Baker, Ray Stannard
Comfort, Will Levington

MICHIGAN—*Cont'd*
Ferber, Edna
Lardner, Ring
Macy, John
White, Stewart Edward

MINNESOTA
Eastman, Charles Alexander
Fitzgerald, F. Scott (St. Paul)
Lewis, Sinclair
Oppenheim, James (St. Paul)

MISSISSIPPI
Bodenheim, Maxwell
Young, Stark

MISSOURI
Akins, Zoë
Churchill, Winston (St. Louis)
Eliot, T. S. (St. Louis)
Henderson, Alice Corbin (St
Louis)
Hughes, Rupert
Hurst, Fannie (St. Louis)
Johns, Orrick (St. Louis)
Moore, Marianne (St. Louis)
More, Paul Elmer (St. Louis)
Teasdale, Sara (St. Louis)

NEW HAMPSHIRE
Brown, Alice

NEW JERSEY
Brooks, Van Wyck
Frank, Waldo
Garrison, Theodosia
Kilmer, Joyce
Sedgwick, Anne Douglas
Sharp, Dallas Lore
Williams, William Carlos
Wylie, Elinor

NEW YORK
Bacheller, Irving
Beebe, William

NEW YORK—*Cont'd*
Benét, William Rose
Brownell, W. C. (City)
Burroughs, John
Bynner, Witter
Conkling, Grace Hazard (City)
Conkling, Hilda
Crane, Nathalia (City)
Crapsey, Adelaide
Cullen, Countee (City)
Deutsch, Babette (City)
Eastman, Max
Erskine, John (City)
Hagedorn, Hermann, Jr. (City)
Hecht, Ben (City)
Irwin, Wallace
Johnson, Owen (City)
Kreymborg, Alfred (City)
MacKaye, Percy (City)
Moeller, Philip (City)
Mumford, Lewis
Nathan, Robert (City)
O'Neill, Eugene (City)
Peabody, Josephine Preston
    (City)
Sterling, George
Untermeyer, Louis (City)
Werner, M. R. (City)
Wharton, Edith (City)
Wheelock, John Hall

NORTH CAROLINA
Green, Paul
Steele, Wilbur Daniel
Weaver, John V. A.

OHIO
Anderson, Sherwood
Babbitt, Irving
Boyd, Thomas
Bromfield, Louis
Brooks, Chas. S.
Gifford, Fannie Stearns Davis
Kemp, Harry
Torrence, Ridgely

OHIO—*Cont'd*
Untermeyer, Jean Starr
Watts, Mary S.

OREGON
Markham, Edwin

PENNSYLVANIA
Allen, Hervey
Anderson, Maxwell
Benét, Stephen Vincent
Boyd, James
Burt, Struthers (Philadelphia)
Connelly, Marc
D., H. (Hilda Doolittle)
Daly, T. A. (Philadelphia)
Deland, Margaret
Hergesheimer, Joseph (Phila-
    delphia)
Huneker, James Gibbons (Phila-
    delphia)
Jeffers, Robinson
Kaufman, George S.
Kelly, George (Philadelphia)
Martin, Helen R.
Morley, Christopher
Repplier, Agnes (Philadelphia)
Rinehart, Mary Roberts
Singmaster, Elsie
Stein, Gertrude
Van Dyke, Henry
Widdemer, Margaret
Wiggin, Kate Douglas (Phila-
    delphia)
Wister, Owen (Philadelphia)
Wood, C. E. S.

SOUTH CAROLINA
Heyward, Du Bose

TENNESSEE
Krutch, Joseph Wood

TEXAS
Benefield, Barry

368

XII. Authors of Foreign Birth

Bercovici, Konrad (Roumania)
Björkman, Edwin (Sweden)
Burnett, Frances Hodgson (England)
Cahan, Abraham (Russia)
Carman, Bliss (Canada)
Cournos, John (Russia)
De la Roche, Mazo (Canada)
Giovannitti, Arturo (Italy)
Harris, Frank (Ireland)
Kennedy, Charles Rann (England)
Leacock, Stephen (England)

Lewisohn, Ludwig (Germany)
Minnigerode, Meade (England)
O'Higgins, Harvey (Canada)
Ostenso, Martha (Norway)
Roberts, Charles G. D. (Canada)
Santayana, George (Spain)
Seton, Ernest Thompson (England)
Strunsky, Simeon (Russia)
Van Loon, Hendrik Willem (Holland)
Wilkinson, Marguerite (Canada)

SPECIMEN REPORTS

A: On a Volume of Poems

Bibliographical Information

　　Renascence, by Edna St. Vincent Millay.　Copyright, 1917; ed. used, New York, 1917.

Type

　　All lyrical.

Length and Form

　　There are three poems that contain over two hundred lines each; of the sixteen others none exceeds thirty lines in length.　The forms are regular: rhyming couplets or stanzas of four, six, and eight lines; blank verse; simple rhyme schemes: abab; abcbdb; etc.

Themes and Attitude

　　Love, death; attitude,—a sense of futility and weariness that is somehow always checked by an intense optimism.

Setting

　　Always vague.　Natural backgrounds play a large part in most of the poems.

Style

　　Considerable metrical dexterity; diction generally fairly fresh if rather romantic; technique able but not highly individual.

Interpretative Comments

　　Miss Millay's first volume is most interesting in the light of her later achievement.　*Renascence* was written while she was still in college.

Present Judgment

　　A promising but not a brilliant first volume.

Personal Reaction

　　I don't think she has terribly much to say.

Date　　　　　　　　　　　　　　　　　　**Signature**

Jan. 8, 1929.　　　　　　　　　　　　　　F. J. Brown.

B. On a Novel

Bibliographical Information
The Age of Innocence, by Edith Wharton. 1st ed., New York, 1920; ed. used, New York, 1922.

Type, Period, Scenes
Social study; early '70's; New York.

Theme
The conventions and codes of the old New York aristocracy.

Plot
Newland Archer is engaged to May Welland but he conceives a passion for her cousin, Countess Olenska, who has been the victim of a European marriage and is now an "off-color" member of the Welland aristocracy. Archer is married to May Welland, however, and the clear-headed and sensible Countess goes abroad. Thirty years later, Archer has the satisfaction of seeing his own children free from the narrow conventions that bound him.

Principal Characters
Newland Archer, dilettante, who is nevertheless able to see through and hate the world he lives in; Ellen Olenska, whose clear-headedness and honesty attract Archer; May Welland, the perfect product of the '70's, who marries Archer; the Beauforts, the Mingotts, the Wellands, clear-cut characters who provide motif and atmosphere for the age of innocence.

Structure
Chronological development; very little extraneous material.

Style
Clear-cut; apt adjectives and penetrating phrases; serene, austere, and disciplined.

Interpretative Comment
Memories of Mrs. Wharton's girlhood among the families of the aristocracy of which she writes gave her considerable material for the study.

Present Judgment
The time and scene of the novel seem to me to suit admirably the talents of Edith Wharton.

Personal Reaction

The narrowness and the disgusting sham of an aristocracy who "dreaded scandal more than disease" does not interest or appeal to me at all.

Date

Feb. 23, 1929.

Signature

LORA CHURCHILL.

C: On a Volume of Short Stories

Bibliographical Information

Bring! Bring! and Other Stories, by Conrad Aiken. 1st ed. and ed. used, New York, 1925.

Types

Psychological studies.

Periods and Scenes

Contemporary; London, New York, and indefinite places along the New England coast.

Themes

Psychological studies of abnormalities and obsessions in relation to love, death, art, etc.

Plots

Hardly any; the studies emphasize a mood or portray a subtle trait of character. The slight external events are completely effaced by the subjective material.

Character and Characterization

Men and children especially complex; women not so clearly or vividly developed. Stories told in the first person are especially effective.

Setting and Atmosphere

Sometimes setting plays a large part; sometimes it barely enters in at all. Atmosphere, however, is in every instance the very life of the story.

Interpretative Comment

Mr. Aiken is also a distinguished poet; the subtle and musical style of these stories testifies to that.

Structure

Little extraneous material.

Style

Graceful; melodious and subtle; strikes right note on every occasion with precisely the right word.

Present Judgment

Interesting psychological insight, together with an admirable sense of proportion and restraint.

Personal Reaction

While I was intensely interested when I read the stories, I was left afterwards with a feeling of dissatisfaction; where I had seen significance while I was reading, I felt trivialities afterwards.

Date	Signature
Feb. 19, 1929.	GRACE RICHMOND.

D: On a Play

Bibliographical Information
The Emperor Jones, a drama in eight scenes, by Eugene O'Neill. Copyright, 1920; ed. used, New York, 1924.

Type, Period, Scenes
Tragi-comedy; contemporary; West Indian island.

Theme
A study of terror.

Plot
"Emperor" Brutus Jones, an escaped convict from the States, dominates an island of negroes by his cleverness and good luck. Finally, the natives, wearying of his tyranny, set out to kill him. The play concerns itself with the pursuit of "the Emperor," his growing terror, and his ultimate death.

Principal Characters
Brutus Jones, Emperor—tyrant and grafter who is, nevertheless, not a coward; Henry Smithers, white trader—a weak and treacherous Cockney who fears, hates, and admires "the Emperor." The Little Nameless Fears; Jeff; the Convicts; the Prison Guard, etc., are indispensable machinery whose parts are dramatized in the "Emperor's" monologue.

Structure
The whole organization of the play is novel and vivid. The first scene is expository and yet full of action. Scene two introduces the Little Formless Fears and the beginning of terror. In the next five scenes varying shades in the intensity of terror are developed. In the last scene, the dead "Emperor's" body is brought in by the native soldiers.

Style
The stage-directions are vividly worded; they have atmosphere and color. The dialogue is terse and vivid, well adapted to the terror theme.

Interpretative Comment
The beat of the tom-tom is lost, of course, in reading. "The Emperor Jones" is a symphony of poetry, music, and sculpture in motion,—it ought to be seen.

376

Present Judgment

A great play, revolutionary, wiping away the taboo on monologue, and effecting a great unity of impression. The beat of the tom-tom rivals the knocking on the gate in *Macbeth* for effectiveness. A great piece of original artistry.

Personal Reaction

Intense. It represents to me a superb combination of the three vehicles of human expression: the rhythm of music, of language, and of art, creating a single profound rhythm of terror.

Date	Signature
Jan. 15, 1929.	GEORGE BRODSKY.

E: On a Volume of Essays

Bibliographical Information
> *Under the Maples*, by John Burroughs. Copyright, 1921; ed. used, New York, 1921.

Type
> Nature studies.

Content
> Personal observation of life in nature—of trees, birds, bees, etc.

Structure
> Compact; each sketch is centered in a particular aspect of nature; the mass impression is of a unified whole.

Point of View
> Intensely personal; full of enthusiasm and warmth; deep desire to identify himself with things he writes of.

Interpretative Comment
> Most of the essays were written during the last two years of the author's life. The title expresses Mr. Burroughs's love for the maple trees under which most of the essays were written.

Style
> Warm; detailed; full of explanation and illustration.

Present Judgment
> Full of serenity, observation, and an interesting semi-philosophy; well worth reading.

Personal Reaction
> There is something intensely kind and appreciative in these pages; the flavor, the vitality, and the reality of the book make it absorbing reading.

Date
March 13, 1929.

Signature
LEON WRIGHT.